KRAUTLAND CALLING

An American POW Radio Broadcaster In Nazi Germany

HAL LISTER

EAKIN PRESS ★ Austin, Texas

FIRST EDITION

Copyright © 1989
By Nana Lister

Published in the United States of America
By Eakin Press
P.O. Drawer 90159 ★ Austin, TX 78709-0159

ISBN 0-89015-660-3

✦ƐP

Library of Congress Cataloging-in-Publication Data

Lister, Hal.
    Krautland calling : an American POW radio broadcaster in Nazi Germany / by Hal Lister
    p.   cm.
    ISBN 0-89015-660-3 : $16.95
    1. Lister, Hal.   2. World War, 1939–1945 — Personal narratives, American.   3. Prisoners
of war — Germany — Biography.   I. Title
D811.L515   1989
940.54'72'430924 — dc19
    [B]   88-16432
                                                                                              CIP

"Krautland Calling . . . Krautland Calling. This is your nightly message and music program brought to you on the medium wave length, 290-meter band, 1031 kilocycles, every evening at this time. Sergeant 'X' here with your favorite recorded music, messages from our buddies in POW camps, and occasional patter to brighten your evening."

So began a nightly half-hour broadcast for the three and one-half months of early 1945 that an American prisoner of war spent under almost idyllic circumstances in a beautiful mountaintop hamlet. Everything would have been wonderful except for his POW status.

An adventure of excitement, romance, intrigue, and danger was built around and led up to those weeks high in the Black Forest.

"In war there are no unwounded soldiers."

— Jose Narosky
Si Todos los Tiempos
Marymar, Buenos Aires

Contents

A DIRGE OF VICTORY

Lift not thy trumpet, Victory, to the sky,
Nor through battalions nor by batteries blow,
But over hollows full of old wire go
Where among dregs of war the long-dead lie,
With wasted iron that the guns passed by,
When they went eastwards like a tide at flow,
There blow thy trumpet that the dead may know,
Who waited for thy coming, Victory.

It is not we that have deserved thy wreath.
They waited there among the towering weeds.
The deep mud burned under the thermite's breath.
And winter cracked the bones that no man heeds;
Hundreds of nights flamed by, the seasons passed,
And thou hast come to them at last, at last!

(From Lord Dunsany's "Unhappy Far-off Things,"
copyright 1919, Little, Brown & Co., and reprinted
by permission of Lady Dunsany, Kent, England,
October 2, 1961)

Foreword

Choose subjects you know a lot about, good teachers of writing always say.

Hal Lister was a good teacher of writing and he knew a lot about war. In *Krautland Calling,* he describes what it was like to fight Hitler in Italy as a GI — a GI who was thrust into a most unusual role, as you will see.

Reading his words, I kept hearing Hal's gruff voice and seeing his intense expression — his blue eyes somber behind horn-rimmed glasses — as he told me about events in the book.

You must understand that Hal did not like to tell war stories. Not only did he hate war but he detested any hint of bravado, any macho celebration of the glories of combat.

What Hal projected, fiercely, those blue eyes beginning to flash, was his pride in having done a vitally important job as well as he could. He had met the challenge head on. He had put his life on the line. He did not judge others, but he did judge himself, severely. The fact that he did not find himself wanting was clearly an enormous source of satisfaction.

Again, don't misunderstand. He was not boastful — anything but that. He was proud. There's a difference.

Hal focused this kind of intensity on another of his passions, his love for the English language. The battlefield where he proclaimed and proved his love was a classroom in "the pit" — the basement of this grand, old school.

There Hal taught incoming students the basics of journalism. Newswriting 105 was and is and always shall be the name of the course. Everyone must take it, not only budding reporters but advertising students and photographers, students who often protest that they would never write a news story in their careers, so why should they learn how to do it? We Missourians know the answer to that: because it is good for your soul.

Hal was tough. Some students felt his course was like taking basic at Fort Dix, only without the Garands. God help you if you misspelled a name or got sloppy.

He had earned the right to be demanding, not only at Anzio (although surely there) but by getting his education the hard way. After the war, he went to the University of Wisconsin-Milwaukee for a couple of years, but had to drop out to take care of his wife Nana and their growing family.

Hal edited suburban newspapers around hometown Milwaukee. He liked that, but the money was bad. To keep going, he would sell insurance and magazines for a while, and then go back to newspapering.

And so at forty-five, brooding over the way his life was going, he decided to finish up his degree and become a journalism teacher.

By that time the Listers had five children. Hal had to work nights selling carpeting for Sears. He also somehow found time to direct professionally and act in community theater groups; his flair for show business that he discovered in the army never completely left him.

In 1969 Hal moved to Columbia, Missouri, to finish his undergraduate degree at the School of Journalism and get his master's. A heart attack in 1971 discouraged him from going on to get a Ph.D., but by that time he had discovered where he belonged — in the pit teaching Newswriting 105.

In 1985 Hal retired from the school and packed Nana off to the University of Tennessee-Martin, where he began teaching journalism again.

The Listers liked living in Martin fine, they insisted, but they prudently kept open a line of retreat by retaining their house in Columbia. They came back to visit from time to time, including one warm April day when Hal was installed as a professor emeritus at the university and I had a chance to say a few words about him to his colleagues.

I talked about Hal's love of language and his hatred of war, and how he had won the Bronze Star with two clusters and three Purple Hearts and how he had twice been captured by the Germans and twice escaped. Although he was Jewish, and the Nazis knew it, he was well treated while in enemy hands.

I told the people about Hal's experiences in combat because they were such an important part of him. I could feel him studying me closely all the while. Afterwards, he thanked me for what I had said. I am proud of that.

Then one time when Hal and Nana came back I could see that there was something wrong with him, something worse than the bad back he got during the fighting in Italy and that forced him to walk with a cane.

He had a brain tumor. Toward the end, lost in his own world, he would talk on and on about the war and the scenes described in this book, a book that he had been writing, and rewriting, for years.

On November 10, 1987, Hal Lister died in Nana's arms.

JIM ATWATER
Dean, School of Journalism,
University of Missouri-Columbia

Preface

The events described in this book are true experiences, most of them of the author; others of close friends under unusual circumstances. Names have been changed completely in some cases; thinly disguised in others.

I wish to extend my sincere thanks to the many talented writers, editors, and supervisors of official documents which describe in graphic detail the flow of some of the adventures listed in parts of this volume.

In particular, thanks are due the many men responsible for the superior publication of "The History of the 30th Infantry Regiment in World War II" and "The History of the 3rd Infantry Division in World War II." Writers of these highly descriptive diaries of these gallant organizations, at the time of the events described herein, were the staff members of Infantry Journal Press of World War II.

Among the individuals who contributed so greatly, though unwittingly, to the several descriptive passages which have been borrowed (with permission) from the two unit histories mentioned (and their ranks at the time) were:

Lieutenant Colonels Walter T. Kerwin and Grover Wilson; Majors Hugh A. Scott and Frederick C. Spreyer; Captain Rupert Proehme; Lieutenant Donald G. Taggart; Technicians 4th grade James A. Claunch and Merrill S. Harrison; Private First Class Emil Hung; and Privates Edward D. Fetting and William L. Cunningham.

All but Captain Proehme, a lieutenant when the author knew him during the pre-Anzio Beachhead invasion days of training at the tiny villages of Bagnoli and Pozzuoli, Italy, were members of the staff of the 3rd Infantry Division office of the A.C. and S., G-2, Historical Section and Information and Education departments.

Lieutenant Proehme was responsible for the production of the 30th Infantry Regiment story in his capacity of regimental historian, primarily under Colonel Lionel McGarr, regimental commander.

Both histories were copyrighted in 1947 by the Infantry Journal, Inc. (now the Association of the United States Army), and the few paragraphs that have been reprinted herein are published with the express consent of that organization.

HAL LISTER
April 1981

1. The Volunteers

THE BRITTLE CRISPNESS of the air caused me to gasp, to feel the burning as I breathed in deeply, to lose my step momentarily. I climbed out of the tiny automobile while the vicious mountain wind blasted my already numbed face.

The first German soldier had preceded me out of the car, and now the two of us awaited the driver who was cursing in his native tongue, a sound I never quite became accustomed to.

Moments before, the beetle-like Volkswagen convertible had become hopelessly trapped in the high snow bank as it attempted to negotiate a poorly cleared, banked curve. After several moments of trying to extricate the tiny vehicle, the traditionally energetic Germans gave it up as a bad job. We would walk to our destination, they decided.

"*Also, komme,*" the driver said to the cold air, his eyes glued to the road at his toes, his chin buried deeply in his collar.

I stood shivering in the sub-zero night air. My only protection against the biting cold was an unlined combat jacket and the already obsolete shoe pacs, designed not for winter use but for amphibious operations. Supplies had been slow in reaching our weary soldiers, resulting in a shortage of more practical, heavy-duty combat boots.

We began our long climb up the winding mountain road which

was barely visible under drifting, blowing snow. The moon was frosty bright and cast a weird, opaque haze over the crusted dunes throughout the valley. In the distance, the little-traveled highway twisted upward into an evaporating serpentine path.

Long accustomed to forced marches over great distances, I walked with the inbred automation of the combat infantryman, considerably experienced at pure physical weariness nearly to the point of exhaustion, never quite becoming inured to it. My fellow dogfaces and I, on endless occasions, had walked for miles, seeing nothing on either side. Then, instinctively and immediately, we awakened at the first sound of danger. Men at these times plodded in their sleep behind the invariable uniform of the somnambulist directly in front of them.

As we climbed, I found my legs automatically assuming the reflexive movements I had learned from so many months of walking up and over innumerable African, Sicilian, Italian, French, and now German mountains. Little effort was required, and what was used was subconscious, as I followed my guides along the steady twenty-degree incline.

The automation of my movements liberated my mind for reflections. My memories were of other recent climbs. It seemed years ago. In reality, it had been only a matter of weeks — nine, to be exact.

On December 29 the second section of the regimental platoon was on observation post duty in a Catholic church just to the west of Kaysersberg. Whether Kaysersberg was situated in France or Germany depended greatly on which geography textbook one read. For nearly seventy years, the region of Alsace had wavered between both national governments.

Currently, it was more German than French. The ancient building in which we were billeted, and from whose steeple we made our daily observations, had performed yeoman service as an observation post, first for the Germans, now for the Americans. Its spired steeple was still standing, nearly completely intact. The three-foot-thick walls offered an imaginary solace against the high-velocity, high-explosive 88-millimeter shells which had become so commonplace.

The delayed Christmas treat — Christmas dinner in the form of the unaccustomed luxury of 10-in-1 rations — had been brought forward the night before, because nothing moved in daylight hereabouts unless protected by heavy fog or ground mist.

The supplies had been dumped unceremoniously on the steps to the basement quarters beneath the old church. Ration hauling to a front-line OP had joined the ranks of other such unpopular and often unhealthy assignments as ammunition hauling to front-line machine gun outposts. The supply crews simply deposited their wares and disappeared in the direction of Kaysersberg.

We had become relatively comfortable in the nearly warm cellar of the church. At least we were able to relax somewhat below the ground, a position that made candlelight a practical luxury.

Since my promotion to sergeant three months earlier, I commanded the small group of intelligence and reconnaissance specialists who were beginning to find our specialty palling.

Our one diversion in the after-dark, non-observing hours was our nightly poker games. I smiled as I witnessed Holdie's unhappy grimace when the third consecutive hand came my way.

"For Christ's sake, you got a marked deck or sump'n?"

"You shouldn't play if you don't like to lose, my boy," I chided him in return.

I pulled in the disorganized piles of bank notes and square invasion currency paper, including a couple of 100-franc bills and a few 50-franc invasion notes. It was easily the best pot of the evening. I estimated it came to more than $18. It was a fitting high point in our six hours of playing.

"You win the deal too, oh, great white leader," grunted Adams, pushing the well-worn deck across the makeshift table to me. I rifled the cards, slid them to Adams for a cut, and began dealing them out, face down.

"Seven card, nothin' wild. Ante ten francs," I advised my colleagues.

The barely audible whistle of the sound-power phone caused our entire group to lapse into nervous silence. Tension hung heavily in the air. The instrument seldom delivered anything but bad news. Some casualties resulted nearly every time it had whistled in recent weeks.

"Lister," I answered, holding the phone a few inches from my left ear. It had an unnerving habit of whistling on its own, should the speaker at the other end speak too loudly.

"This is Captain Etherton," the voice said. "Pick yourself two men and get over to the CP on the double."

"Yes, sir," I responded. I replaced the receiver in its leather case and turned to the five men seated quietly about the table waiting for the other shoe to drop.

"OK, it looks like another routine patrol. Whose turn is it?" I asked steadily.

"How many you need?" Holdie said quietly.

"Two. How about you and Cavella?"

"What do you mean?" Cavella started, rising from his seat. "I was out last night. Goddamn it, ain't there any other outfits in this damn army?"

"OK, simmer down. I'm looking for a couple of volunteers. Kleine, you and Weber haven't been out for a couple of days."

"For Christ's sake!" Weber nearly gagged in his fury. "I been up in that goddamn steeple dodgin' those fuckin' eighty-eights for the past couple of days. That's no goddamn holiday, you know!"

"Good. This will give you a chance to stretch your legs. Come on," I said, rising from the table.

Neither Kleine nor Weber moved immediately. Then, realizing the futility of further argument, they wearily assembled their equipment and followed me to the blanketed entrance of the basement.

I went through the blanket first, carefully closing it tightly behind me to prevent the escape of even a minute flicker of candlelight into the night's blackness. I could hear the others coming after me. I quickly pulled the outer blanket aside and slipped through into the deserted blackness of the street. I replaced the outer cover carefully at my back as the other two men entered the area between the two light shields. I was buckling my rifle belt as Weber and Kleine came through the outer archway.

We stood silently, our collars up, hunched in the bitter cold. Strapping on our equipment, we contemplated the night's work. We had to cross the street, already cluttered with rubble. The piles of debris that littered the streets of this ancient city consisted principally of slates from roofs of historic buildings. I was told by one of the few remaining natives of Kaysersberg that the city had been occupied over a millenium ago. I estimated that the slates from the roofs had been replaced with each war that history had brought through this part of Alsace.

"Let's go," I mumbled quietly.

Silently the others followed me. We made our way along the shadowed street, keeping well under the dark shadows created by the reflection of the moon on heavily eaved buildings. It was extremely

4

dark on our side of the street. The moon hadn't begun to throw its frightful and devastating brightness onto this side of the roadway yet.

Suddenly, someone about four buildings beyond us carelessly moved a blanket from the window it was covering. For a sickening moment, the candle within that room threw the glare of a beacon into the entire street.

"Son of a bitch!" Weber muttered. "Those bastards are gonna get their asses shot off."

"And ours," Kleine said.

We waited nervously for a reaction from the Kraut lines. It wasn't long in coming. First we heard the dull, distant thumping of the cannon's muzzle blast. Seconds later, an all-too-familiar scream filled the air above us.

"In here, quick!" I shouted, tumbling into a shadowy doorway. The other pair fell on top of me. The shell's whistle rose to a terrifying, screaming crescendo as the heavy cargo of death and destruction roared in. It struck somewhere near the top of the building next to us, showering us and the street with more slates and large pieces of torn stucco.

"Let's go, huh?" pleaded Kleine. I put a restraining hand on his arm, fully understanding anyone's desire to get the hell away from a target.

"Hold it," I cautioned. "They've been throwing battery fire at night. That was only one shell."

There were no more shells, though . . . this time. The enemy observer apparently had decided simply to liven up the night as he stared down on Kaysersberg from his lofty, hilltop vantage point.

I moved cautiously to the sidewalk, stepping over a small stack of roof tiles. I headed toward a building which kept us in shadow, but which stood opposite the bakery building. As we reached the front of it, I automatically moved my Tommy gun from my shoulder and tucked it under my combat jacket. The others did likewise. Even the few seconds it would take us to cross this narrow, moonlit street would give us away to an alert artillery observer on a hilltop about a mile away. The glint of moonlight on naked metal barrels could reflect enough to alert him to movement and invite further barrages.

We reached the bakery building with no further trouble. One by one, we cautiously and quickly moved through the double-blanketed entrance, letting ourselves into the crowded, smoky, dimly lit command post.

Captain Etherton, a tired, old man of twenty-eight, had been a

West Pointer. His men respected him as became the due of every Academy graduate I'd met.

The captain was seated on his bunk which consisted of three bags of potatoes he had found in the bakery supply room. Like the men in his company, the captain had a grubby, two-week stubble covering the lower half of his face. The campaign didn't permit the luxury of personal hygiene.

The situation in the Kolmar Pocket, of which Kaysersberg was a part, was tense and growing more critical each day. To the north, the Germans had broken through the American lines with a last-ditch, all-out counter-offensive, slowing in the area of a Belgian town named Bastogne. It was feared that a similar, simultaneous effort might be launched in and about Kolmar. This accounted for the extreme caution all along the line.

I looked about the dingy CP room carefully. As my eyes adjusted to the murky, flickering candlelight, I saw four other GIs, each wearing the blue and white, diagonally striped shoulder patch of the division. I hadn't seen these particular riflemen before.

"Lister, these fellows are from Able Company," the captain said, anticipating my curiosity about the quartet. "They're going out with you on this one." He turned to the riflemen. "This is Sergeant Lister. He'll be leading your patrol." They stood by silently, showing no emotion. We exchanged nods of implied recognition.

As I watched, the company clerk was switching weapons with the A Company men, giving each of them a Browning automatic rifle.

"Where to tonight, sir?" I asked, an uncomfortable lump making its presence known in my chest.

"The bridge again. Same general area as last night and the night before."

"This is pretty heavy firepower for such a routine patrol, isn't it, Captain?" I pursued tentatively.

"Well, it's not quite as simple as I laid it out. Actually, Charlie Company picked up a prisoner a while ago. This Kraut told 'em his outfit's due for relief at 0200. That gives us about an hour and a half to get an OP set up in the forward slope of Hill 632, just beyond the bridge. We want to catch both the incoming and outgoing companies in mid-exchange. I figure it should take you about an hour to get above the bridge on the other side of the creek." He pointed to the spot on the large map mounted on the wall of the room. "Then, with any luck, you'll be in good position with at least fifteen minutes to set up your radio equipment. Play your cards right and we can blast the shit out of both those outfits."

The next few minutes were spent briefing us and explaining the conditions under which we would be working for the rest of the night. The riflemen were to protect our observation post while our I&R unit took care of artillery direction into the trap we hoped to set for the two German companies.

The paradox of my job never failed to amaze me. Specifically, I was trained, as was the rest of the platoon, as a combat intelligence and reconnaissance scout and observer. My basic training commander explained that such scouts were not to get involved in fire fights unless they couldn't avoid them. Our assignment generally concerned obtaining information, a project that could be hampered by direct contact with the enemy. Still, whenever our patrols went out, we were equipped with abnormally large volumes of firepower in case of trouble.

As soon as the briefing ended, the captain rose, wished each of us good luck, and shook hands all around. I turned the SC-300 radio over to Weber.

"Take care of that baby," I warned him unnecessarily. "She's likely to be our ticket home."

Weber grunted and strapped the heavy piece of equipment on his back.

One by one the seven of us edged out of the carefully blanketed command post doorway. The others followed me, single file, staying close to the buildings that overhung the sidewalk. The first outpost we expected to reach was about 200 yards from the CP. As we approached the area, a sharp whisper split the silence.

"Halt!"

We stopped in our tracks. This was the sentry at the machine gun post on the ground floor of the shelled-out wine shop. The whispered voice came through again.

"Ebbetts," came the challenge.

"Field," I replied with the countersign.

"OK, take off," whispered the gunner.

I waved my crew on and we proceeded past the first of the two outposts we would be seeing. Silently and rapidly we rounded the next corner. A smoldering army six-by-six truck still lay smashed in the middle of the street where a barrage had caught it just before dusk the previous night. Fortunately, the flames had died, but the smell of burned flesh, burning rubber, and death still permeated the entire area, stronger than ever since the wind had died down.

"Did they get that poor bastard out of there?" Weber whispered.

"I doubt it," I replied, also in a whisper. "He got it with the first round, the way I hear it. Never knew what hit him. There's no point in sending other guys out here in the open . . . at least not until she cools down a little."

We moved silently, nervously past the destroyed vehicle. I was glad to note that what remained of the truck's cab was in full, heavy shadow. No matter how many of them I saw, I never became fully accustomed to dead men, especially the violent dead, even Germans.

"Halt!" came the whispered command, more urgently than the other challenge had sounded. The nearer the front-line jumpoff spot, the more nervous were the guards who manned the outposts. We halted.

"Ebbetts."

"Field."

"OK, move out. Hey, how long you gonna be gone?" It was the same kid as on the other two nights I'd taken this particular patrol.

"Quite a while, probably," I replied in a quiet whisper. Sound traveled amazingly long distances, especially on such crisp, cold nights. "In fact, you might see some fireworks in a little while. Might help keep you awake."

"I sure as hell hope so. I could use something to break up this goddamn monotony. Why in hell don't they put two of us on these goddamn outposts, anyway?" the young soldier grumbled.

"Maybe they don't have two of you to spare just now," I reminded him, fully aware of the tremendous pounding C Company had taken in this area in recent days. The company was down to about forty percent of strength.

I gathered my men about me and pointed ahead into the vague shadows. I quietly advised them of their route.

"We'll head out for that large evergreen cluster over there. From there, we'll make for that pile of rocks about fifty yards beyond it. Follow me from there. All clear?"

I looked carefully at each man until I received a nod of assent.

"OK, keep low . . . ten-yard intervals."

Unshouldering my Tommy gun, I dashed for the shadow of a large cluster of pine trees. Weber slid in behind me just as I moved out for the boulders. With an agreed jump-off point, we followed even rows of frozen grain stalks down the slight slope to a line of high shrubs about seventy-five yards distant. From there we should be in shadow all the way to the bridge.

I signaled, "Keep your interval and silence." Neither command was necessary, however, because the air was electric with the tension of entering the dangerous unknown. In a low crouch, our procession continued across the relatively open expanse of ground until all seven of us were lying beside the thick bushes bounding the river bed.

It was a matter of seconds before we reached the end of the shrubbery and stepped down into the ditch beside the roadway across the bridge. Stealing along the ditch, we saw the bridge just ahead of us. It was a small stone structure with a low, concrete railing. The shallow water level gave me an unexpected feeling of relief. The tiny stream apparently flooded in springtime, judging by the distance between its banks. Fortunately, it now represented only a trickle at the bottom of a ditch. The thought of wet feet in the bitter cold, and the resulting likelihood of trench foot, plagued the long-suffering dogface who had little enough opportunity to change his shoes and socks in the course of any given week or month.

As patrol leader, I was the first to reach the abutment and to slide down the near bank into the stream bed. The ground was springy despite the temperature. Apparently, the sun had thawed it somewhat during the day. Patches of crisp, white-bordered ice lay on the stream surface.

As I reached the far bank, I used it as cover while I glanced cautiously over the top. Nothing untoward was evident. I waved Weber on, whispering to him at very close range, my lips nearly touching his ear.

"No footprints along here."

Weber nodded understanding. The others had dropped into the stream bed and were lining up behind us. I surveyed the area we were to climb. Approximately fifty yards separated us from the beginning of our final objective. There was thick undergrowth at the base of the hill and heavy snow had drifted against it.

I noted a string of thin poplar trees which seemed to border a small, tributary stream fifty yards to our right. I decided this would be the most practical route to follow to the base of the hill and, perhaps, right up the hillside. Quietly we struck out, following the direct path to the trees.

Possibly the cold, possibly our anxiety caused us to move rapidly. We covered the ground to the base of the hill in just two minutes.

Keeping within the shadow of the heavy undergrowth, we followed the bed of this small tributary stream upward. I headed through the undergrowth and over the rocks which covered the stream bottom, thankful for the layer of heavy snow that covered any loose, snapping twigs on the forest floor.

We climbed with seeming effortlessness, noiselessly, and stopped only when one or the other of the party indicated a shortness of breath by pulling on the clothing of the man ahead of him. We rested several times in the next few minutes, avoiding the panting of breathless men. Such labored breathing could be heard for great distances and, within the surrounding trees, I sensed enemy troops.

We reached the hilltop clearing within eleven minutes of starting our climb. I slowed, looking behind me to make sure that all of the men were keeping up. Weber inched up a few feet to my left, perspiration on his face reflecting in the occasional moonbeams that broke through the trees. Kleine was right behind Weber. The A Company men were closing the gap between us as they approached the head of the patrol.

Suddenly, the silence was shattered by the oilcloth-tearing, staccato chatter of German machine guns. I dropped to my belly instinctively, but not before I saw at least four lines of tracers coming at us. There was no question about it. We'd really walked into one this time.

I chewed my way frantically into the snow-covered leafy forest floor, my heart pounding, ready to burst. Almost subliminally, the thought ran through my mind, *The sons of bitches. They were waiting for us all the time. A setup. We stupidly walked into a setup!* I heard the others scrambling desperately behind me. Weber had hit the ground once and rolled off the path, automatically sliding out of the straps that held the bulky radio on his shoulders. He would be hiding behind the radio right now. I'd done the same on several earlier occasions. I wished I had as bulky a wall in front of me. All I had was a slender tree and my Tommy gun held sideways in front of my head.

Kleine also had fallen, but rolled nowhere under his own power. The first burst from the nearest machine gun had literally ripped his face in two.

I listened for the A Company men behind Kleine. I glanced cautiously from behind the tree that partially sheltered me, using it as a shield. I saw two feet lying in the middle of the path, toes pointed skyward. A few feet beyond I could make out another dark shape huddled

10

on the ground. Obviously, neither man could see the bright moonlight in whose glow they lay.

I thought momentarily about these men who had followed me to their deaths. They didn't know me. I didn't even know their names!

I heard a low moan from the bushes to my left, on the far side of the path. So, apparently, did the enemy gunners. Their fire tore through the shrubbery, silencing the moan.

They weren't through, I was sure. I was right. Another two-minute burst began and I dug myself even further into the ground. All at once, I felt a tugging along the side of my right leg. Almost simultaneously, my hands were jarred as the stock of my Tommy gun was shattered by bullets.

As suddenly as it had started, the firing stopped. The silence was deafening. Not even echoes remained. The entire ambush had taken approximately four minutes. I heard guttural orders and the crunch of boots on crisp snow. I nervously fingered what remained of my weapon, wondering about any survivors from my seven-man patrol. I realized, as I felt for the trigger guard, that my weapon was useless, having been badly damaged by enemy slugs.

A sharp crackling noise immediately to my left made my head jerk around. Within a very few feet stood a young, efficient-looking German soldier, dressed in the heavy, dark green uniform of wool I had seen on recent captives from a paratroop officer training regiment in the area. The young Kraut held a machine pistol in a steady grip, the business end less than two feet from my head.

"*Hände hoch!*" he ordered brusquely. "*Aufstehen, aufstehen! Los, los!*" He waved his piece menacingly. I complied quickly.

My captor continued waving his burp gun anxiously as if he were afraid to spend too much time out in the open. Other Germans were moving through the woods now, seeking survivors among the fallen Americans behind me. I clasped my hands behind my neck as we made our prisoners do. With great relief, I saw Weber limping toward me followed by another German. Weber was favoring his right foot where a slug apparently had cut through his heel.

His limp suddenly reminded me of my own leg and, on checking, I found I had a slight flesh wound that was bleeding fairly heavily. I pressed a part of the wool fabric of my trouser leg against the wound to stem the flow of blood. My trouser leg was ripped in even slices from my hip to my foot.

I was prodded in the back by my guard and, taking Weber's arm around my shoulder, I served as my buddy's crutch up the remainder of the hill toward our original objective.

We followed others of the defending German company across the hilltop clearing, past the fateful machine gun emplacements, beautifully camouflaged, and up another slight slope to our right. Weber winced with pain every time we stepped upward over the remaining 300 yards, until we arrived at a larger clearing at the crest of the hill.

Another American, one of the riflemen, was shoved ahead, joining our little group as we approached an area covered with well-fortified bunkers in a clearing. Each bunker had a heavy layer of logs and sandbags across its roof. This obviously was their company headquarters.

The young rifleman looked around him nervously, obviously terrified. I was too stunned by the developments of the past quarter-hour to fully comprehend what was happening. I did realize clearly that, where there had been seven vibrant, living young men fifteen short minutes ago, there were only three badly mauled prisoners now; men who had left their four comrades lying silent and stiffening on an obscure path on an equally obscure hill, somewhere in Germany or France, depending on which war one was witnessing.

We were led to the mouth of a dugout which, by its size, I surmised was the command post. We were motioned to sit beside the blanketed entrance, an order we were delighted to obey instantly. I welcomed the opportunity to get Weber off his feet, and my own leg was beginning to throb, although the blood seemed to have coagulated sufficiently to present no further problem in that regard.

A rustle of activity at the bunker's entrance announced the impending arrival of our interrogator. The thick-set man who crawled out of the dugout wore the epaulets of a German major. He was powerfully built, in his early forties, I judged, and without the stern expression one might expect; at least, without the expression we always effected when first encountering enemy prisoners. If they are set at ease early, they lose their fear and become more reticent to confide secrets the interrogator wants exposed.

"Well, and what have we here?" the major asked. He noticed Weber holding his heel and wincing. "Is that man wounded?"

"Yes, sir," I replied.

"We will have to see about that, won't we, Sergeant?" the officer continued, using the same cultured English accent I had noticed among many of the higher-ranking Kraut officers I'd encountered. It was an accent that conveyed the study of the language with an English national whose own accent betrayed such higher education. The major whispered an order to a nearby soldier who left immediately for a distant bunker. In fact, his every word had been little more than a whisper, now that I thought about it. I felt the hair on the back of my neck suddenly bristle. I became extremely nervous, with an infantryman's gut instinct in the presence of unseen danger.

Then I realized what created that queasiness. No one here was speaking aloud. A quick glance about the clearing explained why.

It was obvious that this entire mountaintop had been well zeroed in by American guns, judging by the condition of the trees surrounding it. Hardly one of them had escaped the loss of considerable bark, torn away by shrapnel or concussion. Piles of broken branches littered the forest floor throughout this compound area. Several trees had been knocked to the ground by repeated hits.

"The medical officer will be here shortly to look to your injuries," continued the major quietly. "While we are waiting, perhaps you can tell me, Sergeant, how many of you were there?"

I said nothing. Weber was in too much pain to answer or, for that matter, to listen to the question. The major slowly and deliberately turned his attention to the still obviously frightened young rifleman beside Weber. The A Company man, under the pressure of the officer's scrutiny, suddenly blurted out, in a voice much louder than he intended, "There were seven of us, sir!" His voice reverberated throughout the compound and into the trees beyond with an unbelievable force, compounded by the silence that had been present for so long.

The reaction to the shout was instantaneous and unanimous. As if an electric signal had sounded, every German in the clearing disappeared into the nearest dugout. The major frowned at the rifleman and quietly and quickly slipped back into the bunker from which he had emerged a few moments earlier. I immediately knew the reason.

The sound of the man's voice had surely carried the short distance to the next hilltop or the one beyond. And somewhere in there was an American artillery observer, listening and looking for any signs of life in this forested area. The sound of a man's voice was solid proof that this hill was occupied. His job was to depopulate it.

Weber and I were looking around quickly for a defilade position of any kind, another automatic reaction based on experience. We were rigid, listening for the inevitable thuds of exploding muzzles. Actually, the guns themselves would be several miles away, so there would be a slight delay while the observer telephoned back to the battery to advise that he heard a loud voice over here. The waiting gun crews then would perform their expert, deadly tasks.

I pulled Weber down behind the major's bunker, taking what cover it afforded. It extended about three feet above the ground although most of it was well below ground level. We were on the near side of the structure, farthest from what we identified as the American lines.

In the distance, I heard the dread "thum, thum, thum, thum" of a howitzer battery being fired. This would be the incoming mail. The A Company doggie stood rooted to the spot on which he had started this entire debacle, his eyes wide with terror. He was paralyzed with fear.

"Get down, you damn fool!" I shouted at him as the whistles grew rapidly louder. "That's incoming stuff!"

My last words disappeared into thunderous explosions as the shells shrieked in, drowning out any other sound. The gunners were right on target and they knew it. This hilltop obviously had become ritualistic to the GI cannoneers. The shells ripped through what remained of the hilltop forest, whining almost to the point of impact, then awakening with a deafening scream just before they burst into thousands of white hot, jagged-edged, deadly pieces of spinning metal. The concussion was what got the young rifleman, I was sure.

It made no difference to him, of course. His body whipped over the bunker, barely clearing Weber and me as we lay tightly hugging the ground, pressed against the structure. The body struck a large tree stump behind us with a sickening crunch just as another quartet of shells roared in. Confusion was rampant. The air reeked with the stench of burning cordite and scorched wood. Tree limbs flew everywhere. Bits of shrapnel were striking objects on and above ground as they whizzed by and over us.

I could feel Weber shivering beneath me as the terror of the situation overcame the pain of his wound. My mouth and throat ached with dryness and my chest strained at the banging of my heart.

One of the shells must have landed immediately on the far side of the major's bunker, shaking the ground beneath us. I jerked my hand back, realizing suddenly a painful sensation in it. I knew I had not been cut by whirring shrapnel, but saw the three black spots where pieces, nearly spent, had landed on the back of my right hand, still hot. I shook my hand instinctively, but they didn't fall off, leaving ugly, festering, dark spots where they had been. I pulled out my badly deteriorated handkerchief and bound the sore hand as tightly as possible.

When the burned powder smell and smoke began to clear and the barrage obviously had lifted, the Krauts climbed tentatively out of their dugouts. A hurried look about satisfied the major that he had lost none of his own men. Then he turned to us and noticed the body of the rifleman lying in an awkward position against the tree stump just behind Weber and me.

"Oh, my, that's too tragic. But then he did bring it on himself, *nicht?* Well, now, we'd better get you two to the rear before there is any more of that, don't you agree?"

I was relieved to see the major wave two guards over and hold a hurried, whispered conversation with them. They then turned to us.

"You will accompany these men. They will get you to Kolmar. From there you will have facilities to ride. You two are lucky. For you the war is over." The major saluted informally, turned and reentered his bunker as the two guards nervously began shuffling Weber and me to the rear.

The major's closing remark was one I had heard on both sides innumerable times. Virtually ever prisoner of war heard it often during his confinement, particularly in the early stages.

Our four-man party struggled down the steep hillside on the reverse slope. Several times the guards had to lend me a hand to keep Weber on his feet. His wounded foot was weakened and he found it difficult to maintain his balance, particularly on the precariously narrow path we were using to descend the mountain.

Several minutes later, which seemed like as many hours, we reached the level area at the bottom of the hill. The nearby village apparently had been evacuated of civilians and served as a supply depot for forward troops in these hills. Piles of materiel lay everywhere covered by camouflage nets. Actually, the nets were unnecessary since the heavy cover of trees managed to hide the supplies well. And this particular area was out of range of artillery fire. It was a perfect defilade position since guns couldn't fire tightly enough to drop shells this close to the mountain's reverse slope, and mortars couldn't travel this distance.

We were shoved into a dingy barn and told to sleep on the straw-covered floor. It was the first chance I'd had to look at Weber's foot. It had stopped bleeding. The cold air apparently had congealed the blood as it had my own flesh wound. Weber still showed the effects of searing pain, however, and was suffering acutely from the difficult downhill trip. In short order, he fell in a weary collapse on the soft, warm straw. I was grateful for several reasons.

I had developed a strong feeling of friendship for Weber, one of the few remaining survivors of the original company with whom I had stormed ashore on a hostile, Vichy-French-held coast just above Casablanca more than two years earlier. We had come through much together.

At the moment, I felt strangely paternal toward my injured comrade, even though at twenty-four Weber was more than two years my senior. We both would have been in line to return home on rotation furloughs within two weeks. This could have been the end of a pretty full war. Now it was another type of end.

I closed my eyes as I thought back to the beginning of it for me.

2. "Aw right, youse people"

WE'D GONE THROUGH a great deal. We'd managed to retain the well-earned plaudits that had been heaped on the division for generations. My own situation was peculiar, but then, that could be said by virtually every man in uniform.

With only three months of stateside duty after induction, which included basic training, the interminable lying around vegetating in maddening replacement centers, and the lack of any sort of leave, I had been assigned to the U.S. 3rd Infantry Division, a regular army outfit with a proud history.

We landed on November 8, 1942, on the hostile beaches of Fedala, just north of Casablanca, in time to join the French for four days of half-hearted resistance. I recalled the ridiculous picture many of my buddies and I presented later when we removed our helmets in safety for the first time since the invasion.

"Aw right, youse people. At ease. At ease!" The middle-aged first sergeant, with his ample, beer-laden belly overflowing the regulation GI belt, bellowed at every miserable wretch lying or standing about the boat deck. "Fall in over here. Youse're gonna get haircuts now."

The top kick was typical of the peacetime, thirty-year men I had seen so often during my short army career. Most of them were working with cadre members in basic training camps. Men such as this sergeant had been up and down the promotion ladder almost bi-monthly with each drunken payday spree. He was a "born soldier," whatever that was. Had he not been on the government payroll during the Depression's unemployment years in this guise, having no talent or inclination for anything resembling physical labor, he'd have been on some other government dole, like as not.

As the first sergeant roared his orders at the deckload of seasick, untried, uniformed civilians, apprehensive about approaching their first real combat, he shifted his weight from leg to leg to compensate for the graceful rolling of the once proud luxury liner.

The S.S. *Monterey,* sturdy and sleek of line, had been a pre-war cruise ship, traveling from California to Hawaii. Now she had been pressed into military service and had ugly but necessary three-inch and twenty-millimeter guns mounted on former observation platforms, manned by merchant Marine gunners. She had been disemboweled, her luxurious below-deck trappings replaced with countless rows of multilevel bunks bolted to deck, ceiling, and bulkheads.

"Youse people over there," the top kick continued. "Start down them stairs. Line up in the hall on the next floor down. The lootenant there will tell yez what to do next."

Several young merchant sailors standing nearby winced as they heard their sea jargon bastardized by this landlubber.

Grumbling, the men formed a sullen line, still unaware of what they were expected to do. Confusion was rampant, as it had been since each of them first donned olive drab. Their line was formed with the same sheeplike precision that every other event in their lives had assumed in recent months.

Everyone seemed to care little at this point whether he was at the front or rear of the queue. It certainly made no difference to me. There seemed little of importance awaiting us at the front of the line, and at least we were in a different environment in the ship's corridor than we had been out on deck. Even that modicum of variety was welcomed.

Life for all of us had become one continuous lineup. We learned to recognize our comrades in arms by the backs of their necks rather than by their faces.

As we reached the lower deck, we were brought to attention by the loud pronouncement of a giant of a man. 2nd Lt. Edward J. Firestone, Jr., a native of Prairie du Chien, Wisconsin, had played left tackle on the championship LaCrosse State Teachers College team for three years. He held three track letters each in shot-put, hammer throw, and football. He also had been named to the all-conference squad for two successive years.

He could have won his varsity football berth simply on the basis of his immovable bulk, had he been so inclined, I was certain. His academic grade point average probably had been a charitable low C.

Firestone was big and he was tough. He stood easily six feet seven inches tall and must have weighed in the neighborhood of 285 pounds. It was fitting that he should be commissioned after three years of ROTC at LaCrosse. He had stated a preference for the paratroops, but, unfortunately, airborne decision makers insisted that nobody in their ranks be as flat-footed as Firestone. He had second-degree fallen arches and a trick football knee that kept slipping out at awkward times.

Therefore, he had been commissioned and assigned to the necessary, though admittedly less glamorous, Quartermaster Corps where he served in non-hazardous, unrewarding duty throughout the war, remaining an unappreciated second lieutenant until his discharge. This situation, he had become convinced even at this early stage of the war, was the fault of every subordinate who was unfortunate enough to cross his path. In addition, Firestone was considered an A-1, first-class, unadulterated son of a bitch by every enlisted man and most officers who met him.

As senior officer in this section of the ship, he had assumed the obligation of ministering to every enlisted man in the area. He did this with an officious joy as he announced the latest directive to the transient troops now en route to the Dark Continent.

"Hold it, you people," he shouted. "At ease, at ease. That goes for everybody!" Lieutenant Firestone never talked when he could shout. "Now hear this!" he admonished his charges further. He had heard the expression over the ship's public address system several times and, despite its Navy flavor, decided he liked the sound as it rolled over the airways.

"Now hear this. You people are on your way to North Africa."

He surprised nobody with the enormity of his pronouncement.

"You'll find Africa a very dirty place. Eighty-five percent of the natives have venereal disease, and the other fifteen percent have lep-

19

rosy. You are ordered to get yourselves as clean as possible and to stay that way. Therefore, you'll line up in this corridor and Lieutenant Taggatz down there . . ." He pointed to the end of the hallway to another junior officer standing there, ". . . will give you haircuts. These will be real haircuts and let's hear no bitching about 'em, is that clear? Now, let's go and get on with it."

The young tonsorial officer stood resolutely and anxiously awaiting his first victim. In his eager right hand he held a hand-powered hair clipper. The first unfortunate to assume the indicated position on the lieutenant's high stool found his head being crossed and recrossed with no apparent plan. He moodily stared back at the long line of unsmiling buddies awaiting their own turns. Shortly, the floor surrounding the barber's stool was littered with thick piles of black hair.

"OK, next. You go over there, soldier." The lieutenant nudged the now nearly completely shorn recruit off the stool, directing him to another stool a few feet away.

Beside the second post stood another example of the endless and ageless breed known as regular army before World War II. This one, wearing his three stripes and two rockers prominently, scowled at the first victim to cross his path, plumped the youngster on the stool, lathered the stoic man's head, placed the shaving mug on the shelf beside him, and proceeded to cover the entire pate before him with luxuriant, soapy lather. Then, reaching into his left shirt pocket, the sergeant withdrew and deftly flicked open his straight razor. With meticulous care and swift precision, he made sure that not a single, offending follicle escaped.

So passed the entire day until the total assemblage — approximately 426 unhappy, homesick, seasick recent recruits — were shorn with such efficiency and thoroughness that in the dash from the Higgins Boats a few days later, into the face of French artillery, mortar and machine gun fire, their heavy steel helmets slid back and forth on their slippery heads.

When combat excitement died and we finally had time for less demanding chores, I marveled at the hitherto unfamiliar knobs and bumps I found on my own and other heads. It took my hair nearly three weeks to grow back to even reasonable crew-cut length. When it did, I suffered agonies from the itching discomfort on my head and other private parts of my body on which I had permitted depilation.

After the invasion and intitial, brief campaign, parts of the division, my company included, shipped northward to a place called Oujda, and were briefed on the forthcoming eastward trek to be made via the railed vehicles known to World War I veterans as 40 et 8s. These were familiar to me from conversations with American Legionnaires during my boyhood. These vets also had traveled in France aboard such rolling stock, capable of holding forty men and eight horses.

Our tour took us through such exotically named places as Sidi-Bel-Abbes, the headquarters city of the French Foreign Legion, Oran, Arzew, and Bizerte, ending our journey in the vicinity of a pass known as Kasserine.

This frightening, noisy, miserable, and terribly expensive place in central Tunisia was the site of the first and worst real drubbing we took at the hands of the experienced veterans of the elite Afrika Korps. However, after Yankee regrouping under the flamboyant Patton (whom the tankers loved and the infantrymen hated), the compliment was returned, resulting in the capitulation of more than a quarter million German troops in April 1943.

With the surrender of the bulk of Germany's staunch and sturdy bully boys, we neophyte warriors thought the war was nearly over. After all, hadn't the toughest elite fighting force of the entire powerful Wehrmacht thrown in the towel en masse? We believed we would be home for Easter. That was Easter 1943. The war still had more than two frightful years to run.

In the intervening months, I walked an estimated 6,000 miles, most of them uphill, it seemed. There had been amphibious landings — three of them — in Sicily. The first was the gut-splitting affair which put my regiment at a dirty little coastal village called Likata. Most of the landing party in my first wave made the uncomfortable assault, vomiting from the combination of fear, seasickness on the very heavy, stormy summer sea, and reaction to the diesel fumes that engulfed us as we traversed the Mediterranean out on the fantail (T. J. Mooney called it the "back porch") of the LCI aboard which we made the short journey from Bizerte. Fortunately, we were spared the additional discomfort of having to wade in to the beach in hip-deep water. The skipper of the craft had done what he was ordered to do — ram the ship right up on the beach so the bottom was torn out, but so the ramps on either side of the prow landed on sand to facilitate our dash into attack.

We stormed inland after bouts with artillery units and rearguard infantry platoons and, later, made two more surprise landings well behind enemy lines on the north coast of Sicily.

The thirty-eight-day campaign ended with the division taking advantage of a well-earned and promised rest, only to have it cut short when we had to put on our combat boots and travel across the narrow strip of water to historic Salerno to relieve the badly mauled 36th (Texas) Division which had been taking the same pounding we were about to get from the palisades above the beach.

We hiked up the Italian boot as if we were walking on eggshells. We passed ancient and modern ruins of historic storybook towns, liberating village after village, most of which were completely unfamiliar to virtually all of us. We were followed by rear echelon troops which capitalized on every uniform. Cartoonist Bill Mauldin was to call them "garritroopers," because they were too far back to be shot at, yet far enough forward to be credible in the combat gear they had managed to shortstop on its way to the fighting men.

The men of the Rock of the Marne (the appellation given the 3rd Division during World War I when it was the only allied unit to hold against furious German counterattacks along the Marne River in France) plowed ahead to the bloody Volturno River and to the quiet towns north of it, seemingly thrown against the sides of mountains.

First, we encountered heavy resistance from well-entrenched units of Germans around the hillside village of Pietravairano, nestled in the saddle of a mountain range perpendicular to our path. The village fell to an expensive frontal assault.

Then, climbing over this mountain in pursuit of the retreating Krauts, we looked across a valley and the mountain range on the far side of it, in the saddle of which was another picturesque village. This one was Presenzano. Then would come repetitions of the same up-and-over procedure through such significant names as Casserta, Venafro and, finally, the biggie — the spot at which everything in Italy stopped, except death and discomfort — Cassino.

We fought our vicious way up and over Mount Rotundo and Mount Lungo only to gaze into this once quiet valley. At the other end lay the remains of the village called Cassino. That one, I recalled with a shudder, had been a real bitch.

After that, there was the luxury of being relieved and the endless dry runs from the Higgins Boats down at Bagnoli and Pozzuoli, Neapolitan suburbs. That we were invasion-bound, we all knew. Conjecture made our destination Yugoslavia, France, England, and everywhere else in Europe, except the actual site of one of the most memorable, infamous hellholes of the entire war.

Upon leaving the docks of Pozzuoli early on the morning of January 21, 1944, we heard strong rumors of Florence being our destination. Early the following morning, we absorbed the brochures we were given aboard ship — brochures extolling the art treasures of that northern city and admonishing us about our behavior while there. It was a move clearly and successfully aimed at throwing enemy espionage at the Neapolitan docks off our real mission. Our combined troops of the British 1st, American 3rd, and elements of the 82nd Airborne Division landed just a few miles from the original debarkation point, at a favorite beach resort of antiquity, Anzio, allegedly Nero's favorite recreation site, and the one from which some historians maintain he watched the flame-lit sky over Rome, thirty-five miles to the north.

This landing at Anzio and her sister city, Nettuno, was peaceful and constituted a complete surprise for the enemy. In fact, we laughed later when we remembered that the first two casualties in those early morning hours were a pair of anxious doggies falling down the steps of what they hoped was a wine cellar.

Too few troops landed at first at Anzio-Nettuno, so our initial surprise, which really caught the Germans flatfooted, died aborning. Our lines would have been stretched too thin had our invasion body taken advantage of our surprise and attempted to implement our plan. It was to move the full distance of about fifteen miles, cutting the vital Highway 6 and an adjacent rail line which stretched across our front at the base of the mountains.

At Anzio I earned my first and second Purple Hearts, as did most of the men in my company. It was there, too, that I was captured the first time.

The southern France invasion, just short of seven months after the Anzio landing, had been a bit louder than Anzio was. Then the war had stopped for our outfit as we "toured" the lower Rhone Valley. But as we approached the Vosges Mountains, we found the war again, with a vengeance.

My recent ambush took place in the Kolmar Pocket, and was the climax of a long, hard drive to the very doorway of Germany itself — the Rhine River.

3.   A Remarkable War

I WAS AWARE THAT we were approaching the end of our climb. The biting cold had numbed my ears and fingers. I estimated we had been walking for more than an hour. My two Kraut companions were trudging doggedly ahead. We were on a more level road now.

Twice within a few yards, my feet nearly slid from beneath me, almost throwing me to the ground. Only vigorous, instinctive reflexes saved me the added discomfort of a collar or sleeve full of snow.

Then a village loomed ahead of us in the darkness. As I approached it, I thought the little settlement resembled European picture postcards I had seen. It was built around a circular main road, the loop of which held a large lagoon. The lagoon, or millpond, was frozen over, and I could see where snow had been cleared on its icy surface to provide an ice-skating rink. The buildings of the town bordered the outside of the loop with only an occasional structure on the inside of it. At the far end of the loop were larger, public buildings. This had all the earmarks of pre-war tourist country.

We passed an impressive medieval structure on the face of which was inscribed, *"Rathaus."* I knew this was the city hall.

We turned a corner and climbed a snow-covered, cobbled street past another huge building across the front of which, in large, Gothic letters, "Hotel Lamm" was announced. The street narrowed as we approached and prepared to enter a large, square building that had to be a school.

We entered the huge front double door. I followed my German guides along a dark corridor and into a large room that had been a classroom. It was lighted only by two candles on a table, the only piece of furniture in the chamber. The table was on an inclined podium, about eight inches higher than the floor of the rest of the room, and located about where the teacher's desk normally would be.

Around the entire room lay a bracket extending about seven feet from the outer wall, within which was piled clean, fresh-looking straw. Several men lay asleep on and under blankets which had been spread on the straw within this frame. They had assumed various positions of discomfort.

The room was alive with the sounds and smells of sleeping men. I immediately recognized the now all-too-familiar odor I had known so often. Every German position we had ever overrun had been permeated by the same peculiar aroma or combination of odors. I never fully identified any of these smells, although we often suspected they represented the accumulation of tobacco and ersatz sausage with black bread, which comprised the bulk of the Kraut field diet.

On the front wall of the room stood a thick, tiled oven from which emanated a friendly heat. I headed directly for the welcome warmth. One of the Germans with me reached for a long roll of deep-red sausage. With a heavy trench knife, he cut a large, thick chunk from the roll. He placed it aside while he tore an equally thick slice from the loaf of black bread beside it. He placed the two together, forming a curious, bulky sandwich. He took an enormous bite from it, and, with mouth bulging to overflowing, motioned to me to come to the table and help myself to a similar concoction.

I needed no second invitation. I waited until the second German had made himself an equally awkward meal and made my own sandwich as quickly and generously as I could. I wasted little time wolfing it down. It was the first time I had tasted really solid food in weeks and, despite the fact that both the sausage and bread were artificial — a necessary condition at which the German nation had become amazingly adept — the novelty of the unaccustomed food proved to be a delicious treat. I'm sure the true taste was quite frightful, but then, we also had found British bully beef quite palatable as a change from our C rations, while the British found their food distasteful after being limited to it alone for months and years.

I had been on a two-month diet of rutabaga soup and black bread, very little of each, daily. It had cost me some fifty pounds in that time, I guessed. As a result, I soon found that my eyes had exaggerated my stomach's capacity. I filed the uneaten remainder of my sandwich in my combat jacket pocket against further hard times.

I was completely nonplussed. This was obviously not a prison camp, although I reasoned, this might be the guard room of one. But I had seen no sign of any such installation around this building as we entered in the breaking dawn.

As the heat of the oven reached me, I opened the collar of my combat jacket and that of my uniform shirt. It was then that I realized I wasn't alone in my uniform. Several of my boarders from the filthy straw of the transient camp back at Waldkirch had accompanied me. They had not succumbed to the freezing weather as I had hoped they might, but had merely hibernated until this newfound heat rejuvenated them. They had lain dormant in the linings of my clothing and in my body hair.

In addition, the lice had laid their eggs in the body-contact linings of my clothing, particularly in the armpits of my shirt and the waistband of my trousers. They also had laid their eggs in armpit and pubic hair. I felt the unpleasant itching sensation that announced their curious nocturnal wanderings.

I squirmed uncomfortably. The frantic movements of the nearly microscopic vermin caused me to itch over my entire body. I remembered as I scratched that lice were next to impossible to kill. Older hands at dealing with them — those fellows in the prison camp who had come out of the Tennessee hills or the slums of large industrial cities — knew how to deal with them.

My introduction to body lice had occurred in the filthy hovel that had served as quarters for the dozen or so men at the temporary prison camp at Waldkirch bei Freiberg — Dulag (for *Durch-lager*, or "through camp") 62. Under the expert guidance of those who had known lice before, we would conduct nightly contests by the light from the open door of the pot-bellied stove, reflected in the flames from the wood fire. It was our only form of recreation and consisted of one of the men opening the small, front-feeding door and the others baring their abdomens and trying to catch as many of the fast-moving bugs as possible as they skittered across bare skin.

"That ain't no way to kill a li'l ole louse," Sgt. Molder Grubbs, the Tennessean, had snorted, teasing the neophytes among us as we tried to deal with the matter. His specific remark had come in response to what I had thought would be an effective solution. I had caught a louse between right thumb and forefinger and had flung it on the hot metal of the stove. The creature had bounced right off and disappeared into the dark reaches of some other straw mattress.

Grubbs picked one of the tiny creatures from his own abdomen. "This heah's the way," he counseled, crushing the louse between the nails of his thumb and forefinger. "Theah, now. That'll do it every tahm!"

I scratched my groin again and looked at the two Krauts who had brought me here. One was spreading his blanket between two sleeping soldiers next to the doorway. The other, his blanket under his arm, was pointing to another opening in which he suggested I was to sleep. The man threw another blanket to me. Then he moved to the far end of the room to prepare his own sleeping accommodations.

I divested myself of my combat jacket and shirt which I laid close to the man sleeping on my left. My trousers I laid with equal care practically over the sleeping German on the other side. Shortly, clad only in my undershorts, I lay flat on my back, my hands clasped behind my head, staring into the flickering shadows of the dawn on the high ceiling.

I pictured my combat experience in hundreds of miniscule, panoramic, and disjointed views. I relived artillery barrages under which I had cringed and my heart seemed to pound harder. I shuddered as I pictured the machine gun duels in which I had been caught or in which I was a participant, the red tracers of the American guns, the white of the German weapons. I heard again the *duh-duh-duh* sound of the 400-round-per-minute American weapon, the sound of tearing oilcloth of the Deutsche machine *gewehr* with its 1,100 rounds a minute. I felt the panic momentarily I had experienced a few times when it was necessary to cross a no-man's land sector measuring less than 100 yards in width, while trying to avoid the masses of bullets thrown by German automatic weapons.

I saw again the unidentified A Company dogface, a young man with little or no combat experience, dying brutally back on that Alsatian hilltop on what may well have been his very first patrol.

I thought of that son of a bitch of a smirking *feldwebel* at the camp in Waldkirch, a lousy sergeant, that was all. He had conducted himself as if he were some kind of a goddamned bird colonel . . .

It had been a crystal morning when my comrades and I, five in all, walked into the front gate of Dulag 62 at Waldkirch. Weber had been taken to the hospital in Neu Breisach on the Rhine. The other four fellows who had been picked up along the way to the Rhine from our place of capture joined us just before the river came in view. Just at midnight, New Year's Eve of 1944, we found ourselves directly in midstream on a mule-drawn ferry barge. I knew it must be midnight because of the sudden wild and exuberant burst of skyward tracer fire from dozens of machine guns along both banks of the Rhine.

The enemy was celebrating the opening of the Christian year 1945 at the instant it was born. So these bastards still remembered that He in whom God was alleged to have manifested Himself was Jesus Christ, after all, and not the Viennese paper hanger as they had been told.

We had ridden on a rickety relic of a train, crowded with transient civilians and furlough-bound soldiers, each laden with pitiful tidbits of personal treasures. The ancient vehicle lurched along at approximately four miles per hour for a couple of miles until the track ran out at a bomb crater. At that point, all the passengers, ourselves included, resignedly debarked with no complaint, circled the crater, and began walking along the next short stretch of track until we came to the next few railroad cars with their tiny engine, patiently huddled there awaiting cargo. Thus we proceeded from crater to crater, crowded aboard those ridiculous little passenger vehicles. The inside of these cars reminded me of the old Toonerville Trolley comic strip car. This process continued throughout Germany in these days of saturation air strikes by Allied planes, unchallenged by any Luftwaffe ships. The general public and military travelers alike seemed to have become completely accustomed to this incovenience.

At Freiberg, my companions and I were herded off the train to begin the twelve-mile march to Waldkirch. As we sat aboard that railroad car and as we left it, what passing interest we were shown by both civilians and soldiers alike was not hostile. Nor was it particularly friendly. It was almost as if the population was moving in a near trance.

"Zis was ze first Cherman city bombed in ze war," advised the elder of our two guards. "Ze Englanders, zey fly over und drop zeir bombs on ze houses und schools in 1940. But zey didn't bomb ze *fabricken* . . . er, factories."

He was the only guard we had met in days who spoke any English at all. He made me cognizant of the desperate manpower situation now facing the Greater Third Reich. All rear echelon troops I had seen, as well as many combat units, contained men well past forty years of age. Our guide was at least fifty-five, I judged. I could recall instances in the Vosges, particularly around Besancon and in the Belfort area south of here, where company-sized German units had surrendered, simply because their commanding officers had been killed or severely wounded. The dregs of extreme youth and age were facing the Allies as Germany's most desperate pre-occupation era wound down.

I looked toward the west, following the pointing finger of our guide, and saw a long line of dull, flat, one-story buildings covering the horizon at the base of the wooded hills. I took the story of the bombing of the civilians with a heavy dose of salt. It wasn't that I thought it couldn't happen, but if it had, I was sure it hadn't been intentional, as had been implied. Nothing, certainly, compared to what manned and unmanned German aircraft had done to Britain, Rotterdam, Warsaw, and points in between.

The road we were traveling was picturesque, bordered by narrow fields of some sort of grain, now frozen and snow-covered. The fields extended a few hundred yards on either side of the road, ending abruptly as they came face to face with the typical southern Black Forest wooded hills, disappearing into nebulous blackness as they rose above valley floors. From this position at the bottom of the "V" in the valley, the trees looked as if they stretched upward into infinity.

I was glad the walk had been forced on us, a peculiar reaction for an infantryman, to be sure, because most of us had promised ourselves we'd never walk again if we could help it, once the war was over. My reason was that the train had been unheated and my combat jacket offered little protection against the bitterly cold weather. Then too, the temporary stitching job I had been able to perform on my trousers back at Neu Breisach was far from professional. The crude seams between bullet cuts had broken open, and the longer I sat on the train's wicker seats, the more cold air filtered through onto my bare legs. I cursed the day I had stubbornly refused the issue of long johns back at the company supply room in tepid November.

The final bend in the road brought us in sight of the camp. It was a dreary, forbidding affair consisting of two large, barracks-like buildings and a few small, prefabricated huts. The entire place was surrounded by a double fence, ten feet high, made of strands of barbed wire, roughly two feet apart. I saw two guards in their gray-green, ankle-length greatcoats, pacing stiffly before the gate. Over this gate was a sign proclaiming "Durchlager 62." Other guards were scattered in pairs all along the fence. I saw no evidence of prisoners in the exercise yard and assumed they had been kept indoors because of the extreme cold.

One of the two guards opened the huge padlock holding the gate chained shut. He and his companion, completely oblivious to us, seemed much more concerned with keeping themselves warm during their tour of duty. They would walk a few steps, stamp their feet several times, and beat at their shoulders with heavily mittened hands. They wore their gray-green work caps with the ear flaps pulled down and tied under their chins.

We were conducted to one of the smaller outbuildings at the rear of the compound and ordered to wait. The older of our guards climbed the four wooden steps and entered through the heavy wooden door. He returned shortly and called me to the door as the ranking member of our prisoner group.

I entered the building and immediately noticed a small, littered room heated by a large pot-bellied stove. About the room were a few pieces of office furniture which, by their diverse appearance, had been commandeered from a variety of sources.

The German non-commissioned officer behind the desk on my right wore the white-bordered epaulets of a *feldwebel*. He was a gaunt, hawk-faced man whose cold, steady eyes betrayed absolutely no feeling. *An even-tempered man,* I thought. *Always bad.* I estimated the man to be in his mid-forties. He wore the German equivalent of our Purple Heart on his uniform front, an oval wreath with another design in the center. He, too, had seen combat.

"Your pay book, please, Sergeant," he said evenly. He had his right hand extended toward me but was looking at papers on his desk.

"They took it from me, Sergeant," I replied, unable to resist the reminder that we were equal in rank.

"Who did?" he asked, looking up at me evenly.

"The front-line soldiers who captured me," I responded.

The fact was, I hadn't seen a pay book since basic training. In fact, I never knew any of our troops to use them. We were paid simply upon calling out our name and serial number to the paymaster. That was on those rare occasions that we saw a paymaster. It seldom was oftener than every two months.

"Then please empty your pockets here on the desk," the man said in clipped English, precise and studied. It reflected learning from a Briton, probably in school.

I emptied my pockets. I still had three crushed cigarettes in my mutilated Chesterfield pack. I also had three match books, none of them full. From my left rear pocket, I dragged my only handkerchief, a well-worn, bloody, bedraggled rag. It had been through the mill with me for a long time. I had washed it, or tried to, repeatedly in icy streams, but without soap it proved an impossible task.

"And your identity discs too, please," the *feldwebel* continued, completely bored by the entire exchange.

I slid my dog tags over my head, wondering as I did what I could expect as the German non-com's reaction to the "H" stamped on them. I continued dropping my pitifully meager personal effects on the dark wooden surface of the desk.

My old brown leather wallet, which had seen infinitely better days, I placed on the desktop last. All at once I had a most uncomfortable sensation. I suddenly felt a frightening premonition as I wondered if I had ever destroyed that damn newspaper clipping from the *Milwaukee Journal* that my mom had sent months ago.

The German sergeant picked up the dog tags and studied them quietly for a moment. His face was still emotionless and he seemed to be delaying any reaction purposely. Then he looked squarely into my eyes and I knew my stay in Durchlager 62 was going to be something of a tribulation, to say the least. The German, his eyes suddenly beginning to concentrate on me, said in a steady, controlled voice, "I see you are a Jew."

"Yes," I replied, quietly nervous. This was no time, I knew, to demand my rights or to try to defend the underdog, especially since I happened to be the underdog at the moment.

My heart was in my throat as the Kraut reached for the wallet. He opened it and pulled out the pictures of Mom, of my fiancée Nana and her family. Studying each photo carefully, the German seemed to be searching for some Semitic characteristics in each face with which he might damn me. Then he turned to the rear compartment of the billfold, removing several pieces of occupation currency. He looked at each piece disdainfully. Then . . . Oh, goddamn it! There it was. That goddamn *Journal* article. I hadn't destroyed it after all! My heart felt as if it might burst at any second.

The German non-com carefully and methodically unfolded the six-month-old newspaper clipping that I hadn't looked at for nearly as long. After what seemed an eternity of silent reading, during which the man seemed to be memorizing the account, the Kraut lifted his eyes to meet mine, steadily studying me for a moment. He seemed to be relishing this opportunity to exert his psychological pressure on me. Then, slowly enunciating each word so as to create the maximum nerve-tingling impact, he read aloud from last June's *Milwaukee Journal* clipping, which had run after my escape from my first imprisonment in Italy.

"Another contributor has qualified for a column in the *Army-Navy News*," he read. "A four-page home-town newspaper, the *Army-Navy News* is prepared, edited and published monthly by the serviceman's committee of the Jewish Community Center." As he said the last three words, the sergeant smirked and glanced at me with his right eyebrow cocked. Then he continued the reading.

"In a typical column, a soldier told of having read his copy of the *Army-Navy News* while flying around the world three times. Another serviceman read his aboard a submarine deep under the Pacific. A third told of reading his copy while seated in an army dentist's chair having a tooth drilled."

The *feldwebel* glanced without complete understanding at the last paragraph once more, questioning its meaning. As if suddenly realizing what it actually meant, he looked up at me.

"This is a remarkable war you people fight."

Without waiting for a reply, he proceeded to read on.

"The latest contributor is Pfc. Hal Lister, 23, son of Mrs. Hilda Lister, 2325 N. 50th St. Lister wrote from Italy as follows: 'Since I wrote you last, I've had another little adventure. I was captured recently and wounded. After fifteen days as a prisoner of the Germans, during which I read my copy of the *Army-Navy News* in a Kraut prison camp, I was fortunate enough to escape. It's a relief to be back to regular chow with my buddies every day. I nearly lost the habit as a guest of the Krauts. They definitely are not gentlemen.' "

Uh-oh, I thought uncomfortably. *Me and my big damn opinions!* I once had been told never to put into writing what I was thinking. What sound counsel. This was a valuable object lesson in defense of that theory.

The last paragraph of the article seemed to amuse the *feldwebel* who smirked thinly. But when he looked up and into my eyes, there was no humor in that implied trace of a smile. He looked down again and continued reading aloud.

"I had a chance during my imprisonment to observe their morale and the amount and condition of their equipment, at least, in the area ahead of my division. As a result, my own morale is up about 150 percent. You've no idea how much on the run they really are."

Inwardly, I winced. The *feldwebel* completed his presentation, then deliberately crumpled the clipping into a small ball without looking up. He placed it on the far corner of his desk as if he were holding something extremely distasteful. He looked at it a moment in silent contemplation, holding it delicately balanced on the desk between his thumb and forefinger. Then, reaching into his breast pocket with his free hand, he pulled out a box of wooden matches. He lighted one by whipping it along the underside of the desk, and then held it against the crumpled ball of newsprint. The paper flamed slowly at first, then brightly, as the yellow tongue of flame licked hungrily at every exposed surface.

The two of us remained completely engrossed in the tiny fire until the flames died with a puff of smoke wisping nearly to the ceiling. Then, as if our mothlike hypnosis in the flame had been broken suddenly, we looked again into each other's eyes.

"That is a very interesting account, Herr Lister," the sergeant said. "However, I do not think you will have the opportunity to write of such an adventure here. Now, pick up your belongings and wait outside!"

He fairly spat the last sentence out, glaring venomously until I closed the door behind me. I moved with discreet speed, stuffing my meager possessions in any accessible pocket.

It took less than half an hour for the remainder of the Americans to be interrogated. Then, once again, we were assembled outside the office as our guard marched us toward the small, dilapidated structure we had noticed upon first entering the compound. As we entered the flimsy building, we took a few moments to accustom our sun- and snow-blinded eyes to the dark interior. We finally oriented ourselves with the aid of a bit of light that shone dustily through the single, greasy window of the one-room structure.

I looked about slowly, carefully, cautiously trying to find a possible escape outlet. There was only one entrance. The building was constructed of worn boards and probably had been an equipment shed before being put to its present use. It smelled of the many men who had occupied it earlier.

The lone room measured about twelve by twenty feet. Except for a small, cleared area before the window, the room's walls were completely covered with heavy timbers from which were suspended crude shelves. These shelves extended about seven feet from the wall and were covered inadequately by filthy straw. In several places, both layers of the double-decked shelves showed only dirty lumber through minimal straw covering. The straw, too, looked as if it had been here for a very long time. That meant my colleagues and I would shortly be sharing these sleeping facilities with many varieties of vermin. We were not disappointed in this assumption.

As soon as we all were inside, the guard closed the door and latched it from the outside. We stood at the window, forlornly watching the guard disappear around the far corner of the building. No one spoke for several moments as we sadly surveyed what was to be our new home for God knew how long. Then, one of the men, a young, dark complexioned lad, jumped on the upper shelf.

"Hey, ain't this nifty? Look, you guys, bunk beds and everything."

"You're gonna have company up there soon, buster," Grubbs told him. Then, turning to me, he said, "Hey, Mac, youah rank heah. What do you think? Is this where we spend the rest of the wah?"

"I doubt it," I told him. "This is probably just a temporary stopover for transient prisoners. They probably get a big gang here before they ship them out to a stalag."

"What's that?"

"A stalag? It means *'Stammlager.'* That's a permanent camp. *Lager* means camp in German. Like *Konzentrazionslager* — concentration camp. That sign over the gate says *'Durchlager.'* That's 'through camp.' "

The southerner nodded and looked around at each face, making sure all of them understood. As he stared first at one face, then another, he began humming "Wabash Cannon Ball," a song I had quickly learned to detest when it seemed to be the only one available on the recreation room jukebox back at Camp Roberts, California, during my basic training days. God, that seemed a long time ago. It had been. More than two years, in fact.

Grubbs proved to be the personality boy of the group as he made everyone feel that each man's load would be lighter if all could talk and sing and otherwise keep their depleted morale as high as possible.

"Hell," he would say. "I ain't nevah seen no problem that could be solved by worryin' about it."

He had rural Tennessee country jokes for nearly every occasion, or at least a homespun word or expression that would bring a smile to the miserable wretches around him. The men and I grew to rely on Grubbs to see us through those particularly demanding, debilitating days.

Having been stripped of most of our personal possessions upon our respective captures, none of us had toilet articles with us. We were supplied a small pan and a daily water ration for the entire group, which was hardly adequate for one man. The single small bar of gritty pumice soap given us on our second day disappeared shortly after with constant use by all five of us.

It was on our third day that a guard came to the door and called me to come outside alone. He led me to the rear of the building where I was discomfited to note the German sergeant standing beside a shallow trench talking to an SS officer. They were speaking softly, their heads close together as if hatching some gigantic plot. Occasionally, they would guffaw at some immense touch of humor.

As I approached, they stopped conversing and stared at me with obvious distaste.

"Ah, here is the Chewish Chentleman," sneered the *feldwebel* to the officer. His inflection was heaviest on the last word, not the first, strangely enough. I wondered about it at the moment. "He is going to show us how he thinks chentlemen should be treated, are you not, Mr. Jew Lister?" He stared at me now with open animosity on his face. The SS officer appeared vaguely amused by the entire sequence.

"Pick up that shovel, Herr Chentleman."

I looked at the small trench and the shovel lying beside it. With scarcely a thought about the sub-zero weather and my gloveless hands, I began my attack on the frozen earth.

Through the first half hour, I felt them standing behind me, watching silently, smirking. I didn't look at them. Sometimes they would exchange a private joke and chortle in unison, looking directly at me.

My hatless head began to feel the cold and my ears were pinching badly. My physical discomfort, though, was minor compared with the premonition that the sight of the skull and crossbones and paired lightning bolts on the officer's collar drew forth. His insignia identified him as an *oberstormfuhrer* — a first lieutenant.

I couldn't stop wondering why an SS officer should be interested in me. Nor was there any clue from the youthful-looking, black-uniformed lieutenant.

After a thirty-minute session with the shovel, my body was dripping with perspiration. My ears had stopped smarting and my hands were raw with cold on their backs, raw with the steady contact of the rough shovel handle on the palms.

Finally the two Germans left me alone and walked back into the headquarters building. I chanced a glance over my shoulder and saw the German guard watching me from the corner of the building that housed the American prisoners. There was no way out of the camp at this moment, I knew. I could only bide my time.

The pogrom of the shallow ditch continued for eighteen endless days, except that the shallow ditch became a deep, long trench. Its length and depth doubled, then tripled.

Throughout the entire experience, my companions were kept indoors, becoming irritable with boredom and lice. Their diet of a four-ounce piece of black "sawdust" bread and a small portion of watery soup did little to improve their dispositions.

The only thing that kept up any degree of high spirits was my travail as, at the end of each of my long working days, when I was marched back to the barracks, half frozen, hands raw, ears white-tipped with cold, body quaking with the effect of the bitter weather on my damp clothing, they would gather around to ease my burden.

"Here you go, ole buddy," Grubbs would say as he handed me an extra piece of black bread spread with a thin layer of *schmalz* — an onion-flavored lard spread. Where he got it or how he managed to scrounge such a delicacy was beyond my understanding, but I'd take it and revel in the exotic taste. The fact that Grubbs had gone to great personal risk to obtain this treat for me made it taste all the better.

Other occasions showed the close feeling that had developed among us. When I returned from my day in the trench, the men waited at my bedside with a bucket of heated wash water to bathe my sweating body before I lay down on the lousy straw tick. This treatment would give me enough strength to help me face another freezing, ten-hour day in the trench.

On the evening of the eighteenth day, my sixteenth of digging and refilling that goddamn ditch, the elderly guard who had been with us from the beginning came to the door of our shack, unlocked it, and stepped inside. He held a piece of torn paper.

"Come, all of you. Pack your belongings." He smiled, not unkindly, at his little joke. Our only possessions were the filthy, lousy clothes we wore.

"Where we goin', Pop?" Grubbs asked jovially.

"Who knows? Perhaps to join your *Komeraden* in a *Stammlager*. Come, already. Come."

"Well, at least these beards will keep our necks warm. That is, until we get where we're goin'," one of the men said. He moved to help me off the shelf where I had fallen into a deep, weary sleep.

"*Nein, nein,* he does not go, your *feldwebel,*" the guard hastily advised the man. His voice was sympathetic, but firm. "He *bleibt hier.*"

"What in hell you mean, man?" Grubbs demanded, belligerently.

I, meanwhile, had been jolted fully awake by the announcement. I wondered, ominously, why I had been singled out to remain behind.

"I know nossing. I follow orders only," the old man replied.

We bade each other farewell sadly. Together, the group left the building, each looking back at me as he passed through the door, fully sympathizing with me. My troubles obviously weren't over even now. A gnawing fear was growing in my belly.

Leaving me here could mean several things. It could mean, for instance, they planned to knock me off and dump me in some shallow grave somewhere, just because I was Jewish. Or, because I had been a prisoner and had escaped. Or, that I found the Krauts not to be gentlemen. Whatever moved them could result in my demise. Nobody would witness, nobody would be the wiser. I was at their mercy with no witnesses. *Jesus,* I thought, *talk about elements of paranoia!*

The others were marched to the gate, loaded aboard an ancient relic of a wood-burning truck and driven away. They waved to me until I lost sight of them. I stood at the dingy, streaked, and dusty window for nearly two hours, staring into the deepening dusk as if I expected the truck driver suddenly to discover he was one passenger short. The truck didn't return.

Instead, two other large vehicles drove up to the camp shortly after dark. The gate was swung open and a large contingent of French troops was herded in. They were conducted to a larger building in the compound and disappeared into it. All of them seemed to wear the same regimental insignia, as well as I could make out as they passed beneath the yard light on the pole in the center of the compound.

Their capture probably was the result of a major attack or counterattack by the Germans.

Once again, I was alone in the darkness, now eerie with contemplation and fear. I tried to sleep but couldn't. I longed for a cigarette but had none.

Suddenly, I recalled how Grubbs had demonstrated the "hill folks" way to roll smokes out of the ends of straw, using small scraps of paper. I gathered together a few sticks of straw, crushed them, and dampened my fingers in what remained of the wash water. Then I pulverized the resulting combination, spreading it within a strip of paper from the pile of kindling. As I lighted it with a paper strip inserted into the stove, the searing heat poured down my throat. The straw flamed and smoked. However, it did take my mind off my current predicament temporarily and it gave short-lived relief from the terror growing within me.

I awakened earlier than usual the next morning, after a particularly unsatisfactory night's sleep. The few times I managed to drift off, it was a disturbed sleep with no rest and with frighteningly realistic dreams. Faces were close and real and familiar as they died in terror and pain. I jerked upright to a sitting position, my body wet with perspiration even though the fire had gone out during the night, and the building was at its usual morning cold and clammy worst.

I listened intently for the now familiar footsteps of my guard. So would come the traditional opening of another day of labor. The footsteps were approaching now; the door opened. Instead of the usual guard, however, an SS trooper stood in the opening this morning. He motioned silently to me, his face betraying no feelings. I followed the wordless directions, hurriedly laced my boots, and followed the man out the door.

Instead of heading toward the ditch, we walked to the camp's main gate. A few hastily exchanged words between the new guard and the men at the gate, and the huge double door was swung open. This was my first time outside the camp proper in nearly three weeks, and I was confused and very frightened at the reasons for it. I also pondered the likelihood of an escape now that there was a one-on-one relationship. I realized, of course, that, while we were about the same height, I had lost considerable weight because of the heavy work and poor diet and was quite weak. Surely I'd be no match for this SS guy who was armed besides. But the thought did occur as we moved farther away from the barbed wire. I was terribly nervous. I didn't like the way this was developing at all.

For some reason, the air felt warmer this morning than it usually had. Perhaps this, too, was psychological. Neither of us spoke a word as we walked straight toward the village from the camp. We marched side by side, in step all the way, to a building I knew must be the local school. It was a large, three-story edifice of aging red brick.

We entered the structure's front door and walked up a narrow flight of stairs until we stood before a swastika-draped door on which hung a sign lettered, *"Haupt Büro."*

The guard knocked and, without waiting for an answer, opened the door. With a sideways nod of his head, he motioned me inside the incredibly small and crowded office. He then closed the door behind him.

The long, narrow room contained little furniture and what was there stood crowded at its far end. The near end was filled with all sorts of packing crates. The heavy desk stood nearly the full width of the chamber. Two chairs and a bookcase completed the furnishings. Behind the desk sat a pleasant-looking, clean-cut man in his middle fifties, I estimated. He was dressed in a gray, double-breasted, civilian suit, the first I had seen in many months. His tie was a patternless dark, almost slate gray.

He gave no visible or immediate reason for the heavy foreboding feeling that overwhelmed me. Still, I began to feel increasingly uncomfortable. Never had I been in the presence of a non-uniformed German official although I had been interrogated often. This could mean only one thing, I reasoned — Gestapo!

"How do you do, Sergeant Lister. Thank you for visiting me. Won't you sit there?" He stood and indicated with his extended right arm an overstuffed leather arm chair immediately before and facing the desk. I sat haltingly as my host followed suit. Then, reaching into the upper drawer of the desk, the German pulled out a pack of Embassy cigarettes. My mouth watered.

"Would you like one, Sergeant?" He extended the opened pack toward me, showing what had appeared to be a friendly smile.

But rather than disarming me as it might be expected to, it only strengthened my fear and suspicion. From my personal experience, as well as from everything I'd read and heard, this uncharacteristic situation was motivated by something other than simple compassion and generosity.

Nevertheless, I nodded silently, unable to take my eyes off the cigarette packet. I accepted a single cigarette from the proferred box.

The man took out three more and reached across the desk to lay them before me.

"Here, I'll tell you what. Why don't you take these back to camp with you?" He pushed the box in my direction. "If you want any more while you are here, feel free to take them from these."

Cautiously, I accepted the light the German offered. Overwhelmed by this unexpected bonanza, I guardedly realized that he was being gracious with some deep motivation. I waited for the next development as I drew deeply on the unaccustomed smokes. It wasn't long in coming.

"Lister. Lister. That's a rather unusual name for a Jew, isn't it, Sergeant?"

I hesitated a moment. The man's eyes still seemed friendly. The question appeared to be one of mere curiosity. I cleared my throat nervously, flicking ash from my cigarette at the same time.

"My father wasn't Jewish," I said quietly, not looking at the man.

"I see. But that has nothing to do with you being brought to visit me. Sergeant, may I please see your pay book?"

Suddenly, all vestiges of friendliness disappeared. My inquisitor was all business now.

"I told the *feldwebel* back at the camp that it was taken from me by the people who captured me."

"Ah, so. Yes, that is correct. I remember now that Sergeant Hoffman told me that. But you see, Sergeant Lister, if you have no pay book, perhaps you are not even a soldier. We have no way of contacting those soldiers who captured you to verify your story, now, do we? Do you see my position?"

My head was spinning now with possibilities, all of them unpleasant. Of course, I recognized the tactics. First, ease up, disarm by kindness, then imply threats. All classic examples of how to get information or whatever one wanted out of a prisoner. After all, prisoner handling had been part of my business for the better part of two years.

But this was different. At my rank and in my position in the hierarchy of command, I could hardly be expected to have at my disposal the sort of massive state secrets that would make the particular treatment I'd been given reasonable or practical. I thought of the unhappy ditch-digging duty, the isolation, the removal of all other Americans, the cigarettes, the implied threat now being made. What could I know that would justify this series of extremes in treatment? What could they possibly want of me to put me into this kind of emotional turmoil? I was absolutely in a quandary.

At this moment, however, I was truly frightened. There had been injected into this new relationship a very disturbing element. I was being set up, it seemed.

The German leaned back in his chair, his hands folded as if in prayer, his chin resting lightly on his joined fingertips. He seemed to be pondering his own last question to me.

"But I had on my dog tags and my uniform," I protested.

"Oh yes, Mr. Lister. That is quite true. But, you see, it is quite possible for a soldier or anyone else for that matter, to obtain the identity tags and uniform of a dead soldier on or near the battlefield, is it not so?"

My thoughts raced frantically. *This son of a bitch is trying to set up a spy charge against me to justify shooting or hanging me!* I thought, not thinking far enough ahead, however, to realize that he hardly needed such elaborate schemes if my disposal was his goal.

"I don't know anything about stealing uniforms or identification from dead soldiers. These are my own identification tags. My name is on them, the same name as on papers in my wallet. In fact, I had a newspaper clipping in my article which the *feldwebel* burned. It had my picture in it. Ask him. He'll tell you!"

The man didn't react at once. He continued looking at the ceiling in the quasi-prayerful attitude. Then he turned his eyes back to me, still giving no hint of his true feelings. I suddenly felt a modicum of relief, but wasn't sure just why.

All at once, it dawned on me, again, without my knowing the specific clue or reason. This man was playing cat and mouse with me just as he undoubtedly had with countless other prisoners over the past couple of years. They weren't going to execute me! Of this I suddenly felt quite confident.

"Yes, that is true, isn't it, Sergeant? Well, let us not belabor a moot point, what do you say? I am satisfied that you are who you say you are."

He smiled patronizingly. I was fully alert now, listening for every word my interrogator had to say. The pressure had been applied, had actually worked to some extent. Now the Kraut had to tip his hand.

The man reached into his center desk drawer and withdrew a carefully folded manila envelope. With delicate, meticulous hand movements, he gently and carefully unfolded it, reached into it, and withdrew a small square of red cloth with a large yellow bird, a stylized eagle, dominating the center of it. It was the shoulder patch of the 45th Division.

"Here, Sergeant, do you know this insignia?"

I was astounded. Certainly I knew which division this patch represented. The 45th had been on our flank throughout Italy and France. That must be it, I reasoned. He was testing me on the easy ones first.

"No, sir, I don't."

"I see." The man's face bore more of a tongue-in-cheek smirk than a frown, although it wasn't a friendly look at all. "Then you wouldn't have seen these either?"

He slowly withdrew from the envelope the blue arrowhead with the gray "T" centered, and the red and black arrowhead with the buffalo head on it, the patches of the 36th Texas and 34th Oklahoma Divisions. These he tossed across the desk so they fell just in front of me directly in my line of vision. All three shoulder patches were of outfits that had flanked my division in many campaigns, or with which my 3rd Division had made numerous contacts in combat situations. The German's smile narrowed, then disappeared entirely.

"Sergeant, let us not fool each other, eh? I know these units. I know them as well as I know you know them. This one is the American 45th Division. Here is the 36th Division. They were to your division's left and right, respectively, in Italy and France. And it was to relieve the 36th Division that your own organization was sent in against our defenses at Salerno. This was after you had been promised a rest after that Sicilian campaign, not so, Sergeant?"

He had his facts straight. He knew what he was talking about. No sloppy espionage here. The inquisitor then described several other shoulder patches in his envelope and the organizations they represented.

"So you see, Mr. Lister, I know everything, eh?"

"Then why did you have to ask me?" I countered quickly. I felt the need to smile experimentally as I said it. I was relieved to see the German return the smile. For a very brief moment there, I had a vague and comfortable feeling that we had an implied respect for each other, this man and I, even though there was no overt action or word to substantiate the feeling.

"I simply wished to determine if the treatment I understand you have been exposed to at the hands of that boor, Hoffman, had softened you, as you fellows say. I was curious to learn just how cooperative you might have become."

"Why was I brought here?" I asked him, looking directly into the man's eyes.

"Primarily to dissuade you from any notions that all Germans are bestial, actually."

"I haven't said all Germans are bestial," I replied. I also didn't believe the man's latest fabrication. Goddamn it, the man obviously wanted something. Why in hell didn't he simply spit it out? What could it be?

"But you couldn't have avoided thinking it at times, is it not so? After all, if you've seen only such examples as *Feldwebel* Hoffman, I feel sorry for you. He is a clod. An old soldier, you know. But there are those of us who are quite sensitive and intellectually curious. I hope you will recognize this as time goes on. After all, it will be lonesome for you now, at least for a while. I know the feeling of lonesomeness. Er, is that the right word?"

"Loneliness," I corrected softly.

"Ah so, *jah,* that's it, loneliness. I have only these ignorant farmers they have assigned here to talk to. Oh yes, I thought you also might enjoy looking at some of your American comics."

He leaned sideways to retrieve another large folder from his bottom desk drawer. He opened it and pulled out the material. He carefully unfolded the first piece of paper which I immediately recognized, even upside down, as an editorial cartoon from the front page of the *Chicago Tribune.*

"These happen to be intellectual comics. They not only entertain, but also deliver an intelligent message. Here, have a look for yourself." He reversed the paper so it faced me on the desk.

The top cartoon verified my first impression. It was right from the front page of the *Tribune.* I had seen similar work scores of times. In fact, when I was a child, my father had been Milwaukee distribution manager for the *Tribune* and we always had the paper in the house. However, these wartime messages made quite clear that the publisher, Colonel McCormack, still felt greater antipathy for Bolshevism than for Nazism. All these cartoons were at the expense of the Russians, not the Germans, and I could have sworn that, at last report, it was the Russians who were our allies, not the Krauts.

Each of the cartoons depicted in some way exaggerated caricatures of Russian symbols in negative roles. The first, an old item by now, was in the *Tribune* dated January 28, 1943, at the time that the conference in Casablanca, Morocco, was being held between President Roosevelt and Prime Minister Churchill.

This cartoon showed Joe Stalin standing in contemplation, holding a sheet of paper entitled, "Offer of a part in the Casablanca theatricals." He was looking out a window across the street from which was a "Casablanca Theater," with a billboard announcing, "Starring Roosevelt and Churchill." On the wall behind him was a poster proclaiming, "Russian Theater of War presents Josef Stalin, the man of mystery."

The other cartoon was from the *Tribune* dated January 23, 1943, and showed Stalin standing in a shadowy doorway looking into a room filled with caricatures of various crowned heads of Europe, including the queen of the Netherlands, duchess of Luxemburg, and the kings of Albania, Greece, Italy, Norway, Thailand, Yugoslavia, Don Juan Hapsburg of Spain, and Otto Hapsburg of Austria. Before Stalin stood a little man in white tie, tails, and tophat, labeled, "Royalty-fawning New Dealers" (McCormack also disliked Roosevelt's New Deal), holding a rolled scroll of "plans." A similar but larger scroll was being held behind Stalin's back by the Soviet leader. It was entitled, "Stalin's Own Post-war Global Plans."

The caption above the first cartoon, about Casablanca, was "The Old Actor with a Previous Engagement." Over the other cartoon was the caption "The Enthusiasm for Royalty May Not Be Shared by Comrade Joe."

Other cartoons in the group weren't quite as sophisticated in their thinly veiled messages. These simply depicted various bearded, ominously dark-cloaked little men holding spherical black bombs with glowing fuses. In several of them, Russia was depicted as receiving money or goods from the USA in some surreptitious manner.

I had considered myself lacking in political acumen or knowledge up to that time. Nevertheless, I did formulate questions which never left me. I tried to understand how the newspaper's editorial cartoonist could be more anti-Russian than anti-German while the United States was at war with Germany, and Russia was her ally. I didn't question a sympathy that was antithetical to Soviet imperialism, only to this choice at this place and this time in history.

"Rather clever, don't you agree?" my host asked somewhat eagerly.

"I guess so," I responded, tentatively.

"Good. We will show them to your comrades."

"Who?"

"The American soldiers. We are preparing them as part of an educational leaflet program to be sent over your lines in aerial burst artillery shells. You see, we obtain this American newspaper through Sweden, a neutral country. Now, as you can see, not all Americans consider us their enemies. You must realize who your real enemy is in this war and in all history. You will have great trouble with the Communists before the end of hostilities, mark my words!"

I had heard this philosophy often. Almost invariably, however, it came from German prisoners we were about to send to our rear areas. I must confess, though, that I had thought about this question and didn't disagree completely with the Nazi's philosophy concerning Russia. In fact, I believed, as had many of my buddies for some time, that Russia was the lesser of two evils by an extremely narrow margin. Still, I didn't believe it would be judicious to voice such sentiment under the present circumstances. I surely couldn't side with the Germans under any circumstances.

"Now, how would you like to visit with me each morning as long as you are in Waldkirch? Perhaps we could have a smoke together and look at some more pictures. In fact, you might pick out those which you feel deliver the clearest message to entertain your comrades over there, behind American lines."

I was amazed at the minor subterfuge the German had attempted. The poorly disguised buildup had been much cruder than I had been led to believe would come from the allegedly well-organized German propaganda machine. Still, after my recent weeks of experience, I welcomed the opportunity to sit in a soft chair in a warm room, with an apparently inexhaustible supply of cigarettes.

"Do you suppose I might have a shave?" I asked.

"Oh, but of course, my dear fellow. I will arrange it for you as soon as possible. But you will visit me again, will you not?"

"Sure, why not?" I was amused at his asking. All he really had to do was order my presence, but instead, he chose to invite me to visit.

In my recollection, no Kraut propaganda I'd seen fired over the lines to date had ever converted any GI I knew. Earlier, in the Vosges Mountains, I recalled one particularly gory piece which showed a line drawing in which a death's head skull was smiling down on a mass of American soldiers' bodies. On the reverse side was a photograph of rows upon rows of white crosses and Stars of David. Beneath these was quoted President Roosevelt's famous pre-war statement: "I assure you again and again that no American boys will be sacrificed on foreign battlefields."

In spite of that type of pointed material, however, the bulk of the stuff the Germans provided offered more laughs than anything else. If any anger was caused by these efforts, it was anger directed at the Germans.

The same had been true in Italy and Sicily with Axis Sally's radio programs. She provided excellent current recorded American popular music, sentimental philosophizing, and a truly homey touch for the doggies who occasionally were able to hear the program.

Only when she so accurately listed the actual objective of a forthcoming attack, hours before the scheduled jumpoff time, did it prove unnerving. There was some strong morale deterioration when, a few short hours before we were to start a major offensive, we heard the enemy's propaganda machine explain in painfully accurate detail where the attack was scheduled to go, what the objectives would be, and who would be waiting for us at the site.

"There is one other piece of information I wish to check with you, Sergeant Lister. When you were interrogated originally, you told the sergeant at the Dulag that you were a radio announcer, is it not so?"

I smiled. I hadn't exactly told them I was an announcer. I harkened back to the first time I had been captured during the breakout from the Anzio Beachhead nearly eight months ago. I had been interrogated by the front-line outfit's people briefly. The officer going through the motions of questioning me did not speak English.

"Was ist dein Civilist Beruft?" he had asked.

I knew what *Beruft* meant — occupation. But at the time, my German vocabulary lacked the word for "salesman." So, in a series of monosyllabic German words and short phrases I did know, I tried to explain to that officer that my upraised right index finger represented a man who made something. With a nod of my head, I then indicated that my upraised left index finger represented a man who wanted what the first man made. I was about to arc between the two, telling him that the first man must tell the second about what he made. This he did by newspaper (I knew *Zeitung*), by radio (with a soft-"a") and, I was going to say, indicating myself, *"bei ein Mann. Das bin Ich."* However, I never got beyond "radio." The officer interrupted to ask me if I was a radio *sprecher* — radio announcer.

By that time, I figured, what the hell. "Yeah, I'm a radio *sprecher.*"

Now I looked at the German across the desk from me and, again, figured, what the hell. What's to lose? "Yes, I guess that's right," I said. "I guess I did say that."

"That's fine," he replied, smiling, apparently closing this element of the converstaion. He seemed to file the information away for future reference.

Later, I was struck by the wide diversification of information this fellow covered in the course of a single afternoon's discussion. In each instance, he would cut off the subject as soon as he appeared satisfied with an answer.

The interviews continued for the next six days, each succeeding day giving me a golden opportunity to increase my cache of cigarettes against less productive times. I now had nearly twenty of them wrapped in paper in my right breast pocket. They could sustain me in place of food for several days should I get out of here, I rationalized.

Meanwhile, I was free of that damned ditch. My host and I looked at cartoons and political messages until I thought I'd never want to read the editorial page of any newspaper after the war, but particularly that of the *Chicago Tribune.* Other material we checked came from pro-Nazi sources in Germany.

One morning I awoke at my now customary time, in my customary solitude, performed ablutions under the same, dreary, monotonous circumstances and waited for the door to open on the now routine events of each day. This morning, however, no one came to my door except one of the guards with my morning repast.

I had become accustomed to the one-meal-a-day schedule. I never did grow accustomed to the constant gnawing sensation within me. I estimated I had lost more than fifty pounds in the few weeks I had been at Durchlager 62.

Just as darkness began to creep over the camp, with no sign of release from my shed, I noticed a large wood-burning truck drawing up to the gate of the camp, squealing to a halt. I pressed my nose against the dirty window, anxious to see if other GIs were coming in. I longed for the companionship of other Americans by now, after more than a week of being virtually alone most of the time.

Instead of unloading companions for me, however, the truck disgorged only one man — its driver. Several passengers, both military and civilian, were seated on the open rear deck of the vehicle in the blowing snow. Most of them, I could see now, were civilians, although there were a few soldiers of various enlisted ranks. An officer could be seen through the windshield, sitting in the passenger seat.

Each passenger carried the inevitable bundle of important personal possessions of dubious intrinsic value. Since the only vehicles now moving in most of wartime Germany were requisitioned for the military, the drivers had become accustomed to accommodating hitch-hiking civilians and unattached troops.

I couldn't imagine why this truck was parked just outside of Durchlager 62, little more than forty feet from my dirty window. In fact, my immediate reaction was of extreme trepidation, especially when I saw clearly under the bright lights over the gate the dreaded black, natty uniform, high, polished black boots, and the skull and crossbones, double lightning bolt collar insignia of the SS.

After a brief, hurried visit with the guards at the gate, the driver followed the direction indicated by their pointing fingers with his eyes. He looked toward my window, then beyond it to the headquarters building. He was admitted to the enclosure and walked swiftly to the CP.

He moved out of my line of vision, but not before I could see that he was, or appeared to be, little older than I. Since he had passed from my sight, I returned my attention to his vehicle. It was another of wartime Germany's emergency measures, so many of which were seen wherever Germans had been seen in the past year or so. It was a type of vehicle which never seemed to complete a journey on which it embarked. Instead of a gasoline tank, it was fueled with wood, fed into a huge boiler mounted just behind the cab.

The aerial superiority of the Allies had rendered Ploesti's oil fields useless to Germany's war effort. Therefore, the common procedure was for the driver of such a vehicle, upon noting his truck needed fuel, to stop the truck, dismount, walk to the edge of a roadside forest, chop down a small tree, and bring the pieces of the trunk and heavier branches back to the truck. These then would be fed into the boiler's fire pot. This accomplished, the driver simply had to wait until a sufficient head of steam built up to continue his journey.

My reflections suddenly were interrupted as the door of my shack was flung outward. The guard motioned me out and indicated that I was to accompany the SS truck driver standing nearby. The driver stood stoically beside the guard. He was a young man of about twenty-four with a dull, expressionless, baby-red, beardless face.

"Gehen sie mit," the guard said. *"Sie gehen jetzt weit aweg."* He was smiling. This did little to improve my already depleted morale or to assuage the thumping in my chest.

I wondered why my departure was so sudden and unceremonious and why the *feldwebel* hadn't taken part in it directly. I was sure he had his hand in the move, of course. And, above all, why in hell was the SS involved? My feeling of fright continued to grow.

Still, from what I could see of the truck, it was conceivable that I might find a chance to make a break which was impossible within the barbed wire enclosure of the camp. Certainly they wouldn't displace the officer in the truck's cab just to give me a guarded place to sit. Since the troops on the truck's bed wore a wide variety of uniforms, indicating several branches of military service, and the driver was SS, it seemed unlikely that any of the passengers had been assigned to guard me in such a disorganized amalgam of people.

The driver pointed to the rear deck.

"Setzen sich dahinten," he said in a low, guttural voice, not looking at me.

I climbed aboard, finding space to sit between two soldiers and opposite three well-bundled young women. It had begun snowing heavily again, and all passengers huddled into their own coverings. In the gathering dusk, I noticed that the civilian women seemed extremely unfriendly, judging by their poisonous stares at me.

Then I heard one of them remark to her companions, something about her brother being a prisoner in the United States. She said something about my "good treatment" and that she hoped her brother was faring as well.

The animosity of the women was unmistakable. The three glared at me again. Much of their conversation was lost in the wind which kept whipping in vicious gusts across the open flatbed platform on which we all huddled.

Suddenly, I felt twinges of embarrassment. I rubbed my chin and was painfully reminded of the heavy growth of stubble I had acquired over the past week. I was supposed to be provided with shaving material, my interrogator had said a couple of days before, but it was not forthcoming. I silently bemoaned the formidable appearance I must present just when I would have hoped to appear deserving of sympathy.

I recalled how negative our impressions had always been of the German prisoners who remained surly and sullen. As a result, I hoped to put up as positive and jovial a front as possible. But under the circumstances, this was anything but likely since I felt neither pleasant nor comfortable.

Several of the civilian passengers and all of the soldiers on the truck dismounted at the first stop, the railway station in the village of Waldkirch proper. Two young men in civilian clothes and two older women climbed aboard. In the cab, only the driver and one other soldier remained, the officer having left the vehicle with the others at the depot.

I edged closer to the back wall of the cab so it might offer some windbreak against the biting cold as the wind tore at my ragged uniform. I shoved my rigid hands as deeply as possible into my trousers pockets, but this did little other than to irritate my already raw, frostbitten skin. I wished the other cab passengers and these people on the deck would leave so I might be invited into the cab where it had to be warmer.

Finally, my moment came. Another stop was made. This one was on the main street of a small village about ten miles beyond Waldkirch. The fleeting glance I got at the nearly snow-covered sign we passed on entering the town indicated that this was Emmendingen.

Instead of being invited to enter the cab, however, I was told to dismount and follow the driver. The truck had died en route, apparently, in the tradition of every German vehicle I had seen since coming overseas.

The driver waved the remaining passengers away with no trace of apology or concern. He indicated they'd have to walk the rest of their way. Then he turned and began trudging through the snow to the other side of the street. His attitude indicated neither unhappiness nor disappointment, only the same phlegmatic posture he had shown since I first saw him. There appeared to be no animosity in the man — at least, not toward me. He showed only the resigned acceptance of a poor circumstance that I noticed was so common among the German people I had seen. Perhaps long years of suffering what the war had brought them in the way of depleted assets, unrepaired mechanical devices, food and creature comfort shortages, gave them this unemotional viewpoint.

The driver took the mid-winter adversity completely in stride, content to leave his vehicle parked in the middle of the street for the rest of the war, as far as he was concerned.

And throughout this entire experience, he ignored me completely. If I had chosen to walk in the opposite direction, I felt sure he wouldn't think much of it one way or the other.

We walked to the nearest house on the far side of the street. I stood on the sidewalk while the driver, apparently oblivious to the fact that he was responsible for a prisoner of war, knocked on the outer door.

I was astounded at the apparent freedom in which I found myself. Of course, I had no idea where I was or how to get to anywhere else. Still, nobody was guarding me, literally, and the entire affair smacked of the most inefficient, informal handling of a prisoner I'd seen in either army. In fact, the whole episode looked for all the world just a little too pat for my liking. The driver did wear a pistol in a latched holster on the back of his belt, but he had made no move toward it.

The man spoke quietly to the woman who opened the door of the house. I couldn't see her clearly in the shadow. Then the driver turned to me and motioned me into the house. I was shivering uncontrollably at this point and needed no second invitation. I mounted the steps hurriedly and followed the Kraut through the darkened arch. The woman closed the door behind us and followed us through the darkened and obviously unused sitting room. This, I assumed, was a situation brought about by acute fuel shortages in the nation as well as equally pressing problems of transporting what fuel was available from the Ruhr Valley to the rest of the country.

We entered a brightly lit kitchen where two other people sat in comfortable warmth about a center table. The room was heated by a large, porcelain-tiled oven standing against the far wall. It was about seven feet high and two and one-half feet wide and deep. It was fueled by compressed coal dust that had been formed into briquets. Two or three of these were inserted into the level fire pot at a time. Civilians trudged weary miles to obtain as few as a dozen of these briquets. The high priority needed to obtain this fuel was the same as that required for every other available retail product in the country, it seemed.

I glanced about at the two others seated in the kitchen, an elderly man and a young woman. They had been listening to the radio which they shut off as we entered the room. The driver asked the woman's permission to use the telephone and was granted it immediately. He crossed the kitchen to the indicated small alcove where the phone was kept on a shelf. He turned as he was about to pick up the device. Indicating me, he pointed out, without malice, *"Er ist ein Kriegsgefangener. Amerikanisch."*

With relief, I saw there was no animosity in their faces when the civilians learned about my prisoner status. Instead, the older woman who had admitted us to her house offered me a cup of steaming chicory coffee, the first warm liquid I had tasted in a long time. I thanked her and held it to warm my hands and let the fragrant steam surround my face. Then I wolfed it down as quickly as my burning throat would permit. When I glanced up again, I saw the old man staring intently at the oilcloth table cover, seemingly lost in reverie of some sort. Glancing about, I found myself caught in the intense stare of the younger woman.

She was an attractive girl in her early twenties with a full figure clearly apparent beneath her heavy, shapeless dress and bulky wool cardigan. She smiled shyly, although she didn't divert her eyes when mine caught them. I returned her smile, suddenly feeling terribly conspicuous because of my filthy, unkempt appearance. I wished I could have washed and shaved. In fact, I began wishing a great many things I hadn't thought about for a long time.

The wheels of fantasy began to turn in my mind. I started to hope that the relief vehicle for which the driver obviously was calling would be unavailable until morning. I fantasized a scene in which I was cleanshaven in a new, pressed uniform, locked in a room with this lovely young woman, the first I had seen this close in many, many months . . .

The driver concluded his conversation and turned to the older woman. He explained that a people's car would be calling for us later in the night. Meanwhile, would the *"Gnädigte Frau"* mind if we waited here in the warmth of her comfortable kitchen?

Of course she wouldn't. This was quite a break from what must have been a deadly monotony in her wartime life full of deprivation of experience as well as material goods. The two women seemed genuinely pleased to have us with them. Although I, the enemy, hardly presented a picture of any sort of beauty, they seemed truly sympathetic, apparently recognizing my circumstances.

I learned, by piecing together bits of the rapid conversational exchanges among the women and the driver in an unfamiliar dialect, that both women were widows. The younger woman had been married to the brother of the other woman. He was killed in a tank battle near Stalingrad. The older woman lost her husband in North Africa. The old man was her father-in-law, she told the SS driver. The incongruous trio lived together for economical and familial reasons and, apparently, because there was no real reason not to.

The waiting began to feel unbearable because of the sudden reawakening of my body guests, now crawling out of clothing linings and warm body hair. The only ones who really had escaped from Waldkirch were the lice. The heat of this kitchen brought them back into feverish activity. I could feel them scurrying across various intimate parts of my anatomy, and it was only with the greatest self-control that I refrained from scratching myself furiously.

The knock at the door sounded after about an hour of this torture that seemed like an eternity. When the newcomer was ushered into the kitchen, he proved to be another young SS enlisted man, I guessed, a late teenager. He was bright and personable. His smile was broad and infectious and aimed at everyone in the room, me included. He was, in every visible way, a direct contradiction of the driver who had brought me here.

The new man was joking with the hostess immediately upon setting foot in her kitchen, adding a genuine note of good feeling to the evening. It seemed forever since I'd been a part of such glad feeling. His name, I learned, was Emil Arentz. He was nineteen and, when he smiled, which was almost constantly, he showed clean, white, glistening teeth.

Arentz happily accepted the proferred cup of chicory and drank it leisurely. Then, draining the final swallow, he turned to the driver and, with an expression which admitted a reluctant realization of duty, nodded toward the door. Both German soldiers arose, and I followed suit. As we reached the front door of the house, I felt rather than saw movement just to my left. I turned to find the younger woman quietly standing beside me. Just before I stepped through the door after the German soldiers, I felt her touch my hip with her hand. I reached down and squeezed her fingers gently. She returned the pressure. I didn't look into her eyes, but I could feel her staring at me. I was sorry to leave her and her lovely, warm, comfortable kitchen.

Outside, the new snow was falling more heavily now in large, slow, soft flakes which settled gently on my nose and hair. In front of the house was a small, peculiarly shaped car, the popular German Volkswagen. It hardly looked big enough for the three of us with our bulky winter wear. I was the tallest of the three, at least two inches taller than Arentz, whose height I estimated at about five feet, ten inches. The other Kraut was about two inches shorter than he.

Arentz held the driver's door open for me and pulled the seat forward so I could climb in back. It was cramped, although I had the entire rear seat on which to spread out. I hunched up against the growing cold and anticipated colder weather before we reached whatever destination fate had in store.

Arentz squeezed behind the wheel, with the truck driver grunting in beside him. The other German's name, I had learned this evening, was Traxel, Werner Traxel.

The little vehicle started eventually, after two or three efforts. Arentz eased it into the frozen ruts in the middle of the road. It was quite apparent that he'd have preferred to drive differently if conditions were other than they were. In fact, he gave ample evidence of a heavy foot on several heart-stopping occasions, despite the inclement weather.

We started our steady climb up the narrow mountain road, almost immediately passing the outskirts of the village. Approaching several extremely sharp curves on the slippery, snow-covered highway, the little car skidded dangerously close to the precipice and continued ahead into the sightless black of the snowy night.

Weariness finally overcame me and I was conscious of only occasional snatches of conversation between the two Germans, that of Arentz being rapid and animated; that of Traxel confined to dull, monosyllabic replies.

We crossed a railroad track after what seemed an endless stretch of straight road. We passed a sign that announced "Triberg." As we reached the far side of that city, we crossed what appeared to be the wide, main street of the town. At this point, Arentz pressed the accelerator too hard, sending the tiny car into a spin. It ended deep in a snow bank. Finally, the two Germans extricated it and we continued on an upward, winding path around hair-raising "S" curves. At one of these, the car was suddenly out of control again and much deeper in a snow bank than before. No amount of effort on the part of the two soldiers could rekindle a spark of life in the tiny engine.

Finally, the three of us got out of the car to trek the remaining few uphill miles to our destination — Schonach.

I glanced about the schoolroom slowly. Not a sign of life could be seen anywhere. Occasionally, a man would snore or groan lightly in his sleep. Arentz, now snuggled into an open place across the room from me, already was asleep. Traxel had long since fallen asleep in his chosen spot.

I scratched my groin and fell asleep too.

4. Broadcast Experience

INCREDIBLY BRIGHT SUNLIGHT was my first impression, as its unbearable glare suddenly thrust itself into my consciousness. It was so stark that I turned my head to the side and shielded my eyes with an upraised arm.

I cautiously opened one eye, then the other. The first thing I saw was a seemingly endless expanse of straw. Wherever I looked there was a heavy scattering of it. I then became aware of the movement of many men and their mingled conversation.

I sat up and looked around the schoolroom. Most of the German soldiers were standing about the pot-bellied stove in various stages of dress. Some were chewing their morning sausage and bread and drinking chicory from metal canteen cups. Others were filling the air with huge volumes of thick, white smoke from their acrid, vile German regular-issue cigarettes. The smokes were in yellow packets labeled *"hoco."*

Arentz was standing near a window with two of the other soldiers, exchanging quiet pleasantries. Every so often, one of the others would burst into a loud guffaw, further testifying to Arentz' way with a story. Then Arentz, noticing I was awake, crossed to the stove and retrieved a large bundle, bringing it to me. It was my uniform. My heart leaped at the thought that some miracle had caused it to be deloused during the night. A quick check of the belt lining dispelled this hope, however. There they were, the rows upon rows of microscopic white eggs and the occasional nit running across my line of vision, almost obscured by its tiny size and amazing speed. Actually, it was almost a gossamer movement that barely caught the eye unless one were looking closely. Arentz had done me the courtesy of piling my uniform near the stove so my clothes would be warm first thing in the morning.

Arentz helped me to my feet and, as I dressed, the young fellow tried to convey to me the urgency of the situation and the need for speed. I still was in a complete quandary about my situation. This treatment as a prisoner of war was anything but typical in my experience.

For one thing, there had been no harsh orders from either of the men who brought me here. There was no threat, implied or otherwise, from any of these fellows. And they were all SS men! But they were nothing like the SS infantrymen and panzer grenadiers I had met repeatedly on numerous battlefields.

Then, too, there wasn't another American soldier in sight. And last night, coming up the mountain past that sign that had identified Schonach, I had noticed no sign of a camp or of barbed wire.

My introduction to this room full of sleeping SS troops had been most informal considering my status. Few of them paid me any but the most passing interest and completely without any sign of animosity or even curiosity. Their casual glances set my mind at ease somewhat, but served to confuse me still further.

One of the men across the table reached out, with a grunt, handing me a cup of steaming black liquid. I suddenly realized how hungry I was and eagerly tasted the drink with a smiling, *"Danke."* The cup was brimming with chicory. It wasn't coffee as I knew it, but it was very welcome. It took few swallows to down the hot liquid despite the burning sensation in my throat. In the time I had been a prisoner, I had learned to eat and drink very rapidly what modest cuisine I had been offered. That, in some small measure, served to create the illusion of dispelling the hunger.

Finally, Arentz caught my attention and indicated it was time to leave and quickly. We left the schoolroom side by side, moving down the corridor to the building's huge double doors. We walked into the brightly sunlit cobbled street. From the steps of the building, I had a delightfully panoramic view of incredible beauty as I gazed over the entire valley down the mountainside we had climbed last night. It was a clear, crisp, and cloudless day, and the world was covered with soft, friendly mounds of cottonlike snow.

Down a slight hill I saw the building we had passed in the early morning hours — the Hotel Lamm. It was a huge, multi-faceted, rambling frame structure, the outer walls of its lower story covered with dirty gray stucco. I saw what appeared to be bedroom windows on the second and third floors, and large, sectioned picture windows surrounding the entire end of the first floor. This, I assumed, was the dining room and kitchen area of the hotel.

The road up which we had come in the early morning darkness stretched beyond the village, running in a neat circle I had observed in the early morning hours. Lining either side of the road I had climbed were quaint chalets and square, unimaginative stone houses. All were at least two stories high.

In the center of the circle created by the road lay the beautiful little millpond fed by two or three deep, tributary streams rolling down from the ridges above. I could see water running in some of them, apparently stirred from ice by the strong sunlight.

The entire view was breathtaking. It resembled nothing more than a huge tennis racket, the handle represented by the road we had traversed up the mountain from Triberg.

I followed Arentz across the courtyard and into the rear door of the hotel. We climbed the stairs past closed doors, crossed the hallway beside the second-floor landing, to a door identified as "201." Arentz knocked and stepped back. A stir from within was followed by heavy, uneven footsteps. The door jerked open, and Arentz pulled himself to attention, his eyes rigidly forward.

The man who stood in the doorway appeared amazingly young and fragile-looking, particularly in light of the epaulets he wore. His insignia indicated that he held the rank of *oberstormfuhrer,* or SS first lieutenant. His extremely youthful face was almost effeminately pretty with sharply delineated black eyebrows, incredibly long, black eyelashes, and a thin, aquiline nose. His cheeks were devoid of any sign of a beard . . . no stubble, no shadow, only unbelievably soft-looking skin, brightly highlighted by a red circle on each cheek. His slick, black hair was combed severely back almost into a shining skull cap. His head was small and well-shaped. So slight did he appear, in fact, that his actual height — approximately that of Arentz — completely escaped anyone looking at him for the first time. He gave the impression of being very small and thin.

He seemed genuinely delighted at the prospect of company. His smile was that of a small boy who realized that his long-awaited treat had arrived finally. He nearly bubbled with delight as he held out his long, thin hand to me.

"Ah, good morning, good morning. This would be Mr. Lister, would it now? Did you sleep well? I hope you did. This place doesn't offer the ultimate in comfort, I'm sorry to say, but we'll make more pleasant arrangements later."

"Good morning, sir," I stammered in amazement. "I slept fine, thank you." I was overwhelmed by this reception and friendliness, and from an SS officer at that. Surely this guy knew about me. I obviously had been brought here for some reason. Perhaps they needed me for something. But why so damned friendly? This entire situation was growing increasingly unnatural at every turn.

"I am *Oberstormfuhrer* Walter Best," the lieutenant continued, his voice almost uncontrollably effervescent. "I am in command of the military aspect of this project. But first we must do something about your appearance, what do you say to that? When was it you last shaved, Mr. Lister?" Then, without waiting for an answer, he continued, "And that uniform! Good heavens! It is simply dreadful. We definitely must do something about having it stitched and cleaned, mustn't we?"

The lieutenant's nose quivered as he said this, and I was conscious of even more of my sartorial shortcomings. I felt very self-conscious.

"Well, we go downstairs and meet the others now. You will like them, I am sure. They make a most interesting group. And Lieutenant Trautmann will take care of your personal needs. He, too, is in the dining room. Come now, please." He spoke in a cultured English accent with barely a trace of the German idiom.

Still standing in the doorway, he now slammed the door behind him, just a little too hard, and walked deliberately around me. Arentz and I dutifully tagged along behind him as he descended the stairs. I marveled at the large number of Germans I had met who spoke almost flawless English. Best was far from an exception in this regard.

At the bottom of the stairs, Best stepped to the threshold of the dining room. He enthusiastically pulled it open and made a studied, grand entrance. The room was a large, table-littered chamber with high, sectioned picture windows looking out over the delightful valley scene. The heavily wooded Black Forest mountaintop was overwhelming in its beauty.

Several people sat around a few small, square tables that had been moved together to form a long banquet board. They appeared very informal and at ease. They all rose as we entered the room. Best held his arms at length expansively, including everyone in the greeting.

"Good morning, my dear friends. Good morning. I hope you all slept as wonderfully well as I did. *Ach,* this lovely, clear morning air, eh? This morning I have the pleasure to introduce to you our new guest, Mr. . . . er, Sergeant Hal Lister, of whom we have spoken already."

He turned to include me in the sweep of his right arm, being most careful not to touch me with his extended hand. With his eyes he directed my attention around the table as, one by one, the traditional German hands were held out for traditional German handshakes and occasional clicking of heels from some of the men. This was delivered with a simultaneous stiff bow of head and shoulders.

Best did the honors before each person. He began with the fascinating-looking, tall man in the uniform of an air force private. The man stood at least five inches taller than my six feet. He had a tremendous head topped by a vast mane of unruly gray hair. He literally had a leonine mane that curled over his incongruous blue uniform collar.

"Here is Herr Helmut Bruckmann," Best said.

"How do you do, my dear fellow," the big man replied courteously, shaking my hand firmly. I stood dumbfounded by the scene before me.

"We have been most anxious to meet you," Bruckmann continued with a peculiar one-sided smile that twisted the right end of his mouth into a sort of leer. He had deep-set gray eyes that I thought were the most penetrating I'd ever seen. The man's firm handshake was thoroughly masculine. He released the grip immediately, however, as if to indicate an end to the act of initial introduction.

Next in line came another private, this one in Wehrmacht gray-blue. He was shorter than I and quite stocky. What little hair he had was pulled over the rapidly expanding island of skin in the center of his head in an attempt to cover its surface. He also had a fringe of hair circling his head like a laurel wreath.

"Mr. Charlie Schwedler," Best continued, in a matter-of-fact, bored tone.

"Hi there, Hal. Glad to meetcha," replied my newest acquaintance in an unmistakable and unsuccessful, crude attempt at an American vernacular accent.

The immediate impression I had of Schwedler was unpleasant. He sounded as if he had spent some time in the States and evidently had picked up enough American pronunciation and idioms to mimic an American. He didn't quite bring it off, though. His handshake, too, left much to be desired. It reminded me of a limp lettuce leaf. Everything signified to me just what my first impression of Schwedler told me: he was insecure, insincere, clammy, and thoroughly untrustworthy. And all this from just two short statements!

I stiffened to attention as I approached the next person in the line. She was beautiful, blonde, sparkling. She also was quite a bit heavier than she should have been, particularly about the breasts and hips. I noticed the way she arched her back, emphasizing her more obvious attributes. She smiled, exposing even rows of square, white teeth. Her smile was altogether friendly and feminine. Her mouth was large and sensuous, with a light coating of lipstick.

"This is Frau Inga Domann," Best pointed out.

"How nice to meet you, Sergeant," she said. "We have been looking forward to meeting you." Her voice was smooth, low, and exciting. Her cordiality seemed genuine enough and once again, I felt frightfully self-conscious, particularly in light of the intimate manner in which she seemed to be observing me.

Best had moved around the far end of the table. He nodded to two *unterstormfuhrers* — second lieutenants in SS uniforms.

"Here is Lieutenant Trautmann." He indicated the nearer of them. The older man, possibly approaching fifty, had a fatherly quality about him, a softness that conflicted with the lightning bolts on his collar.

His handshake was firm and friendly, as his smile seemed to be. I felt an immediate, impulsive liking for this slender man with the dark circles under his sad eyes. The man's gray hair was thinning noticeably, particularly in the front. It was nearly completely silver at the temples. I returned his smile.

Trautmann's accent was thicker, more Teutonic than the others I had met so far.

"We must do something to make you more comfortable, *nicht wahr,* Sergeant Lister?" he said, taking his eyes from mine and moving them down the front of my body. It was then I realized I had been shaking hands with my right hand, but simultaneously scratching my fly with my left. This subconscious habit had carried over from Dulag 62.

Another military member of the entourage stood beside the two SS lieutenants, the second of whom obviously spoke halting English and merely nodded when I was introduced to him. His name was Küttner. But the next man was an interesting specimen.

He was tall and thin to the point of emaciation. He had a huge Adam's apple, a large nose, wore heavy horn-rimmed glasses over his watery eyes, and had slicked-down, blond hair with a severe part on the left side. He was dressed in the uniform of a Luftwaffe corporal.

"And here we have the Baron Wolfgang von Nordenflycht," Best said, a trace of a smirk on his lips.

"Herr Baron," I said, extending my hand.

"How do you do, Sergeant," the man said in a high-pitched voice. He had a lisp. His German accent was unmistakable.

"The baron has a famous relative in your homeland," Best continued, smiling at von Nordenflycht.

I looked sharply at Best, then at the younger man, the unspoken question in my eyes. Von Nordenflycht anticipated my question.

"Perhaps you have heard of *mein* uncle, H. V. Kaltenborn?"

"Kaltenborn, the newsman?" I asked in surprise.

"Yes."

I recalled the pre-war stories about America's premier newsman arriving in Berlin a couple of years earlier. Hitler, furious at the tenor of the noted American news dean's stories about his glorious Third Reich, had refused to permit Kaltenborn to leave the airplane. Kaltenborn had stayed aboard the plane, so the story went, at the Berlin airport and returned to Paris, thence back to New York. He had become a diplomatic hero in my eyes as well as in those of most Americans.

Noting the surprise on my face, von Nordenflycht smiled awkwardly.

"He is an uncle by marriage, Mr. Lister. His wife is my mother's sister. I lived with them in 1933 and 1934 when I attended Columbia University in New York."

Best broke into the reflection with a nervous clap of his hands.

"So, Mr. Lister. That completes the introductions. Is it not as I have said? Are they not interesting?"

I merely nodded agreement, still completely puzzled by my treatment.

"And now, thank you all for waiting," Best continued to the

group. It was an obvious dismissal. The party broke up and everyone dispersed. All, that is, except Bruckmann.

Best nodded to me and explained, "Mr. Bruckmann will tell you about our operation here, Mr. Lister. I must go now. You will excuse me." Without waiting for a reply, Best snapped to attention, clicked his heels, bowed from the neck, and turned sharply on his slickly booted heel, leaving the room.

Bruckmann sat quietly for a moment, seeming to observe me. An amused grin again seemed to lift the edge of his mouth. Finally, he turned and called over his shoulder to the heavy-set, aproned woman standing near the door to the kitchen.

"Frau Greiner, *nach eine Tasse cafe, bitte.*"

Frau Greiner, apparently the innkeeper, who looked very much like my childhood recollections of Mama Katzenjammer in the comic strip with Hans and Fritz and the captain, moved rapidly to the sideboard, her head bobbing, causing the tightly wrapped bun on the back of her head to wobble up and down comically. She obtained a clean cup and spoon and brought them to the table, placing them before me. The coffee pot already stood in the center of the table on a small candle-heated, metal device. The brass pot held about four cups. Bruckmann filled both our cups, setting mine before me.

I felt awkward and stupid in my inability to grasp what was happening. And every one of these people had behaved as if I had been forewarned and pre-advised about the situation. Such friendly treatment was unparalleled in my experience with the Germans or in any experience involving them about which I had ever heard.

This diverse gathering puzzled me as well. I was too contented for the moment, though, to question it deeply. I knew that, whatever there was in store for me, it would be divulged eventually. Meanwhile, I was satisfied with the way things stood at the moment.

I enjoyed sitting in a comfortable straight-backed dining room chair. The fragrant aroma of the chicory aroused in me a suddenly noticed hunger. I glanced around the room at the others who had gathered, for the most part, at a distant table in another corner of the room after Best dismissed them. They were talking animatedly, waving cigarettes at each other, the smoke mingling over their heads in rising clouds, pouring through the sunbeams that lighted the room. The smoke fanned out at ceiling level.

"Mr. Lister, what did the *oberstormfuhrer* say your first name was, please?" Bruckmann interrupted my thoughts.

"Hal, sir," I replied, snapping back to attention before the big man.

"Well, then, if you do not mind, I shall call you Hal, eh?"

"You bet. I mean, yes, sir."

"And for heaven's sake, stop calling me 'sir.' After all, as you can see by this ridiculous uniform, I am only a Luftwaffe private."

"Mr. Bruckmann, just what is going on here? Why am I here?"

"Going on?"

"This whole situation. You must admit it isn't the customary treatment for a prisoner of war."

"Ah, so. Well, my young friend, don't you worry about this just now. I'll explain everything to you in good time. But the first thing we must do is get rid of those horrible whiskers, eh? And you must be made more comfortable, don't you agree? We must get your other, er, problem cared for at once, eh?" He was glancing at my abdomen. Again, I was scratching at the damn lice without being aware of it.

"I'll certainly buy that!" I said enthusiastically.

Bruckmann, without taking his eyes from my face, raised his right hand and snapped his thumb and forefinger together just once. Immediately a chair scraped across the room behind me and, all at once, Lieutenant Trautmann stood beside us, having crossed the room in a virtual split second.

My quandary grew intense. How could it be that a Luftwaffe private could summon an apparently subservient SS lieutenant simply by snapping his fingers? A very strange situation existed here, one that would demand extremely cautious watching on my part. I had no idea what I was into. The fantasy continued to grow.

"Lieutenant Trautmann will take you down to Triberg for a bath and some supplies now, Hal. You will go with the rest of the men. It seems that, somehow, during the night, they were invaded by an army of tiny enemies. Can you imagine such a thing?" He smiled broadly, greatly impressed with the humor of the situation.

The warmth of the dining room had been pleasant but the cold air outdoors was a welcome change. I knew the cold would deactivate the lice and put them back into a temporary dormant stage. The lieutenant and I walked quickly across the courtyard to the waiting truck. The rest of the military people from the schoolroom already were aboard, good-naturedly stamping their feet and laughing among themselves. It gave me a warm feeling to realize that, single-handedly, I had loused up an entire SS unit.

I was helped onto the truck bed by eager hands. Once I had acquired sound footing and had joined the merry, jostling throng, I saw Trautmann snap a chain across the tailgate and walk forward to climb into the truck's cab. The engine ground into life and the large vehicle lurched forward, rattling and groaning its way onto the road to begin its downhill trip to Triberg. As we passed the last house in the village, I looked back to see the sign I had seen hazily the night before. No matter what happened hereafter, I'd never forget my introduction to Schonach.

The clumsy vehicle jumbled its noisy way down the hairpin curves up which I had hiked only hours earlier. Each turn threw all of us on that crowded platform together, but no irritation was evident. Several of the soldiers boisterously shouted raucous army jokes back and forth.

Finally the truck reached one of the outskirt streets of Triberg and approached a huge, five-story building on the north side of the street. The truck jerked to a squeaky stop, and the men jumped down. I joined them. Few civilians were to be seen on the street, and we paid little attention to them or them to us. The sight of soldiers had become quite commonplace in recent years. At a signal from Trautmann, we filed into the building which I recognized as a hospital.

At the end of the long first-floor corridor, we were herded into a huge, square room. I followed the lead of the Germans who were removing their uniforms. I stepped out of my shorts and stood naked among them.

"It's damn near impossible to tell one army from another without a score card," I mused to myself.

The uniforms were picked up by three white-jacketed attendants who proceeded to hang each on its own hanger, suspended from a circular rack in the ceiling.

One of the attendants, meanwhile, was moving about among the soldiers who seemed familiar with this routine. He was carrying a large can of jellylike, red substance which each man took in his fingers and then rubbed roughly into all bodily hair. I followed their example, first rubbing the stuff liberally into my pubic region, then quickly into my armpits. However, the almost immediate reaction to the unaccustomed powerful antiseptic was one of vocal shock. I shrieked loudly as the substance burned into my skin wherever I had applied it so generously. My fellow nudists enjoyed my discomfort with good-natured gales of laughter.

We then shuffled into another vast chamber, although smaller than the first, and with a much lower ceiling. Row upon row of symmetrically arranged shower heads hung from the ceiling. Each man selected a spot beneath one of the heads. This was an exercise I approached with relish.

Suddenly all sprays burst forth at once with hot, clear water. I applied the welcome sting of lye soap all over my body. I luxuriated in the unfamiliar joy of cascading hot water pouring over me. This was my first complete, hot-water bath in more than four months. I reveled in it.

The shower lasted about twenty minutes. Then one of the attendants shouted in a husky baritone, *"Also, fertig, fertig."*

Those who still had soap on their bodies rapidly rinsed it off. The water flow suddenly stopped. The men filed back into the larger room, picking up large, rough, gray towels in the doorway as they passed through. I followed suit. When we all were dried and terry-cloth-rubbing red, we sat together on a long bench lining the wall. There were twenty-three of us altogether. I looked around for the lieutenant but failed to see him. I assumed he was waiting outside.

Two attendants walked to the far wall of the room and opened the two huge metal doors, revealing the heat room, similar to the inside of a large oven. The walls were lined with fire brick and painted an antiseptic white. As the door was opened, the attendants quickly stepped behind the doors. Waves of intense heat swept through the room, making each of us gasp for breath. I couldn't recall having felt such intense heat in my life without flames, as now permeated this chamber.

The racks of uniforms were pulled from the heat room gingerly by the attendants, using long poles with hooks on the ends, sliding the still steaming clothing along ceiling tracks. The uniforms were sorted and grabbed eagerly by individual owners. I reached for my uniform, distinctive among the forest green German outfits. My first touch was greeted by the burning sting of material too hot to hold. I jerked my hand back because I had touched a button that burned my hand. I carefully felt the cloth again and found it was beginning to cool.

Finally, either because the material actually was cooling, or because my fingers were becoming accustomed to the temperature, I was able to pull my clothing from the hanger, anxious to check the linings. Piece by piece, I carefully inspected the now thoroughly purged clothing. As I found each piece completely free of infestation, I put it on. I was holding my shirt in front of me, inspecting the armpits, just as

Lieutenant Trautmann entered the room. He was carrying a large bundle under his arm. He called to me, tossing the bundle toward me.

I caught it, curious as to its contents.

"Here you are, Mr. Lister. I thought you could use these things."

The lieutenant stepped back to observe in amused silence, much as a doting parent might watch his delighted youngsters anxiously opening Christmas presents before the tree. I opened the bag and delightedly pulled out treasure after treasure. First, there was a small face towel. Then came a safety razor, a comb, a toothbrush, a bar of gritty hand soap, a bar of grittier shaving soap, a small tube of toothpaste, and a package of five double-edged razor blades. It was a glorious and unexpected bonanza.

"You might as well shave in here," the lieutenant advised. "The men must go back to the truck. I will see to them. You and I will drive back together. I have recovered the auto in which you drove here last night." He left the room after the last of the stragglers from the Schonach group.

I needed no further invitation to shave as I turned on the hot water in the nearest basin, the steam rising swiftly, clouding the mirror. I arranged my shaving treasures on the narrow shelf beneath the mirror and reveled in the ablutions that took longer than I anticipated. The thick, unkempt, matted growth on my face pulled as I tried to cut into it, despite the heavy lather I rubbed onto it. Particularly sensitive was the area just under my nose. I had nearly forgotten what I looked like clean-shaven and, despite the pull and pinch of the poorly constructed razor and even more poorly matched blades, I managed to enjoy the experience thoroughly.

Then, for the first time in months, I studiously sought out the part in my hair and combed the heavy matted growth carefully into two respective sides of the part. The pompadour wave on the right side of the part fell into place with little prompting, despite the long lack of attention it had suffered.

This completed, I felt like a truly new person. I put all the pieces of my newly acquired toilet kit back into the bag in which I'd received them, just as the lieutenant entered the room. The officer took a long look at me, searching for defects, it seemed. Then, his face wreathed in an admiring smile, he said cheerfully, "By heavens, do you know, you aren't at all a bad-looking fellow. I never would have dreamed it." We laughed together.

"Herr Lieutenant, you don't know what you've done for me," I said gratefully. "I really appreciate it."

"Oh, I think I do. You see, I spent nearly a year at Ostfront . . . er, on the Eastern Front in Russia." I had heard from German prisoners we'd taken about the hellish living conditions on the Russian front, particularly in Russia itself.

Together we left the building and entered the Volkswagen of the previous night, which was parked in front. It now was unencumbered and free of any snow drifts.

Lieutenant Trautmann turned the ignition key and started the engine of the little car. We moved slowly toward the outskirts of town, firmly gripping the now snow-cleared cobblestones of the street.

The lieutenant stared intently ahead as he approached the first inclined turn in the road.

"What did you do in civilian life, Sergeant?" he asked without looking at me.

"I was a salesman, sir."

"Ah, so? I thought it had to do with something in radio." He pronounced the last word with a German long "a."

"Well, I did do some radio work in school, but I felt I could make a better living in sales. What was your profession, Lieutenant?"

"I was a philosophy instructor at the Gymnasium in Koblenz."

"Gymnasium?"

"*Jah,* it is a school between the lower, elementary level and the university. An advanced form of secondary academic education."

"Oh. We call it high school. Are you a party member, Lieutenant Trautmann?" I was curious and actually felt comfortable with the man despite his collar insignia.

"Party member? What is that?"

"The Nazi party."

"What is the Nazi party, please?" Trautmann asked, his brow furrowed into a quizzical look.

"You know, the political party in Germany."

"Nazi. Nazy . . . hmm. Oh, I think I see. A contraction of National Socialist Deutsche Arbeiter Partei. The German Workers' Party. Yes, Nazi. Yes. Well, I am a member, yes."

"Why, Lieutenant? I mean, you, a man of intellect."

"What has intellect to do with such things? One of the greatest intellects in history, and my favorite pre-Reich philosopher, agreed with der Fuhrer."

"Who was that?" I asked, incredulous.

"The Greek, Plato. He was one of my favorites, anyway. I am sure he was a deep source of inspiration for der Fuhrer. For example, Plato wrote . . . 'I proclaim that justice is nothing else than the interest of the stronger . . . in all states there is the same principle of justice which is the interest of the government; and as the government must be supposed to have power, the only reasonable conclusion is that everywhere there is one principle of justice, which is the interest of the stronger.' "

"But does that automatically mean persecution of the weaker?"

"Persecution? What persecution?"

"Well, the Jews, for one thing. Labor unions for another. Or natives of countries your armies have overrun. Millions of people persecuted . . ."

"Nonsense, my boy. That is Bolshevik propaganda. The Jews of Germany were taking advantage of our entire population by controlling our economy. And everyone knows they were Communists or Communist sympathizers. Our Fuhrer has said so too. Labor unions curtailed German production for the growth of the Greater Third Reich. They have done this throughout the world, even in your own land of the free. So they had to be sacrificed for the good of the whole state. They were against Germany's best interests. As for other European nationals, this is war. They are the vanquished, we the victors. That is all there is to that. Oh yes, on this matter of religion. There are many justifications for our opinions of the Jews. Martin Luther gave us several. So did Richard Wagner. Both were outstanding Germans. Both hated Jews fervently."

"Does that make it right?"

"What is good for the party and the state, that is what makes right."

Throughout this dissertation, Trautmann presented his interpretations of facts while looking straight ahead so as not to hinder his driving. He treated this whole thing as a lecture to an anonymous audience. He seemed in his element once more, at the head of a class, a class of one captive student this time. I wondered about the man's obvious integrity, his clearcut sincerity whenever he talked to me. But here he was parroting the brain-washed, trite phrases I had heard from many German soldiers of all ranks. It was almost as if he were presenting a memorized valedictory rather than a discussion on logical philosophy as I had thought I might expect from a man with his credentials.

"Of course," Trautmann continued, "I have never personally held with or participated in riots or Jew baitings. That is in the realm of the brutes and bullies. I have little sympathy for their methods. We, in education, prefer no dealings in such matters. In the matter of following der Fuhrer's political theory, however, it is predestined that we educators should become the thought leaders, particularly in controlling the weaker intellects."

"But Herr Lieutenant, as an educator, aren't you more concerned with proper thought development than with thought control? Or shouldn't you be?"

Suddenly, I realized I had gone too far in this ludicrous situation. I was sure I had stepped out of line, not in theories, but in the expression of them to a pro-Nazi SS officer under present circumstances. Trautmann's eyes narrowed slightly as he glared at the roadway ahead. The village came in sight as we rounded the last bend in the highway. I had the feeling I had misread the depth of Trautmann's seeming friendship. Our discussion was ending on a sour note.

Trautmann had matured under a strong nationalistic political philosophy, much of it brought about by the events of his youth. He grew up in the dire poverty that had overtaken his entire nation after World War I, with severe restrictions placed on the Germans by the victorious Allies. He had seen the starvation, the deprivation, the worthless money. He had been one of the millions of Germans ripe for the picking by an astute political leader. And now, at age forty-five, he had been conditioned by a dozen years of alleged uphill improvements.

Suddenly, he turned to glance at me. "You know, Sergeant, for subjects to do what was commanded of them by their rulers is just . . ."

His voice became soft, quiet and controlled, as if he were attempting to convert the classroom incorrigible. "Now that certainly makes sense, does it not? Because, you see, Plato said that too."

I bit my lip to keep from getting in any deeper. But I was taken with the fact that this man, schooled in an exacting but personal human science, could twist any philosophical observation to his own viewpoint simply by quoting unfamiliar passages out of context. In this instance, his captive audience was unfamiliar with the work quoted. I was not conversant with Plato's writings and couldn't call the lieutenant to account for any discrepancies in his translation or interpretation.

Trautmann seemed uninterested in continuing the discussion as the little car made its final swing around the circle of Schonach's principal road, into the parking lot behind the Lamm. Both of us alighted and were about to enter the hotel when Trautmann laid his hand on my arm, restraining me.

"You are concerned that perhaps you were insubordinate?"

"Yes, sir, possibly . . . although that certainly wasn't my intention."

"And what would you fear if I should report you to *Oberstormfuhrer* Best?" Trautmann asked it with a smile. He seemed to be playing a game in the interest of psychology. He still appeared to be as conversationally friendly as he had most of the day.

"Some sort of reprisal, I suppose," I replied hesitantly.

"And what could be his most fearful reprisal?"

I thought for a moment of everything that had happened to me in this incredibly violent war and what it was that I always had feared the most.

"I guess death would be the worst thing."

"Aha! I knew you would say that!" Trautmann replied enthusiastically. He appeared victorious in his satisfaction with my expected response. "And what do you suppose that clever Grecian fellow would have to say about that? I'll tell you, and you will find that it completely refutes your own theories. Plato said, 'The fear of death is indeed the pretense of wisdom, and not real wisdom, being the pretense of the unknown.' He further believed that, 'A man who is good for anything ought not to calculate the chance of living or dying; he ought only to consider whether, in doing anything, he is doing right or wrong — acting the part of good or bad . . .' You see?"

Trautmann smiled in a way I hadn't seen before, as if he were subconsciously quoting at last the true beliefs that plagued him rather than those expected of him by his superiors.

The lieutenant's hand was on my left elbow as we entered the hotel. The conversation undoubtedly had ended for the present. I was sure, unfamiliar with Greek philosophy as I was, that no shallow motives existed in Plato's writings, at least none such as had been attributed by Trautmann. I was sure the thoughts had been misrepresented at least, to make them appear consistent with modern Nazi ideology.

Before we entered the dining room, I asked for and received permission to borrow some of the books from Trautmann's personal library in his room upstairs, particularly those of Plato and other philosophers. It was an area of my background that had been completely neglected. I knew I could never counter Trautmann's assertions and his

70

assured manner unless I was armed with some of the same sources of information.

Later in the day, Trautmann presented me with several volumes. All were in German except one — "The Apology" — which was in English. I decided to tackle the unfamiliar author in this simplest form first. Then, if I could work my way knowingly through the entire volume, I would take a pass at having one of the others translate difficult German passages in one of the other books for me.

I was sure Trautmann would grant me the dubious privilege of further discussion on the subject, but couldn't be sure he would translate quite as objectively as I would like.

Later, as I sat alone, I wondered why I should assume such a seemingly monumental undertaking in my present circumstances. A picture flashed across my mind. It was a scene from an early Sherlock Holmes movie I had seen as a youngster. Basil Rathbone was Holmes; Nigel Bruce was Dr. Watson. The scene had depicted Holmes seated before a table on which there was a large mason jar. Inside it were several houseflies.

Holmes had been playing disassociated notes on his violin in an effort to discover the effect of the sounds on the flies. As the notes gained in intensity, the detective watched with fascination as the insects moved in ever-tightening circles. In reply to Watson's query about the experiment, Holmes had said, "The active mind, Watson, is a healthy mind. Rather than stagnate as you do with your pipe, old fellow, I prefer to satisfy my scientific curiosity by testing the reactions of common houseflies to different sounds."

I had been a young lad when I had seen that picture and, although I didn't recall the plot of that particular Holmes adventure, that single line of Holmes' had remained in the back of my mind for years. The active mind is a happy mind. Perhaps this was my motivation. Then, I mused aloud, "Simply because it's there." I chuckled at the motivation given by mountain climbers for their dangerous hobby.

I entered the dining room where Trautmann had told me Best was waiting. As I stepped into the large room, I found the entire group from earlier in the morning assembled about a single, long table. Bruckmann rose, a broad smile on his face.

"By heaven, Lister, you certainly don't look like the same person."

I glanced at the others, all of whom seemed equally pleased, judging from facial expressions. My transformation gave me a distinct feeling of personal accomplishment and pleasure, even though it had been developed with the simplest of actions — a bath.

My eyes stopped on those of Inga Domann. Her eyes held a thinly veiled look of decided interest. Or was it my imagination?

Bruckmann took my arm and led me aside to a distant table, away from the others. They returned to their own conversations.

"Now, perhaps we discuss your situation here, Sergeant Lister, eh? Let us review the arrangements. First of all, you served in several campaigns, did you not?"

I was telling him nothing he didn't already know when I replied, "Yes, sir."

"Well, when you were in Italy, did you ever hear our Sally on the radio?"

"The bitch of Berlin."

"Er, yes. I believe that is what she was called by you Yanks, at least some of you on occasion. Now, tell me, what of her programs?"

"Oh, we didn't hear her all that often. When we did, we enjoyed the music. She played American pop music, you know."

"And what of the prisoner messages?"

"You mean of Americans in German captivity?"

"Precisely."

"We didn't pay much attention to them. We knew they were phony."

"Aha, Hal. That is the very problem we have here, you see. This is the same story we have heard from every prisoner who was in Italy. And all because of that fool, George, her companion on the program. She insists on keeping that oak with her to read the messages. He is exactly what he sounds like, a guttural fool. That is why you are here."

"I don't understand." That queasiness in the pit of my stomach was returning. Suddenly, I was on the threshold of all this mystery.

"Well you told our people that you had radio experience. If that is the case, perhaps you would agree to broadcast such prisoner messages for us here. You see, we are setting up a shortwave radio station here in Schonach.

I was flabbergasted. I never thought my fib would result in such dramatic repercussions, particularly since it had been a white lie purely of expedience.

"No, sir, not this boy," I insisted. "I have no intention of spending twenty years in the pokey for collaboration. I won't broadcast any propaganda!"

"Now, don't be concerned, my boy," Bruckmann replied patiently. "We are not asking you to do any propaganda broadcasting. We'll take care of that end. Actually, nobody will be likely to be listening to the silly things anyway. It's just that the Americans are broadcasting messages constantly from our men in your camps in America. We would like to reciprocate in kind, that's all. We can do it more convincingly if we have an experienced man like yourself, who sounds like an actual American soldier, broadcast the prisoner messages. If you like, we plan to have you driven to the camp in Villingen at least once each week to pick up messages from your fellow prisoners of war. You can check it with the American officials there, if you like. That way, there can be no doubt in your mind. What we do before and after your program need be of no concern to you, isn't that true?"

Bruckmann waited for an answer from me. I still remained utterly confused by this whole bizarre situation. I hesitated as I mulled over the proposition. After all, I wouldn't be the first person taken in by a glib con artist, and Bruckmann had all the earmarks of just that, a likeable swindler. Sensing his advantage, Bruckmann bore in.

"Actually, you know, Hal, if you don't do it, we will find somebody else who will. We have a great many prisoner of war camps with a great many prisoners. Surely, among them there is someone else with broadcasting experience."

There certainly was logic in that. I thought hard about his arguments. They weren't being nice to me and making me an attractive and unusual offer for any reason other than that they needed me. That was obvious. I thought about Dulag 62, Feldwebel Hoffman there, the lice, and Schonach with its complete lack of guards or barbed wire. In fact, it was that thought that finally convinced me to investigate this offer. The only deterrent to escape here was the chest-high snow throughout the hilltops and the forest. This snow would have to melt before too much longer, while the barbed wire in a prison camp, which was my alternative, would be there for a substantially longer time. All this rationalizing going on in my mind, coupled with Bruckmann's assurance that no propaganda would be required of me, convinced me at last to ask for a visit to the Villingen camp.

As a matter of fact, I reasoned that I really should be registered at a camp officially anyway. My status at Waldkirch had been strictly transient.

"When could I go to Villingen?" I asked as noncommittally as I could.

"Oh, we'll go at once, my boy. At once."

"Well, if the American ranking officer there says it's OK, I'll be willing to do it."

"Splendid! We'll be getting started on programming in a week or two. First, of course, we'll get you to Villingen for all that business. Now, come over here to the others. We'll have to tell them the good news."

I arose as Bruckmann did and crossed the room just behind him.

"What do you think, my friends?" He stood before the others at the long table as they expectantly watched him. "Hal is going to stay with us. He's agreed to do the program."

I was a bit concerned about his automatic conclusion to our tentative agreement before I talked to some American in a position of authority.

Most of the gathered participants offered congratulations as they crowded round me. All except Inga, who merely sat back in her chair contemplating me. She smiled directly into my eyes as our eyes met. The complete incongruity of the scene struck me again.

I was a prisoner of war, a Jew, standing in the comfortable dining room of a quaint hotel in the enemy's homeland, surrounded by a highly multifarious assemblage who seemed genuinely delighted that I had voluntarily chosen to stay with them. I tried to think of a way to explain this situation to my buddies back in the outfit. *They'd never believe it,* I thought. *In fact, neither would I.* I couldn't help wondering, momentarily, where the outfit was now.

"Sit down here, Hal, my boy. Sit over here, next to Inga," Bruckmann directed with no apparent motive other than drawing the group back to their places around the table. Inga smiled and said, "Yes, Hal. Sit here and we'll talk about it."

I slid into the empty chair beside her. In the course of the next two *tête-à-tête* hours during which most of the others fell into their own two- and three-person discussions, I learned as much about Inga as she did about me.

I found that this exciting, beautiful woman had broadcast over most of the German propaganda stations throughout Europe at one time or another. She was a German native who had been taken to the United States as a child and reared in exclusive American schools until 1935, when her parents were divorced. Her father, a university professor, had taken her on a world cruise then, covering the Orient, India, the Middle East, the Mediterranean, and ending in Switzerland, where she had been enrolled in a private school for girls.

She was thirty-two, she admitted, and had been married and divorced just before the outbreak of war in 1939. She had lived on an island in the Baltic Sea which her father owned, and her background and education were considered more conducive to her present work than to the operation of a machine in some factory.

She was an utterly fascinating woman, one whose physical attractiveness made her immensely popular in the circles in which she traveled. Her present attitude toward me seemed to be that of an adventuress who had discovered a new toy. The way her knee occasionally bumped, or rubbed briefly, against mine might have been an accident. Or it might have been further indication that she was on the prowl. I was afraid to react, lest I had misunderstood her message, or worse, lest she had no message at all. I was sure the German open-handedness would not include sexual fraternization.

I recalled with discomfort the German decree of which I had heard concerning the death penalty for any non-German caught fraternizing with a German woman. I was damned sure a Jewish American POW would land somewhere at the top of the prosecutor's list. I decided simply to let nature take its course. The whole situation was becoming disturbingly disarming for me. I sat back in admiring silence, listening to and watching Frau Domann.

"We must work together here," she was saying. "There are so many ideas I have to improve our efforts."

I couldn't help wondering just where her improvement ideas were centered. I glanced around the room as casually as I could and felt relief that nobody seemed to be observing us.

5. "Keep your messages short"

"IT IS ONLY THREE more kilometers," Lieutenant Trautmann said as he expertly guided the little car around the wooded curves of the Schwarzwald lowlands. He and I were headed toward Villingen, the site of the nearest American POW camp to Schonach. Actually, this camp had Allied soldiers of several nationalities, except the Americans were there in the greatest numbers.

We had been driving for more than an hour, much of it in hazardous weather on dangerous mountain road curves. I was pleased at the caution exhibited by the lieutenant as he held the steering wheel tightly with both hands. Trautmann stared straight ahead, his hands at ten and two o'clock, and showed the care usually seen in an older driver who has had his share of exciting times behind a wheel and has outgrown them.

There had been no other settlements or groups of houses since we left Triberg, and the countryside was awe-inspiring in its late-winter beauty. Towering evergreens shaded the road from all sides, their branches drooping low under the weight of heavy layers of snow. Nowhere could I see clearings along the roadside. The trees were so close to each other in their virginal settings that I wondered how they breathed. I would have assumed they'd choke each other in the incredibly thick, sunless forest.

I began to worry about an escape route once the opportunity presented itself. I had no doubt one would. But I couldn't leave Schonach via the highway. While there wasn't an abundance of military activity in the little mountain hamlet, there would likely be much of it on the roads out of Triberg, of which the Schonach road was one. I'd be conspicuous in my uniform if I were to try to maneuver along any public road during either daylight or evening hours. And, in the forest blackness, German vehicles were moving with headlights blazing, unlike the situation anywhere else in this part of Germany, especially over on the west side of these mountains, on the Rhine. Apparently the fact that the sky couldn't be seen because of the heavy overhang of greenery gave the driver confidence that was unusual at this stage of the war. After all, they probably reasoned, if we can't see out, they can't see in.

If the density of the parts of the Black Forest I'd seen were any criteria, it would be impenetrable for anyone trying to move exclusively along the forest floor. But surely I would find paths among the trees. After all, this was popular pre-war resort country. Surely there were hiking trails and walking routes followed by mountain folks traveling from village to village.

At the moment, with deep snow drifted about the trunks of trees as far into the woods as the darkness permitted me to look, my escape thoughts were a bit premature. I would have to seek what information I could as diplomatically as possible, from whomever I could talk to who would be familiar with the area. In this way, perhaps I could piece together a practical escape route.

We came upon the camp with such unexpected suddenness that I was amazed to see a substantial man-made installation where, only moments before, there had been impassable forest. The camp had been literally hacked out of the grasping woods over several acres of land.

The compound had the same dreary look I had seen around every such installation I'd come across. A ten-foot, barbed wire fence surrounded the enclosure, with another such fence about four feet further in, forming a walkway between the strands, through which a guard, a pair of guards, or a guard and a dog could patrol. The prisoner population was kept inside the inner fence. There were manned machine gun towers at each corner of the compound and midway along the fence on each side.

The numerous barracks buildings were traditional, one-story affairs of dingy, unpainted wood. Hundreds of prisoners could be seen milling about the exercise yard and along the gravel paths that wound everywhere in the camp. In the nearest group of prisoners I could make out American uniforms predominating.

I saw shoulder patches of my division as well as companion units with which I had become familiar. Many unfamiliar patches also abounded. After all, we now were joined with the northern American armies that had come ashore at Normandy while we were liberating Rome. I wasn't familiar with many of those, although some old friends were among them. I saw a couple of Big Red One patches of the 1st Division, the peculiar clover leaf pattern of the 4th and numerous gaudy triangular tank division patches.

In the distance within the camp I noticed many French uniforms with which I was familiar. We had served with the French First Army just before coming to Kaysersberg. Several dark-skinned Arab prisoners were squatting about a portion of the parade ground, apparently playing a game known in their homelands. They ignored everyone else as they laughed among themselves.

Beyond the camp, the ground leveled still more and, in the slight depression that became a wide valley, I saw the picturesque and ancient city spread out to the south.

Heavy, Gothic stones formed the high walls and parapets surrounding Villingen, and I saw several high arches that formed the gates to the town. I noted three tall, pointed church spires, the highest landmarks in the town. The entire panorama had an unreal, book-illustration quality such as those I'd seen in Crusader stories.

"That's a beautiful sight, isn't it?" I asked, staring at the lovely view below us.

"That is Villingen," Lieutenant Trautmann said. "The city is more than a thousand years old. There, beyond the forest. That is Switzerland," he added, pointedly, I thought.

I looked above the village, up over the black trees that made up the southern extremity of the German Black Forest. Then I looked further into the distance where, looming against the sky, literally hanging over the landscape and dwarfing all before them, were the Alps. Although the snow-covered giants gave the impression of nearness — I felt I might reach out of the car window and touch them — I knew they must be at least twenty miles away.

My fascinated stare was broken by the lieutenant who softly advised, "There are a great many border patrols and guard stations from here to the southern border."

I turned my head quickly to find Trautmann staring at the mountains rather than at me. It was almost as if he had been thinking aloud rather than addressing his last remark to me. A hint of a smile curved the right side of Trautmann's mouth, but very slightly.

"Well, let us get on with our business, eh?" the officer pulled the wheel to the right, turning into the short driveway before the camp's wide double gate over which hung a sign with two-foot-high letters proclaiming, "Stammlager VII-B." A sentry approached the window and glanced inside at me. Trautmann reached into his inner jacket pocket and withdrew his official papers. The sentry read them and looked up at the guards at the gate. He waved, and they opened the gate to permit entry of the car.

We drove slowly into the compound and pulled to a smooth halt before the first building, obviously the camp commander's office. It bore the legend across the door, "Buro. Kommandatur."

"You wait here," the lieutenant said. "They won't bother you as long as you stay in the car and in sight of the main gate. That sentry read my orders."

He crawled out of the car and entered the headquarters building. I watched the mingling prisoners moving about listlessly. They looked clean-shaven and, aside from what must have been paralyzing boredom, seemed well-enough cared for. Their uniforms looked relatively neat and, generally, an air of cleanliness was evident.

None of them ventured near the car, even though I saw no guards directly among them. I'm sure I wouldn't have either, under their circumstances. Apparently common sense dictated against any overt move which might be misconstrued as an escape attempt.

Trautmann returned and leaned down to window level.

"All right, Mr. Lister. Everything is prepared. We are to go with this fellow to an American barracks. You will be introduced to the American man of confidence and given thirty minutes to gather material. I have registered you as a prisoner at this camp. Here is your official prisoner identification tag." He handed me a small metallic object through the car window and opened the door for me to climb out.

I looked at the object. It was a rectangular piece of thin metal, about two inches long and about an inch and one-half wide. On it were crudely stamped characters. I held it at an angle so I might read them

better in the glaring sunlight. The simple message read: "VII-B —
Villingen — 30820."

An *unteroffizier* — German corporal — stood behind Trautmann.
He now moved around him in front of me and nodded down the path
to the second building on our right. I followed him to the front of that
structure. Trautmann held out his arm, stopping me. He had followed
us. We stood still while the guard stepped to the top of the low stoop
and opened the door enough to allow passage of his head and shoulders.

"Hallo, Herr Sanders. Nehmen sie hier, Herr Sanders, herous!"

The door opened from the inside and an American master sergeant came through it. He was a man of about thirty, short and bulky
with straight, sandy hair. He wore the bright orange and black shoulder patch of the 106th Tank Destroyer Regiment — a lion's head, jaws
crushing a tank tread.

He stepped out with the air of officiality one might expect from
the ranking representative of an entire delegation. He approached me
and extended his right hand.

"Hi, Sarge. I'm Elliott Sanders. I'm con man here."

"Hal Lister," I replied. I smiled and shook his hand enthusiastically.

"We'll have you fixed up in no time. We have a couple of extra
bunks in here," Sanders said, taking me by the arm as if to move me
indoors.

"Just a moment, Sergeant," Trautmann said, stopping Sanders in
his tracks. "This is a different situation than you think."

Sanders looked at the lieutenant, puzzled. Trautmann turned to
me.

"Why don't you go with the sergeant and explain the situation to
him, Mr. Lister? I'll wait at the headquarters building. Remember
now, we have thirty minutes only today."

He turned and motioned the guard to follow him. They walked
stiffly to the orderly room, side by side.

Sanders turned to me, a puzzled frown on his face. "What in
hell's that all about? Are you in some kind of trouble? And with the SS
yet?"

"No, nothing like that. It is a queer deal though." I was having
difficulty finding the proper opening to cover the series of weird circumstances that had overtaken me. "Let's go inside, and I'll try to explain it to you."

Sanders held the door open for me as we entered the barracks. The inside of the building consisted of a low wall between the first cot and the rest. The wall consisted of four small boxes the size of orange crates back home. It gave Sanders a measure of privacy.

"Squat here," he said. "This is my CP," he advised, with a grin.

I sat in the middle of the bed, while Sanders sat at the foot. For the next few minutes, I explained the weird set of events that took me to Schonach in the first place and the reason I was here today — to get his blessing for the project which would keep me in a guardless village, free to escape as soon as the snow melted. I assured him, as Bruckmann had me, that I would have no direct propaganda involvement.

"Now wait just a damn minute here," Sanders interrupted me. "You mean to tell me you're gonna be broadcasting propaganda for them fuckers up there?"

"No, that's just my point. My part of the schedule, as I've had it explained, will be to read a few POW messages and play a few records. Oh, the station is a propaganda station, no doubt about that. And my program surely will be bracketed with propaganda programs of some kind."

"Yeah, well nobody believes that shit anyway," Sanders nodded.

"Not only that, but there are no guards. The only military up there is this SS engineer outfit that's building the station. As soon as the snow melts a little, say in early or mid-April, I should be able to walk out of there like a big-assed bird."

Sanders stared at his shoes for a moment. "Well, I'll be damned! That's the goofiest goddamn story I ever heard."

"Well, what do you say, Sarge? It's just crazy enough to give me a chance to escape that I'd never have if I came down here. I'd like your clearance, though, in case any question ever came up later."

"Shit, man, I sure can't blame you and wouldn't want to block a chance to break out. Sure. Here, tell ya what. Take this." He pulled his dog tag chain over his head, opened it and slid one of his tags off, handing it to me. "Now, hang on to this. Then, if anybody gives you heat, don't be afraid to give 'em my name and tell 'em I said it was OK. Hell, you ain't actually doin' the propaganda, so who can blame you?"

The man of confidence was an honored institution in POW camps. Usually, he was the ranking enlisted man who served as the official spokesman for all other enlisted troops of his nationality. Of course, in an officers' camp, he would likely be the ranking brass.

"They tell me they'll bring me down here every couple of weeks or so to let me pick up more messages. I brought some forms today which you can pass out to the guys. We have time for about twenty messages today. I'll pick up a lot more next time."

"How many you gonna read each day?"

"Well, I haven't actually started to broadcast yet, but in unofficial times tests, I figure I can get about three records and ten messages on each program. If I can stock up about a hundred messages, I figure I'll be able to pace it so as to get that many on every couple of weeks. Here, I'll give you these forms now and, in the next week or so, have other guys fill them out. But get me some for now with these others, OK?"

Sanders nodded and took both bundles of forms from me. He laid the thicker pile down on his bedside table. Then he looked about the room. Several men were occupied with various diversions. I could see one sewing a patch on a shirt. Others were writing letters, reading, or playing cards quietly. Two men on a small nearby bunkside table were playing chess with a little portable set.

"Hey, Harley," Sanders yelled. "Take one of these and pass the rest out, will ya? And hurry up and fill 'em out. We need 'em right away."

The man put down his shirt and walked across the room to Sanders, taking the pack of forms. Sanders took in the entire room as he bellowed his next order. "You guys each take one of them things and write a message home. Sergeant Lister here will put them on a short-wave broadcast and your families might hear 'em. Keep your messages short."

"You might as well write one for yourself, Sarge," I said. "I'll put yours on the first broadcast."

"Great. Thanks a lot. I hoped you would." He took one of the forms and began composing a brief, penciled message. When he finished, he handed me the form. "How's that?" he inquired.

I checked the message. It was simple and concise. It had been lettered in neat, block characters. It read:

"Mrs. Elliott J. Sanders, 420 Division Rd., Utica N.Y. From Master Sergeant E. J. Sanders, Stalag VII-B, Villingen, Germany. Prisoner serial number 27645. Dear Emily: I am well and comfortable. Hope you are the same. My love to you and the baby. Please don't worry about me. I'll write again soon. Ell."

"That's just great, Sarge. Let's hope they all keep 'em as short as this. It will give me a chance to get more on each program. How many prisoners are there here?"

Sanders thought for a moment. "Let's see, there are twelve American barracks. We have a maximum capacity of thirty-two men per building. That's 384 with our present setup. Of course, we could get more in at any time, or they might transfer some as we fill up. I've been here a year and a half and that's happened both ways. We have eighteen empties right now. Two of our guys went to the hospital in Triberg with pneumonia yesterday, but they'll be back."

I knew that the GI population of the camp could be altered, as Sanders had said, but not likely by more than five to seven percent.

"We'd better get 'em movin', Sarge," I urged. "They said thirty minutes and I guess time's just about up."

"Right." Sanders stood and looked around the room. "OK, you guys, let's wrap it up. The sergeant has to get going now. Here, Schroeder, you pick 'em up on that end. I'll get these down here."

Each of the men hastily concluded his own personal message and handed it in. There were twenty men in the building at the time. All messages were stacked and handed to me. I folded them and forced them into the right-hand hip pocket of my trousers, lifting my combat jacket to stuff them in.

Sanders accompanied me outside and as far as the end of the path. There, I turned and shook his hand.

"I'll see you week after next, I hope," I said.

"Fine. And good luck up there. I wish I was goin' with you. Take care of yourself."

Trautmann was waiting on the porch of the headquarters building as I approached. The two of us climbed wordlessly into the Volkswagen, and the lieutenant skillfully manipulated it in that cramped parking area into a series of backward and forward motions that permitted us to drive forward out of the camp gate. There was no reaction from the guards as we drove by them, nor did Trautmann give any indication of recognizing their existence. Obviously, his SS uniform and a message from an SS commander carried considerable weight, especially among rear-echelon Wehrmacht troops.

The drive back to Schonach was quiet and uneventful except for a brief exchange about the mission. The lieutenant was interested in the types of messages I had obtained. I unfolded and read a few of them. Most were quite unimaginative, stereotyped good wishes. They contained pleas to relatives not to worry. I hoped advance notice, which had been unavailable this time, would improve the originality of the messages on the next visit. I planned to alter some of these messages slightly just to give their delivery a little variety without changing the meaning in any way.

I was somewhat disappointed when I noticed Trautmann's obvious preoccupation with distant thoughts and his apparent disinclination to continue our philosophical discussion of a few days earlier. We arrived in Schonach in time for our midday meal. Today, Frau Greiner had prepared boiled potatoes, green vegetables, and a small piece of pork for each plate, including mine. It was delicious.

6. No Wild Indian

I KNOCKED AT THE heavy oak door three times.

"Herein," came the deep-voiced message from within.

I entered to find Bruckmann seated comfortably on the couch, his shoes off, his big toe peeking through a hole in his right sock. He was drinking tea from a huge china mug. He stood hurriedly, rearranging his uniform which had been left comfortably unbuttoned.

"Ah, Hal, my boy. Good to see you. Forgive the way I look. But you are right on time. I like that. It's a good thing to be punctual. It shows a marked respect for the other person's busy schedule." He pronounced it the British way, "shedule."

Bruckmann opened a tin box. "I got this precious stuff from my wife in Augsburg yesterday," he said, spooning bulk tea out of the box into another mug. He poured water from the steaming kettle into the china teapot on the table, thence into my mug, letting the tea steep about a minute first.

Taking the cup, I seated myself on the ottoman beside the couch as he had indicated with a nod of his head.

"Did you get your messages organized?" Bruckmann asked.

"Yep. Everything's all set. I've interspersed three records among the five messages. That and the opening and closing theme time out to just twenty minutes. That's what you said I had, isn't it?"

"That's correct. Actually, we have a little leeway by cutting or extending your theme song. By the way, have you selected a theme song as yet?"

"Well, I listened to a lot of records. One of my favorites back home was Artie Shaw's arrangement of 'Copenhagen.' I noticed it among Lieutenant Küttner's collection up at the studio. It's catchy, brassy, and would be an attention-getter."

"Well, I guess that would be all right. You think it is popular among Americans?"

"Oh yes, it's extremely popular among my generation."

"And it has no political implications that I can see, isn't it so?"

"No, it's nothing but a rhythm number. It doesn't even have anything to do with Denmark. I don't really know where the title came from. I've heard the lyrics several times."

"Really? How does it go then?"

"As I recall them, the lyrics go something like . . .

> 'Way down in old New Orleans,
> You'll find shoulder-shakin' queens.
> And when they roll their eyes,
> You wake up in paradise.
> And when that old leader man . . .
> I said, when that old leader man
> Picks up his saxophone,
> All the shoulder shakers moan.'

"That's about all I can remember of the introduction. Then the chorus goes something like this:

> 'Professor man, won't you play Copenhagen,
> 'cause that one tune sure had me runnin' wild.
> Nobody knows how that tune burns up my clothes.'

"Then there's a bunch of stuff about rhythm and blues. But no place in the song does it refer to the city of Copenhagen."

"It sounds like a ridiculous song to me. I really don't understand young people's musical taste these days. How does the music to it go?"

I tried to recall as well as I could the riffs and rolls of the Shaw arrangement as I whistled the tune for Bruckmann. The big man seemed to enjoy the rhythmic movements.

"Well, there are no words on this recording, you say?"

"That's right. No singing. It's strictly instrumental."

"Fine, then let us plan to use that. I like the sound, and it has a lovely, catchy tune that is likely to interest a young audience. Oh, and another thing, Hal. We'd better agree on a name for your program right away."

"I've been thinking about that," I said. "I've come up with one that makes sense to me, provided you approve."

"Indeed? What is that?"

"How about 'Krautland Calling'?"

"Krautland? What means that, Krautland?"

"It means Germany in American military slang. You know, as in sauerkraut."

Bruckmann frowned uncertainly. He wasn't sure he liked the sound. It was an unfamiliar use of the translation of cabbage, and he, quite correctly, felt it might have derogatory connotations.

"Are you sure that isn't an insulting word?"

"Absolutely not," I tried to assure him.

"But Krautland. I just don't know."

I knew it would be accepted by American troops. Throughout the American campaigns of this war, some of the World War I terms used to describe the enemy had been replaced. The British still used "Jerry," the French called them "Bosche," the Italians called them "Tedeschi." I had not heard the once popular "Heinie" or "Hun" applied by anyone. But, in the American army, "Kraut" had become the synonym, and it never had favorable implications.

"Well, you know how poor at foreign languages most Americans are," I continued, defending my title. "But one word we all recognize is 'Kraut.' We know that cabbage is a very popular food in the German diet, and we used that word to refer to German soldiers. Just as you refer to us as 'Yanks,' or the British as 'Tommies,' and some Americans use 'Frogs' for French and 'Guinea' for Italians, we use 'Kraut' for Germans. There is nothing derogatory about it, I assure you," I lied. "I'll guarantee that it will be familiar to every GI who hears it, though."

Bruckmann was considering the word and idea with some uncertainty. There was something about it that bothered him but he just couldn't put his finger on what it was. He couldn't afford a mistake of the magnitude of the program title being an insult to the Reich. However, my sincerity apparently appealed to him. And it would put much more responsibility on my shoulders. Yes, he decided he would permit me to use "Krautland Calling."

"Well, Hal, my boy. How do you like life here in Schonach? It surely is more pleasant than in a prison camp and much safer than in those fighting situations you were in, don't you agree?"

I certainly couldn't fault that logic. In fact, I still found myself in a quandary trying to understand how this had happened to me. I had been here for nearly two weeks and had virtually free run of the town. I was permitted to attend the local cinema in the basement of the Hotel Schwann across the street. A crude replica of a little theater had been established there and current German movies were shown for a week at a time. I had attended the present one three times in an effort to improve my German proficiency.

It was strange to see a foreign language movie without voice dubbing or subtitles in English. The movie I had seen was titled "Verloren," and was a sophisticated love story, à la Noel Coward.

The newsreels, of course, were Nazi propaganda devices, concentrating on bearded, bedraggled Allied prisoners and German artillery barrages on the various fronts which had been established against der Vaterland. From all filmed indications, Germany was winning the war on all fronts, or such was the narrator's invariable message.

One particular innovation to be seen and heard everywhere was the German parallel to the American "Loose lips sink ships" admonition warning Americans of the constant possibility of enemy ears hearing conversation, especially about military matters. The German version, which cautioned citizens to keep their thoughts and information to themselves in case spies were listening, showed a large black shadow running diagonally across the viewers' line of vision. It resembled the radio character Lamont Cranston, "The Shadow," as advertised in posters and in comic books in the United States in the late 1930s.

The stylized shadow was of a man with a wide-brimmed hat and a long cloak. His caped arm was drawn across his face. The printed message emblazoned across the poster was, *"Achtung, der Schwarze Man is hier!"*

I never saw the poster without silently recalling the deep baritone voice of Cranston as he proclaimed, "The weed of crime bears bitter fruit. Crime does not pay. The Shadow knows!"

"And now I have a surprise for you, my boy," Bruckmann was saying, his large mouth stretched into his usual unbalanced smile. "I am taking you to meet Frau Schilli today. We are getting you new quarters because we need all the rooms in the school building for the sender. The soldiers will move into the third floor of the hotel here and into the Schwann across the road. We are placing you in a private home hereafter. We don't want you sleeping on that blasted straw in that wretched schoolroom, eh? How does that sound to you?"

I had been waiting for some move. The German troops with whom I'd been billeted had been moving out of the classroom in twos and threes over the past few days. Apparently they were planning to use the schoolroom for some part of the station's operation. The upper floor of the building already had been converted completely to a radio station, and facilities appeared to be moving in on the ground floor next.

"Where does Frau Schilli live?" I asked. From the window of Bruckmann's room we had a complete panoramic view of the entire village below us.

Bruckmann rose and walked to the window. I followed. The big man squinted, primarily as a shield against the incredible brightness, as he surveyed the beautiful snow-clad landscape. Then, after a moment, as if he had been searching for something in particular, he stopped and smiled.

"Ah, that's her house there. You can just make out a corner of the building there, see? It's the house at the very edge of that side of the left-hand loop of the road."

I saw the house he was indicating.

"That is the Schilli home. There also is a Herr Schilli. Urban, his name is. She is Maria. But he is harmless and won't bother you. He works two shifts each day and is almost never at home. In fact, I found him a completely innocuous, not unpleasant little chap. We'll have you settled in in no time at all."

I finished my tea and set the cup on the low table.

"OK, Herr Bruckmann. I'm ready when you are."

Bruckmann smiled. *"Ach, moment, bitte."* He lapsed into German as he did whenever he wanted to appear facetious. He sat on the edge of the couch and, grunting with the exertion of bending over to tie his boots, completed that project, arose, crossed the room, and pulled on his military greatcoat and heavy leather mittens.

We left the hotel and took the link of the circle road that gave us the most direct route to the Schilli home. We climbed the banked steps to the front door of the dull, gray-white stucco building. Bruckmann knocked authoritatively, and the door was opened by a short, heavy-set woman who appeared to be in her late fifties. She seemed ill-at-ease and completely subservient, almost as if she were frightened by the proximity of two such large men, both of them strangers, although Bruckmann obviously had been here before. She received us nervously into her crowded living room, standing behind us, wringing her hands. She waited for us to finish our cursory analysis of the sitting room into which we had been ushered.

It was a small room, very busy with too much furniture and too many fixtures. It measured about ten by twelve feet in area and looked as if Frau Schilli had made use of it at the expense of every other room in the house. She seemed to have moved many pieces of furniture in here from other rooms. On the front wall, between two small windows, she had a drop-leaf dining room table surrounded by four chairs.

A large, tiled *kackel offen* — an oven for heating the room — was mounted in one corner of the room. On the opposite wall there was a delapidated couch next to which . . . my heart jumped . . . there stood an end table on which reposed an ancient, rectangular, dark wood radio complete with an amplifying horn on top and with earphones attached.

Every wall was literally covered with antique paintings and family portraits. There were no books in the room, although there was a bookcase whose shelves were covered with a clutter of framed photographs and carnival-type bric-a-brac. I looked back to the radio as inconspicuously as I could. I hadn't heard any news of the outside world for more than two months. I hoped the set worked. I felt sure I could manage some very late night or early morning listening if I were to do it carefully.

Frau Schilli was dressed in a heavy black cardigan sweater, under which she wore a dull brown dress. She wore dark cotton stockings and heavy-heeled, well-worn, black shoes. Her entire attitude since she had admitted us was one of utter subservience, and Bruckmann seemed to accept it as his due.

"*Also, Gnädigte Frau Schilli,*" he began in a most conciliatory tone. "*Ich bin Herr Bruckmann von den Buro. Hier haben wir unser Gast. Er ist ein Amerikanische Kriegsgefangener, aber er ist auch ein hochgeborene Mensch, und sie wissen schon was wir mirchten hier, nicht wahr?*"

She nodded, fully aware of the insistence in his syrupy voice. From what I could piece together, I had been introduced as a highborn American POW. It was apparent from Bruckmann's remarks to Frau Schilli that she had been briefed somewhat before my arrival. She probably had been given more of an implied command than an invitation to serve as my hostess.

The magic word seemed to have been "highborn," I noticed, because she broke into an appreciative smile at the use of this stilted phrase. Despite her obvious nervousness, she immediately set about being as affable, almost servile, as she seemed able. She hurriedly shuffled to the table and drew two chairs out from under it, indicating anxiously that we should sit. She then bowed repeatedly and backed out of the room.

Bruckmann cocked a superior, knowing brow at me and said in a quiet voice, "These wretches are highly pleased to have so distinguished a guest in their home. You don't know what a novelty you are in Schonach, my dear Hal. Now I imagine she is preparing a warm drink of some kind for us. They have delicious native concoctions here in the mountains."

"I feel guilty using any of her food," I said, aware of the restrictive and expensive rationing system in force throughout Germany.

"Oh, have no fear, my young friend. Frau Schilli is being compensated handsomely for having you in her home, both in marks and ration coupons."

His explanation was interrupted by Frau Schilli's return. She bore a huge tray on which she had two cups, two saucers, and a heavy earthen pitcher. Steam was rising from the pitcher as she placed the load on the table.

I had started to rise when she entered, to help relieve her of her load, but the pressure of Bruckmann's hand on my arm deterred me. "Such gallantry is out of place here," he said quietly. "She wouldn't understand it and it would make her even more uncomfortable."

I watched Frau Schilli as she busied herself pouring an amber liquid into the cups, placed each cup on its saucer, and passed one to each of her honored guests. She carefully passed us our cups simultaneously as if to avoid the dilemma of selecting one of us over the other in priority.

My nostrils were assailed by the delicious aroma of fruit. It was very refreshing, this odor. I smelled plums or apricots, I couldn't be sure which, but the drink did smell of a mixture of such fruits. I couldn't understand where foods like these would come from up here in midwinter. I did realize they must be stored in a cool cellar somewhere, or perhaps dried for subsequent cooking. Apparently there were orchards in the vicinity.

Frau Schilli placed the ewer on a black metal trivet and leaned back, her hands in her apron pockets, a beatific smile brightening her face, as she seemingly awaited our reaction to her treat.

"She wouldn't drink with us highborn folk," Bruckmann smiled. "She feels she is beneath our station," he said, seeming to enjoy the situation.

I tasted the drink and found it extremely palatable. In fact, I liked it much better than the tea with which Bruckmann had been brightening our sessions together lately. Sugar being at such a high premium here, when available at all, the natural sweetness of the fruit drink made it much more tasty. During the next few moments, as I relished the delicious novelty, Frau Schilli stood by, clucking at my obvious delight in her concoction. She kept clicking her tongue on her upper palate, producing a clicking sound which I took to imply a positive reaction, since she was smiling at the same time.

"What is this, Helmut?" I asked, tentatively using Bruckmann's first name for the first time. He had suggested it the day before, but I hadn't been able to do it until now. It suddenly seemed appropriate.

"*Heisgetrink,* it is called. It is a predominantly local fruit drink which has proven of great interest to tourists over the years. It is made from fruits picked up the hill in those orchards you can see behind the school. The pensions and hotels have served it for some time, but it has started being used by individual families much like this one."

Finally, Bruckmann finished his cupful and arose, accompanying Frau Schilli into the next room. Actually, he steered her there, holding her left upper arm gently but firmly. She didn't object.

He didn't indicate that I should follow, so I stayed where I was until they were out of sight and the door was closed. I then bounded to the radio set and checked the few simple dials. I found the switch that turned the set off and on and found the point at which the earphone wires were plugged into the cabinet with a crude jack arrangement. A switch just above this point obviously switched the set from speaker to earphones.

I turned the off/on switch as far to the left as I could so the volume would be minimized. Then, glancing through the louvered slots on the side of the cabinet, I was delighted to see lighted tubes inside. The set worked. Now all I had to do was plug in the earphones, switch them on, and listen to war news from the American or British stations just across the Rhine. Or, at least, that was my hope. I couldn't be sure about possible mineral deposits in these mountains and their effect on reception.

Bruckmann's voice was growing louder as he approached from the next room. I moved swiftly to my place in the chair I had occupied earlier. The two entered the sitting room, both seeming to beam at me. Frau Schilli seemed particularly overcome by my presence there. I imagined that, even though Schonach obviously had been a pre-war tourist haven, few of the simple natives had ever associated with visiting Auslanders.

"So it is all decided," Bruckmann advised me. "You will live in this house with Herr and Frau Schilli. That will be your sleeping room." He nodded to an adjacent room into which he and Frau Schilli had gone for their final, private conversation.

I arose and walked into "my room." I found a long, narrow chamber in which stood a huge, heavy, three-quarter-size bed, an immense clothing cabinet — a *Schrank* — standing against the wall, and a washstand on which rested a heavy, antique crockery bowl. In the bowl was a matching, rose-festooned, white pitcher. The room was comfortable but small. It had a narrow window at the end beside the bed, and at the other end of the room was a door leading, I assumed, to the outer hall. It was on the same wall as the door from the sitting room into the outer hall. Another door, opposite the foot of the bed, led into a larger bedroom, presumably that of the Schillis.

I returned to the parlor and, after a few additional amenities, including compliments for Frau Schilli's *Heisgetrink,* several exchanges of tolerant smiles from Bruckmann and girlish giggles from our hostess, emanating from behind her shielding hand, we left the house. A handwringing, beaming *hausfrau* stood happily in the doorway behind us.

"She was absolutely delightful once she overcame her basic fear of strangers," Bruckmann explained. "When she was first approached about boarding an American prisoner of war, she was nearly frightened to death. After all, an American, you know," Bruckmann continued. "She told me she had never even talked to an Auslander, and to these people, even citizens of Triberg are treated as Auslanders. Why, Frau Schilli told me that, in her thirty-eight years . . ."

"Thirty-eight years?"

"Yes, isn't it amazing? She looks older than fifty, don't you think?"

"She certainly does."

"Obviously, it has to do with the hard life they have here, these locals. They are very hard workers. Anyway, she said she had never been farther than fourteen miles from Schonach. Once, when she was nineteen, she said, she went with her mother and father to a village fair in Haslach, just over the mountain there."

"So she thought Americans had horns and a tail, did she?"

"Not quite, but I think you're not far from the mark. But now that she's met you and found what a charming fellow you are, I have no doubt she'll make your life pleasant enough. At least she knows you are not some sort of wild Indian or gangster or something like that. These are very simple, kindly people. They lead their own lives. I doubt that she and her neighbors and relatives have anything to do even with Frau Greiner or the other hotel or pension keepers. After all, such living is quite sophisticated for people like her."

"Fascinating," I had to admit. "Tell me, do the Schillis have any children?" I suddenly realized, in fact, that I had seen no sign of children anywhere in Schonach.

"No, and she seems genuinely heartsick about it. She told me she loves children. Frau Schilli is not too old to bear children. She said her constant hope is to have a child some day. Oh, and by the way, Hal, these people are Catholics, so you might keep quiet about being a Jew, do you understand?"

The remark didn't seem to be made in an unkind tone, rather as a simple statement of truth in Bruckmann's mind, and in an effort to simplify my getting along with my new landlady. He didn't realize, as I would shortly, that it was this very Catholicism that was responsible for the antipathy to Nazism I would find among most of the local people, and for their kindness to me.

Bruckmann explained further as we walked back to the hotel that Herr Schilli — Urban, his name was — had been a bottom-of-the-barrel inductee to the Wehrmacht two years earlier. He had been sent to the Russian front from where, after contracting a severe case of frostbitten feet, he was sent home. He now worked in a small munitions plant near Triberg, to which he walked daily. He worked on an assembly line which produced parts for aerial rockets.

Herr Schilli was forty, Bruckmann said. He also worked weekends at his lifelong craft — that of clockmaking — in a small shop at the rear of his home. The Schillis led anything but a luxurious life here in this picture-book setting, I decided.

As we returned to the hotel, we passed on the steps von Nordenflycht leaving the building. He was headed toward the school up the hill. He waved and shouted, his slight lisp evident, "Inga was looking for you, Helmut. She was on her way to her room a moment ago."

"Thank you," Bruckmann called back. Then, turning to me, he

added, "You might as well come too. I have work to do and, perhaps, if you are there, she won't want to talk so long about her business, and I might be able to leave to take care of my own. Anyway, you can keep her company for a while. She has been lonesome here. She is used to a much more active social life than is available here. I don't like to seem rude, but when that woman starts talking to you, it is all one can do to get away from her."

"Innoculated with a phonograph needle, perhaps?" I said softly.

He thought about that a moment, then broke into a broad smile. "Ah, that is very clever, Hal. Very clever indeed. With a phonograph needle. Oh, I like that, but I wouldn't dare say it to Inga. But you stay with her a while, will you? Do me that favor."

"Right," I said. I had nothing better to do this afternoon and she was a hell of an attractive woman to sit and look at.

We mounted the rear stairs to the second floor and approached Inga's door. Her room was on the rear wall of the building. Bruckmann knocked. From what sounded like a great distance, we heard her invitation to enter.

She was not in her room. The window was open and through it, we could see the roof of the kitchen just beyond. She had found a sheltered spot out of the wind, protected by the chimney and a low wall around the edge of the one-story kitchen's roof. There, protected from the chilly winds, she had availed herself of the bright sunshine, attired in a luxuriously scanty bathing costume.

My heart began thumping. I felt my own temperature rise as I looked at her. She was stretching on her back, her head resting on a rolled jacket. She wore an extremely skimpy pair of shorts and an almost negligible halter top that barely covered her ample breasts.

It had been a long time since I had seen a woman's body so clearly presented. It had been an even longer time since I had relieved my enforced celibacy. I honestly believed I'd never seen a woman as magnificently constructed as Inga. Her large, Nordic frame was well-molded into just the proper Rubenesque proportions to be both pleasing and highly desirable.

She sat up and smiled broadly at us as we climbed out through her window onto the kitchen roof.

"Hello there, you two. What have you been up to?"

"Oh, various official matters," Bruckmann responded pleasantly.

"I'm so glad you came up. I was terribly lonesome. Come, join me. The sun is wonderful. And it wouldn't hurt you either, Helmut. You have a frightful parlor pallor."

"Parlor pallor?"

"You have unhealthy coloring, or lack of it. Really, Helmut, you should take more sunshine."

"Well, my sweet, some of us have to work while others soak up sunlight."

"Oh, poo!" Inga exclaimed. She laughed and turned her attention to me. "And what about you, Herr Sergeant?"

"He would be a more likely prospect for your health cult," Bruckmann interjected. "I'm afraid that, even in season, I am as white as the purest lily, my dear. I'm not much of an outdoorsman, in any event, you see. Besides, the work I have to do today must be finished shortly if we are ever to get on the air. There are many loose ends, as Hal here would say, that I must see to before we begin our programming. I thought you had something of importance to discuss with me. Wolfgang said something about you wanting to see us."

"No, darling, I just wanted some company, somebody to talk with, and you're so scintillating as a rule." She looked at me. "Well, Hal, since you are going to stay, you might as well get your shirt off. The sunshine would do you good too."

Bruckmann smiled knowingly at me. "Yes, indeed, Hal, you are welcome to discourse with Frau Domann the entire afternoon if you can stay awake." He broke, laughing, quickly darting through the window.

I watched the tall man cross the bedroom, go through the door, and close it after him. I turned back to Inga. As unobtrusively as possible, I took stock of her obvious attributes. The scanty outfit she wore only served to emphasize her bountiful endowments.

I looked around nervously and, seeing nobody, removed my shirt. I felt relatively secure in the shelter of the rooftop windbreak. Glancing toward the upper floors of the hotel, I noticed the third floor windows first. I immediately recalled that the German soldiers billeted up there were never in their rooms during the day.

Inga shifted her position to make room for me on the blanket she had spread on the roof. As she did, her left thigh moved directly along my right leg, brushing the length of my thigh, sensuously. She leaned forward to help pull my undershirt out of my trousers. Her skin felt smooth and warm as it brushed against my shoulder, and I felt the firmness of her breast as it rubbed my upper arm. As she moved about, her halter shifted, exposing the smooth, white, round mounds beneath. I could see her right nipple, pink and erect. I quickly averted my eyes.

Her hands were amazingly soft as they brushed against my bare chest. Gently sliding my undershirt over my arms which were stretched over my head, she almost caressed my skin wherever she touched it . . . or was I experiencing a fantasy? Actually, the whole episode was quick and smooth. She really wasn't making any overt moves of a sexual nature, was she? I was growing increasingly confused. Did I dare? After all, a German woman with highly placed friends and acquaintances . . .

Folding my shirt neatly and laying it aside, Inga turned back to me. She gracefully lowered herself until she was leaning on her left elbow. I still couldn't identify anything intentional she was doing, but, from the start, I felt there was some sort of bond between us.

Come to think of it, this was a mature woman of the world. She moved in sophisticated social circles. She had been around a hell of a lot more than I had. Was she toying with me, perhaps? Or was she even aware of me in any sensual way? I was growing concerned . . . and frustrated.

I was affected both emotionally and physically by this beautiful, seductive woman who, with nearly every movement, managed to rearrange her position so as to accentuate her already fully visible charms.

"Now lean back and be comfortable for heaven's sake. Tell me, what have you and Helmut been up to?" A nebulous smile flickered across the corners of her full, luscious mouth. Her lips were scant inches from mine. I wondered, again uncomfortably, if she might be teasing me or testing me. She certainly was opening up with a variety of weapons from her arsenal.

What concerned me most was the nagging fear that there was more than an innocent flirtation going on here. Obviously, her physical beauty, intelligence, and social position assured her success with any man she cared for, especially the officers. Surely she was aware of the alleged ruling against fraternization. Equally certainly, she knew I was a prisoner and a Jew.

Noting my hesitation, she pouted slightly. The pout, I noticed, was nothing but "lip service." Her eyes sparkled with merriment as they had since we first met.

"What is it, Hal? Don't you like me?"

I sat still, staring intently into her eyes. I wasn't sure what she was leading up to, but if this was to become a test, I surely didn't want to fail it. I was too close to a perfect escape setup to be shipped back to some prison stockade now, or worse. I had no desire to jeopardize my chances here in Schonach.

Suddenly, she appeared to lose her balance, leaning full on me. Her breasts pressed against my naked chest. She planted her lips fully on mine, her tongue snaking in and out of my slightly parted lips. Momentarily surprised, I lost my own balance and, in regaining it, put my arms around her shoulders. She shifted her hips and moved closer, pressing firmly against me.

My left hand instinctively sought the bow that held her halter in place. I wondered only momentarily what would happen if she should suddenly scream. She didn't. Instead, she shrugged her shoulders so that the halter fell into my lap. Brushing it aside, she leaned back, sitting upright, her arms extended behind her. Her weight was on her hands, which she placed on the deck to her rear. Her breasts stood firm, full, and upright. She showed no sign of self-consciousness or embarrassment, nor should she have, with a body like that.

Her smile removed all doubt from my mind. It was a smile both of conquest and surrender. I longed to lie beside her, to fondle her, make love to her. I held my legs tightly together so as not to reveal the impact she was having on me. I needn't have tried. It was impossible to disguise.

Then, regaining my senses, I once again realized my tenuous position here. I rose to my knees, trying not to look directly at her.

"I think I'd better be going," I faltered.

"Are you afraid of me?" she asked somewhat petulantly, I thought.

"Well, yes. In a way. Oh, not the way you think. I think you are a tremendously beautiful and desirable woman. It's only that, under the present circumstances, it doesn't seem very practical. I shouldn't be here alone with you, you know that."

I reached for my undershirt and uniform shirt, but she had anticipated the move and swept them away from me, holding them behind her, again emphasizing the upward thrust of her breasts as she did so. Suddenly, with a laugh, she jumped to her feet and bounded to the window. With a teasing glance over her shoulder, she slid over the ledge into her room.

As I climbed over the sill, she was locking the bedroom door to the hall. She turned and faced me, her back pressed against the door.

Then, deliberately, keeping her eyes focused on mine, she moved her hands to her hips, unbuttoned the side buttons of her tight shorts and, with a deft swing of her hip, flicked them open, wriggling so they fell to her ankles.

She stepped out of them and stood nude before me. I marveled at the full beauty and perfection of her body. Her skin was smooth and white, the gentle swell of her belly was emphasized by the movement of her right leg, slightly ahead of her left.

She glided across the floor smoothly on her long, well-formed legs. Standing before me, she kissed me deeply as she unbuckled my belt.

7. I'd Rather Be a Dog-Faced Soldier

I WAS SEATED ALONE in Bruckmann's room. The big German had excused himself to answer a call from Best downstairs. I looked out of the window across the beautiful valley stretching toward Triberg.

I could recall other mountains and other snow-covered valleys, none of which had been as attractive because of the conditions under which I had viewed them. This was the first time I'd seen such scenery in a non-combatant circumstance. I luxuriated in the appreciation of such breathtaking beauty from this high vantage point.

"What an ideal observation post this would make," I mused.

I began whistling quietly as I looked out on the landscape. Then I suddenly realized what I was whistling. "Dogface Soldier," the official song of the 3rd Division. I heard it had been written by a couple of guys in the outfit while we were back in southern Italy. The first time I heard it had been at Cassino. I thought out the clever lyrics as I continued whistling the catchy tune . . .

> "I wouldn't give a bean
> to be a fancy-pants Marine.
> I'd rather be a dog-faced soldier like I am.
> I wouldn't trade my old O.D.s

for all the Navy's dungarees,
for I'm the walking pride of Uncle Sam.
On all the posters that I read
it says the Army builds men.
They're tearing me down to build me over again.
I'm just a dog-faced soldier with a rifle on my shoulder,
and I eat a Kraut for breakfast every day.
So feed me ammunition,
Keep me in the 3rd Division,
Your dog-faced soldier boy's OK."

I smiled as I recalled the immense moral factor this song had become on many long, forced marches. Just as the men seemed to be lapsing into subconscious doldrums, the ones that accompanied most such marches, or long, unrelieved stints on the lines, someone farther back in the column would begin the song, and men all along the line would pick it up, both melody and lyrics. Everyone seemed to learn the lyrics almost the first time the song was sung. It wasn't unlike the massive harmony achieved by German soldiers as they marched.

Then, with a chuckle, I recalled the parody written on the song by a couple of my buddies in regimental headquarters. Those words, too, I repeated to myself:

"I wouldn't take a million
to be a dirty old civilian.
I love the Army, I think it's simply great.
I wouldn't trade my combat boot for any old double-breasted suit.
I'm crazy and I want a section 8.*
On all the posters that I read
it says the Army builds men.
But look at me now and send me back home again.
I'm just a dog-faced soldier
with a pain in my right shoulder,
and I see the medics every single day.
I complain about my vision.
Good-bye, old 3rd Division.
Your dog-faced soldier's P.L.A.**"

The final verse then would be repeated with new words, which went:

* Section 8: Medical discharge, usually related to mental disability.
** P.L.A.: Permanent Limited (non-combatant) Assignment.

"So feed my ammunition to the 45th Division
and send me back to the U.S.A."

Suddenly my attention was diverted from these musical wanderings by a flurry of movement on the road below the window. A large, black sedan, a staff car of some sort, had pulled to a stop near the rear door of the hotel. Several people were climbing out of it.

The door to the room burst open and Bruckmann bounced in. He hurriedly crossed to his dresser, then to his bedside table, gathering papers and other material, leaving others in his wake. He hardly seemed to notice me until, just as he accumulated the last of his papers and stacked them neatly, he moved toward the door, calling over his shoulder, "Oh, Hal, the new people are here. Why not come down and meet them in a few minutes? I have to welcome them now."

He left, closing the door behind him. I turned back to the window to review the group below. They stood there uncertainly as if awaiting someone. There were four of them, two men and two women.

My curiosity was piqued immediately when I recognized that the outfit being worn by one of the men was a GI combat outfit. However, it was obvious, even from this distance, that he wasn't an American soldier. The sloppy appearance of the man and the blue overseas cap he wore identified him as a member of the French Army. Closer examination from my vantage point convinced me that he was an Arab. He was dark-complexioned, short and stocky, with Semitic features. He wore leggings instead of combat boots or shoe packs. He stood silently by as the other three conversed excitedly, pointing to the countryside about them.

The other man wore a threadbare, herringbone-patterned tweed topcoat and a shapeless brown felt hat. He was slight of build, and I couldn't see his face.

The two women were equally hard to identify. They were huddled in their cloth coats, their fur collars hiding their faces. One of them wore a large-brimmed hat which hid her face entirely. The other was hatless, her shoulder-length, auburn hair glinting in the sunlight as it was blown by the slight breeze. Then she turned and glanced upward, along the lines of the hotel. As her eyes took in the window from which I was observing her, I was struck by her astounding beauty. She had a very youthful face with delicate, fine features. She seemed unhappy as she glanced beyond my window, not having seen me in passing. She dabbed at her eyes with a tightly clenched handkerchief and turned back to the others just as Bruckmann stepped out of the building and walked down the steps to greet them.

He shook hands with all of them except the uniformed man. Then, pointing with his right arm, he guided them into the rear door of the hotel.

I stood before the mirror on Bruckmann's dresser. I had just shaved and combed my hair. I adjusted my shirt at the waist to make sure it was tucked in tightly. I leaned over and adjusted my trousers at my boot tops. Then I stood again and rearranged the white scarf I had begun affecting the past week. It was a piece of white jersey-like material that Frau Schilli had given me to keep my neck warm. Actually, it did keep the biting early-morning wind from my throat, but I had to admit, it helped make the picture of my uniform much more attractive. I felt like some of those fly-boys we used to see in Napels, or the rear echelon types Bill Mauldin used to call "garritroopers."

A quick rub of my cheek with the palm of my right hand convinced me that I had used my razor to its limited capacity. I opened the door and descended the stairs.

As I entered the dining room, I saw that Bruckmann had seated the newcomers at one of the tables near the windows and was in the process of helping Frau Greiner serve coffee. They had removed their outer garments, draping them informally over nearby unoccupied chairs.

I immediately sought out the young woman whose face had so attracted me from the window. She sat facing me, listening intently to Bruckmann as he moved about the table distributing cups and spoons.

My entrance caught the eye of the big man who smiled as he saw me. But he didn't stop his lecture to his new guests.

". . . So those of us attached to the American or English senders will converse almost exclusively in English. The others may speak French if they prefer. That covers our instructions concerning language."

Bruckmann waved to me. "Here, Hal, come over here, my boy. Meet our new guests."

All four people at the table turned to face me. The little man in uniform, I saw at once, was filthy, his uniform completely soiled. However, it was evident that he wasn't a prisoner, based on the informality with which he comported himself. He probably had been a defector from the French First Army across the Rhine. He had an unhealthy look about him, his face pockmarked by some pox or other earlier in his life. When he smiled in anticipation of a greeting, his occasional, uneven teeth showed black marks where decay had eaten them away.

I turned my gaze to the others. The other man wore an unpressed, single-breasted suit with heavy cuffs. It was much too big for him. He had a slight frame and tightly curled blond hair lying in tiny ringlets all over his head. He was clean-shaven and reminded me strongly of someone I had seen somewhere. An aristocratic air hung over this man who sat drumming his fingers nervously on the table. Then it suddenly struck me that he looked like a movie actor. His facial features were very much like those of actor Leslie Howard, whom I had enjoyed so in *Petrified Forest,* Bogart's first picture. The man's delicate expression made him almost the perfect double for Howard, in fact.

The woman whose face had been hidden earlier now was hatless. She was older, in her late thirties, I judged. She was fairly attractive but very tired-looking. Her face had a dissipated look. Heavier than the other girl, this one had an almost cherubic quality with heavy, round cheeks and wide eyes. She wore a look of constant amazement. I imagined that, in her youth, she might have been considered "cute." It seemed incongruous now, especially since this didn't appear to be a romantic escapade on which she and the others were embarked.

My sweeping glance then came to rest on the younger girl. I gasped involuntarily as I realized that her stunning, exquisite beauty was even more pronounced up close than it had been from an upstairs window. She presented an appearance of innocence and fresh-scrubbed cleanliness. She had gorgeous almond-shaped eyes with an almost Oriental lift to the outer corners. Her high cheek bones and small, tilted nose gave her an exotic look which I found completely entrancing. She returned my self-conscious smile.

Bruckmann had served everyone by now and stood behind the civilians.

"Ladies and gentlemen," he said, "this is Sergeant Hal Lister. He is an American and will be handling the prisoner messages on the American Redaction. Hal, this is Mademoiselle Inga Guttman," he said, indicating the older woman. She smiled a sickly, ineffectual grin.

"And here we have Mademoiselle Christianne Verbruggen." His glance was aimed at the young beauty. I met her eyes with an electric thrill.

"And here, Hal, is Mr. Steven Humphreys. He will work on the British sender and will do some work for the American sender as well."

The little tweedy man held out a fragile hand as he partially arose from his position at the table, reaching across to me. It was only a gesture, as if it were something automatic and expected under such circumstances.

"And this," Bruckmann continued, a trace of distaste in his voice, "is Ali Mal Barrot." The dirty, uniformed body lifted itself lazily to a partially upright position, but made no attempt to shake hands. He smiled almost as if he recognized a fellow Allied soldier. Possibly, I thought, this fellow, wearing American ODs, felt he had a kindred spirit in me by virtue of our similar trappings. I felt revulsion as I saw him up close.

"Ali Mal will broadcast to the Arab troops from North Africa who are serving with the French Army across the Rhine," Bruckmann continued. "The ladies, of course, are assigned to the French Redaction. Now then, sit with us if you like, and get acquainted, since we all will be working together."

The fact that Bruckmann's invitation had implied an alternative to staying, indicated to me that my presence wasn't really desired. "If you like" Bruckmann had said. Normally, when he wanted something, he requested rather than ordered it done. But his implication was strongly in favor of his having a private conference with the newcomers at this time.

Accordingly, I apologized and rejected the invitation, claiming other business and moving to the door of the dining room. I left the building, breathing deeply of the clear, cold, morning air. I stalled over my first cigarette of the day, holding it tightly until the approaching fire nearly burned my fingertips. Then, discarding the short butt, I turned back into the hotel and reentered the dining room. Nearly fifteen minutes had elapsed, and I hoped Bruckmann had taken care of his initial business by now.

Entering the room, I noticed Bruckmann and the Englishman seated alone at the table where I had left them. The Arab was nowhere in sight. The two women were standing at the front of the dining room, looking out of the window at the panorama of the valley. I walked slowly toward them. Neither of the men looked up as I passed them, so deeply engrossed were they in their conversation.

Christianne turned as I approached, smiling the same shy smile I had seen earlier. The other woman followed her glance and saw me approaching. She moved discreetly away, a half-smile on her lips. She sat alone at a nearby table, her attention concentrated toward the view out the window.

"Did you take care of your business, Sergeant?" Christianne asked. Her voice lilted into my consciousness. It was perfect. It sounded exactly as I would have expected it to sound — soft, and with a charming French accent.

"Yes, I had to get something from upstairs," I lied, not really knowing why. Her accent was not exactly what I had come to know from dealings with her countrymen.

"Where are you from?" I asked her directly, smiling as I did.

"My home is in Versailles, although I was born in Belgium," she replied. "I recently came from Strassburg with my family."

"I was in Strassburg a couple of months ago," I said. I recalled the bitter Vosges Mountains campaign which had led to the capture of the beautiful large city on the river.

"My father was Gauleiter there until the Americans approached. Then we had to leave and come into Germany. When they said I must go to work, my father managed to get this work for me rather than something in a factory."

Frau Greiner circled the table at which the older woman sat, bringing her another cup of chicory coffee. She looked at me and my cup as if to see if we wanted refills. I implied refusal, and it was accepted noncommittally with a shrug as the German woman turned and shuffled back to her kitchen.

"Do you like your work?" asked the girl.

"Well, it's better than being in a prison camp," I explained. "How about you?"

"Well, I haven't done anything yet. I traveled from Strassburg to Munich with my father and mother. Then last week, they came to my apartment and told my father that he must go to Berlin and I must go to work. That was when my father called Herr Bruckmann, whom he had known before in the diplomatic service."

"Diplomatic service?"

"Oh, yes. Herr Bruckmann was in the propaganda ministry first, a very high-ranking official, I believe. He was either a colonel or a general or something like that. Anyway, he met us in Vichy and gave my father the assignment in Strassburg. That was last year in April. Herr Bruckmann was in America, I believe. He was in the German embassy in New York for several years. Then Herr Goebbels personally called him back to Berlin. My father says that Herr Bruckmann is only two places below Herr Goebbels in the propaganda ministry."

I suddenly understood the enigma of Bruckmann. Things began

to fall into place with Christianne's astounding announcement. For instance, it explained the obvious superiority of the man in the uniform of a private in the Luftwaffe over SS officers, based on the deference Best always showed Bruckmann. Best, I assumed, thereby was merely icing on the cake. He commanded only the military technicians here and Bruckmann was the commandant of the entire operation.

I failed to understand why Bruckmann would assume so ridiculous a disguise, assuming that such a low rank might create a more comfortable atmosphere of camaraderie with people he needed, such as me. I had to admire the man's brass and easy-going manner all the more now.

I was thinking of this amazing news of Bruckmann's status when I heard chairs scraping. Bruckmann and Humphreys were rising, having finished their discussion. I saw them shake hands. Bruckmann turned toward me and waved. Then, turning again, the big man left the dining room. Humphreys resumed his seat and began perusing some papers Bruckmann apparently had left with him.

I turned my attention back to the girl. "Who is this Humphreys? Do you know him?"

"We met in Munich only a few days ago. I heard that he worked with the Englishman in Holland."

"What Englishman?"

"The broadcaster. You know, Lord Haw Haw."

My eyes narrowed as other facts suddenly fell into place. By God, I was traveling in some pretty fast company! The situation had decidedly uncomfortable implications. I had run into personalities with very strange contacts here in this scenic village. Axis Sally, Lord Haw Haw, Goebbels, the diplomatic service — it all conjured up a weird, distorted vision involving strange bedfellows and, in my relative lack of sophistication, left me somewhat breathless.

Bruckmann reentered the room. "All right, everyone. Your rooms are ready for you, if you would like to freshen up a bit. You'd better go and unpack and get a little rest. We will meet down here again later." It was not an order — quite. Still, it sounded like a more demanding expression than a simple suggestion. I knew from the tone of authority Bruckmann employed that he wanted them to go. They knew it too, because, to a person, they rose and left the dining room.

Christianne had given me a lingering look and a fleeting smile as she went out the door. Bruckmann preceded them, conducting them into the rear hall and, presumably, up the stairs.

Arentz entered the dining room from the company office at its rear. He saw me and came over.

"Ah, *gut morgen,* Sergeant. How is it today?"

"Fine, Emil."

"Phew! It's hot in there," Arentz said, nodding toward the office. "And that Spiess . . ." he lowered his voice and rolled his eyes skyward, indicating an appreciation of the furious temper of the first sergeant of his company in that other room. Apparently Arentz had just been chewed out by the top kick. German non-coms seemed to make a living out of screaming at their men.

"What happened now, Emil?" I asked, amused.

"*Ach,* that Spiess. He expects miracles. These old-time professional soldiers. They are all alike. What do they want anyway?"

The remark was reminiscent of similar attitudes in the American army, I recalled. It was a peacetime draftee's constant complaint about the pre-war career army man.

"I thought you enjoyed the army," I teased Arentz with a smile. It was the closest I could come to the commonly quoted, "You found a home in the army" that we employed in such circumstances.

"*Nein.* I wish I was back on the farm."

"Where is your home, Emil?"

"Just north of Breslau. We had a nice dairy farm there. I was to inherit it some day when my father retired. Then the army comes. 'Do you want to go in the Wehrmacht,' they ask, 'where you get four cigarettes and 100 grams of bread a day, or do you want to go in the SS, get a nicer uniform, get ten cigarettes and 250 grams of bread each day?' What would you say to this?"

I must confess, there was a certain inescapable logic when the matter was spelled out that simplistically.

"Well, I suppose I'd take the larger amount. That would be a natural thing to do."

"*Jah,* that's what I think too. Only, to get the larger *verflägung,* er, how you say . . . rations . . . Anyway, to get more, I have to join the SS. So all of a sudden, I am SS man. But I'm not SS man inside, you know."

I was surprised. First of all, I was surprised to learn that the highly vaunted SS had been reduced to conscripting SS men. However, the way the war had been going for Germany in recent months, it seemed logical enough that these troops, too, must be severely depleted by now.

The top kick stormed out of his office, his face a red, glaring mask. "Arentz!" he roared.

The young SS inductee sprang to his feet and dashed across the room to follow Spiess into the company office. I chuckled at the thought of turning Arentz into a soldier. He and I had become quite friendly since our meeting back at Emmendingen. And I had been delighted to realize how much English he knew. He hadn't let on about this skill until we'd been acquainted about two weeks.

Later in the morning, I walked up to the school building to watch the electricians wire the last of the connections to the record turntables. This was becoming quite the professional operation. I was impressed with the efficiency with which each man did his job. These fellows, in this SS engineering company, obviously had been selected for individual talents, and each showed craftsmanlike skill and pride in his work. I looked over the glass panels which separated the broadcasting studios from the small audience chamber beyond and from the much larger recording studio which held a huge concert grand piano.

The floors throughout the studios were carpeted with heavy, lush, woven fabric. Every window had been completely draped in twenty-foot, floor-to-ceiling velvetlike material. It seemed no expense was spared in the construction of the studios. Engineers and workmen were everywhere, making last-minute checks, altering various connections and otherwise making adjustments at this eleventh-hour inspection by a newly promoted Captain Best.

I stayed around the building until late afternoon. Then I left, heading directly for the Schilli house. I hoped to have an opportunity to listen to the BBC or the Armed Forces Radio Network before Herr Schilli came home and while Frau Schilli would be busy elsewhere in the house.

During news broadcasts the past few nights, I had heard that the Allies had crossed the Rhine over a bridge at a place called Rhemagen. It couldn't be much longer, I was sure, until they moved eastward, reaching well into the area to the north of Schonach. That would make an escape much more practical for me than having to figure a way to cross the Rhine. I hoped only for thawing weather in the next few weeks to permit passage through the currently snow-laden forest.

I entered the Schilli living room to find my hostess comfortably seated at her table, busily darning her husband's socks. I suddenly realized that I had never seen her simply relaxing. She always was bustling at some sort of chore.

"Hi," I said, greeting her pleasantly. She was a lovely, warm little woman, and I felt a genuine affection for her, much as one might for an old maid aunt.

I had been trying to accustom her to a few popular American expressions so that, even if she couldn't comprehend their meaning, she could grasp the intent and feel the inflections. My German still was halting and anything but grammatically correct, I knew. Still, compared with her complete unfamiliarity with English, it was our best means of carrying on a conversation. She listened to my attempts very patiently, although, occasionally, she couldn't help giggling at my innocent errors, either in interpretation or pronunciation.

She smiled back at me. "Hi," she responded. *"Werden sie eine tasse tay* (tea) *trinken?"*

"Nein, danke," I motioned her to keep her seat. I sat opposite her, stretching my legs.

She watched me carefully for a few minutes, some secret motive prompting her to smile even more broadly than usual. She seemed to be keeping some immense secret from me and enjoying the game in thorough, simple, childlike pleasure.

Then, as if unable to contain herself any longer, she shyly reached into her apron pocket and drew forth four precious cigarettes which she tenderly placed on the table in front of me. She then withdrew her hand and watched me intently, anxious for a favorable reaction.

"Da," she said triumphantly. *"Sehen sie mal was Ich hatte gefunden."*

I was delighted at the unexpected gift which she indicated was all for me. I couldn't imagine how she had come by them. Cigarettes, like nearly every other commodity throughout Germany and, especially in backwoods villages such as Schonach, had become virtually impossible to obtain. I was especially pleased in the knowledge of what she had had to sacrifice to provide me this pleasure. Neither she nor her husband smoked, and the ration coupons and money which must have gone into this exorbitant investment certainly could have been used to greater personal benefit by Frau Schilli.

I had given her my chocolate ration from last week's Red Cross parcel obtained in Villingen. I was immensely gratified by her overwhelmed reaction. She and her husband hadn't tasted chocolate in more than two years, they said. I had to caution them at the time against overindulgence because of the highly concentrated nature of the bar contained in the Red Cross parcels. It was intended to last a long time, and the nutritional value of it was great. Too much taken too quickly could easily upset the stomach of a well-fed combat man, let alone an undernourished prisoner of war.

We were issued such chocolate rations before each amphibious assault, to use for a couple of days if the need arose. On occasion, we distributed them to children in the area after the battle. Too often, we saw the painful, sometimes disastrous results of gorging on unfamiliar treats.

I reached for the cigarettes, mumbling sincere thanks. This obviously made her feel she had repaid the chocolate debt. She anxiously opened the drawer of a box of wooden matches, withdrew one, and inexpertly lighted it, holding it gingerly between the thumb and forefinger of her right hand. She made no effort to shield its flame from drafts and, when I leaned forward to place my hands about her in a windshield effect, she blushed and giggled. I placed one of the cigarettes between my lips and allowed myself the luxury of a deeply drawn first drag.

Frau Schilli leaned back contentedly, watching as I smoked in great enjoyment. When I seemed completely at ease, she sprang the surprise on me that she had been saving. Having paved the way with her well-intentioned gift, she felt it a judicious moment, apparently, to make her request.

"Hal," she faltered, still smiling, although not quite as comfortable as before. *"Ich möchte fragen sie mal etwas."*

"Jah?" I waited, completely unprepared for her bombshell.

"Ich werde English lernen." She said it quickly and quietly, dropping her eyes to her lap in embarrassment.

I jerked upright. I hadn't dreamed that she would even consider the possibility of learning English. I certainly wasn't capable of teaching her, being as unfamiliar with German as I was.

"Werklich?" I asked, dumbfounded.

"Todsächlich!" she answered, positively.

I knew I couldn't be so cruel as to simply refuse. Yet, I was unable to explain clearly the enormity of what she was asking. I began to think desperately of various diplomatic means of discouraging her, or better still, having her discourage herself.

I figured the most logical approach would be to expose her to some of the overwhelming inconsistencies of English. I thought of several. Then, with a smile, I knew I had the right answer. I reached to the window sill for a small pad of paper and a pencil.

Placing the paper directly in front of her, I began lettering short words, one below the other. She watched, fascinated, fearful, uncertain of my agreement. Then, as she saw that I evidently was beginning her first lesson, she sighed and, with a broad smile, put her sewing basket on the table and prepared to give me her undivided attention.

I had written, or lettered, four words on the paper. They each contained the "ea" diphthong. They were "pearl," "heat," "head," and "heart." When I had them all written, I moved my chair around beside hers so we were side by side and each looking at the paper from the same angle.

I was sure that this simple lady would be so steeped in her mountain exclusivity, nurtured by ancient custom and simple practice of a language thoroughly consistent, that it would be impossible for her — or so I hoped — to comprehend any language as complex and inconsistent as English.

"Also," I began. *"Sagen sie mal dieser."* I pointed to the first word, "heart."

She studied it for a moment carefully. It was as if she feared it was a trick word which would give her charter lesson an inauspicious start. Then, taking a deep breath, she braved the unknown witchcraft that this strange phenomenon might hold for her, and blurted out in her literal, pronounce-every-letter German pronunciation, "Hey-art."

I knew this had to be her response. German is a very consistent language with no room for deviations. As kindly as I could, I shook my head from side to side.

"Nein," I told her. *"Das heisst 'hart.' "*

She looked puzzled, but gamely repeated it just as I had pronounced it.

"Hart." She rolled the "r."

"Gut," I said, trying to generate some enthusiasm in my impossible task. Then I uncovered the second word.

She smiled confidently. After all, hadn't she just learned the peculiar pronunciation of English with that other word which looked very much like this one? She took her breath and exploded, "Parl!"

She sat back, smiling proudly at her accomplishment. Her joy died immediately, however, when she saw the disappointed expression I effected as I shook my head again.

"Nein."

She bravely took another stab at it, lapsing once more into the more familiar German pronunciation of such a word. "Pay-arl?"

"Nein," I responded. *"Das heisst 'purl.' "*

Now she was completely puzzled. She faltered noticeably as I unleashed the third of my four-barreled weapons. Such a thing could never happen in her own language. She had lost her confidence entirely as she hesitantly began the series of unheard-of pronunciations in this crazy language. She studied "head."

"Hay-ahd?"

"Nein."

"Hahd?"

"Nein."

"Hurd?"

"Nein." It was all I could do to keep from laughing aloud. But that would have been unkind, and this poor woman was becoming much too frustrated to understand the humor of the situation. She looked back at me, her eyes verging on tears.

"Das heisst 'hed,' " I told her.

She shrieked, throwing her hands high over her head.

"Lieber Herr Gott," she said. *"Hier ist ein bestimmt verüchte Sprache. Das kann ich nicht lernen. Nie mals! Nie mals!"* She pushed the paper away from her, stood and, grumbling good-naturedly under her breath, made her way hastily out of the room.

So ended my singular episode of language instruction. The idea never was brought up again.

8.   Opening Day

THERE WAS CONSIDERABLE excitement in the Hotel Lamm. It was a Monday morning, and the long-awaited opening day of the radio station was at hand.

Bruckmann had told me to be ready to broadcast this evening, and a script conference had been scheduled for early this morning. Everyone from all three senders was present.

Bruckmann finished his side conversation with *Oberstormfuhrer* Best just as I entered the dining room and exchanged a more-than-friendly glance with Christianne. During the preceding ten days, this lovely girl and I had found we had much in common. We had become close in many things. We were much closer in age than either of us was with anyone else there. She was a year younger than I.

We had taken to walking together through the village and the surrounding countryside to the edge of the still-snowbound forest, usually on pleasant, sun-filled afternoons. I was cautious enough to wait until we were out of sight of the hotel before holding her hand.

Just two days earlier, we had stopped to sit on some boulders in a warm, sheltered area beneath a small, secluded stand of fir trees. We spent a lovely afternoon in this idyllic setting discussing our respective homes. I explained about Nana, to whom I'd become engaged immediately prior to entering the army, and whom I hadn't seen for more than two years.

Christianne asked about Nana and the engagement. Had I not had a furlough to visit my fiancée? I told her I hadn't, which was true.

"How sad," she said sincerely. "Young lovers should be together."

"And you?" I asked. "What of your love life?"

"I have no romantic attachments. Always we have been too mobile. My father always was moving and taking employment in different places. We didn't stay in one place long enough for me to develop such liaisons," she said. She didn't seem particularly unhappy with this announcement, however.

Throughout this discussion, there was a feeling of being here and now, an unspoken agreement of more than a platonic relationship developing between us. Shortly before we left the hotel, for instance, she had reached forward in a proprietory gesture to brush a lock of my hair off my forehead. Now, as we rose to return, she did the same thing.

Thrown temporarily off balance as she stepped on a small stone, she fell toward me. I caught her and held her longer than was necessary to reestablish her equilibrium. We kissed.

It began experimentally. I didn't want to upset this girl and I hoped my feeling of more than strong camaraderie was already obvious, was not simply another of my fantasies. She responded to my kiss, hesitantly at first, then with a strong passion. She worked her tongue between my lips as girls of her land reportedly had since the art of osculation began.

We leaned against each other, and she did nothing to discourage further exploration of her lithe, young body. It was obvious and gratifying to me that Christianne desired me as much as I did her.

"Ladies and gentlemen," Bruckmann broke into my reverie. The big man was standing in the middle of the dining room, tapping on his cup with a spoon. As he attracted everyone's attention and all fell silent, Bruckmann announced, "We all know that we begin broadcasting this evening. The American sender will begin his show at five-thirty. The French sender goes on the air at seven o'clock. The Arab sender will deliver his message at nine-thirty tonight."

A murmur passed through the group.

"Now we must rehearse briefly to check the time element. Each of you has prepared his own portion of his respective show. Therefore, if you people from the French sender will retire to the other end of the dining room, the American and British groups will hold forth at this end. Oh, Mr. Humphreys, you will start your program in Studio Two at six o'clock, all right?"

Humphreys nodded assent.

Once again, Bruckmann's pronouncement was issued as a subtle order rather than a request. Every person in the room responded in exactly that way too.

The Arab stood and crossed the room to a far table where the two French girls sat. As she rose, Christianne half-turned to look at me. Her expression bespoke soft admiration and something more. She raised her right hand unobtrusively to pat her hair into place and, as she did so, she seemed purposely to accentuate the exciting swell of her breasts beneath a sheer, white, linen blouse.

I noticed that I wasn't alone in my admiration of an act that I was sure was intended for me alone. Every male eye in the room seemed to be surveying Christianne hungrily. I observed *Oberstormfuhrer* Best especially.

A poorly disguised animosity had grown between the young captain and me in recent days. I was sure that my relationship, or just my friendship with Christianne, was the cause of it. I was unsure whether it was as personal as jealousy because he wanted her, or if it was more professional. That is, it might have been based on a disapproval of such liberties being allowed a prisoner of war, particularly a Jewish POW. I'm sure I'd have taken a dim view of such goings on if the situation were reversed. But, once again, Bruckmann's position appeared to have prevailed because, while the big man appeared unconcerned, in fact, unaware of the development, Best said nothing to me about it. I was sure he had complained to Bruckmann who, in all likelihood, had charmed him out of his petulance with an explanation of how much I was needed by the station.

At any rate, I determined not to put Christianne — or myself, for that matter — in any unnecessary jeopardy. I certainly didn't want to do anything that might endanger her or make her stay here in Schonach unpleasant. I had discouraged any further open meetings with her, preferring to meet someplace where we could be alone instead.

When both groups had settled in their respective corners, Bruckmann addressed our Anglo-American group which consisted of Inga Domann, Charlie Schwedler, von Nordenflycht, Humphreys, and me.

There had been absolutely no indication in the exchanges between Inga and me since our afternoon together that such an event had even transpired. Apparently it was a momentary fling to satisfy an immediate urge. I was relieved by that turn of events.

"Do you all have your scripts with you?" Bruckmann asked. We nodded affirmatively.

"Good," he continued. "Let us time the actual broadcast now. Hal, you have exactly twenty-eight minutes. Since you open the show, suppose you present your portion first."

Bruckmann held up his right forefinger as he consulted a stopwatch. Then, dropping his hand suddenly, he pointed right at me. I was quite nervous. First, I whistled a few bars of the theme song, as well as I could imitate the recording of it. Simultaneously, I consulted my written script.

"Krautland Calling . . . Krautland Calling. This is your daily message and music program brought to you on the medium wave length, 290 meter band, at 1031 kilocycles every night at this time. This is Sergeant 'X' bringing you our nightly presentation of your favorite recorded music, messages from our buddies in prison camps, and occasional patter to brighten your evening. Here's our opening number tonight. I hope you like it."

I waved to Bruckmann, who immediately began timing the two minutes and forty seconds required to play Tommy Dorsey's "Song of India," as I had listed it on his copy of my script. As the seconds dragged by, I couldn't help smiling as I remembered the way in which Bruckmann, this supersophisticate, had accepted my explanation of the name I suggested for the program. Certainly, if the programs were heard at all, the GIs in the audience would get a real bang out of this program from the German side called "Krautland Calling." I know I would have.

Bruckmann raised his right hand in warning of the approach of the end of the record's time. I stood by, paper in hand, waiting for the pointed forefinger. It came. Again I referred to my script.

"Well, gang, I hope you enjoyed that as much as I did. It's one of a set of numbers he's been doing so terrifically for the past few years. I believe it belongs with 'Sweet Sue,' 'Marie,' 'This Love of Mine,' 'I'll Never Smile Again,' and 'Night and Day.' They'll really be classics in the future, don't you agree? But stick around, and we'll have some more from the Sentimental Gentleman of Swing. This is a reminder that I'll be on the air every evening at this time with nearly half an hour of this kind of stuff, jokes, prisoner messages, and music for your listening pleasure. And now, here's a message from one of our buddies in a Kraut prison camp here in Germany. The first one is from Master Sergeant Elliott Sanders, serial number 27645. He's in Stalag VII-B, Villingen, Germany. Sergeant Sanders sends the following message to his wife, Emily, at 420 Division Road, Utica, New York: 'Dear Emily — I am well and comfortable. Don't worry about me. My love to you and the baby. I'll write again soon. Ell.' By the way, you doggies over there in the Vosges area of France, Sergeant Sanders is with the 106th TDs in the 3rd Division. If you come across any of them, you might pass the word. He's probably still listed as missing in action. He's alive and well and in a POW camp in southern Germany. I talked to him just the other day. And now, back to the music. Here's a sentimental piece from our pre-war courting days, remember? It's Sammy Kaye's 'My Prayer.' "

I signaled Bruckmann again and the big man began timing the record. As it finished, the others sat straighter in their chairs. I read another two prisoner messages, repeated both prisoners' home addresses and names as well as names of next of kin, and signaled Bruckmann to time the closing theme. Then, I stood and moved away from the group, my part of the program completed.

The others launched into a cleverly written propaganda skit which had been contrived by Bruckmann and the Englishman, Humphreys. In the skit, a cannibal king of a southern Pacific island had sought handouts from American soldiers and Marines who had landed there in combat with the Japanese. One of them advised the king that, if he joined the United Nations, the United States would give him all sorts of valuable gifts in the form of lend-lease aid, simply for declaring war on Germany.

Bruckmann read the role of the king, Inga was the queen, Charlie Schwedler played the cannibal prime minister and Humphreys portrayed the visiting UN delegate, on loan from the San Francisco conference presently under way. Bruckmann had made sure the name of the conference city in this instance was pronounced "San Fiasco," rather than San Francisco.

The gist of the story was that the world peace body, the organizational conference of the UN, had just declared that any country which entered the war against Germany would be eligible to join the United Nations and automatically, thereupon, would receive the largesse of the United States, which, the script went on, almost single-handedly supported the world organization.

Seeing his chance to become a profiteer, the cannibal king immediately agreed to terms, despite the fact that his entire fighting force consisted of four warriors, armed with spears, and a single, leaky war canoe. The sketch was fraught with cynical but occasionally clever dialogue.

As the final strains of "Copenhagen" had closed my part of the program, Bruckmann had beamed. Now, as the short closing announcement of the entire evening was made, he smiled broadly at every person in the room.

"Right in the nose," he exclaimed. "We used eighty-nine minutes and forty-five seconds and we can rectify this minor difference with an additional few seconds of theme music before the dramatic interlude. Why do you smile so, Hal? What did I say that was so humorous?"

"Nothing much," I replied, grinning broadly. "Only the expression is 'on the nose.' "

He frowned momentarily, then burst out laughing. "Of course," he said. "How foolish that was. 'In the nose,' indeed! Good gracious!"

Bruckmann was highly pleased with the entire rehearsal of the American-English sender crew. He excused himself and went over to the French group to hear how they were making out. The Englishman went with him. Schwedler rose and left the table to sit with Wolfgang.

"Big deal, huh?" I said to Inga, who sat nearby. "So now we're radio stars."

"It will be all right," she said, consolingly. "We will have a good program, and when we finish this evening's work, why not stop up in my room? I have a new bottle of cognac which I received this morning from my father. Perhaps we could toast our new program."

"Fine. Who else will be there?"

"Else? Who else should be there?" She flicked her eyelashes at me flirtatiously. "Seriously, though, Hal, I do want to talk with you alone, a serious matter. You will come up?"

"Sure. I'll be there." I winked at her, and she smiled in return. I wasn't very comfortable about it. She hadn't really talked to me alone since our recent assignation up in her room. I'd have to be extremely cautious in front of Best, Bruckmann, or any of the other Germans. Meanwhile, I wished there were some other way for her to tell me her important news. In any event, I couldn't do anything to jeopardize my situation here and be shipped to a prison camp, or worse. If I were to escape easily, Schonach had to be the answer. I was fully aware that I wasn't indispensable, only the most convenient prisoner they happened across when they started looking.

"Inga," I said softly.

"Yes, darling?" she purred.

"What's with you?"

"With? What do you mean?"

"You're in a position here to demand whatever you want. You could have any of these people, the officers, anybody. Yet you insist on teasing me. How come?"

She studied my face for fully a minute before she answered.

"Perhaps it's your youth. Perhaps your style. Perhaps your naïveté. I don't know. Why not just be satisfied that you are my friend? No commitments or serious thoughts. Isn't that all right?"

I smiled at her gently. "It's quite all right." I didn't feel that it was, though. I didn't completely trust Inga. There was no telling where she could take this thing if she wished and what she could accuse me of. I suddenly realized that having all this freedom, of not being accounted for every moment, also had disadvantages.

Bruckmann returned to our table to announce that *Mittagessen* would be served early in order that we might hear the French program and rest before that evening's actual broadcasts began. In fact, Frau Greiner was setting the long table already.

Conversation at lunch was animated, with everyone inserting ideas for improving respective programs simultaneously. The meal seemed to end as quickly as it started, with all present anxious to get to their individual rooms to prepare for the live broadcasts.

Early that evening, we joined forces to approach the school in a body. We arrived in time to watch the final mechanic fasten the last bolt to the floor. The French-Arab group and von Nordenflycht moved into the audience chamber and took front-row seats. I went into the small studio and sat in the chair before the turntable and control board. Bruckmann had told me on the way up the hill that I would open the show. On other nights, they might have a dramatic presentation before my show as well as after it.

With a single dial on the control console, I could blend in or out whatever music I had selected for the turntable. I could bring it up behind my voice, fade it in or out, or just keep it as soft background to my dialogue.

The actual program ran smoothly except for a couple of muffed lines by Schwedler who, at best, was no actor anyway. That he had hoodwinked his employers into believing that he was a showman proved him a better salesman than thespian. Meanwhile, many older and relatively more infirm men than he were facing front-line fire tonight and every night.

As we walked back to the hotel after the show, Inga managed to detach herself from the others, holding back to walk beside me. The French group had already left when the program ended to prepare for their own show later.

"You haven't forgotten my little treat, have you?" Inga said.

"No, or anything else," I replied, feeling uncomfortable.

She squeezed my arm just above the elbow, digging her nails into the skin through the thickness of my combat jacket and OD shirt.

"Well, just in case you need a memory freshener, hurry up to my room." She flounced away to join the others for the last few yards to the hotel door.

Each went his own way upon entering the building. I eventually, and as unobtrusively as possible, made my way to the rear staircase. Inga had ascended these steps moments earlier. Passing the company office on my way to the stairs, I was disturbed to notice Spiess looking at me through the glass doors. I boldly waved to the dour sergeant as if I were fully entitled to be there and, perhaps, was on my way to a business conference. The other grunted as he returned to his paperwork.

Three light taps at Inga's door were answered with her voice bidding me enter. She was just fastening the waistband of a blue satin negligee that left very little to the imagination. She must have raced to make the change in the time since I'd last seen her.

She was pouring cognac from a square bottle into two cut-glass tumblers. I imagined that she must have taken the stairs two at a time and literally flown into her room. I saw no sign of her discarded clothing and assumed that she had made time to neatly and carefully hang away everything she'd been wearing. I knew her as a fastidious, meticulous person where her clothing was concerned.

Tingling with the recollection of our earlier encounter, which had been accomplished with no alcohol whatever, I again decided to play a defensive game. I made no advances other than to light her cigarette before picking up the proffered cognac glass. She took her glass and sat on the edge of the bed. After draining the drink, she placed the empty glass on the bedside table. I sipped the strong liquor and found it warming, although I didn't care for the exotic taste. I had never tasted cognac before, at least not what I assumed was good quality stuff.

Leaning back on her elbows, Inga struck her favorite pose. It seemed to me she was smiling sagely at me. Her posture accentuated the swell of her breasts and, to further enhance the pose, she rolled slightly to her right hip. Her carelessly looped belt opened. With studied nonchalance, she moved her right leg slightly so as to bring it out of the concealment afforded by the filmy garment. She made an altogether appealing and revealing picture. If only circumstances . . .

I casually finished my drink, as casually as my banging heart would permit. I reached down and unlaced my boots, keeping my eyes on her all the while. She was smiling at me steadily. I kicked off my boots and began unbuttoning my shirt with a much greater show of casualness than I felt, and placed it on the back of the chair. As I turned to face her, I unbuckled my belt, letting my trousers drop to the floor. I turned my left side to her as I did so. Somehow, I still felt embarrassed undressing in front of a woman, despite the silliness of that posture. I stepped out of my pants and crossed the room to her.

Inga, meanwhile, had swung her body around so that she lay full length on the bed, her negligee completely open. She was naked beneath it. I'd never seen anything so magnificent. It was sheer sensuous opulence. I stood beside the bed, drinking in her Nordic beauty. She had closed her eyes. I bent forward and, with a hand on each of her hips, swung my left leg over her so I could straddle her.

As our bodies joined, her only indication of being awake came in the form of her labored breathing. She grimaced, gritting her teeth. Then, suddenly, she threw her arms around my neck tightly and breathed into my ear, "Oh Karl, Karl, darling. No commitments."

As Karl's surrogate, I asked for none.

9. A Real Turkey Shoot

DURING THE FOLLOWING few days, Frau Schilli's neighbors had fallen into the habit of visiting the house late in the afternoon, before I had a chance to leave for the studio. Their initial visits had been prompted by normal human curiosity concerning a visiting celebrity. Later, their interest expanded as those who had loved ones — husbands, brothers, sons, and other relatives — in prison camps in Allied countries, particularly the United States, sought the comfort of hearing of satisfactory living conditions there from someone who might know.

Many of the Schonach men had been conscripted early in the war. Several had been in the Afrika Korps, most of which had been sent to the States after their capitulation at Bizerte in the spring of 1943.

The neighbors' questions centered around these people, the treatment they were receiving, their living conditions, and the like. If I answered these properly, I could offer solace to many worried women of varying ages.

Actually, I hadn't seen any such installations because the first of them had been built after I left the States for North Africa. But I had heard many stories from late-arriving replacements, particularly those who were assigned to the infantry after their Army Specialized Training Program education had been interrupted by federal budget tightening. One, in particular, from Milwaukee, had advised me of the prisoner of war camp that had been constructed at Billy Mitchell Field, the city's airport.

These ASTP replacements advised us that the Kraut prisoners back home were paid eighty cents a day, did a modicum of work, and lived a life of relative ease. Considerable bitterness had resulted in the minds of the combat men who were suffering indescribable hardships in an effort to destroy the German military machine as a fighting force.

Nevertheless, my reiteration of that second-hand information concerning German POWs in the States pleased my audience greatly. As a result of the psychological relief I was able to offer, I became a favorite of the ladies who occasionally sneaked some choice tidbit out of their meager rations. These gifts didn't actually come in the form of a bribe. Rather, they were well-intentioned contributions to my own happiness from sincerely appreciative new friends.

One woman in particular, though, bothered me considerably. She was an elderly widow who had two sons. Both had been attached to the German 19th Army in the southwestern part of France. Their last letters had arrived postmarked Bordeaux, early the previous September. With German communications in their present disastrous state, she hadn't been advised as to the status of her boys. She imagined them killed or wounded or at least missing in action. But the complete absence of any official word sent her to the Schilli house, where she pleaded with me for some glimmer of hope about her loved ones. Perhaps I knew of them being in prison camps in the United States?

I doubted it. I didn't tell her, but I really pictured them as being part of that frightful carnage I'd seen above Montelimar last fall . . .

The day had broken heavily overcast with the threat of discomfiting rain. The division received orders at the last moment to move toward and liberate the southern French town of Montelimar. Intelligence reported the entire German 19th Army attempting to escape from a pocket that had been created by General Patton's Third Army from the northwest and General Patch's Seventh Army, including my 3rd Division, from the south.

The two massive American forces were rapidly closing like a pair of gigantic pincers, and in the bite was the area immediately surrounding Montelimar. The 3rd, in the vanguard position in the Seventh Army, was leading its advance on the vital rail and highway center.

The line of escape from their former Bordeaux area headquarters would take the German forces through the Rhone River valley, the village of Montelimar itself, just north of Avignon, northeastward toward the Belford gap, through Besancon and Strassburg, right to the Rhine. The 19th Army failed in its attempt.

My patrol of regimental I&R men, ten strong, was attempting to reconnoiter the size of the rumored convoy making the break. The patrol was to contact elements of the regiment's first battalion which covered the particular front in question in the hills just north of the town.

The intended point of rendezvous was a road junction in a small valley of the Jabron River, a tributary of the Rhone, running westward through Montelimar. As we came down out of the wooded hills toward the junction, we realized that our rendezvous would not take place as scheduled. There were three goddamn Kraut tanks on the road below, big bastards!

"When the hell are you gonna learn to read a goddamn map?" snapped Gill, who now was a corporal. I signaled the men back under the protective cover of the trees while I rechecked coordinates on my map. At least the Krauts hadn't seen us. We had been out for over six hours trying to locate this particular junction and, twice, had been forced into lengthy detours due to an unexpectedly large concentration of Kraut armor in our path.

"Well, goddamn it, Joe," I said. "My coordinates are right. It's the fuckin' Krauts who're moving around lousing us up." I kept rechecking map positions. "They aren't supposed to be this far up. Not yet, anyway. Not according to Major Sevaresy."

The major, our intelligence officer, had laid out what he expected he would find based on early Piper Cub observations of the area. We should have had time to set up an OP before the expected parade of Krauts began to show up below us in the valley.

"Well let's write a letter of complaint to the good major," Gill said. "Maybe he'd reconsider and get the Krauts the hell back where they belong. What the hell, tell him to call the German high command to report their goddamn panzers are blocking our way."

Fortunately, we hadn't been seen, although the tank commanders could be seen standing, exposed to the waist, in their turrets.

All at once I realized what had gone wrong. In our several circuitous but necessary deviations, we had moved several miles off course around Montelimar so that, instead of approaching it from the east as we had intended, we now were coming toward it from the north.

A careful study of the road below, as it related to other landmarks, indicated conclusively that this must be Highway 7 leading northward from the city. This was the actual escape route alleged by division intelligence, and the fact that my patrol could get as close as we had indicated that intelligence had bogged down somewhere. The site was to be an observation post we and the 1st battalion artillery officer would establish in our effort to discover and direct fire against the fleeing Nazis. Instead, by accident or some unexpected quirk of fate, we had reached the spot hours ahead of the original target time. Or, perhaps, the Krauts had moved faster than we anticipated. In any case, here we were, and there they were.

There wasn't too much traffic on the road below. These tanks could simply be the advance guard sent out to clear the way for the rest of the column.

"I wonder if that's part of the gang that's pulling out," Gill said, to himself as much as to the rest of us.

"I suppose so, although I don't know why they aren't batting ass northward if they are," I responded. I looked anxiously about the area for signs of German troops. The tanks, meanwhile, were making no move to leave.

Suddenly, as we watched, the first tank's motor roared to life after the peculiar, wheezing windup which always reminded me of the midwinter cranking of a frozen car engine. The other tanks, in turn, began wheezing and coughing into life. Soon, the roar of their oversized, heavy-duty motors began reverberating across the valley's narrow floor and bouncing back against the hill on which our patrol hid.

The tank commanders didn't seem particularly interested in any targets. Instead, they leisurely looked to their rear as if waiting for something imminent.

Following the line of the Germans' stares, my heart jumped and I dug my fingers into Gill's arm as I turned his attention down the valley to the south. Gill, wincing with pain, jerked his arm away, but not before he, too, found the fascinating view before him. We had just seen something that caused the hair on the backs of our necks to bristle.

"Jesus, Joe, look at that!"

"Holy Christ! What in hell is it? Memorial Day?"

Less than a mile away, approaching slowly and steadily, was a bumper-to-bumper procession of every conceivable type of German and commandeered French wheeled vehicle. There were trucks, tanks, passenger cars, many of them with horses tied behind, and several large guns being towed by strange little tracked vehicles like miniature armored personnel carriers. Men and machines began clogging the highway as far back as the eye could reach.

"Hey, Hal," came the frantic whispered call from behind us. I turned to find Restivo excitedly waving his arms to draw attention. He pointed anxiously toward the woods to our rear. "Someone's comin'!"

Gill and I left our vantage point hurriedly, dashing back to the rest of our people who now stood nervously fingering the triggers of their weapons. We all looked toward our rear, trying to make out movement in the dense foliage and underbrush.

"Restivo. You and Hunt over here behind that large fallen tree. Warner, you go with Gill and Kershek into that ditch over there. Whoever is coming is headed right for us. Everybody take cover!"

All of this was spoken in tense, loud whispers. We all dropped into whatever defilade and camouflaged position we could find, all alert to the situation. Then, out of the heavy undergrowth burst two GIs. They glanced from side to side, then ahead where the sky shone through at the edge of the heavy woods. One turned back and called over his shoulder, "Hey, Lieutenant. We're practically out of it. Another fifty yards or so."

As the man had turned, I noticed the 3rd Division patch on his left shoulder.

"Hey, you guys," I called as loudly as I dared. "Keep it quiet!"

The two froze in their tracks.

"Pancho," I called with the day's challenge.

"Villa," one of them responded, nervously glancing about to try to spot the unseen challenger.

Gill and I rose and walked toward them.

"You guys came busting out of there like you were going to a beach party. What the hell's all the racket about?" Gill asked them angrily.

"What's going on here, you men?" asked the young lieutenant who burst out of the bushes just then. He was followed by two more enlisted men, one of whom carried an SC-300 radio. The other carried two Garand M-1 rifles, his own and the radio man's.

"What's your business up here, sir?" I challenged, after saluting the officer.

"I'm Lieutenant Meade, 7th Infantry artillery observer. Who are you?"

"Lister, sir, 30th Infantry I&R. We got detoured a couple of times but got to our objective ahead of schedule anyway. And did we hit a bonanza. Come over here."

I nearly dragged the lieutenant across the few remaining yards of partially wooded landscape to the edge of the hill. I pointed down the road. The German procession still moved along steadily. Apparently the entire column was slowing to the pace of its slowest members.

The lieutenant stared for a long time, gasped, and broke into a broad grin. He exclaimed in a loud whisper, without taking his eyes off the scene before him, "My God, they were right! We received a G-2 report of this evacuation this morning. One of the Piper Cubs spotted it down the valley further. But they couldn't reach it with our big guns at the time. Here, Reilly," he called quietly to one of his men. The radioman rushed forward.

"Set up right over here behind this tree." The lieutenant pointed out a spot behind a huge oak. "You're going to be damned busy, so get yourself settled comfortably. Sergeant, would you and your men stick around a while? They may have infantry outposts out this far up and I only have four riflemen with me. I can see you all have automatic weapons." I nodded agreement.

"By God," he continued. "This is going to be a real turkey shoot. I don't want any damn Krauts interfering until we're through."

"Right, Lieutenant," I said. "There are eleven of us. Gill," I called to Joe. "Get our guys and the other two with the lieutenant dug in to a large semicircle around this observation post. I doubt than anything will be coming up this far, but let's be sure anyway."

Gill hastened to set up the defense perimeter, dispersing the men into well-organized, two-man units in a large ring around the rear and sides of the OP.

I returned to the artillery officer who was studying a detailed, large-scale map intently. He had the convoy pinpointed exactly as far as I could tell over his shoulder. The lieutenant had double-checked every available landmark and measured distances on the map's roads based on known actual distances between cities on either side of us. Fortunately, the road had a peculiar S-curve almost directly in front of us, which diverted traffic slightly away from us, but no more than a few hundred yards, before it turned north again. All of it now was well within artillery range. I estimated the road beyond the curve ran straight as an arrow for about three miles.

The road was at the bottom of a sharp V-shaped valley. Along the bottom of our side of the valley ran a single railroad track on which several flat cars were being pulled laboriously by a tiny locomotive. On the rail cars were every kind of artillery weapon, tanks, and other equipment.

The tanks we saw below us originally had pulled out and were now up the road about a mile and moving forward slowly. They appeared to be leading the entire parade.

The lieutenant's radioman was ordered to call back for all the regimental and divisional artillery fire available. I later discovered that this meant all 105- and 155-millimeter guns, both howitzers and rifles, as well as heavy mortars that were close enough to be effective. Thus, firepower of relatively nearby rifle company mortar sections also was brought to bear.

In the ensuing few hours, I witnessed a true example of the "shooting fish in a barrel" allegory. The first shells followed the path prescribed by the lieutenant's expert directions, roaring over our OP to fall among several trucks which were bunched in the middle of the road below us. The explosions destroyed several of the vehicles as well as two other, smaller vehicles.

Immediately, drivers and passengers in other nearby cars and trucks abandoned their transportation and headed on foot for the ditches beside the road.

Other shells now roared into the target area, exploding all about the sitting-duck vehicles and troops with brilliant white flashes. Explosions now were occurring all along the line of march as shells began coming in from several sources both to the north and south of our position.

In addition, ammunition in many of the vehicles being struck also began exploding, compounding the noise and confusion.

I nudged the lieutenant and, when he looked around at me, pointed up the line, showing him a sensational series of explosions that were throwing equipment and men and horses in all directions. The officer nodded. "Everybody's in on this baby," he called back over the noise of incoming shells and their explosions, the roar of which continued to reverberate back and forth from one side of the valley to the other, thundering endlessly.

The lieutenant was nearly laughing aloud in his exultation. This was the biggest, most lucrative target he'd ever been involved with and he was responsible for its destruction, right here before his eyes!

"By God, Lister, I swear we've caught the whole damn Kraut

army in this one!" he called to me, excitedly.

Below us on the road, utter confusion reigned. Several wounded horses lay mortally injured, kicking their legs in their death throes. Others lay where they had been hit, their entrails spread over the entire area. Then, from the left, three fighter-bombers bearing the American star insignia, swept over the column just above treetop level. They were less than 200 feet above us, it seemed. They dropped their loads, further devastating the convoy.

Later, as I rejoined my outfit and we advanced through this horrendous debacle, we saw unbelievable and frightful carnage. An estimated 1,000 horses had been pulling carts or trailing behind slow-moving motor vehicles. Many of them had been stolen from the French as the German army moved through the countryside. When the shells rained in on them, most of these animals were killed. A few, with their entrails dragging or otherwise horribly mutilated, had to be put out of their misery with merciful bullets as we came upon them. Some were miraculously unharmed and nosed curiously among bodies of their dead fellows, or grazed contentedly in narrow pastures beside the road.

Smashed, fire-blackened trucks, halftrucks, sedans — some still burning or smoldering — clogged the road where they had been cut down by artillery shells while trying to make their escape amid the frustrating, overwhelming, heavy traffic.

Along the railroad tracks, parallel to the road, sat six giant railway guns, four of which were the familiar 280-millimeter monsters, sisters of the famed "Anzio Express," which had shelled the evacuation hospital on that beachhead in Italy. In fact, these shells which we swore were the size of jeeps, did considerable damage within a full mile of the tent evacuation hospital the first time I was wounded and awaiting movement to Naples.

Two of these big guns in this French valley were 380-millimeter jobs, similar to that which one of my patrols had destroyed in a cave a long time ago.

Along the entire length of this scene of massive destruction, an outrageous stench of burned and burning wood, scorched metal, stinking dead, and singed flesh and clothing assailed our nostrils. Even the "Avenue of Smells" along some of the roads well into the hinterlands bordering the Anzio Beachhead in late April and early May, nearly six months earlier, with the dead sheep and cattle, had not been such an affront to the nose. The stench made the eyes of every passing dogface water profusely, and more than a few of us vomited beside the road that day.

The peculiar, sickly sweet odor of burning human flesh permeated the entire roadway all along the procession scene.

What equipment wasn't destroyed was captured intact. This included innumerable guns of many large calibers, as well as several of the magnificent and dreaded 88s. The prisoner total for three days of concentrated attack came to more than 1,000. These German prisoners came from a wide assortment of divisions and attached units, all within or attached to the 19th Army.

Every one of the prisoners who miraculously escaped death or injury in that misadventure bore the same stunned, stupified expression we had seen among prisoners after the breakout from Anzio the previous May.

The massacre above Montelimar proved to be a costly one for the German 19th Army as well as for the entire Nazi war effort in its dying months.

As I talked with Frau Schilli's neighbors, I explained as unemotionally and seemingly objectively as I could that I didn't know anything about the 19th German Army or the lost sons of Frau Schilli's friends. The grieving mother gave me a mirthless smile. She seemed satisfied for the nonce and would go on hoping.

I felt uncomfortable in my knowledge. But I believed I had done the right thing for her at this time.

10. Young Love

THE PROGRAM WENT into its second hour. We had been broadcasting for nearly three weeks and the pattern was well-established. Of late, I had become increasingly aware of Best and the man's unpredictable, although dependable, nervous temper tantrums.

Highly irrational, the captain was best avoided and left alone. This was especially true on those days when he'd come storming into the studio speaking to no one. On such occasions, he'd lock himself in the large recording studio and thump himself down on the bench before the studio grand. There he would remain for hours, pounding heavy classical themes of Wagner and Chopin. The man seemed to be an accomplished musician.

I had wanted to speak to Best for days, but couldn't find a time when the captain wasn't either too busy or emotionally unstrung. Therefore, despite a feeling that something unhealthy was brewing in the overall situation at the station, I went to Bruckmann.

"Helmut," I faltered, uncertain as to the most effective way to broach the subject. I had become rather self-conscious in the big man's presence of late, not being certain of his actual status in this alien land.

"Yes, my boy. What is it?"

"I've been thinking of ways of improving my program. You know, add some variety."

Bruckmann, the promoter, was interested at once. After all, to improve the program in any way was to improve the results he obtained in his efforts for his nation. He put aside the heavy volume he'd been perusing, turning his full attention to me. "Tell me about it, please."

"Well, don't you think it would be a good idea if we varied the music occasionally?"

"But, of course, you have been doing that. You have a complete selection of popular phonograph records, don't you? You have fox trots, waltzes, jazz, and all that, no?"

"Well, I was thinking more of a different kind of variety. What would you say to alternating live music with the records?"

Bruckmann pondered the idea for a moment, nodding his head slowly as it began to make sense to him. It was appealing, he had to admit. It might well give the program the personal, sentimental touch it needed to appeal to an unknown, distant audience. Then, with a patient, conciliatory smile, he reminded me, "An excellent idea. But the only musician here is our *oberstormfuhrer,* and I doubt that he would be interested in performing in public with his ridiculous temper, that fool."

From the glint in Bruckmann's eyes, I couldn't be sure if he was being defeatist or simply teasing me. Since he continued to seem quite friendly, I decided to pursue the discussion further.

"I was thinking of something a little different. I was thinking that we might make up a little combo. You know, three or four instruments working together. If we could get a couple more American prisoners up here, say one who played piano and one on some kind of horn, a trumpet or saxophone, I would play drums. I used to in a high school band. There must be hundreds of musicians among the American POWs in your various camps."

I stood quietly, waiting for the suggestion to sink in and bring forth a response.

Bruckmann smirked as if to admit that he had known of the direction my suggestion would take from the beginning.

"That might not be a bad idea at all, Hal. And I can see how lonely it must be here for you with none of your own people to talk with."

Bruckmann's crooked smile hinted at allusions to Christianne and, possibly, Inga, although I couldn't be sure. Actually, on second thought, I didn't think he'd accept Inga's involvement with me as easily as he bought the French girl's. After all, I was an enemy prisoner. I was a Jew. No matter what histrionics Bruckmann effected to convince me that he was just a willing worker on this project, he still was an official of the party. I decided I didn't want to push this issue at all. After a moment's thought, the big man sighed, rose, and banged his flat hands on his knees as he did so.

"Well, it's something to ponder, isn't it? Let me talk to the *oberstormfuhrer* about it. Perhaps we can arrange something of this sort, eh?"

I left the big man's company feeling hopeful. It had been almost too easy, but I was sure Bruckmann hadn't guessed my actual motive behind this request. I had been formulating escape plans for some time now, particularly with the threatening approach of spring. I had decided the move out would be more practically handled, would be smoother and easier, if there were two or three of us together on the march to the north. At least the stock of food and supplies I was building could be carried more easily over a great distance with a couple of backs to share the load.

It was late February. In another month or so, I estimated, spring would be setting in and with it, the snow in the forest would likely begin to melt. I had heard BBC broadcasts over Frau Schilli's radio in her living room during early morning hours. The Schillis were sound sleepers and I would listen through the earphones. These broadcasts, and those of the Armed Forces Radio Network, had told of the Allies crossing the Rhine and now of attacks in the vicinity of Stuttgart. In fact, my outfit was making these attacks.

According to a map in a geography textbook in one of the school classrooms, Stuttgart was about twenty-eight miles north of Schonach and in the same general valley system in which the village was situated. I had torn the pages with the map from the book and now had it folded in my right breast pocket.

Three days elapsed before the subject of live music came up again. This time it was Best who broached it. I was seated in the dining room of the Lamm having coffee one morning when the captain entered. Making for my table, he obviously intended to speak to me. I stood and saluted.

"Ah, good morning, Mr. Lister. Do you mind if I join you?"

"Of course not, sir."

"Herr Bruckmann tells me you went to him with an idea about having more of your countrymen brought here. Wasn't that a bit presumptuous?"

"I'm sorry, sir. But every time I approached you with the idea, you were busy. I thought Herr Bruckmann might be seeing you more often than I did, that's all."

"Well, it's neither here nor there. The fact is that he tells me you wish to make a live orchestra here in Schonach."

"Not really an orchestra, sir. I was thinking of a small, three- or four-man ensemble to play popular music."

"Yes, I see. That should be quite good. Yes, that's fine. I believe it might brighten up your program a little. I have been thinking of such a thing myself. Therefore, I have called the commandant of the Stalag in Villingen where you are registered. He has promised to look out for musicians among his prisoners, both now and in the near future. I'm sure he will accommodate us soon. How does that sound?"

"Fine, Herr Hauptstormfuhrer. Thank you."

"Now then, we aren't quite so bad as you think, eh? You see, we can be kind too."

"Yes, sir."

"All we ask is the proper respect and a little thoughtfulness. You understand me, eh, Mr. Lister? You behave yourself and we have no difficulty, right?"

It was obvious that he had a single-track mind. I silently nodded to his implied warning. *Yes, sir, you bastard,* I was thinking. It might have to do with one of the girls or perhaps with the abundance of personal freedom I was enjoying. I'm sure both rankled him to no end. At least, my apparent liaison with Christianne did. Again, and for the same reason, I was sure he didn't know anything about Inga and me, any more than Bruckmann did.

Without a further word, with only a curt nod of his head, Best very unceremoniously rapped the table top with the knuckles of his right hand, arose, and swept grandly from the room. He was done with the conversation, and this was his way of effectively closing it.

The likelihood of two musicians being found at Villingen, just a few miles away, was not terribly great. However, with the speed at which fronts were moving in various Western Front battles, I was sure I'd be getting company in the near future.

I began organizing coded notes describing what would be needed for an escape attempt. I estimated that, by traveling only at night and sticking to the forest as much as possible, three people might make Stuttgart or its environs within five days without knocking themselves out. Much would depend on the condition of the battle zone as we approached it. We'd worry that out as we got closer to the city. This left only the problems of provisions and opportunity. Neither presented any formidable obstacle that I could see.

In anticipation of the break, I had stolen a *rücksack* from one of the German soldiers. In it, I had a map and a bottle of wine, as well as some of the provisions from my Red Cross parcel. There was a can of concentrated powdered egg, a bar of highly concentrated chocolate, some biscuits, and the like. In the bag also were a can of powdered coffee and a can of cheese with an attached roll-type can opener that would work with other cans which had their own roll tabs. All this I had stored beneath the bridge on the main road from the hotel to the Schilli house. I had placed several large rocks around and over the treasure so it wouldn't be seen easily.

The idea to use the bridge as a hiding place had come to me as Christianne and I were walking hand in hand one afternoon. We had met by prearrangement at the hotel before anyone else came down for lunch. We decided to hike along a little-used narrow wagon cart track running up out of the village over the ridge northeast of Schonach.

After walking slowly down the main road, we crossed the bridge and stopped to look down into the swirling rapids of the incredibly clear, growling mountain stream as it rushed down to the millpond and southward toward Triberg. Despite the speed of the water, I noticed that its level wasn't much higher than usual. It was then that I decided I had found the ideal hiding place for my cache. It would remain cool and unobserved beneath the bridge, in spite of continued thaws which seemed to only deepen the stream bed instead of widening it.

We continued up the path until we reached a clearing amid the steeply hilled woods. We stopped on what seemed to be the ridge line and looked back. From here we could see for miles in three directions. Only to the north was our view blocked by a somewhat higher and more densely wooded hill.

Even the hitherto impassable forest was beginning to beckon. The heavy snow cover was melting noticeably. I knew that only a little time remained now before an escape was possible.

"It's beautiful, isn't it?" Christianne asked, her eyes taking in the breathtaking panorama below us.

"It is. I can understand why this was such a tourist attraction before the war," I responded.

"Whey my father heard I was being sent here, he told me he had been here once long ago. That was before he met my mother. It was for a skiing weekend. He often talked of it when I was a child too."

"I don't ski," I told her. "But I could see spending many happy times here if circumstances were different." I was looking down at her now. She sensed my eyes on her and looked away, back to the valley, apparently pleased at my attention. My arm encircled her waist, drawing her closer to me. She came willingly, resting her head on my shoulder. I thrilled at the gentle caress of her breeze-blown hair against my cheek. She smelled of the perfume of natural cleanliness. Despite the relatively primitive conditions and lack of creature comforts in Schonach, Christianne managed to keep her hair, indeed, her entire body impeccably clean and desirable.

We followed the path slowly, more deeply into the darkness of the forest, uphill along this ancient trail. In a few minutes we reached another, smaller clearing and the village and entire surrounding countryside were hidden from view. So, in fact, were we.

"Are you tired?" I asked softly.

"No. I could walk like this forever with you," she said, pressing her head closer to my shoulder.

We were approaching a small shed a few yards off the path and just beyond the clearing. It appeared to be a three-sided ski shelter or firewood storage shelter of some sort. It obviously hadn't been used in a very long time. It seemed to be structurally sound, I noticed as we drew nearer to it. More by instinct than design, our steps veered toward the shed. It was a tiny place, measuring no more than five by twelve feet.

The interior walls were lined with straw-covered, wooden benches. The straw had long since seen better days and apparently had been here for many months, to say the least. I brushed the straw off the bench lining the rear wall and, looking about for a fresher and more suitable covering, spied a fallen pine tree just beyond the open side of the building.

I gathered huge armfuls of softly needled pine branches and carried them inside to deposit on the bench. As I worked, Christianne stood quietly at the open side of the building, gazing intently into the thick, black depths of the woodland.

I walked to her when I had prepared the site. Impulsively, she turned to face me. She melted into my arms and we stood together like this, tightly holding each other, saying nothing, for several minutes. Slowly then, I led her to the rear of the shed by a minute pressure on her elbow.

Our lips sought each other hungrily and, despite the season and the cold outside the shelter, we were comfortable in the warmth of our young love. My hand moved gently up beneath the rough material of her heavy sweater and found her breasts. She held me more tightly. Slowly, we sat on the newly made pine bed and, still locked in a fervid embrace, we leaned against the back wall. Then Christianne slid farther down until she was resting on her back among the pine boughs, with me lying over her. This was the nearest we would come to the private dream world sought by all young lovers. We were completely alone in this primeval forest, a million miles from everything but the distant stars. There was no war. There were no enemies. We loved with all the gentle exuberance of our youth. I was tender with her.

Much later, it seemed, I sat against the wall, smoking leisurely. Christianne lay beside me, her head in my lap. Our physical need satisfied, we found the solutions to other yearnings as we held important young discussions.

"What will you do after the war, my darling?" she asked.

"I don't know. Perhaps I'll complete my journalism studies. I've always wanted to write. Now I have a story to tell. I know it sounds presumptuous, but I like to think that I might help to prevent some of the things I've seen from being repeated."

"Has it been so terrible, this war? I haven't seen it closely, of course. It never came where I was."

"It has been terrible. I've lost good friends. My heart has ached often from sadness and fear."

"And when it ends," she persisted, "when it ends, you will return to l'Amerique and you will marry . . ."

It wasn't a question. She was staring at the ceiling of the shelter. It had been an unhappy statement of intuitive fact.

"Likely."

I, too, failed to look directly at her as I answered. Instead, my eyes became hypnotized by the gyrations of a tiny gray squirrel that was busily rooting about in a small thicket nearby and finally seemed to have discovered what he was looking for — some choice viand. I looked beyond the little animal into its green-black, nebulous world. No flicker of sunlight penetrated the forest depths here.

"So, you do have a sweetheart?" Christianne asked softly.

"You are my sweetheart," I replied.

"Yes," she sighed with resignation. "You are right. We mustn't talk of such things, or think of them. We must think only of now. This is our time and place, isn't it, Hal?" She half-rose and looked deeply into my eyes. "Please say it is!" There was quiet desperation in her voice.

"It is, I swear it," I said in a whisper as I held her to me, kissing her moist eyes. My lips wandered across her cheek to her hair.

"What about you, Chris?" I asked, whispering into her tiny ear. "What will you do?"

"I don't know. I have thought about it but it gets too difficult. There is no answer. So I stop thinking. I can't return to Versailles, I think. My father was sympathetic to the government in Vichy. Now he would be considered a collaberateur with the Boche in the eyes of our family and former friends there. I don't really know where I will go or what I will do. I live for each day only, for now. I don't like to think of the other."

The conversation was approaching the same inevitable, distasteful, morbid conclusion which it had so often before. I, too, had thought of Christianne after the war. I hated to think of this beautiful, delicate girl wandering about Europe, displaced through no actual guilty act of her own, the victim of the errors of men of another age. The fact that she had no answers for the unvarying political accusations which would come promised to make her fair game for all sorts of unpleasant consequences I preferred not to contemplate.

I stood and turned, reaching out my arms to her. She held my hands and allowed me to pull her to her feet. She stood on tiptoe to reach my lips with hers. The kiss was soft and tenderly warm.

"We'd better be getting back," I warned. "We don't want them to notice that we were out alone together."

"All right. But first, thank you for today, my darling. And kiss me again. I'm afraid these times will not happen too often again. The *oberstormfuhrer* has been acting strange to me lately."

"How?" I asked, concerned.

"He has stared at me for long periods of time. I have felt it and, when I turn to look suddenly, I catch him at it. The other day he held my hand, but I took it from him. And last night, he invited me to his room for a glass of wine. I told him I had a headache. But he frightens me." Christianne's brow furrowed into three tiny ridges.

I, too, was frightened for her. I knew of Best's interest in the girl, but could think of nothing to do about it at the moment without jeapordizing her safety . . . or mine.

She held her mouth up for my kiss. Our lips clung together with all the hungry, urgent desperation we both felt and with the hopelessness we both recognized.

"This is our time, Hal," Christianne whispered, her lips close to my ear. "I love you." Her eyes were closed as I pulled her head back to kiss her again. A single tear squeezed from beneath her left eyelid and rolled slowly down her flushed cheek. I kissed it away, wishing I could eliminate her other problems with similar ease.

Neither of us spoke again until we reached the point in the path directly above the hotel. I leaned over and kissed the crown of her auburn hair. The sun, now higher in its orbit, reflected into the softness and gave her face a beautiful, red-blonde halo.

"You'd better go on ahead," I suggested to her. "I'll go around the school and come in the rear door of the Lamm."

She nodded and, without looking back at me, squeezed my hand and began running down the hill. I noticed that, as she ran, her shoulders seemed to droop listlessly.

I smoked another of my precious cigarettes, giving her further time to reach the hotel. Then I walked around the school building and down to the rambling structure, entering it by the rear door.

Most of the staff members had arrived for lunch and were distributed around the tables. I glanced at the *Kuckuck's Uhr* on the wall and was surprised to see it was still early in the day, so much time had seemed to stand still for a while in our forest glade.

Bruckmann was the first to notice me and he waved a hand in friendly greeting, indicating at the same time that my presence was desired at his table.

I crossed the room, nodding morning greetings and bidding, *"Guten Appetit"* to those still eating. I sat opposite Bruckmann. Inga was seated on the other side of the table. Her eyes caught and held mine longer than I thought judicious. Wondering if anyone else had noticed, I felt a sudden concern about her intuition. I had an unpleasant feeling that she knew or suspected about Christianne and me.

"Good morning, my boy," Bruckmann said lightly. "You slept late, eh?"

Before I could answer, Inga interrupted in an unaccustomed, near saccharine tone. "Oh, no, my dear. Hal was exercising, weren't you, darling? He went for a walk." Her voice changed, almost flighty now. "You know, Helmut, it wouldn't hurt you to take early morning walks. It makes you bright for a full day's work, and I have noticed you are getting a bit of a tummy, darling."

Her smile would have melted butter. Her eyes, though, held no humor. All I could think of as I tried, unsuccessfully, to avoid them was the cliché about hell, fury, and the woman scorned.

"Never mind my figure. When you reach my age, you forget about little things like, er, how do you Americans say it, Hal . . . Oh, yes, the window bay."

"The bay window," I corrected quietly, with a smile.

"*Jah, jah.* That's it. The bay window. That's most appropriate, you know?"

Best, who had been sitting at a distant table with two other soldiers, rose and approached us.

"Well, Mr. Lister, we have good news for you. I just received a telephone call from Villingen a short while ago. They have found your two musical comrades for you. How do you like the news, eh?" He smiled, proud of his typical Teutonic thoroughness.

"That's wonderful, *Herr Oberstormfuhrer.* When will they arrive?"

"I expect sometime tomorrow. I told the commandant to have them sent first to the hospital in Triberg for, you know what, eh?" He chuckled in reminiscence of my own inauspicious arrival several weeks earlier. "Then I will have Lieutenant Trautmann go for them when they are cleaned up a bit. And now, if you will excuse me . . ."

He turned swiftly and strode from the room, but not before I saw his face undergo the sudden change from bright good humor to a murderous glare as if an inner pressure was pushing against his jaw and eyes. I had noticed this particular look often lately.

As Best arrived at the door of the dining room, the two enlisted men with whom he had been sitting earlier, both of whom appeared to be newcomers, jumped to their feet and raised stiff right arms in a Nazi salute. Best stopped, glanced over his shoulder at them and, in a single gesture, threw a tired right arm partially up, flipped his hand backward over his shoulder as if utterly bored with the whole business, clicked his heels, and bowed his way out of the room.

"These pompous fools," Bruckmann sneered, more to himself

than to us. "I'm so sick of their continual discipline and proper Prussian mannerisms. The eternal militarists. If only they would realize how much more is accomplished through diplomacy than through physical might, how much happier and powerful the Reich would have remained."

Inga looked suddenly angry. "Be careful, Helmut. I don't care how highly placed you are. That's treason. You'd better think before you speak of such things!"

"My dear Inga," Bruckmann said, a sneer curling his lip. "Do you for one moment think we have the slightest hope of winning this ridiculous war?"

"Whether I do or not, this is no time or place for you to be speaking so. After all, Best's men only do what he instructs them. And he, himself, is a dedicated party man. You know that."

"I also know he has become quite tired and emotionally disturbed lately," Bruckmann said, the sneer remaining.

Throughout this discussion, I felt like an interloper. These were words I wouldn't have thought were intended for my ears. Yet, the diatribe had gone on as if I weren't even there.

Then Bruckmann turned to me. "Well, at least Hal has had good news today, eh?"

"Good news?" I had become deeply involved in other thoughts.

"*Jah.* Your new friends coming to stay with you here. Isn't that good news?"

"Oh yes, that."

"Well, before they arrive, perhaps more of the business should be accomplished, what do you say? Have you completed your script for tonight?"

"Most of it," I replied. "Of course, the music will have to wait until I know what these fellows can play. But I have several prisoner messages for tonight and four good records. You know, without a stop watch, it's been rather difficult for me to time it properly."

"Oh, this is a minor problem. You use your dials and controls. I will give you the time. Don't bother yourself with these technical details." He leaned forward in a confidential manner. "Besides, in all truth, nobody probably will ever hear these silly programs anyway."

"What was that?" Inga asked, having heard only the first part of Bruckmann's last line.

"Nothing for your tender ears, my dear," he teased her with a genial smile. "And what have you planned for today, my dear Inga?"

"Arentz is driving me to Triberg. There are some things I must buy there."

"When are you planning to work on our script with me again?" Bruckmann asked.

"Oh, we have plenty of time. I should be back shortly after mid-afternoon. I have to go now. There goes Arentz for the auto." She stood, glanced first at Bruckmann, then at me. She turned on her heel and strode hippily toward the door across the room. Just as she reached for the knob, the door opened and Christianne entered. For just a brief moment, the two stood looking at each other.

Christianne had changed her outfit. She now wore a one-piece blue jumper with a white blouse beneath it. I thought she had never looked so young and fresh. Just before Inga closed the door, she looked at Christianne for a long moment. The French girl, who had moved her gaze into the room and had settled it on me, didn't notice the older woman's stare. Then, meaningfully, Inga glared back across the room at me. My eyes couldn't avoid hers, although I was trying to return Christianne's gaze.

Inga slammed the door behind her as she went out.

11. An Unlettered Oaf, Our Fuhrer

"I MUST ADMIT, my boy, although he is an unlettered oaf, our Fuhrer has a way about him that appeals to the masses. My own tastes, of course, always leaned toward the more intellectual approach."

Bruckmann was being extremely artless this evening, with some assistance from the better part of a formerly full bottle of young Rhine wine. He had managed to consume that much following the broadcast earlier in the evening. After the program, he invited me to his room. Together we finished part of one bottle, and Bruckmann had opened a second which he stored on his window sill for cooling. I had accepted none of the second bottle while my host swallowed prodigious amounts with each gulp.

"The man is of a very small stature, you know. I remember standing just behind him among some other diplomatic corps personnel one afternoon in the stadium in Berlin. The man actually spoke for seventy-five minutes — ranted, I should say. And, in all that time, he said nothing. But he absolutely hypnotized the peasants in that audience, some 20,000 of them, by the way, with his platitudes. It was ridiculous. Ridiculous and frightening, too."

Bruckmann was beginning to slur his words. I wondered more about the man and his superior attitude as I got to know him better.

He had to be a party man, I reasoned, if the rumors of his former high station were true. But he seemingly wasn't a pro-Hitler member.

I closed my eyes, deep in thought. I pictured Bruckmann, lard-ass Hermann Goering, club-foot Goebbels, von Brauchich, the man who looked like a rat, von Ribbentrop, the rat who looked like a man, and several other plenipotentiaries, all standing around in dutiful silence behind the little maniac as he strutted and postured and screamed his wild invective at a fascinated mob. It conjured up a frightening, ridiculous picture. But Helmut seemed to fit right into my fantasy.

I harkened back to another occasion when I had been given the opportunity to witness a national leader who had inspired his audience without saying a word to the men directly.

The afternoon sun had blazed over Casablanca. The entire division had been called out to pass in review for some half-assed congressman or something, according to the latest latrine-o-gram.

We had fought a hard, though short battle on the North African Atlantic coast, had done considerable hot, sticky mop-up and patroling on ensuing days, and now, just in time for our first rest in a couple of weeks, we were stuck with a formal goddamn review! Most of our fellows hadn't reached voting age, so they had little interest in a rear echelon reviewer, even if he was some damn congressman.

Following our first sounds of hostility, we were given some time to examine this exotic land. There were many sights, sounds, and smells of a fascinating new country to keep us occupied. We learned about Medinas, the old native quarter which squatted anachronistically amid the modern cities of western Morocco; about French food and customs, French men and women; about mangy, overworked burros; ugly, spitting, nasty-tempered camels; wooden plows; Arab beggars; chicory coffee; and the thousand subterfuges by which a people accustomed to a colonial luxury attempted to shore up their living standards.

And now we were stuck with a review in full dress uniform before some visiting dignitary. Suddenly, a murmur ran through the front ranks.

"Battalion!" came the call from the battalion adjutant standing well in front of the seemingly endless files of troops.

"Company!" echoed the company commanders in unison, before their respective units.

"Tooooon!" bellowed the accumulated second lieutenants to their waiting platoons, relaying the warning of an oncoming order.

Every man on the parade ground tensed in preparation for the second step of the command. We were about to be called to ramrod stiffness.

"Ten-hut!" came the battalion adjutant's command to attention. As a man, the often-drilled young men snapped rifles to their sides, pulled aching feet snappily together, and directed eyes straight front.

A flicker of perspiration dropped down my brow, running from beneath the heavy steel helmet, following furrows in my face to a low spot beside my nose, hanging from the end of the nose. I blew upward, trying to dislodge the stubborn droplet. Although it fell away, others were not far behind in this incredible African sun, aided no end by the heavy wool Class A uniform.

Across the parade ground, I could see the tanks and troops of another unit lined up. The guidons and identifying flags proclaimed them to be members of the 2nd Armored Division. There were more than 30,000 troops on display, I estimated. To my knowledge, not everyone in the 3rd Division had been called out, but even so, this was a pretty large turnout for run-of-the-mill dignitaries. This, I assumed, had to be somebody pretty important.

Just then, my contemplation was interrupted by the massed 3rd Division band which burst into the stirring notes of "Hail to the Chief."

"Holy balls!" whispered Fred Anderson, standing beside me. "It's the president himself!"

The procession of jeeps rumbled into view from across the parade ground, passed quickly before the massed 2nd Armored troops, then whipped across the open space between us, past the band, slowing as it turned to cross in front of the 3rd Division. There were seven jeeps altogether, each with a large flag mounted on a high standard. All but one were generals' flags. The single exception was the president's standard.

There, in the front seat, within thirty feet of me, sat the man who was a legend, a world figure. His flop-brimmed, battered gray felt hat buckled in the breeze. He sat facing his right at a forty-five-degree angle, a frown crossing his very distinctive face, his familiar lantern jaw thrust forward.

Franklin D. Roosevelt, wearing a gray business suit, also wore a black armband around his left bicep, mourning for his mother, Sarah Delano. The procession passed the entire length, about a mile, of the formation of combat men representing all the separate units in the parade. Gen. Mark Clark and Gen. Jonathan Anderson, Fifth Army and 3rd Division commanders, respectively, shared positions of honor in the back seat of the lead jeep.

The president's message, which was delivered in person to ranking officers and by proxy to the rest of the men in these units, contained many heartfelt phrases, all of which respectfully stressed the importance of the Allied mission on a strange continent, the end result of which had to be to contain and soundly defeat the Nazis. From all reports, it was a spirited message delivered in level, distinctive, Rooseveltian tones.

My second recollection of an inspiring address by a brave and gallant leader began on a muggy, hot evening near Bizerte, Tunisia, a few months later.

The evening sun had dropped behind the tired, dusty green olive trees, but the heat driven into the ground by its piercing rays during the day was still radiating upward. It brought perspiration to the tanned faces of the men sitting in a large group toward the northeastern edge of the 3rd Division bivouac area.

We sat in a huge semicircle. It was composed of every officer and many of the non-commissioned officers of the division. To the front, a line of chairs conformed to the shape of the formation. Upon these chairs sat the ranking officers — the regimental commanders and the two brigadier generals of the division. The majority of the audience sat on their upended steel helmets.

It was not a particularly noisy gathering, I recalled. The prevailing heat forbade exuberance. Rather, it was a silent, speculative group. On olive-drab-clad backs, white salt stains of dried perspiration indicated the exertion and temperature of the times.

A loudspeaker microphone had been placed in front of the group. Two rosettes of amplifying horns were mounted on poles at opposite ends of the audience area indicated by the clearing. A large, red-faced man with a bushy mustache — Col. Don. E. Carleton, division chief of staff — stepped up to the microphone. Before he began to speak, a sudden rush of withering hot air struck the assemblage.

"Gentlemen," said the colonel, tentatively at first, then with greater enthusiasm as he heard the playback over the speakers.

"Gentlemen, the first sirocco. A hot wind that sweeps north across the sands of the Sahara, with the heat of a furnace, to die over the Mediterranean. A good omen."

There was a slight murmur of laughter as the meaning of his analogy fell upon the gathering. Then the laughter diminished as quickly as it had begun. There was a silence. The colonel fidgeted slightly, waiting. Then he looked to his right, straightened, and called out, "Ten-hut!"

We all scrambled to our feet.

"Gentlemen, the commanding general."

Gen. Lucian K. Truscott, now commander of the division, heavyset, steel-gray haired, took his place at the microphone. A beam of light from the dying sun shot through an opening in the olive trees and rested on his face, causing him to wrinkle his features in a characteristic grimace. He looked over the entire group before him slowly.

"Gentlemen," he began, speaking very deliberately. "We are on the eve of a great adventure. We are about to set forth upon the greatest amphibious expedition the world has ever known. We are going forth to engage the enemy and to defeat him . . .

"I say to you, as I look upon you, that we are ready. Let us review briefly the training of the last few months . . .

"You have engaged in five-mile-an-hour marching — which my staff officers tell me is commonly referred to the 'Truscott Trot' — until you now are able to march great distances over long periods of time, and arrive at your destination ready for combat . . .

"You have learned what it is to follow your supporting artillery closely, and your men have learned not to be afraid of it . . .

"You have learned how to land on your assigned beaches, quickly disembark, and move inward rapidly to seize your objectives . . . I repeat, we are ready . . .

"On the eve of this great adventure, do we find ourselves anticipating failure? No, instead, we anticipate success, a success beyond our utmost expectations. We do not know the word 'failure.' We know only that we will be successful."

It was nearly dark when the general ended his speech.

Later, walking back to our tents, 1st Sgt. Len Morasco and I paced, side by side, silently. We exchanged not a word until, just as we reached the company orderly room, and the top kick was about to turn into it, I paused beside him. We looked at each other.

"Goddamn," Morasco said quietly. "He's one hell of a guy, ain't he?"

"Makes a good speech too," I admitted. "I only wish the rest of the guys could have heard it."

"Are you inspired about the landing tomorrow?" Morasco asked.

"No, not particularly. Just scared," I confessed.

"Me too," the top responded.

Morasco caught a machine gun slug in his throat at 0748 the next morning. He was dead before his body hit the ground.

12.   Saying Howdee Do

FRAU SCHILLI WAS shaking me vigorously. I grudgingly came out of the soundest sleep I had experienced in recent months, despite the fact that it had been a most disturbing night. I felt anything but rested. My recurrent dreams of battle scenes gave me little real restful sleep. Last night, I recalled, I had been back on the rock. Mount Rotundo, overlooking the hellish valley which lay before the tiny village at the base of the high cliff on which the Montecassino Abbey stood.

The village was Cassino. I had lived through weeks of heavy bombardment and counter-attacks all over again during those few hours of unconsciousness. The efficient German gunners somewhere beyond the Abbey had been doing their devilish best to keep my sleep a nervous one. I could recall the dream as clearly as if it were the actual progression of events during those days nearly a year and a half ago.

We had been pinned down on the forward slope for the better part of a week. Supplies had to be brought up at night and with the greatest caution. Any sound which came from the mountaintop would echo across the valley, bringing forth volley after volley of heavy, death-dealing shells, fired indiscriminately and all well-placed, thanks to several weeks of zeroing-in preparation by the efficient German observers.

Since digging in was impossible on the forward slope of this mountain of stone, we had embossed foxholes of sorts by piling loose stone and rock on top of other loose stone and rock. These did little to protect us from a close-landing shell, but proved effective against nearly spent fragments of shells.

My stomach was tightly knotted. Only minutes before, I had seen Bob Davidson's last minute of life. Bob held out as long as anyone else, for nearly three hours. We were all being tortured by the groans of a wounded buddy lying further down the slope, audibly bleeding to death. His life's blood pulsed out of the shredded ends of veins which were severed when his left leg was ripped from his torso just below the crotch. Although Manning, the wounded man, had hundreds of other pieces of shrapnel peppered throughout his body, the most noticeable was this large, jagged piece that had moved in on him at whirling, supersonic speed and trapped him as he arose to retrieve his canteen of water just beyond his foxhole.

Davidson listened to Manning's soul-searing shrieks of agony for the first twenty minutes of the barrage. When the injured man's energy sapped and left him only strength enough for pitiful tortured moans, Davidson took it as long as he could. There was just no way to drown out that sound. It would live for as long as he did, in his consciousness.

Every man in the company lived through the three hours of torture, knowing full well that it would be suicide to venture out after Manning until dark. There would be no other opportunity as long as the man lay exposed on the hillside, because of the dreadfully efficient tank and artillery fire. The Krauts could put an 88-milllimeter shell in a guy's back pocket at 1,000 yards with unerring accuracy, and they'd fire at a single man. They knew it. We knew it. And they knew we knew it.

Davidson was in the nearest foxhole to Manning. Suddenly, he reached the limit of his ability to endure the moans and, with the desperation that comes of near madness, Davidson burst from the protective cover of his inverted foxhole and ran stumbling down the few yards between it and Manning's.

They caught him with an 88-millimeter shell waist high after missing him with their first shot by three feet. The shell exploded beyond him before anybody heard it coming. That was the way of the

88, because it had such high velocity.

Davidson, midway between the two foxholes, suddenly disintegrated before our horrified eyes. He had been staggering down the rocky slope barely seventy-five yards from me when the second shell "whooshed" in. Afterwards, we considered ourselves relatively fortunate to find that part of him which must have been his upper trunk. His dog tags lay bent and scorched against ruptured flesh. The rest of him had been scattered over a hundred-yard area of a central Italian mountainside.

I remembered later that old, familiar feeling of guilt about being glad that Davidson hadn't been a particularly close buddy. Was it that, I wondered, or was it that I was relieved that it had been Davidson instead of a close friend? Or, perhaps, had I preferred the solace of seeing someone else get it instead of me? These and similar thoughts plagued all of us constantly in combat situations. We knew how pointless it was to wish that nobody would get it. Many numbers came up each day. It was a matter of waiting out the selection process. That's the way this game was played.

"Was ist, Hal? Sind sie krank?" Frau Schilli was asking excitedly as she pushed against my shoulder. She was concerned, I realized, because I apparently had been moaning or crying out in my sleep.

Fully awake now, I realized I was soaking wet. I must have perspired throughout that reliving of Davidson's death. Smiling to relieve Frau Schilli's mind, I shook the sleep cobwebs from my brain and assured her that it was nothing but a bad dream. I was pleased at the proficiency I had achieved in her language in recent weeks. I even had learned several of the idiomatic expressions peculiar to the Schwarzwalder dialect. They were unlike anything I had heard before among German nationals. She, in turn, had become increasingly patient and understanding about my bumbling attempts at learning German.

I began to sit up, but stopped suddenly as I remembered that, beneath the lightweight eiderdown, I was completely nude. I wished that this room didn't separate the Schilli bedroom from the sitting room. It provided the only access to the kitchen from their bedroom too. This meant a constant stream of traffic through my sleeping chamber, resulting in a complete lack of privacy. My objection had little to do with modesty, however. It was simply that I preferred the right to be selective in my immodesty.

Then, as I rethought that last mental exchange with myself, I laughed aloud. I compared my complaints with those of other GIs in German prison camps. Or with my own experiences at Waldkirch and elsewhere.

Lately, Frau Schilli had been abandoning much of the original formality she had shown when I first met her. In fact, she had resorted to becoming "cute" in her attitude toward me in the past week. Occasional pats and pinches would accompany the morning wakeup greeting that served as my alarm clock.

On second thought, why then, I wondered, had she reverted to the formal *"sie"* when she awoke me this morning? Perhaps it was the result of fright because she thought something might be wrong.

Generally, she would rise earlier than I did, begin her morning chores and, when my time came to awaken, she'd steal against the side of my bed, slide her hand under the eiderdown, and pinch me in the nearest available spot on my anatomy. In a couple of instances, she had been embarrassed by an untimely contact.

Normally, this would have been considered an ideal setup. The lady of the house was home all day by herself. Her husband left at dawn and returned after dark when he indulged in his meager supper and retired immediately. That was a six-day-a-week schedule. On top of that, there was the hostess beginning to feel playful at a time when I was alone in the house with her. The greatest difficulty in all this was that this was far from the ideal erotic setup.

In the first place, I had enough of my own romantic problems to solve. Furthermore, as kindly and gracious as my hostess was, she certainly was no trip to Hollywood. No, this lady, this Frau Schilli, was not to be considered a likely romantic partner even under the most perfect circumstances. My problem, then, was to discourage her romantic and playful intentions gracefully.

I decided to outwait her this morning. I sat up staring at her. After about two minutes of my unflinching gaze, she conceded nervously and retreated to the sitting room, where she busied herself at setting the table.

I threw aside the eiderdown and swung my legs over the side of the immense, high bed. The lack of central heating in the house caused all rooms other than the kitchen and sitting room to retain the bitter cold of the previous night long into the new day. Eventually, the sun would serve to warm other parts of the house.

I hurriedly donned my shorts and trousers and pulled on my

socks. I stood before the small mirror mounted on the wall above the masonry ewer on the service commode. Picking up the heavy pitcher, I poured frigid water into the matching bowl. Thus I began my daily ritual of torture as the cold water, combined with the poor quality of shaving soap and a rapidly dulling razor blade, combined to pull and tug whiskers from my face rather than slice them clean.

I couldn't bring myself to throw away a used blade, with the result that I continued using them long beyond their normal life span. I began shaving, as I did routinely every other time I shaved in my life, as I suppose all men do ritualistically, by shaving against the grain on the left side of my neck. Then I got the right side, then the middle. Then I started downward on my right cheek, then the left cheek, ending in the area of the chin which was the most challenging. Finally, I dispensed with my under-nose area quickly and deftly.

At least the crude conditions provided for my toilette served one positive purpose, however. If nothing else, I consoled myself, this procedure served to shock me to wakefulness every morning.

The smell of potato pancakes frying suddenly permeated the air. I silently blessed Frau Schilli who, despite any other deficiencies, had proved herself a most adept chef, especially after learning that potato pancakes were among my strongest *lieblingessens*. This was particularly true in light of the pitifully limited and unvarying supply of foods available to her.

I was buttoning the last two buttons on my shirt as I entered the sitting room. Frau Schilli had set the table and there, invitingly arrayed on my plate, were four handsome, large, thick, crisp-edged, succulent potato pancakes.

"Do you know, the only time I ever take breakfast seriously is when you surprise me like this?" I said to her in German.

She giggled, pleased at the compliment, entertained by my frightful attempt at her language. Her face was brimming in a beatific smile, as she felt fully satisfied that her efforts were not in vain. She hadn't been able to do enough for me, it seemed. I believed, from her actions and those of her friends, that my visit with her, as a "highborn, distinguished" guest in her house, would elevate her social standing in the community. It was entirely likely that, once they assured themselves that I was, in fact, a pleasant, ordinary, human being, these simple folks would consider my presence a plus for their village.

I thought out my next question, to make sure I would establish the correct connection in translation. Then, swallowing my final heaping mouthful, I turned my attention fully on her. It seemed to fluster her momentarily.

"How is your brother's wife?" I asked.

"I think her time is soon," Frau Schilli answered. "Perhaps today, Erik thinks. He has taken her to the hospital in Triberg."

This would be the first baby in the family. Frau Schilli was barren and anxiously awaited the birth of her first niece or nephew, she had told me. She had no relatives other than her younger brother. His wife was about to deliver, which threw the entire neighborhood into a turmoil.

I was happy for them and for myself because I knew that I would leave here one day soon. When I did, she would have the anticipated infant on whom to lavish the love and affection I had enjoyed for these weeks. In fact, this promised to be the most thoroughly and frightfully spoiled child in all of the Greater Third Reich.

"He comes here today for more clean clothes," Frau Schilli went on. I had been shocked earlier when her brother arrived one evening armed with a huge bundle of blood-soaked rags. These carefully accumulated primitive conveniences were intended to ease the personal hygiene needs of the new mother. No modern feminine conveniences such as were taken for granted in more urban communities were even within the ken of these poor, simple mountain people. I was to discover further hardships, such as several hours after the birth of his daughter, Erik delivered his grisly bundle. He had walked the steep, three-mile trail from Triberg with the bloodsoaked rags, then dutifully walked back down with them after his doting sister had scrubbed them by hand and folded them lovingly. His wife then would make further use of them.

"Hey, I have to rush," I suddenly exclaimed, glancing at the large Black Forest cuckoo clock on the wall over the couch. "Today I meet my new comrades."

I tickled her under the chin, causing another frantic giggle, picked up my combat jacket from the couch, and ran from the house.

It was a fine, clear morning with a bright, friendly sun shining with promise on the snow-covered forest. The promise of an early thaw became stronger each day, raising my ever-increasing hopes. Now that I was about to acquire my two companions, the planning and execution of the escape would be simplified greatly. At least, that was my hope.

I yawned suddenly. The combination of the yawn and the biting breeze caused my eyes to water. I rubbed at them with the backs of my hands.

I had managed little sleep the previous night, thanks to the exciting news on BBC and the Armed Forces Network. I arrived home well past midnight and, making sure the Schillis were asleep, I tiptoed back into the sitting room in my stocking feet. I lay on the couch for nearly three hours in the darkness, intently listening to the radio through the ancient earphones.

Armed forces radio had alternated with the BBC in the presentation of popular music and news, respectively. There was plenty of both. I was happy to have reached the Schilli house later than usual because the hour assured me of an undisturbed session of listening. I was just in time to catch the sign-on theme played by the band of the recently missing Maj. Glenn Miller. The introductory chords began just as I clamped on the earphones.

"This is Sergeant Ray McKinley
sayin' 'Howdee Doo!'
The boys in the band sayin' 'howdee' too.
Sergeant Johnny Desmond's
here to sing tonight.
You can bet your life, buddies, everything's all right."

The familiar strains of the traditional Miller "Moonlight Serenade" theme nearly brought tears of homesickness and nostalgia. The heavy saxophone section outdid itself, it seemed, as it had in those long past, pre-war days. They moved gracefully through "At Last," with Desmond on the vocal, then performed a spirited rendition of the "St. Louis Blues March."

Then, with the clipped, efficient, concise accents of cultivated boredom, the *veddy* British announcer came in with his latest BBC news bulletins.

"On the western front, the Remagen crossing now has been fully effected, and the strong bridgehead across the Rhine has moved well into the homeland of the Nazis themselves." The announcer pronounced the word in true Churchillian style — "Nazzies."

"Strong supply lines are pouring across the wide river tonight," the man's voice continued unemotionally. "The fight has moved well into Germany proper and pitched battles keep the combat troops busy.

Casualties are reportedly relatively light among the Allied troops during these first days following the crossing of the German threshold. On the Italian front, only routine patrol action is reported in the vicinity of Florence . . ."

I was elated at the first report of action to the north. The successful crossing of the Rhine meant that, with the reported capitalization on it, there was promise of an earlier escape than anticipated, which, in turn, meant the likelihood of returning to Allied control that much sooner.

I thought for a moment of the announcer's last statement. *I'd like to meet the bastard who sent in that report. "Routine patrol action," indeed,* I thought bitterly. I had read such overly simplistic reports many times after my buddies and I returned from such an alleged "routine patrol." It was routine only to those who read about it, many miles from the scene, many days later.

I turned off the radio and paused, as I undressed, lost in unhappy reflections on one of the most frightening of those routine patrol actions . . .

13. "Find that son of a bitch!"

WHAT LITTLE SLEEP we had managed was as fitful as was to be expected in severe combat circumstances. We lay in the shallow defilade we had chanced on just before dark last night. Ground mist laid heavily on us, saturating our badly worn uniforms. This was our third day out and there was no telling how much longer we could afford to continue this search.

Sgt. Les Standish commanded the patrol. I was still a corporal and second in command. Standish was lying on the ground, his combat jacket covering his head in order to prevent any light from his flashlight escaping while he pondered the map. There was no telling, even with the present, practically impenetrable fog, how far such a light beam could be seen here in "Injun Country."

We were in an area generally south of the Anzio Beachhead, or, at least, on its southern periphery. Our patrol had originated from our position on the right flank of the beachhead. Most of the ground we covered had been extremely swampy. This, I assumed, was the area just beyond the effective reach of Mussolini's highly vaunted drainage canals throughout the Pontine Marsh area of the beachhead.

When we were given this assignment, it was stated quite simply.

"Find that son of a bitch! We've got to get rid of it one way or another!"

The major was furious when he mentioned the huge gun hidden somewhere here in these foothills of the Appenine Range. The weapon was estimated to be at least 280 millimeters, perhaps much larger, judging by the size of the shell it fired. This shell was estimated by some who had been in the vicinity of its explosion as "about the size of a large jeep," or "as big as a large wine barrel."

Whatever its size, its effect was terrifying to contemplate as it fired regularly, twice each day, into the now overcrowded 150-square mile area inland from Anzio/Nettuno. With the crowded conditions of the beachhead, it was almost impossible for the Krauts to fire this monster without hitting something and doing considerable damage. The tragedy was that several recent rounds from this gun and one like it firing from, we were sure, the vicinity of the railroad yards of Rome, about thirty-five miles to our north, already had fired rounds into the evacuation hospital's tent city, killing several helpless evacuees and nurses indiscriminately. When these behemoths poured their cargo of death into the skies, aimed toward the beachhead, they unleashed an initial furious explosive force as well as untold and uncountable volumes of spinning, white-hot metal.

I surveyed the rest of the patrol while Standish was studying his charts. We all knew we were well behind enemy lines, such as they were in this sector. We knew, too, that we were nearing our objective. The tenseness was becoming increasingly obvious to all of us.

Restivo and Adams lay quietly behind a huge boulder, vaguely visible in the dim early morning mists. Below me and a little to my right, I could see Forman and Fortino taking cover behind a low stone wall. The others were out of sight, but I knew they were near.

Standish threw back his jacket and raised himself on one knee as he folded the maps, putting them inside his jacket.

"OK, Lister, I think I've got it. We'll jump off from here as soon as we can get 'em organized. I want to get across this valley before the mists clear. That way, we have a better chance of getting over there without being seen."

The sergeant rose and moved to his left, rounding up the men waiting there. I did the same with the men in the opposite direction. We assembled in the low area where we had been marking time behind whatever cover we could find in the murky semidarkness.

There was no knowing here, deep within enemy territory, just where the Krauts might be. We had barely missed contact with a German patrol early the previous day. The group of twenty or so German soldiers had stamped by us as we lay breathless along the forward slope of a ridge. The Krauts were just beyond the peak of the hill. Actually, little more than patrol activity was expected in this area because of the virtually impassable terrain for large-scale operations. The enemy had disappeared over the hill into the distance, their metallic gear pounding against their sides as they descended the far rocky slope.

"OK, Lister, let's get 'em rolling."

"Right." I turned to the men assembled before me. "OK, you yardbirds. Off your dead and on your dying."

The men groaned quietly under their breaths as they wearily assumed the same order of single-file march they had practiced since our patrol began. As fatigued as we all were, we knew we would have to continue patrolling until we accomplished our mission or, better still, until Standish would call it off and order us back to our outfit. Since this never happened, we had nothing to do but get the damned assignment over with as successfully as possible. We had nothing but hope and experience to carry us forward.

Standish had explained the situation to the rest of us before we left the battalion CP. Now, he pointed out in whispered directions how we stood on a low ridge and were about to descend the slope to one of the unvarying and inevitable valleys which ran down to the sea on our right. Across the indeterminate valley floor we would find another, similar mountain. At the bottom of each of these mountains, especially in this Pontine area, we were sure to find low, marshy land, certain to soak our feet. But, all important, at the bottom of one of these lines of hills, we would come to a railroad track which tunneled through it. There, we were all sure, we would find this big bastard we were searching for. It had become a personal grudge now, this battle between each of the twelve men in the patrol and the big gun.

The gun had to be in a tunnel somewhere because several air reconnaissance missions had failed to find it from their vantage point on high.

"How far you figure this time, Sarge?" asked Adams.

"We can't be sure. Not more than five or six hundred yards, according to the map. But whatever it is, we gotta cross it while it's still foggy. Let's move out now and get down as quick as possible. And as quiet!" Standish said meaningfully in a loud whisper. To me, he whispered, "We better pray we get across this valley before the damn sun comes out. They're bound to have ouposts if this is the one."

"I still think this is a stinkin' deal, sending out twelve men to do the job of a whole goddamn company," hissed Restivo.

"Quit your bitchin'," Standish hissed as he glared at the malcontent. "How in hell do you figure a whole company could get through here until we find the goddamn way?"

It was bad enough being in charge of an undermanned twelve-man patrol which had drawn this rotten recon job going through swamps, up and down rock-strewn mountainsides, always hiding, always avoiding direct fire fights which might mean detection and the subsequent destruction of our effectiveness as a reconnaissance unit.

It was tough enough taking that kind of responsibility without having to listen to constant griping. Standish had been in the thick of combat since the North African landings. Very few of that original gang still remained in the outfit. As for his patrol, there were only Standish, Fortino, Weber, and me from that original group.

I felt for Standish. Since I had received my second stripe, I had a small taste of the responsibility which plagued the sergeant at every turn. When you gave a man an order, it might be the last one he'd hear in his entire lifetime. That was a terrible pressure, especially if your order contributed to his demise. Standish was beginning to show the strains of it.

We were silent with the omnipresent, sickening fear which occupied our every thought and accompanied every move. It was the same fear which caused every infantry doggie to sleep with his back to the enemy in a fetal position. That way, he might not be hit in the crown jewels. This was the same fear which made a dogface unable to stand, sit, or lie down without making sure, instinctively, that there was some actual or imagined barrier between him and the Krauts.

"See anything, Les?" I asked Standish as we moved to the crest of the hill.

"No. Damn fog's too thick yet. But I keep hearing motors down there somewhere. OK, let's move out."

We formed our line automatically. Each of us had gone through this maneuver a hundred times or more. We automatically assumed the customary five-yard interval, although occasionally, the distance between men shortened as the fog made a closer contact possible. When we couldn't see more than a couple of feet ahead, it was important we didn't lose contact with each other and wander off in different directions.

Standish led out, with me right behind him. Fortino, Weber, Restivo, Adams, Kleine, Anderson, Holderbaum, Krauss, Doyle, and Hanson followed, in that order.

I had argued against putting the three greenest men on the tail of the column, but Standish maintained it made no difference under the circumstances of this patrol.

"If we get trapped on this deal, it won't make a damn bit of difference who's on the ass end," he had said succinctly. "Ain't nobody gettin' back then anyway. I bet the whole gang gets through or nobody does."

This defeatism wasn't like the Standish who had led me on other patrols. The man had a premonition, I knew. I had seen it happen to others, and they were generally proved right about it.

We half-stumbled, half-slid down the rocky hillside, trying desperately to make as little noise as possible. Each of us had been over enough of these gravel-strewn hills to know enough to protect our equipment by holding it tightly against our bodies. All, that is, except Holdie, Doyle, and Hanson. Loose equipment could be damaged and damaging if allowed to bang against rocks in passing. The sudden clang of metal on stone could be heard for fantastic distances, alerting every enemy troop within hearing range.

We reached the bottom of the hill in a little over three minutes with only one minor casualty. Doyle sprained his ankle slightly by stepping on a small, round stone. Krauss helped the limping man the rest of the way by serving as a crutch, offering his shoulder for Doyle to lean on.

The soil on the valley floor was spongy under the cover of the stifling mist. I consulted my watch. The luminous dial told me it was 0552. Somewhere above this fog was a sun which was due to appear clearly within about fifteen minutes. In another half hour, it should begin pouring its heat down on our ground cover, dispelling the protective blanket.

Standish knew his job was to get his men across the open area toward the highway on which we had heard sounds of movement earlier. He knew it had to be somewhere just ahead of us because the occasional noise of passing trucks was getting louder.

We weren't sure just what we would find in the way of protective cover over there, but where there was a road in this country, outside of major cities, there invariably was a ditch beside it. In this God-forsaken area, with its rainy winter season, the ditches generally would be quite deep, providing possible standup cover. This would be especially true this close to the ocean, as the accumulated drainage of the mountains converged in increasing intensity and volume on the lowlands.

"We'd better use hand signals from here on. So tell the men to close it up. Pass it back," Standish told me. I passed the message back along the line of men who each instinctively drew closer to the man in front of him.

The "no talking" signal brought every man to nervous attention and alertness. Whenever this signal was given, it meant we were very close to Krauts. At the moment, we didn't know just how close, but their nearness was a certainty.

The chill of the mist hung heavily on all of us. Traveling as lightly as possible, we had only our combat jackets to warm us, to protect us against the early morning damp cold. Still, none of us wished for the warmth of the bright sun at this moment. We welcomed the mist as an ally just now.

Standish moved ahead cautiously, just within range of my vision. Suddenly, he dropped to the ground as the sound of a heavy German vehicle was heard growing louder in the distance. I, too, fell prone, looking back over my shoulder and waving down the men I could see. I heard the muffled grunts of the others in the haze as they hit the dirt. The heavy truck chugged along the highway, unseen in its proximity because of the mist. It was near enough now to throw rocks at as it passed our position. We were amazed at the nearness of the still invisible highway.

We moved out again, this time less than forty feet, before Standish nearly fell into a deep, irregular roadside trench. I followed Standish as the sergeant slid down the steep bank and waited for the others. I stood close to the wall so I could alert any nonobservant man of the ditch. Finally, the dozen gathered in a huddled mass.

We were thankful that little water was running through or standing in the depression. This spared us the added discomfort of a thorough soaking. We moved slowly along the ditch beneath the roadway overhang. Less than twenty feet from where we entered the ditch, we came to a bridge over which the highway curved. We moved into the shelter of its high concrete culvert.

Standish and I held a hurried, whispered conference. It was decided to send two men in either direction to find a way across the road without having to climb up and over. Standish reasoned that, with as deep a ditch as this, the tributary streams which brought the large volume of water off the mountains had to be carried beneath the road somewhere along the line in which we were standing.

Weber and I moved back in the direction from which we had come to check for an upstream crossing point. Fortino and Adams moved slowly in the opposite direction as the remainder of the men sat silently and alertly in the culvert, huddled out of cold and fear. To make matters worse, no smoking was permitted any of us because the smoke would mix with the heavy, humid air and could be smelled for great distances.

"Hey, Hal," Weber whispered, "what do you suppose our chances are on this one?"

"What the hell's the matter with you, you jerk? How the hell should I know? But rest assured, they're probably as good as on any of these patrols." There was no sense in letting Weber feel and pass on to the others any uncertainty on my part. "You ask the same goddamn stupid question on every fuckin' patrol," I continued, angrily. "What the hell am I, a fortune teller or something?"

I knew that Weber and I had been together too long for the man to be fooled by my brusqueness. But it permitted me to rationalize that such discussion, if not exchanged, would keep the frightening thoughts in Weber's mind rather than releasing them.

"Just wondered," Weber continued with a wry grin. "Say, do you suppose I'll get the Air Medal or something after this one? This is my twenty-fifth recon patrol since hitting Italy."

"Yeah, you'll probably get transferred to heavy weapons for a week as a reward. Now shut up, willya?"

Our exchange referred to the infantryman's greatest passion — hatred of the air force. Or, as veteran newsman Ernie Pyle had told us around a campfire in the pine forest of the King's Hunting Preserve on a three-day rest a month or so earlier, "Yeah, at least, when you die in the air force, it's with a full belly from a hot meal the night before when you slept on a warm bed in warm pajamas."

Ernie hadn't respected the fly-boys any more than we did. In fact, we sort of agreed with that fabled Englishman who allegedly announced his criticism of American air men with, "The trouble with you blokes is, you're overpaid, overranked, oversexed, and over 'ere!"

It was our firm conviction that people in the air force were excessively decorated too. For every five missions they flew they received an Air Medal, as we understood it. Five Air Medals entitled them to the Distinguished Flying Cross. Both awards thereby were minimized in value. This was particularly true when we compared the time they spent in actual danger of death or injury during any given seventy-two-hour period — probably eight to ten hours, we reckoned. The statistic in our case, more often than not, was much closer to seventy-two out of seventy-two. And with all this, we begrudged the air force people their fifty percent extra pay for hazardous duty just because they flew occasionally.

All in all, it was my firm conviction from discussion of this with scores of infantrymen from many divisions, that the American Air Force was as much an enemy of the American infantryman as the Luftwaffe, taking as much of a toll in lives, largely because of faulty communications between ground and air during massive attacks or counterattacks. But the principle reason for bad feeling was the highly preferential treatment given the fly-boys by the military, the same as was found in the British and German armies.

At any rate, my reference to Weber's being transferred to less hazardous duty referred to the air force practice of inactivating flyers with a given number of missions. In fact, the magic number at the time was twenty. That is, a flyer, after flying his twentieth mission, was relegated to rear echelon or stateside duty.

We used to joke about our situation in this regard. "Perhaps after 200 reconnaissance patrols, we can be sent back to a heavy mortar company." Or, as Bill Mauldin credited Willie, one of his famous twosome of grimy dogfaces, with a saying to a front-line medic, "Just give me a couple of aspirin. I already got a Purple Heart." Such were the views of the dogface to his daily travail.

I was glad of Weber's company. His consistent wit — even forced levity such as this exchange we were having — helped take some of the pressure off both of us.

We came upon the tunnel completely unexpectedly. It ran directly under the road and was about four feet in diameter. We crouched and moved through it quickly and silently, pausing before coming out into the open on the far side. There was another, shallower drainage ditch on this side of the road. I beckoned to Weber, and we moved along it until we found what we were seeking.

A deep V-shaped trench cut into the mountainside disappeared somewhere above us. This would be the pathway for melting snow as it poured its way down the mountainside, along the roadside ditches and, subsequently, out to sea.

I motioned Weber to get back to the others quickly. He left to bring up the patrol. This looked like our safest bet at the moment.

In a matter of minutes, the entire group had crossed beneath the road and was climbing gingerly up the slit in the mountain. We had climbed approximately forty feet when it leveled gradually in front of us. Standish held the group still as he and I moved ahead a few yards to reconnoiter. We returned moments later.

"Christ, it's a natural," Standish said to the group. "There's a big tunnel at the base of the mountain caused by falling rock. Come on, we've got it made now."

We moved forward to find a perfect, protected spot. Something either natural or man-made — more likely the latter — had forced a landslide down the mountain. The falling rock had piled at the base of the cliff and away from the mountainside itself. Beneath an overhang at the cliff's base, the piled stone formed virtually a natural tunnel running along the entire front of the hill. It was a tailor-made path for our forward progress from here on, as far as we could see.

Still no cigarettes were permitted, although we were allowed to talk in hushed whispers, within reason. We could see several patches of light breaking through the pile of stone beyond us, indicating openings in the wall. Some of these were large enough to pass through.

Suddenly, bright sunlight dashed through the overcast sky in several long rays. Looking out in the direction from which we had just come, the mist was disappearing rapidly and, to our right, the entire valley was bathed in bright sunlight. The die was cast. It would be impossible for us to venture out into the open again without being seen as long as daylight remained. At least, we still had the element of surprise on our side. All this, of course, was pure conjecture, and assumed the presence of entrenched enemy troops close by.

Somewhere nearby we suddenly heard the sound of metal scraping on metal. We looked at each other nervously.

"Now keep it quiet, you clowns," Standish hissed to our closely gathered group. "That gives you an idea of how close the Krauts are. Hal," he whispered with a nod. I moved in next to the sergeant and, together, we walked cautiously in the direction of the noise we had heard, keeping inside the cover of our tunnel.

"Jeez," Standish whispered in amazement. "This damn rockpile is a tremendous thing, ain't it?"

I agreed. The path along which we walked was at least four feet wide and completely protected by the boulders which had dropped from above.

We picked our way carefully for another fifty yards until we came to a slight bend in the path and a sizable break in the rock wall. Through the opening, we could see the railroad track leading out along the base of the mountain and, further across the valley, through a pass toward the point inland of the beachhead where we had been able to see it clearly for many weeks.

Immediately to our right, the tracks entered a tunnel into the mountain. Near the point where the tracks curved, they had been cut and a block placed at the broken end near the tunnel mouth. On an aerial photograph, this would look like a piece of destroyed railroad which could have little significance to either side.

We both gasped. There, within fifty feet of us, was the biggest goddamn railroad gun either of us had ever seen. We were absolutely dumbfounded by its immensity.

A crew of German soldiers in shirtsleeves worked on the carriage of the great weapon. The barrel, I estimated, measured all of forty feet in length. The gun was mounted on a railroad flatcar. The gaping hole of the muzzle caught our attention.

"Good Christ! That son of a bitch would hold a fuckin' truck, I swear," Standish said in admiration.

The exaggeration was well-taken. The gun must have been at least 350-millimeter, maybe bigger. That was at least fourteen inches across the muzzle opening!

"No wonder those bastards have been raisin' hell!" the sergeant continued without moving his eyes away from the mammoth weapon. "Can you imagine the muzzle blast that fucker must have?" His rhetorical question was soon to be answered.

I knew the minute I saw the gun what had caused the landslides here.

"I'm surprised it didn't cause a landslide to block that tunnel," I whispered to Standish.

We carefully looked over the hillside above the cavernous opening. It sloped back sharply at this point whereas the face of the rest of the mountain was nearly perpendicular to the ground. This helped to explain the reason the tunnel had been placed here.

I wondered what Standish would do to satisfy our mission. We had found the gun. Actually, we should head back as soon as possible to report it.

"Let's get back and set up the watches," he said. "They've been firing their first round of the day around noon. That will give us about an hour. The next one will go off at about 1500 hours. We'll catch the second show from here."

I couldn't help thinking that Standish had something special in mind between noon and 3:00 P.M., the times of the two routine shots fired each day. Certainly he couldn't be thinking of crossing the valley again with the gun and its crew right here, not in daylight. Could he be thinking . . . ? No, it was ridiculous even to contemplate it. But Standish might just be foolhardy enough to consider attacking the gun itself with only the twelve of us.

Standish had a reputation for valor. He had been decorated four times since we landed in North Africa. He had won the coveted Distinguished Service Cross, two Silver Stars, and a Bronze Star. Any of us would have followed the man anywhere under normal circumstances. The only questions here were, was Standish still as sharp as he had been once, and would the new men be able to give an adequate account of themselves? We still had to get the information back.

"Well," I mused to myself, "We're here; they're there. There's only one way to find out."

We returned to the others and, in hushed tones, began discussing the plan of action which Standish had formulated the moment he saw the monster outside.

"OK, you guys, listen up. Here are the choices we can make. We can wait until dark and try to make it across the valley and home with the information. Or — remember, none of us expected to get this close to that big bastard out there — as long as we're here, we might as well take a crack at it ourselves. What the hell, we got lots of fire power and they can't have too big a crew on that damn dinosaur. Anyway, it's a volunteer deal as I see it. Anybody wants out, you might as well follow this tunnel as far back as you can and hide out down in the ditch there until you can make your way back across the valley. As for me, I'm all for knockin' out that son of a bitch."

"How we gonna do it, Sarge?" Weber asked enthusiastically, completely ignoring the possibility of alternative action.

Weber's question galvanized the entire group into action as the excitement of our pending mission infected every man. We crowded around the sergeant as he squatted on the sandy ground. Standish looked up at me, a broad grin tipping the edge of his mouth. He winked.

"OK, here's the deal. First of all, until they fire their first round in about . . ." He consulted his watch and paused momentarily, counting the tiny black dots as the sweep second hand moved steadily past them. "Now, in exactly thirty-six minutes, as I make it, it will be twelve straight up. We gotta have an OP operation there at the bend of the cave so we can watch their routine. I'll take the first shift. Who wants in?"

Every man raised his hand.

"Now, hang on a minute," Standish said as he looked around at each of us. Three of the men whispered among themselves in the rear. "At ease, you guys. All right, I'll tell you what. I'll take Adams up with me. Hal, you and Weber move up above the cave along this ledge line and try to look down at 'em without being seen. The rest of you guys take it easy here for a while. We'll call you when the action starts. Fortino, take over here."

The four of us moved out, two to man the observation post, and two to look for an OP closer to the gun and above it.

Weber and I left Standish and Adams at the first large split in the path and picked our way through the now cluttered cavern. The floor of the cave began to rise noticeably and, in a matter of minutes, we came to another break in the outer wall almost directly above the gun carriage. We glanced cautiously down on it from about twenty feet above it.

Below, we could see a crew of five men working about the huge weapon and a sixth who kept disappearing into the cave beneath us. We watched for the better part of a half hour as the Krauts polished the breech of the gun and tested the many wheels and other controls which made the big beast live. Watching the two men in the seats mounted beside the barrel, I decided that the large wheel on the right side controlled trajectory, that on the left, traverse.

"Do you realize that with that damn thing's range, a two- or three-inch adjustment on those damn wheels could make a difference of a mile or more in target range?" I whispered to Weber.

"Goddamn them," Weber said to himself, barely audibly, as he stared incredulously at the huge weapon.

Just then we heard the sound of metal wheels scraping and screeching from within the tunnel.

"That must be how they do it," I predicted. "They must bring the shells up on another flatcar. That's why there aren't any other flatcars around."

The sound from the cave grew louder. Suddenly, from the cave mouth, we saw the snout of another flatcar grinding to a halt. A crew of men jumped from the new arrival and began arranging the crane that was mounted to it. The maneuver was an involved one but the two crews worked it with clocklike precision. The crane was swung backward into the cave and, when it came into our view again, it held on huge pincerlike hooks, a large shell. The hooks extended over the gun's breech as the two men in the seats guided the hanging chains by hand. When it was in position, the winch lowered the shell slowly, and the men rammed it into the breech. There followed the other maneuvers I had often seen but never fully understood in American artillery outfits.

Gun crews always seemed to be doing things with what looked like canvas cylinders and bags which I assumed contained gunpowder.

These men were doing the same except, of course, the pieces they were handling were bigger than anything I had ever seen before. When the huge gun was loaded and the breech closed and locked, the freight cars were uncoupled. Then I could hear the locomotive puffing and chugging its way back into the cave. The ammunition car disappeared from view. The entire, orderly procedure had taken less than ten minutes.

The six-man crew of the gun conferred with a chart mounted on a small podium atop the flatcar. When they agreed on an angle of fire and had adjusted all necessary controls, they appeared ready to fire. Still they waited. I consulted my watch. It was less than forty seconds before twelve o'clock. I nudged Weber, and we moved down the cavernous path toward the others.

The explosion came just as I came abreast of Standish, and the force of it nearly knocked Weber, Standish, and me across the cave.

The ground on which we stood shuddered. Stones pelted us as they dropped from the cavern's ceiling. The voluminous thunder was magnified by the position of the tunnel in the valley. The sound waves whirled and bounced across the entire half-mile of valley floor, forcing the marsh grass to bow before the terrible onslaught. The monster shell went spinning invisibly into the sky, bound impersonally for some nebulous but vulnerable target twelve to twenty miles distant.

From the position of the gun and the angle of the deflection of its barrel, it seemed likely that this shell would go even beyond that maximum estimate. As the dust began settling, I could see the Germans resuming their positions on the gun carriage. Standish and I watched them through a chink in the stone wall of the cave. They apparently had become immune to the blast which was nearly deafening even at the rear of the gun.

"Those bastards," Standish said, half aloud. "They just dumped about a ton of hot metal onto the beachhead and now they lean back and relax for three more hours."

"Simmer down, Sarge," I said softly, keeping my eye on the gun crew. "By the time they're ready to fire again, we'll have their number. Come on, relax. Show's over for a while."

Standish grunted and turned away from the opening to accompany me back to the others. The rest of the men waited impatiently in the cave, anticipating whatever activity would be demanded of them in the wake of the immense blast that had just occurred. Standish squatted in the midst of the group to outline his plan.

"All right," he started. "The first thing we've gotta figure out is how in hell we're gonna knock that fucker out. Any of you had any explosives experience?" Nobody volunteered.

"Well then, it seems to me, if we can dump the Krauts on the crew, which shouldn't be any trouble, we should be able to arrange powder so it will explode."

"Will that be enough to blow up the gun, Sarge?" Adams asked.

"Probably not, but if we use enough powder, it might dislodge the carriage from the flatcar and the gun could collapse from its own weight. At least it's worth a try."

Each man was given a specific assignment to perform at the time the next firing was slated. We all were briefed and had the situation re-explained in great detail to make sure there would be no slip-ups. We were on the fifth round of explanations of individual assignments now, ten minutes before H-hour.

"Now then," Standish said, wrapping things up. "Let's get it sharp and clear one more time, the last time. Fortino, you and Adams cover us from that opening up there with the BAR. As soon as the ammo train pulls out, fire the gun. We wait exactly one minute — sixty seconds — after recoil. Then, Restivo, you and Anderson and Holderbaum move in from the road down there, just beneath that large outcropping. You'll be out of their line of sight right until you make the turn under the gun barrel. Meanwhile Krauss and Doyle, go over the tunnel entrance on that path. It should let you down on the far side of the gun without being seen. But get into position fast. The dust should cover all of us because it takes about ten minutes to settle. Hal, you, Hanson, and Weber will move out with me from up here.

Now remember, we have to move like a dose of salts through a widow woman to take advantage of the surprise. Right now those bastards don't know we're here so they're not being too alert. And they'll be too busy adjusting the gun after firing to be looking around for visitors. You guys coming up from below and from the other side should be able to get well within Tommy gun range before they could notice you.

"I noticed when they fired this noon that they're all wearing pistols. That guy up on the carriage seat on this side had a rifle slung beside him on his pivot seat. The guy on the other side had a rifle slung beside him on his pivot seat. The guy on the other side stacked his down on the ground with the others. Weber, you take the guy with the rifle. You fellows coming up from the road on this side, keep your eyes on those birds on the ground and any others possibly in the tunnel. I don't know that they don't have a couple of people in there with the ammo pile. Whatever you do, don't let any of them get to their pieces. I didn't see any burp guns among them but we can't take any chances. And for Christ's sake, remember, we don't have any facilities to take prisoners back! Got it?"

We all nodded grimly. The new men looked at each other uncertainly.

"Remember now, sixty seconds from the blast. Now, get into position."

I looked around at the new men. "You'll be fine," I said, trying to give them assurance I didn't feel myself. "Just remember to move fast and keep under cover as long as possible. And start shooting as soon as you have a clear target."

The men nodded, appreciatively, I thought.

Everyone scrambled to assume the most advantageous position for a fast jumpoff when the moment arrived. They squatted, waiting for the endless pause to be over. Those who were seasoned veterans — that is, who had been in our last campaign — felt the same pangs and qualms we always felt this close to an attack, I was sure. I did.

I was worried about one thing in particular, and I knew that it bothered Standish too. Only sketchy retreat plans had been laid out for the period after the gun might be deactivated. There really hadn't been an adequate opportunity to make an elaborate scheme. But we would be crossing the valley in full daylight and, although we hadn't seen any German troops since the sun broke through this morning's fog, I thought there were or could be many within earshot of the fire fight that was coming. I was concerned about running into a truckload of them or a couple of tanks before we could reach the cover of the distant ridge.

All in all, this was a gigantic calculated risk. I still had my doubts about the wisdom of the attack. Our mission had been to try to locate the gun, not destroy it. We were supposed to return with that information so either division artillery or air force support could take over. In the past, however, air support usually came into suspected areas to find no sign of the gun, which had been rolled back into the tunnel.

But we hadn't realized how close we were going to be able to get to the huge weapon without being observed. At any rate, the plan that Standish had devised off the top of his head really should have a good chance of success, if every man did his job. It could be a matter of shooting fish in a barrel . . . Or . . .

I did remember, however, that entire pitched battles had been launched on several occasions with less information about the enemy objective than we had about this one at this moment.

I wiped a bead of perspiration from my eyelid. I blew away another which had been hanging from the tip of my nose. The air inside our cave was hot and heavy, and incredibly humid. Large, dark spots of perspiration showed on the back of every man's shirt.

The second loading operation of the big gun was completed. We had watched it with great interest. The ammo car was uncoupled and the return through the cave was under way. The seconds dragged agonizingly by. The gun crew was in position, ready to fire. The trigger man applied pressure to the control button and every one of us instinctively flinched, drawing his head into his shoulders, eyes tightly closed to wait for the voluminous blast. Each held his head against the maddening force of the impending explosion.

The deafening reverberation seemed louder than it had at midday. Part of the reason for this phenomenon obviously was the additional excited anticipation we all felt, stimulated by the imminent attack.

Every one of us seemed to be counting off seconds in his mind's eye. The entire area before us was invisible in the thick dust clouds that had been raised by the blast.

I checked my watch. My arm quivered with fear and expectancy. The countdown seemed interminable . . . eighteen . . . seventeen . . . sixteen . . . fifteen.

We were on our feet, our weapons in firing positions, safety levers off. I stood right behind Standish and felt, rather than saw, Weber and Hanson right behind me. The others already were watching for the positions from which they would turn directly on the big gun.

The dust hadn't settled as Restivo, Adams, and Holdie dashed down the hill under cover of a large line of boulders, still in a crouch. They were going to circle below the front of the gun carriage and come up from the near side of it. Anderson counted off five seconds and, with a silent wave of his arm, urged Krauss and Doyle to make their dash toward the road.

"Let's go," Standish said, starting toward the far cavern and the next break in the wall which would bring us out into the open just above the gun and a little to its left. Weber and Hanson and I were right on his heels.

As we broke through the opening, we noticed that none of our people had been discovered as yet. So far, so good. We still had the element of surprise in our favor. It was too late to turn back now. We would need every advantage. Suddenly, the chattering of Restivo's Tommy gun broke the air as the dust began to clear.

A clear shot had been given Restivo and he took advantage of it from just below the gun carriage. I saw two of the three Germans fall as his slugs ripped through them. The third dashed into the cave before being hit. Standish fired at him, but missed.

Just then, one of the men on the breech seats turned and saw Standish just ahead of and below me. Before anyone else could move, the Kraut fired two fast shots at the sergeant with his rifle. Braced against the side of the big gun's barrel, the man then swung his weapon toward me. His second shot caught Standish in the chest and he buckled, crying out as he fell the fifteen feet to the track below. I brought my own Tommy gun up just as the BAR slugs ripped out of the cavern.

"Bless Frankie Fortino," I thought as the Kraut threw out his rifle and spun in the air, seeming to hang momentarily as Fortino's .30-caliber slugs tore through him. Then he plummeted to the bed of the flatcar, bounced off it onto the ground, and lay crumpled and silent, five feet from Standish.

All at once, the flash of a German machine gun burst out of the tunnel. It ripped into the attackers who were coming in from the road in a direct frontal attack. We hadn't expected a machine gun. The long bursts being fired by the gunner in there were telling on our guys.

Restivo fell almost immediately after the gun started firing, a slug through his left shoulder. Doyle and Krauss were dead before they hit the ground. This was an easy turkey shoot for that damn gunner! The GIs were lined up in front of him all within fifty yards. It was almost impossible not to hit some of them.

The rest of the attacking group had hit the dirt and crawled behind or under any cover they could find. Hanson leaned out from behind one of the flatcar's wheels in an attempt to get a clear shot at the machine gun. He raised his Tommy gun just as the top of his head was ripped off by a string of bullets, the first of which sent his helmet spinning down the decline. He was thrown over on his back, his arms frozen in firing position, still holding his weapon.

"Weber, you're closest," I shouted. "Get that guy!"

Weber edged toward the ledge just over the tunnel entrance. He pulled a grenade from his suspender strap, removed the pin, and gingerly flipped it awkwardly in the direction of the machine gun below and behind him.

The grenade exploded on its first bounce, and Fortino was on his feet at once, jumping down to track level, holding his automatic weapon hip-high, spraying into the darkened depths of the tunnel. I sprayed a full magazine of thirty slugs across the flatcar as the last of the Germans began to descend, his pistol in hand.

"All right, move now!" I screamed at the survivors of the attack. "This place will be crawling with Krauts in a few minutes!"

The entire group galvanized into action immediately. Fortino led four men into the cave, returning heavily laden with kegs of powder.

The rest of the men were assigned the unhappy task of carrying our four dead buddies down the hill to the ditch on the far side of the road, stripping them of papers and hiding them as well as possible.

"Here, let's pile those things under here. I don't know of any other way to do this fast," I called to the men staggering under their loads of powder kegs. They piled the kegs in a confined group directly under the left front wheel of the flatcar.

Fortino dashed back into the cave for two more kegs. One of these he threw up on the carriage beneath the breech of the gun. The other he smashed open at one end with his BAR butt. Then, picking up the opened keg, he began backing down the hill, laying a trail of powder with which to fuse the explosion.

Weber and I, meanwhile, broke open the other kegs, scattering handfuls of black powder among them. Then we broke open the keg on the flatcar, pouring powder into the open breech of the gun.

From deep within the tunnel came the sound of a chugging loco-motive and the screeching scrape of metal wheels against the track.

"Let's go, you two," Fortino shouted. He had reached the ditch with the open keg. Weber and I each fired a short burst into the tunnel although we couldn't see anything. Then we ran frantically down the hill toward Fortino just as he tossed a lighted match into the powder on the ground. The white sparks dashed along the black line toward the gun as Weber and I jumped into the deep ditch beside the others.

"Hit the dirt!" I yelled, falling on my face.

German small-arms fire could be heard at the mouth of the tunnel as the noise of the locomotive broke into the open. Simultaneously, a massive explosion rocked the entire valley, throwing dirt and pieces of metal through the air. Large rocks and other debris rained down on us in the ditch, and the air was filled with heavy, acrid smoke. A large stone struck my helmet, bounced off, glanced off my shoulder, and flew to the ground. I barely noticed it.

The explosion had wiped out the mouth of the tunnel, causing a devastating landslide to pour down on the ammo car and its hapless passengers.

Fully fifteen minutes elapsed before any of us dared breathe freely. We looked at each other in amazement. We hadn't expected such a powerful explosion. Apparently, the remainder of the powder kegs just inside the tunnel also had gone.

"Goddamn!" Weber murmured, looking over the rim of the ditch. "Lookie there!"

We all stood and followed his gaze, still stunned by the immen-sity of the blast. We were greeted by a beautiful sight. The left front wheel of the gun carriage flatcar had been blown off completely, caus-ing the heavy weapon to fall over on its side. The weight of the long barrel dragged it faster than the rest of the mechanism could have and the barrel had broken loose, carrying other parts of the gun and the flatcar to the ground beside the track. The mouth of the tunnel was completely closed. No telling how far into the aperture the landslide had filled.

Several German soldiers and parts of others could be seen lying in the position in which they had died in the extreme violence. The ammo car was covered with rock and dirt, and only the smashed snout of the locomotive could be seen poking through the pile of debris that cluttered the tunnel's mouth.

"That noise is sure to attract somebody," I reminded the seven men with me. "Let's get the hell out of here."

"What about them?" Fortino asked, pointing to our four dead buddies, now stiffening in death.

"We can't possibly get them back. They'll be found by graves registration when they come through here. That should be pretty soon. Or the Krauts might bury them with their own dead up there. Anyway, you've got their papers?"

Fortino nodded affirmatively.

"What about their dog tags?" he asked, looking nervously up and down the highway.

"No, leave them. We know who they were. We can't do any more for them now," I replied. "Let's get back with the information."

I led the way out of the ditch, followed, single file, by the others. Fortino had Restivo's good arm around his shoulder, helping the wounded man walk. We moved as rapidly as possible, feeling terribly vulnerable here on this open terrain. The air still was thick with dust.

We were anxious to get to the relative safety of the hills on the far side of the valley before we were discovered by Kraut reinforcements who could be whipping along the highway back there from either direction — inland or from the coast.

It had been a busy patrol, the roughest recon patrol any of us had ever pulled so far. I knew there would be others. Yet, despite the excitement, it would be described as part of a "routine patrol activity" in the Italian campaign.

14. Welcome to Schonach

"GOOD MORNING, MY BOY. How is it this morning? Much excitement, eh?" Bruckmann was extremely solicitous today. He sat alone with his coffee. From somewhere, he had managed to scrounge a hard roll of some sort and was indulging himself in the unaccustomed luxury of making it completely palatable by dunking pieces of it in his coffee. Crumbs floated atop the liquid. Bruckmann seemed unconcerned about them. It was nearly impossible these days to find both coffee and dunking pastries while the one was warm enough, the other soft enough to be appreciated simultaneously.

"Yeah," I replied. "I didn't have too good a night. I had a bad dream. I suppose much of my restlessness is due to the arrival of our guests this morning, huh?"

"Undoubtedly. The anticipation is great, isn't it? I can tell from the state of your nervousness. You are anxious to meet your new comrades, eh?"

"I guess that's right," I said, tentatively. I still wasn't sure who they were bringing up here. For all I knew, they might be Kraut plants, although I couldn't imagine what I represented that was important enough for such intrigue.

"It shouldn't be too much longer for you to wait, I think,"

Bruckmann continued. "Trautmann went down to Triberg to get them from the hospital. They should be back in a little while. You know, Hal, I know how you feel in a way." Bruckmann smiled, kindly, sympathetically, I thought. "I recall when I was attached to the German embassy in New York," he went on. "There was a seven-month period back in 1937 when I was the only person of rank stationed at our office. Of course, there were three others there, but they were dolts, cretins, you might say. I couldn't possibly associate with such people. I truly missed those of my class. Oh, don't misunderstand me. I thoroughly enjoyed all the delightful Americans I met there. Such marvelous parties they gave, those society matrons. But it still wasn't the same without my own people, you know?"

I nodded, as if in understanding. I was amused as I recalled Bruckmann's emphasis on social classes and his insistence on introducing me to Frau Schilli as a highborn American.

It was obvious that Bruckmann was a man of rank, both socially and politically. Probably militarily too, based on the situation in the Third Reich. His bearing proved that unquestionably. However, whether he actually deserved such distinction still was questionable in my mind. But Bruckmann definitely had been accustomed to lofty position, I was sure.

"Why, even during my years in Chicago," the big man continued, "when I was living with my American family, it still wasn't the same as being with my own people." He made no move to enlarge on that reference, so I didn't push it with questions.

Just then, Lieutenant Trautmann entered the dining room through the rear hall door. He looked around the room. Then, spying Bruckmann, he smilingly approached us, a grin of accomplishment on his face.

"Ah, there you are, Herr Lister," he said to me after having acknowledged Bruckmann with a respectful nod. "I have your men in the car just outside."

The reference to "your men" was a slip of the tongue in the mouth of an officer in a discipline-burdened army. I had seen completely unwarranted military respect, exaggerated beyond reason, among German prisoners we had taken. Corporals were given the type of treatment by privates that Americans reserved only for officers of high rank.

Bruckmann arose and nudged Trautmann to the side, out of my earshot. A quiet conference ensued during which Trautmann seemed to be arguing. Bruckmann gave a quiet, curt order in German; Trautmann drew himself to snappy attention, clicked his heels, muttered, *"Jawohl!"* and turned, leaving the room without a backward glance or without looking at me again. Only the hand salute was missing.

"They will come in in a moment or two," Bruckmann said, his mood entirely altered from its original joviality of a few moments before. "We will have to make these fellows feel at home, won't we, Hal?"

I nodded with a bit of a frown. Bruckmann spoke with authority now. It was an unusual tone for him to assume with me. Perhaps it was held over from his apparent altercation with Trautmann.

"I'll lend them my toilet articles," I said, remembering my own first day in Schonach.

"That won't be necessary," Bruckmann countermanded the suggestion. "I had Lieutenant Trautmann obtain some from the stock in Triberg. They will be amply supplied, as you were."

There was a tense pause as we finished our coffee in silence. I knew that some portentous event was about to occur. I'd never seen him so serious and preoccupied before.

"There is something I think we'd better discuss right now, Hal," he started, uncomfortably. He looked ill at ease in the hesitant pause that followed.

I waited, saying nothing.

"Let us not forget, Hal, that you are prisoners of war, you three. As such, it should be remembered that you conduct yourselves as prisoners. It wasn't too bad when you were the only one. The civilian population here didn't think too much about it. But now, with three of you, you will be much more visible. I think it would be better if you limit your freedom about the village, at least, in the eyes of the public."

I breathed a sigh of relief. So that was it. Of course, he was right. This was a weird setup for prisoners of war. It would be easy enough to comply with this order which really sounded more like a request.

"No sweat," I said quickly.

"I beg your pardon?"

"I mean, sure thing. We can arrange to keep busy about the hotel."

"Good boy. I was sure I could depend on you."

"By the way, Helmut," I pressed. "I've been meaning to ask you about something you said earlier."

"Eh? What was that?"

"About your service in the foreign office. Just what was your job there?"

Bruckmann started momentarily, his eyes scanning my face warily. Then, appearing satisfied that it was a conversational question only, he replied, almost flippantly.

"Oh, I was one of those bungling bureaucrats. You know, a sort of cushy desk job."

"What sort?"

"Just an office job, you know. Well, you will miss your coffee altogether if you don't hurry and drink up. Nothing quite as bad as cold chicory." Bruckmann smiled, but his steady, gray eyes announced that the discussion had ended.

I arose and poured a head on my coffee. I helped myself to one of the rare cubes of sugar lying on top of the sideboard beside the coffee urn. It had been some weeks since such an open display of sugar had been seen. In fact, the only sweets we had seen recently had been the artificial — *Kunsthonig* — honey which came in the form of a heavy jelly. *Kunsthonig* had an exotic, flowered scent and tasted like a delicate gelatin.

It was one of the many ersatz products to be found throughout Germany now, the real things being almost impossible to come by. I had obtained about four ounces of it when I presented my card for my *Verflägungsmittel* — my rations. The artificial honey was excellent trading material for cigarettes, I had discovered. However, most of the time, I preferred to keep my supply for myself, consuming it almost immediately after I received it. This, I was sure, in retrospect, was a result of my prison camp days and the necessity under those circumstances of wolfing one's food before a fellow prisoner grabbed it.

Voices were heard in the rear hall as other guests came downstairs from their sleeping quarters. The door was opened by Humphreys, who held it for Inga, Christianne, and von Nordenflycht. The little Englishman smiled as he looked over at Bruckmann, who was standing just inside the door.

Bruckmann invited them to sit with him as soon as they got their coffee, but he seemed to be avoiding me deliberately. It was clear to me that I was to stay by myself, probably to greet the new American prisoners. I assumed they hadn't appeared yet because they were being settled in their living quarters. I was told the new men would be staying in a comfortable room, formerly janitor's quarters, that had been set up for them in the basement of the school.

The Englishman stood and left the table where his companions were engaged in quiet conversation. He approached me, carrying his cup carefully, and sat at my table, silently contemplating his coffee.

"Blast it!" he said. "I can't get used to this bloody imitation coffee. Bloody well sooner have a cup of tea in any case."

"I haven't seen any tea since I was captured," I said.

"Not bloody likely to either," Humphreys responded with a bitter grimace. "These rotters don't appreciate anything with charm about it and God knows, tea is the most civilized drink in the bloody world."

I was surprised at the vehemence I was hearing in the remarks of this normally quiet, almost mousy, little man. It was the first time I had heard him sound angry.

"What's up? Did Bruckmann chew you out?"

"Chew you what?" Humphreys asked, puzzled.

"Chew you out. You know, bawl you out, criticize you."

"Oh, that silly bugger. He thinks he owns the whole bloody German nation to hear him talk."

"Well, look, if you're so unhappy with them, why do you work for them?"

"Oh, my God. I'm not working for them as much as I'm working against the bloody Bolsheviks who are running the damned labor government in Blighty. Besides, the pay here is much better than I could get at home, and there are no air raids here."

"Well, I guess you couldn't rationalize yourself into a better position then, could you? But what good does the extra money do you? There's nothing to buy and, when there is, you have to have a whole bushel of ration coupons."

"Oh, I'm settled on that. I'm entitled to coupons. I have civvy papers, don't forget. Don't you?"

"No, I'm a prisoner of war, not a volunteer worker," I reminded him.

"You don't say. Well, I'll be buggered. I didn't know they treated their prisoners like this. You're the first I've seen, you see."

"Well, don't judge prisoner of war status with my setup here. I've been in their prison camps. That's sure as hell no picnic, even in the best of them."

"Well, I say, isn't this collaboration then?" Humphreys asked perceptively. His eyes studied my face for signs of resentment. He wasn't sure just how far he could bait me, apparently. From his vantage point, he must realize that the Germans here needed me, or I wouldn't be in this interesting situation. And, if they needed me, I might be entitled to more respect than one might expect to give an "enemy" POW.

"Not as far as I'm concerned," I hastily advised him. "I cleared all this before I started. They registered me at the stalag in Villingen. I talked to the American representative there. He gave me complete clearance as long as I wasn't broadcasting actual propaganda messages." I suddenly wondered why I felt it necessary to defend my position to this misguided Briton.

Humphreys persisted. "Also, because I imagine this situation makes possible an easier escape, eh?" He smirked. "Besides, in order to hear your program, the audience must listen to the propaganda too, isn't that true? Isn't that the same thing, really, then?"

I had thought about this often. I always managed to stop worrying about it with a simple thought that my escape would make everything all right. Now Humphreys had seen the obvious too. This situation here did open the way to a natural escape at some near future time.

"Yeah, escape," I said lightly. "I'm just waiting for the new model Volkswagens to come out before I leave. I might as well go in style, right?"

The Englishman smiled and said nothing. He lifted his cup to his lips, then set it down with a frown. Just then, the outer door slammed and footsteps could be heard in the hallway approaching the dining room door.

That door opened and Trautmann entered, followed by two very young, bewildered, bedraggled American soldiers. Lieutenant Küttner brought up the rear.

I stood as the German officers approached me, leaving the two GIs standing alone just inside the door. They looked around the room hesitantly, their eyes wide in astonishment. This certainly didn't represent what they had come to know as quarters for prisoners of war.

Bruckmann arose from his conference with the others and intercepted the officers just before they reached me. He glared at the soldiers as if to chastise them for not bringing their charges to him first, for not going through channels.

"Well, gentlemen, I see you have our new guests cleaned up, eh? Did you not see me when you entered?"

Both SS lieutenants stood uncomfortably before the big Luftwaffe private as if they'd been caught with their hands in the cookie jar. It was a most incongruous situation.

"*Oberstormfuhrer* Best ordered us to deliver them to the American sergeant," Küttner said quietly, not looking at Bruckmann.

Bruckmann's frown cut off any further remarks from the man.

"Well, I'll just have to talk to the *oberstormfuhrer*, won't I?" His mood seemed to brighten visibly then. "So, let us meet our new friends."

Trautmann signaled the newcomers to approach him. They did so hesitantly.

"Gentlemen, welcome to Schonach. It is a pleasure to have you here with us. Please don't be concerned. Make yourselves comfortable. Sergeant Lister here will explain your position to you. I'll see you after a bit."

Bruckmann left us to return to the ladies, his officious introductory speech ended. As I stepped forward to greet my two new companions, the German officers left the room.

I moved to the coffee urn and poured two new cups of coffee. Setting them down on the table, I looked at the new men. The expressions on their faces, under any other circumstances, would have been terribly comical. I sympathized with them as I recalled my own consternation upon first contacting Bruckmann and the others. Bruckmann had been at his forceful, maître d' best with them. Both the men wore grimy uniforms, but their faces showed evidence of recent scrubbing.

"Now take it easy, boys. You have a lot of surprises coming. I'll explain it all to you in good time. Meanwhile, my name's Lister. What's yours?"

"I'm Ernie Goebel. I'm from Chicago," said the taller of the two. He was an emaciated young man about twenty, whose heavy-rimmed glasses perched precariously on the bridge of a painfully thin, long nose. His eyes bulged in their sockets. He was nearly as tall as I but obviously weighed considerably less, despite my bout with the Waldkirch malnutrition. I looked at him, smiling to set him at ease.

"Really? I'm a neighbor. I'm from Milwaukee."

His smile told me he already felt more comfortable.

I looked at the other man.

"Bill Tenkhoff," he said softly, with a trace of a southern accent. "I'm from Mauldin, Missouri."

Both of them wore patches consisting of a small, red keystone.

"What outfit is that?" I asked.

"The 28th. Pennsylvania National Guard," Ernie said.

I hadn't seen it before. They must have come in through Normandy. "Where did you land?"

"Le Havre," Ernie replied. "We landed about a month ago. On the first night on the line, we were overrun, and I was captured. Christ, I never heard a shot fired." He pronounced it "Le Harve."

"Me neither," Bill said. He had stood quietly by up till now, watching what went on but not participating.

"Were you a first nighter too?" I asked him.

Bill nodded. Then, as if rethinking his response, he said, "Er, no. I came in a few days after the invasion. I came in as a replacement. They transferred about a hundred of us to the 28th."

Ernie nodded enthusiastically. "Yeah. That's what happened to me too. When we got to what they said was the front, they pointed to a foxhole of the guy in the outfit who was leaving. I mean, the guy was in the outfit we were relieving, you know."

"I understand," I told him.

"Well, anyway, they pointed to this foxhole, I crawled in and fell asleep. Next thing I know, there's a Heinie lookin' down at me with a burp gun in his hands."

"That the way it happened with you, Bill?" I asked the other fellow. He really had been more reticent than Ernie. He hung back throughout our discussion, appearing more embarrassed than Ernie had.

"Aw, hell. It really was ridiculous the way they got me. I was in the regimental dentist's chair."

"The what?"

"No kiddin'. There I was, about fifteen miles behind the line. Old Major Brojanac was drillin' away on a cavity. Shells were flying all over. Then we heard some machine gun fire. Next thing I know there are these three Krauts with their burp guns aimed at us. They captured us, dental chair and all. I didn't even get my final filling."

Apparently they had been in the bulge which had broken loose up north of the Kolmar Pocket in late December. The Germans, under the leadership of the old Desert Fox, Rommel, had penetrated deeply into the American positions up around Bastogne, Belgium.

As we exchanged news, Humphreys arose from his solitary table and approached us. I couldn't avoid the introduction without appearing rude.

"Fellows, this is Mr. Humphreys. He works here. Humphreys, this is Bill Tenkhoff, and this is Ernie Goebel."

Humphreys gave Ernie sort of a cursory handshake and a clipped "How do." However, his eyes had been on Bill from the beginning of the introductions. He lingered over this handshake, smiled, and said, "Well, isn't it nice that you have some company of your own kind at last, Sergeant?"

The only difference was that, as he spoke to me, his eyes remained on Bill.

Finally, he said, "If you gentlemen will excuse me, I have some work that needs doing. I'll see you later, though. Ta-ta." He left through the rear door of the dining room.

We sat again and I leaned forward after making sure that Bruckmann and the others weren't watching. I rested my cheek on my right hand nonchalantly.

"OK, let me brief you right away so you'll have an idea of what's happening here." I explained in general terms about my own second capture, about being brought here, and what was expected of me according to Bruckmann's initial discussion. I told them about having received clearance from Sergeant Sanders. I also told them about lousing up the SS company of engineers my first night here. They both enjoyed that part immensely. I decided not to discuss the escape plan with them just yet.

"What do you play, Ernie?" I asked the gaunt young man.

"Piano. I played with a combo back home."

"And you, Bill?"

"Clarinet and sax. I played in the high school band and was in the marching band."

"I don't know what they're getting you for a horn. They did ask what you play, didn't they?"

"Yeah. I think that little fat lieutenant that just left said something about a tenor sax. That'll be OK."

"And there's a fabulous parlor grand up at the studio for you, Ernie," I added.

"Studio?" Ernie asked. Both men looked perplexed. Apparently neither of them had been told their roles here.

Once again, I explained their part in the proceedings. Then I told them to be patient. Something good was developing, I told them guardedly.

I learned that both of them were nineteen, that Bill had been in the army for ten months and had come overseas immediately after his very short basic training period had ended. Ernie arrived overseas less than a month ago and had been in the service less than six months. But more importantly, I learned that each had been given his Red Cross parcel just before leaving the stalag for Schonach.

"You'd better stash some of the stuff in those packages. It will last quite a while if you take care of it. Don't trust anyone you meet here. I've been here a couple of months and can't tell yet who my real friends are, if any."

It suddenly dawned on me that I would be included in that admonition, at least until I proved myself. It also occurred to me that, as those words dropped from my lips, I was staring at Christianne, across the room, her slim back to me.

Ernie, the more vociferous of the two, interrupted my train of thought.

"What do you mean, friends? Aren't they all Nazis?"

"Not necessarily," I explained. "Oh sure, they all work for the German government in some way, but they have cliques here. You know, like gangs. I've been able to tell only two of them for sure so far. The SS captain you haven't met yet, and that big guy you met when you first came in. That was Bruckmann. They're party all right, but not for the Nazi theory, I would guess. The captain, Best is his name, is off his rocker, I'm convinced. Part of it probably came from some pretty rough fighting on the Russian Front. I guess he picked up his limp there. But he's really high strung. Stay out of his way if you can. Bruckmann, on the other hand, has never heard a shot fired, I'm sure. But he's an opportunist. He'll milk anyone who'll let him. I'm sure Best is one of those who still thinks Germany's gonna win this thing. I'm equally sure Bruckmann knows better and his interest in this radio station is to soften the treatment Germany in general and Bruckmann in particular get after the war."

"What kind of stuff do they broadcast, Sarge?" Ernie asked.

"That's just it. In Italy, we used to hear messages concerning American warmongers, the 4-F crowd back home, Jewish industrialists, who were profiteering while we were overseas. You know. All kinds of stuff to make us mad or disillusioned. They probably figured we'd quit fighting and surrender if we were disillusioned enough. But these people here have begun swinging their messages against other Allies rather than against America. Sort of preparing us for the trouble we'll have with Russia, France, and England after Germany is defeated. That way, apparently, they figure it will go easier with them if their predictions were right."

"Hey, I heard that. A guy down at the prison camp said something about not knowing why we're fighting Germany when Russia is our real enemy," Bill said, excited for the first time since he had entered the room.

"Hell, I've heard that story told as far back as Sicily from prisoners we took there. And that was more than a year and a half ago. The Krauts were still ahead in the war back then. Actually, there's a lot of truth in that philosophy about Russia, I'm convinced. But I'm convinced, too, that Germany wouldn't be any better an ally for us. What we really should have done, I suppose, is just let the two fight themselves out and come in for the kill."

Both men pondered the point for a moment.

"I remember a bunch of Krauts we ran into," I continued. "These were in southern France. They'd been recruited from eastern Europe. I guess they were anti-Communists, so the whole outfit surrendered and switched sides. And they were Russians. Actually, they were from the Mongolian part of the Soviet Union and, Christ, they were a mean-looking bunch of savages!"

"Jeez, kind of makes you wonder, doesn't it?" Ernie said, sunk deep in thought.

"Well, I'll tell you one thing. I wouldn't trust any of 'em right now," I said.

"Were you scared when they brought you here, Sarge?" Ernie asked.

"Sure. I suppose anybody who says he isn't in a case like this is either kidding himself or trying to kid somebody else. But don't worry. They brought you two up here and that proves that they think they need you, and as long as they need us, we're all right."

"Yeah, but what happens when they don't anymore?" Ernie persisted, a worried frown creasing his forehead.

Bruckmann had arisen from his table and was approaching us.

"Well, now, and are you getting acquainted?" We all nodded. "That's fine," he continued, grinning affably. He sat in the empty chair at our table and began toying with my coffee spoon, drawing small spiral indentions on the tablecloth.

"Do you both understand what is expected of you?" he asked the newcomers, both of whom nodded, somewhat overeagerly.

Sensing that Bruckmann's thin veneer of friendliness was hiding something possibly more sinister, I hastily explained, "I've given them the general picture and explained that they are to play with me in the combo, that's all."

Bruckmann nodded pleasantly, still smiling thinly. "Fine, Hal. Then, if you will excuse me, gentlemen, I will go and arrange for your rations while you are here. Oh, and Hal, you won't forget what I suggested about too much exposure, eh?"

"Right."

"Now, you fellows, I'll be right back to get you. I'll take you to show you your quarters, so don't leave the room, eh?" He crossed the room and entered the company office through the glass doors.

The three of us sat and talked about home and sports for the few remaining moments until Bruckmann reappeared and signaled the pair to follow him. They went out the front door of the hotel. I walked to the window and watched them as they left the hotel and headed up the cobbled road toward the school building. I wondered if Christianne had gone there when she and Inga left the hotel a few moments before. I decided to go up and have a look.

As I climbed the street, I noticed a heavy cloud formation moving rapidly in from the north. The large, black clouds blotted out even the translucent glow which had indicated where the sun was. These could be snow clouds, I feared. If so, they could materially affect any escape plans much longer than I had hoped. I couldn't be sure because of the temperature. It was warming considerably and had been for several days. I estimated the temperature now stood in the high forties.

Then I felt relieved as I heard the unmistakable clap of thunder to the north. If it rained instead of snowed, our position would be improved appreciably. The snow would melt faster than expected and we would be able to leave much sooner. I hoped fervently for an early thaw.

As I entered the school building, a few raindrops heralded the approach of the storm. I mentally crossed my fingers, hoping this might portend a heavy downpour. I climbed to the second floor and walked through the deserted corridor to the main studio door. There was no sign of life inside, so after a brief glance about the large room, I turned to leave.

The door burst open before I could reach it and Best charged into the room. He lurched swiftly, limping badly, across the large studio and literally threw himself at the piano bench. The theme he began hammering out of the keyboard was familiar to me. I had heard it with Nana and her family at a concert we attended just before I left home. Its exciting notes were melded into an active story which I could almost feel. Although it rose in fury as the captain banged it out, I knew that it should be played by an entire orchestra and with variations of volume. Best was playing only the most familiar passage from the work. I recalled the name and missed the frantic crashing of cymbals I had enjoyed during the concert presentation of the number. It was Prokofiev's "Scythian Suite."

The cause of this emotional outbreak on Best's part I could only guess. It likely had to do with Bruckmann. Their confrontations lately seemed to leave Best in a foul mood oftener than not. The two argued almost constantly lately. However, I was amused to recognize that Best sought to relieve his mental pressure by providing a noisy rendition of a Russian musical piece by a Russian composer. At any rate, I vowed to stay out of the captain's way until this episode blew over. Quietly, I made my way out of the room, into the corridor and down the stairs, sure that Best wasn't even aware I'd been there, despite his having looked directly at me as he played.

I emerged from the building to find the streets bathed in a heavy torrent. Water ran several inches deep in the cobbled roadside depressions which served as street-level drainage ditches.

The pitch of the road promised a considerable flow when this accumulation reached the headwaters of the millpond and poured their way down the mountain to Triberg. If this weather continued, I thought, an escape might be contemplated very shortly.

I pictured the effect of the rain on the diminishing snow. If it had the effect on Schonach and the surrounding countryside I hoped it would, it undoubtedly would clear most of the ground cover of the Black Forest to the north, removing the bulk of the deep drifts which had made the forest impassable since I had been in Schonach.

About a week after they arrived, Ernie and Bill accompanied me on an early morning hike to my favorite spot in the surrounding hills — the saddle on the ridge just above and behind the hotel. From there, we could view the entire Triberg valley. Ostensibly, this was an exercise break, and as such, was smiled upon by Bruckmann, Best, and the rest. However, I wanted to brief the two men on my escape plans, now rapidly formulating.

We stopped beneath an immense pine tree and sat on a large boulder in the sun. The sky was cloudless and the warmth of the sun's glare was an encouraging sign. The trees behind us shielded us from the chill morning wind on the mountaintop. Below us, a three-dimensional cyclorama was breathtaking in its beauty. The brightness of the sunlight, countered by the blackness of the depth of the Black Forest in every direction, lent balance to the entire picture.

"Damned if it don't feel just like spring," Bill mused aloud.

"Yeah, especially with those damn snow drifts melting the way they are. Man, I'll tell you, I hate snow and cold, don't you?" Ernie said.

"Only when they're in my way," I replied, looking toward the Lamm where the now nearly snowless roof steamed in the sunlight. "Incidentally, that's what I want to talk to you about this morning. If this weather keeps up, we should have clear sailing in a couple of weeks."

Bill looked troubled. "Say, Hal, I meant to ask you about that. If you're planning a break, how you gonna do it with all the roads crowded with Kraut soldiers and equipment?"

"I don't plan for us to use the roads. I have our road pretty well mapped out." I described in detail the valley in which we were situated. The mountain we were on dropped rapidly into another valley. Eventually, if my maps proved right, this next valley followed a series of smaller defiles in the mountains of the Schwarzwald directly to Stuttgart which, according to the news analyst on a recent broadcast, had been taken by my own 3rd Division. At least the outfit was still fighting there the night before last. "I figure it's about twenty-five miles as the crow flies," I added.

"The only thing is, we ain't crows," Bill continued with his Missouri drawl. "Anyway, suppose we make it out of here without bein' seen. And suppose we get up there to that town, wherever that is. Then what? I mean, how are we gonna get to the Americans? What if —"

"If, if, if. For Christ's sake, if the dog hadn't stopped to lift his leg, he'd have caught the rabbit," Ernie interjected angrily.

"Well, let's not invent problems. There'll be enough without that. Let's not worry about things that far in the future. I figure we'll take those things as they come."

"Yeah but I don't wanna get my ass shot off just about the time the war is gonna be over, especially when I could stay in a nice place like this until . . ." Bill persisted.

"Until what, Willie?" Ernie challenged. Bill was silent. He obviously hadn't considered other possibilities.

"You see, we really have no choice," I went on. "No matter how you slice it, we are doing something that could be considered collaborating with the enemy. The only reason I'm doing it is that it gives me a clear-cut chance to escape. I assume that's the way it is with you two. But just how far do you think your position would take you, Bill, if we sat here waiting and the French First Army crossed the Rhine directly opposite this area and came here to recapture us? And that's who will probably take this area, you know. The Americans are all up around Rhemagen and north of there, according to the news broadcasts I've been hearing. Now, remember this. The French took a hell of a beating in the Blitzkrieg back in 1940, and they've been occupied by the Krauts ever since. To them, there's only one objective in this war. That's to kill every Kraut they can, and that includes anybody working for the Krauts."

"Jeez, Hal. Do you really think they'd be that tough on us?" Ernie asked, frowning deeply.

"Well, I'll tell you this. We took several towns in southern France, just after the Krauts pulled out. Right on our heels, the FFI swept through the towns and pulled out all the gals who had been horsing around with the German soldiers. They shaved their heads and paraded them down the middle of main street."

The two young men sat thoughtfully, Bill staring at a distant pine tree silently. Ernie drew concentric designs in the floor of pine needles with a piece of a broken branch.

"Well, look, guys, and especially you, Bill. I don't relish the thought of going back into combat any more than you do. I wouldn't be very happy, obviously, about getting hit again just as I was rejoining my outfit with the end of the war in sight. But look at it this way. When we get up close enough to Stuttgart to hear small-arms fire, the entire tactical situation may have changed. Our boys might have pushed the Krauts way the hell to the east by then and all we have to do will be to walk down the middle of a highway or hitch a ride on the first six-by-six that comes along. Or, if fighting is still going on, we might be able to hide in the woods until the GIs push the Krauts through us. Then, all we'd have to do is turn ourselves in to the first

Allied outfit to pass. That happened to me in Italy and it wasn't so bad. There's a lot of confusion in a battle area, as you both know."

Ernie broke the tension by asking a question which was of more importance to him than any of the others.

"How about our food supply?"

Ernie had developed an amazing propensity for anything edible at any time and always in voluminous amounts. I was astounded at the man's appetite in light of his unbelievably thin frame. He always reminded me of pictures of Ichabod Crane in "The Legend of Sleepy Hollow."

"We have five good days' rations stored down there in my bag under the bridge. That's if we're careful. And there's still room in the rucksack for a few more small things we might be able to scrounge."

Ernie's eyes seemed to bulge more than usual. Bill's attention was elsewhere, however.

"What's up, Bill? You're a million miles away," I said to him.

Bill had been listening only occasionally, and then only half-heartedly, seeming preoccupied as he stared dreamily down in the valley.

"What's your problem, Willie?" asked Ernie, good-naturedly.

"Nothin'. I was just thinkin'. I'll be glad to get out of here after all. That goddamn Limey!"

"Who? Humphreys?" I asked, surprised. This was the first time Bill had mentioned anybody else in the company.

"Yeah, that son of a bitch propositioned me last night."

"He what?" Ernie asked, incredulously.

"Well, we were down at that Schwann guest house havin' a beer. He invited me. Ernie was readin' one of those German picture magazines, and Humphreys asked me to come with him. Hell, I didn't know what he had in mind. Well, anyway, there we were sittin' and drinkin' beer and talkin' about nothin' in particular, when all of a sudden he puts his hand on my knee under the table. Not like you guys do when we're all kinda sittin' around close together, you know, when you make a point or somethin'. He was feelin' my leg. Christ, I like to went through the ceiling. I almost smacked the bastard. Jeez, it made my skin crawl!"

"Are you sure you didn't just misunderstand?" I asked. I had had some doubts about the delicate little Englishman from the beginning, but didn't want any fights or scenes to affect the possible escape adversely. "It might have been an accidental brushing, you know."

"Bullshit! I had a guy try that on me once in a crap game at Fort Meade. Everybody knew he was a goddamn homo. They all said he picked me because of my curly hair and my baby face." Bill pouted as he spoke, further emphasizing that baby face. He really looked like a smooth-cheeked, angry little boy. I chuckled despite my misgivings.

Ernie leaned forward, interested.

"Well, for Christ's sake, what did you do last night?"

"Last night? Nothin'. I just jerked my leg away and said I had to go to the can. Then he asked me if I knew where it was. He wanted to show me!"

"I'll bet he did," Ernie smirked.

"Anyway, I told him to never mind. I'd find it myself. I told him I had to turn in anyway."

"Then what?" Ernie was exhilarated.

"Then he asked me about going for a walk today, just him and me."

I was becoming concerned about this situation now. It was bad enough having the Englishman justifiably accusable of being a profiteering adventurer with few or no scruples. But if the guy really was twinky, he could become excessively hard to handle. He might be quite emotional if he were crossed. He could louse up the entire escape plan in a fit of pique, I knew.

"Well, look, Bill. Just try to stay out of his way for the next few days. I'll try to keep us all busy with program business to give you no time to interest him. Stick with Ernie or me whenever you can. Maybe the crowd will scare him off. But, whatever you do, don't cross the guy, at least, not obviously and not yet. He could throw the blocks to us but good if he got real sore at us."

"You mean about the escape?"

"Exactly."

"Well, does he know about it?"

"He hasn't been told. But with a mind like his, he'd know it would be the natural thing for us to do and I think he suspects we'll try to make a break sooner or later. All we need is for him to plant a suspicion in Best's mind and we'll spend the rest of our time here in a locked room with a guard."

"Yeah, well, I don't care. I'll smack that little bastard if he — "

"You'll smack nobody if you want out of here. Now, goddamn it, you listen to me. I mean it. We can't afford to antagonize anyone now.

Just play your cards right and we may be able to blow earlier than I had planned."

Ernie leaned back with a grin on his face. "Hey, Willie boy. Why not give the Limey a go? What the hell, he's better lookin' than most of the broads I've seen around here."

He laughed uproariously as he rolled off the boulder and out of Bill's direct line of fire as the unhappy young man threw a handful of snow at him. Then, tauntingly, from behind a nearby tree, Ernie teased, "You know what they say, Willie. What the hell, don't knock it if you ain't tried it."

Ernie ducked behind the tree, chortling loudly. Bill, after a moment of tense anger, realized it was only good-natured joshing and stood up, his hands in his pockets. I also arose and the three of us joined forces to start back to the village.

In the short time we had been together, an understandable, rapid camaraderie had grown among the three of us, all misplaced GIs in a strange environment. Perhaps it was the unique nature of our predicament. Maybe it was the variety of our personalities and the fact that each of us somehow complemented the others. In all likelihood, a good share of it was the result of our conditions in combat and basic training.

Infantry service accomplished this fast-building, desperate friendship more than any other experience I'd ever had. Most combat men I'd met, and I'd met a great many, seemed continually to be promising never to become attached to anyone closely again. It was too hard to lose a buddy, especially a close buddy, and virtually all men who experience terrible hardship and danger together are likely to become close buddies quite quickly.

I led the others to the upstairs office at the front corner of the second floor of the hotel. They selected numbers they would play later in the day from the names of the records I had. The two looked over the list, finding names which Bill and Ernie could play either from memory or by ear. Generally, Bill, who carried the melody lead, was given the selection privilege.

The three numbers they picked for this particular evening's program were "South of the Border," "Long Ago and Far Away," and "Over the Rainbow."

"Well, if nobody ever hears us," I observed, "we're having ourselves a ball and getting experience, right?"

Both men agreed. And, unspoken in their agreement was the realization that this was a hell of a lot better than a barbed wire enclosure.

"You can say that again," Bill grunted, apparently thinking of his non-musical experience with Humphreys.

We finished our selections and went downstairs for lunch. After eating, I proposed a walk over the bridge above the millpond stream. It was a fully exposed spot so our actions would not be considered suspect by the Germans, yet it was far enough removed from the main road to prevent anyone from overhearing important discussions which looked like simple reminiscing to the casual observer.

We walked silently around the road until we came to the footpath leading to the bridge. As we leaned on the bridge railing, looking down into the millpond, we could see the bubbles in the water just beneath the thinning ice cover. I dropped a pebble and it broke right through the skimpy crust covering the pond. It would be completely melted in another day or two. I just knew it.

We spent a pleasant afternoon chatting and enjoying the sunshine. We reviewed several experiences in uniform. Ernie, having been captured on his first night in combat, was completely unfamiliar with combat conditions and limited his participation in the discussion to some of the hilarious experiences he had had in basic training. But he listened with delight like a small child while Bill and I recounted some of ours.

Bill told of the initial hedgerow battles he'd been through shortly after the Normandy landings. The Germans apparently had been last-ditching all the way because it sounded very much like the type of combat I knew well — the type which made a man of a boy extremely quickly, provided he lived through it.

"Hey, Hal," Ernie said excitedly. "What about that Dago army? I heard from a 1st Division guy in England that they were worth their weight in sheepdip."

"Well, that was one of the few funny things about both the African and Sicilian campaigns," I replied. "They did some damage, of course, but I don't think their hearts really were in this war. It was Germany's fight and the Italians knew it. They were treated like poor relations by the Krauts, you know. Anyway, most of them I saw were like comic opera soldiers whenever we ran into them. I can remember several times when we were on forced marches or jeep patrols in Africa. I was first scout in a rifle company at the time. I'd be out about a hundred yards or so ahead of the company on point when a machine gun would open up on me. I'd hit the ditch and fire one short blast from my Tommy gun and, damned, those guys would come charging out of their gun emplacement with their hands in the air. They weren't any real problem. There was one night when a bunch of them scared me nearly shitless, though . . ."

The Sicilian campaign was nearing the end of its thirty-fourth day, four days short of its ultimate conclusion, although none of us fully realized how close the end was, of course. My regiment was in division reserve for a change. In fact, it was the first time during the entire campaign that we'd been given that exalted position.

Four of my buddies and I had drawn the midnight to 4:00 A.M. guard detail at a hastily constructed prisoner stockade. The prison enclosure consisted of nothing more than five criss-crossed strands of barbed wire strung between four-inch wooden stakes, ten feet high and placed about fifteen feet apart.

There had been no time or real necessity to construct corner machine gun towers. The guards simply patrolled the outer perimeter of the enclosure in pairs except for the single man posted at the wide double-gate entrance to the stockade.

There were approximately 250 Italian prisoners inside the wire. On the night in question, all were asleep and everything was still. I had taken the gate guard post. I was seated on the ground, facing the gate from a vantage point about twenty feet in front of it, where I was able to lean against some large boulders, my Tommy gun across my raised knees, and keep an eye on the camp as well as hear any sound for a long way around.

This was a quiet period, the first such we had seen since the landings to the south at Likata more than a month before. I was enjoying a cigarette as I pondered how the rest of the division was making out in its drive eastward toward Palermo. Occasionally, the distant thunder of the big guns would roll across the clear night sky.

It was the first time in nearly five weeks that my buddies and I had felt even relatively secure. The nearest representation of the loosely defined lines, then extremely static in nature, couldn't have been nearer than fifteen miles away.

Suddenly, I sensed a new sound. I tensed, alert and frightened. It was distant, rhythmic stamping. I checked my watch. The combination of bright moonlight and luminous dial told me it was three minutes before 0300. I nervously listened for the pattern as it grew louder. There could be no doubt about it — it was the sound of the precision marching of hobnailed boots.

I knew there were no British troops in this sector, they having gone north along the east end of the island. And Americans did not use hobnails. This had to be either Germans or Italians, both of whom did.

I arose and moved toward the gate, anxiously searching the vague area to my front in the bright moonlight. I sounded out the direction of the marchers. They were approaching from the north, from the direction of the battles we could hear in the distance.

The ancient Roman road that ran beside the stockade disappeared around a bend about 200 yards to the south of the camp where there was a small village. About the same distance to the north, it rolled through a thick olive grove whose trees shaded the road surface itself. This made any movement farther away invisible from where I stood. I looked about quickly to check the positions of the four other guards. Only those on the west side of the stockade had heard the noise and were running around the corner of the enclosure to check with me. The other two were at the distant rear wall.

"What the hell is that, Hal?" asked Navison, the stringy, hawk-faced Californian who had joined our section only two weeks before.

"I'm not sure, but we know damn well they're not ours," I replied quietly.

Diston, the quiet, mild-mannered old fellow from Woodstock, Illinois, came up from the other side. He was one of the two men in the company who shared the dubious distinction of being called "Pop" by the men — respectfully, of course. That happened when a man reached the dignified and venerable age of thirty-five. "Pop" Diston was thirty-eight.

"What could we do against so many of 'em, Corporal Lister?" he asked, his voice level with concern.

"I'm not quite sure. But I'm sure of one thing. That sounds like at least a company."

"Oh, God," Navison said, his voice quavering.

"Well, if they're coming to liberate this bunch of clowns in here, they're welcome to them. I have no intentions of fighting that big a crowd for the privilege of hanging on to these guys in the stockade. Here, Navison, get back to the CP in the village quick. Wake up Captain Savaresy. Tell him what we heard. I don't know what we can do about it, but he has to know anyway. The rest of the outfit's spread all over hell and gone in these hills around here."

I pointed to the boulders to our front. "Pop, just in case there is something we can do, you'd better take cover behind those rocks over there. Don't fire unless you have to. Wait until you can see what's happening. And Navison, as you go past the rear of the stockade, tell Fortino and Adams to get up here on the double. Now take off!"

Navison disappeared around the front corner of the stockade fence. Hardly had he left when I saw the vanguard of the marching body of men approaching from the shadows of the olive grove. They still were too far away for me to distinguish nationality, despite the bright moonlight in a cloudless sky.

I felt very apprehensive in the knowledge that, at best, all I could depend on in a fire fight would be four Tommy guns. The rest of the regiment was spread over a four-mile area, most of them billeted in farm houses and barns in groups of squad strength or less. There was no telling where any of them or other support troops might be at this moment. But if a fight did start, I was sure the noise would attract many others.

At the moment, however, my three remaining guards and I were pretty much on our own, I guessed. There had been no vehicular traffic on the road since shortly after my guard shift had begun at midnight. There were no communications here either, except runner service which I had employed through Navison. I prayed quietly.

I felt my heart pounding and a slight pain begin in my chest. The pain of fear that I had known so many times before, especially under a heavy artillery barrage or during a frontal attack against an enemy-held position, was with me again. It was the constant fear of the unknown when some danger was in the vicinity. Subconsciously, I flicked off the safety catch on the left side of the Tommy with my right thumb, bringing the weapon to port across my chest.

Just then, with the columns of troops, at least a battalion, I now realized, less than fifty yards from me, their helmets shining in unison as far back as my eye could see down the road, I heard the call to halt in a loud voice and, thankfully, one I recognized as Italian.

At least these weren't Krauts. I could see the long lines of heavily equipped men in uniform, their rifle barrels gleaming in the bright moonlight behind their shoulders. They wore full fieldpacks as far as I could make out. I estimated the number at over 1,000 men! The rear elements hadn't emerged from the olive grove into the moonlight, and there was no telling how far back beyond that this column went.

A single figure detached himself from his spot at the left front of the massive column and approached me. I guessed it would be an officer. The man carried no rifle but wore a pistol holster on his belt. I could see the light-colored leather of it shining in the moonlight. He also wore jodhpurs and high, shining, leather boots. He stopped only a few yards from me and asked in faltering English.

"Is this Americano?"

I fingered the trigger of my weapon nervously, pondering the possibility of holding this officer hostage, or of killing him and hoping that might leave the soldiers on the road in some disarray. I still hadn't brought my weapon down from its port position so that, instead of covering the Italian officer, my gun was pointing into the air to my upper left side.

"Yes, sir. *Si, si,*" I stammered.

"*Bueno.* I am Captain Fransconetti. I wish to surrender my battalion."

My mouth suddenly filled with nervous saliva. I swallowed hard. Falteringly, I asked, "Er, how many men do you have, Captain?"

"*Chenta* . . . er, six hundred forty," the officer replied.

I reacted automatically. Without thinking of what I was saying, I blurted out, "Oh, I'm sorry, sir. We don't have room for that many here."

The officer pondered the situation for a moment. He looked back at his men, then into the stockade itself. He stroked his chin, pushed back the stiff-brimmed dress cap, and looked back at me.

"Where we go, then?"

It was a ridiculous situation. Here was this captain with the better part of a whole battalion of troops who wanted to surrender. It was three o'clock in the morning. They were tired, having walked a long way, and standing, heavily laden in the moonlight. And here I was, refusing him admittance to a prison stockade.

"The next encampment is about eight kilometers down this road, that way," I pointed toward the village.

"*Molto bueno.* We go there." The officer turned to return to his troops.

"Oh, Captain," I called to him, stopping him in his tracks. "Before you go, would you all leave your weapons here, please?" I brought my Tommy gun down to my side, pointing at the officer.

"Ah, *si, si,*" he replied jovially. Neither of us seemed to be aware of the total incongruity of the situation. He bellowed a command to his troops in Italian.

At once, the nearest column moved forward toward the stockade in single file. They approached the point directly before the captain, dropped their rifles and other weapons in a pile, and returned to their positions at the road. Column by column, all six hundred-plus Italian soldiers made the round trip, rapidly adding to the growing pile of rifles, submachine guns, pistol belts, ammunition bandoliers, and grenades, as well as three light machine guns and mortars with base plates.

Among the last few to file by were four men each carrying parts to these heavier weapons. These, too, were dumped unceremoniously. The entire operation took about twenty-five minutes. Once every one of the Italians was reorganized back on the road, the captain turned to me, carefully unbuckled his belt and dropped it, the holster with pistol in it, and an extra clip of ammunition onto the stack. Then he turned and saluted me. I returned the salute after awkwardly switching my Tommy gun from my right to my left hand.

The captain, with great dignity and standing fully erect, turned his head toward his men and resolutely marched back to the head of the column. He gave the commands for attention and forward march and led his happy army off down the road in the direction of the village and the next stockade.

Pop Diston staggered out from his hiding place. The others also joined me. The four of us stood, our mouths agape at what we'd just experienced. We looked after the disappearing column of men as it passed before us and moved off into the distance. A song began farther down the line and was picked up by the men at the rear of the line, a marching song whose cadence helped lift spirits and keep them in step.

Pop patted me on the arm. I was still slightly dazed as I turned to the older man. Diston asked quietly, his eyes still on the vast accumulation of weapons, "How in hell are you going to explain this to Captain Sevaresy?"

I, too, was hypnotized by the large cache of arms.

"Damned if I know, Pop. I was standing here through that whole thing and still don't believe it."

"That was the god-damnedest thing I ever saw," said Restivo, his voice filled with awe.

Then the complete absurdity of the situation struck all of us virtually simultaneously. The giggling began with Diston. Then I picked it up, and with mounting volume, we burst into raucous laughter, beating each other on the backs with wild hilarity. The night, suddenly alive with our gleeful shouts, seemed to move into the stockade and, for the first time, some of our prisoners, asleep in their pup tents, began to stir, looking out at us curiously.

"Hey, Hal," Adams called from the far side of the pile. "How about you? Here you just about captured the whole goddamned eye-talian army single-handed. Maybe you'll get a medal or somethin'!"

"More likely a court-martial," Fortino laughed. "If I know them Paisanos, they're shackin' up in that village right now before they take off for the stockade. Us Dagos are hot-blooded, you know. Romance gives us strenth." He pronounced it without the "g."

I looked away from the others and back to the pile of weapons.

"I'll be a son of a bitch!" I said quietly and to nobody in particular.

"You mean to say that 600 of 'em just gave up like that?" Ernie asked, incredulous.

"So help me," I assured him. "Thank God they were Guineas, though. I'd hate like hell to think of how a gang of Krauts that big would have stomped us into the ground. They'd probably have shot our prisoners to boot."

"Did you get a medal for that deal?" he asked.

"No, but I didn't get a court-martial either," I smiled. "I kinda figured I came out even on the exchange."

Bill entered the discussion for the first time.

"Hey, Hal, when did you get that?" He pointed to one of the two ribbons sewed above the left pocket of my shirt, visible now that my combat jacket was hanging open. "That's the Purple Heart, isn't it?"

"Yeah, the old Purple Turd."

"With a meatball cluster," Ernie chimed in. "I heard a guy in my outfit call it that."

"Yeah, they give you a cluster for each additional wound, instead of another medal. Kinda chicken shit, I'd say."

"You were wounded twice?" Ernie continued.

"Three times. I was hit again when I was captured this time, back near Kolmar."

"Jeez, three times!" Bill said, amazed.

"Holy shit! I'll say!" Ernie said, a new look of respect crossing his face.

"I'll say, too," I chided them.

"Any of 'em bad?" Ernie persisted.

"No, not really. The worst was the first one. We were on OP duty on the Anzio Beachhead last February. That's the only one that really bothers me. I was buried for two and one-half hours in a sitting position with huge weights on my back before they dug me out. My back still gives me a lotta grief."

I settled back to remember.

15.   Four Damn Naked Fingers

THE SIX OF US from the First Squad of the regimental intelligence and reconnaissance platoon had settled comfortably in what had been a small storage room on the north side of a farmhouse. Sergeant Tickler was assigning the Observation Post schedule.

"Lister, you and Nottingham take the first watch as soon as it gets light. No more than three hours at a time or you'll start seein' things that ain't there. That'll give you six hours off before your next shift. That way, nobody'll have to pull more than two a day. No point in night OPs up there. The rifle companies have their outposts out."

"Shouldn't we get our equipment upstairs right away before daylight, Tick?" I asked.

"No, I'd just as soon you don't set up till after daylight. You can go up and check it out if you want, but you ain't about to see anything in the dark and you can't use flashlights up there. Anyway, that lieutenant in that tank we passed a while back told me that the Krauts zero in on all these points up here every morning at dawn. They start with that burned out tank we passed down the road. Then they move over to the road junction we crossed on the way past that checkout point, and finally, a couple of minutes later, they lay a couple on this house and what's left of the next one down the line."

"You mean just to zero in their guns?" Fortino asked. "What a waste of good ammo."

"Come on, you jerk," Tickler countered. "I wish to hell they'd use all their damn ammo for zeroin' in. That way, nobody'd get hurt much. Well, anyway, once they start, they go through this routine every morning. At least, that's what that tanker officer said. Then, once they finish their rounds of shelling, you can get your stuff upstairs. Anyway, it's better to wait until the dust settles after the shelling stops."

"What time you got, Sarge?" McCullough asked.

Tickler checked his watch. "I make it 0345. That means about an hour and a half till daylight. Let's have a cuppa coffee before we sack in. Here, you two guys might as well take ten with us."

"Judge" Nottingham and I put down the equipment we had been holding, preparatory to moving it to the bottom of the stairs in the outside hallway. Judge had the SC-300 radio; I had been carrying the map board, the scope, and its bipod. Judge also had the binocular case hanging around his neck. Our Tommy guns had been stacked against the wall immediately after we entered the house.

Judge was proficient at heating water faster than anyone else in the section. He took the small, portable carbide stove from McCullough and had the fire going with an incredibly bright, white light under a full canteen cup of water. Judge had the charming accent and demeanor of his native Lynchburg, Virginia, and was the butt of constant good-natured jokes as a result.

He had graduated from Virginia Military Institute and, as a result, was better organized militarily than any of the rest of us. We were sure he'd be promoted rapidly as soon as his skills were recognized.

We had barricaded ourselves in this little first-floor room that served the former occupants of the house as some sort of supply room. Several large bags of grain were stacked in one corner of the room. Tickler ordered two of them stacked on the wide window sill in front of the blanket in order to provide additional protection against shell fragments. We struggled with their dead weight, but felt considerably more secure once they were in place against the window.

We had arrived at the house in the dark less than an hour before. The squad we were relieving had just pulled out and was headed back to the Command Post, nearly five miles to the rear. On both sides of the house, stretching into distant fields, rifle companies were dug in, their foxholes staggered across the fields. This would seem to offer us additional comfort, knowing that we had considerable, well-armed company nearby. But it also added to our discomfort, realizing as we did that this was as far forward as our troops had moved on the Anzio Beachhead. The enemy was similarly dug in less than 150 yards to our front.

Tickler continued checking the names and figures written on a small pad he had taken from his pocket.

"Gill, you and me'll take the second shift about ten o'clock. Then, Mac, you and Fortino come up in the early afternoon. Now, anybody down here when chow time comes, see to it that the water's on, got it?"

"Hey, Sarge," Judge called lightly, "Watuh's goin' now, that's foah shuah." He removed his canteen cup from the flame and replaced it with the sergeant's. His own was steaming heavily as he tore open the tiny packet of powdered coffee concentrate and poured its contents into the hot water. He reached into his right trousers pocket and extracted an incredibly dusty cube of sugar. Stirring thoughtfully with his trench knife, Judge stared at the cup.

"Gawd dayam," he said aloud, to no one in particular. "Ah shuah would love to have some milk with mah cawfee. Cain't get used to it black somehow."

"Hey, Judge, lemme ring room service for ya," Fortino chided.

According to ritual, Judge finally blew the coffee drinkably cool, sipped from one side, turned the metal canteen cup, and offered me the other side. Meanwhile, Tickler and McCullough were sharing another cup as were Fortino and Gill.

We gingerly approached the strong, black brew. The metal cups retained heat much longer than the liquid within them, it seemed, and one always ran the risk of burning lips and tongue if he were too anxious.

I sat with my back against the wall under the window, lighted my second cigarette, and prepared to enjoy a few moments of relaxation. Tick checked his watch again. He looked around the room to reassure himself that everyone was ready and able to serve. Fortino, Gill, and McCullough already were asleep. Judge was busy adjusting something on his cartridge belt.

Pete Tickler was another of those vanishing citizens I'd met for the first time upon donning khaki. He was the pre-war infantry soldier whose tenure of service and corresponding seniority in the outfit had automatically elevated him from his peacetime Pfc rank to that of tech sergeant in command of a platoon of recon men. He'd held his Pfc stripe for five of his eight pre-war years in uniform. He'd been in the 3rd Division for about ten years and was in his mid-thirties. I swore on occasion that he seemed to resent the war most because he had to associate with so many Johnny-come-latelies, many of them wearing officers' bars or oak leaves on their collars.

Judge and I arose wearily and began strapping on our equipment. Dawn was only minutes away and, as soon as the bombardment was over, we'd have to get our gear upstairs and set up as quickly as possible. Finally, fully loaded, we edged out of the room into the chill darkness of what must have been the equivalent of a living room. There was no furniture, most of it apparently having been burned for warmth by visiting GIs in earlier days on the beachhead. The house was ideally situated as a relief station for the surrounding troops. It was the only two-story building still standing in this part of the beachhead.

Tick quickly closed the door behind us to permit minimal light from escaping. Judge and I had become close friends during our seventeen months together. He was a delightful, serious companion, a well-built, handsome chap with blond, wavy hair. He seldom raised his voice in anger. In fact, the most notable time I could recall was earlier in beachhead days when Judge, in his usual meticulous manner, dug a bunker into the side of a hill.

The rest of us simply dug a two-by-five foxhole about three feet deep, as a rule. But Judge wasn't satisfied with such slipshod housing. Instead, he would dig elaborate quarters. On this particular occasion, he'd literally dug a room, about five feet high, six feet long, and four feet deep. He had cut further into the wall to make a flat bunk on which to sleep and, above it, another indention as a shelf for his toilet articles.

One night, while Judge was on guard duty, a group of us decided to use his room to play poker. We made ourselves as comfortable as possible, secured the double blanket doorway, and lighted a candle.

In the middle of a particularly devastating hand for me, the blanket suddenly was thrust aside and quickly replaced as Judge stormed in.

"Hey, y'all! Get out of mah house!" he shouted in that peculiar Virginia twang. We complied instantly. I, in fact, was delighted because it saved me about eight dollars when the pot was divided evenly among the players.

Judge and I made our way carefully across the dark room in the farmhouse after allowing ourselves a few moments to let our eyes become accustomed to the incredible blackness of the night. The room was rubble-strewn. The building itself, constructed in the regimented pattern of the Anzio Beachhead area, consisted of two identical attached units, backed against each other into a single building. Each single-family unit contained a large, first-floor room in which there was a huge, walk-in fireplace, a family table surrounded by chairs, and cooking pots hanging on pegs around the fireplace.

The only other enclosed room on the ground floor was the storage room in which our squad was billeted. To the rear of the floor, attached to the outside wall of the living room, was an open barn for cattle and farm machinery. It resembled a large, doorless, multi-car garage as seen back in the States.

Sleeping quarters were on the second floor. The houses were built of stucco and stone and were painted in unusual pastel shades. All houses in a given area, apparently a political district of some sort, were painted the same color. In the particular district where our house was situated, each house was painted an attractive yellow. I was not far from the dividing line between this and the next district of the beachhead in which the houses were light green.

Outdoor plumbing still was the order of the day, and the houses contained no running water.

As we passed the fireplace, we observed the still-glowing coals from someone's earlier fire.

"Somebody probably heated coffee here yesterday," I said.

"Golly, that's dangerous, isn't it?" Judge replied.

"They probably used some of that peat we've been seeing in the fields. Remember, we tried it once down near the beach. It stinks like hell, but it burns without black smoke. It just has a little thin, white smoke until the flame catches, remember?"

"Yeah, that's right. I should have known these guys up here would know better than to use smoky fuel this far up."

We found the stairs to the upper story crowded against the far wall. As we climbed, with me in the lead, we came to a large section of the wall that was caved in, probably by repeated shell hits.

"Take it easy here, Judge. Watch your step. There's all sorts of crap here on the steps. The wall probably took a couple of hits right at this spot. Here, let me have the scope."

I reached back to relieve him of the heavy telescope. Judge still had to maneuver the pile of stone and stucco-littered debris on the stairs. We picked our way carefully to the second floor and through the obviously hastily abandoned and litter-strewn bedrooms to the far end of the house, facing the enemy head-on.

Although, technically, three sides of the house faced the enemy on the Anzio Beachhead, surrounded as we were by mountains occupied by German divisions, the enemy to the north was nine miles away, while our southernmost foes were more than four miles away. Only to our direct front, to the east, were we in reasonable proximity to enemy troops. Ten miles behind us lay the Tyrrhenian Sea, our only perimeter not enemy-occupied.

The German front-line elements a short distance from us had riflemen and machine gunners at about 150 yards distant, tanks and light artillery within 500 yards. That much had been observed by earlier OP crews who had transmitted the information to us as we relieved them. The heavier Kraut guns were located farther up and beyond the mountains just ahead of us. Their observers would be located ideally on the hills' forward slopes with superior optical equipment and positions, staring down the throats of the GIs in the forward positions and well able to note virtually any movement anywhere on the beachhead on any clear day. Only constant smoke machines operating in most quarters prevented such direct observations.

The American infantrymen conjectured many times that the combination of equipment and position made it possible for the Kraut observer high on the mountainside to kibitz a front-line card game, being able to read every card.

"OK, Judge, this looks like a pretty good spot right here. There's a big shell hole that goes right through the wall here. It's big enough to mount our scope, and the wall's thick enough to keep it hidden from view." The thickness of the wall, approximately two feet, gave us a convenient ledge on which to stand the bipod.

Satisfied that we could mount an operative OP from this spot, we returned to the business of safeguarding our equipment against the anticipated barrage. We stacked our equipment in the near corner of the room and turned to survey it for anything heavy enough to cover the stack against flying shrapnel. We decided on the heavy metal bed that stood unmade in an opposite corner. Together, we grunted and gasped, pushing the bed frame and heavy springs across the floor until they completely surrounded our optical equipment. Fortunately, the mattress from this bed and from another in the room beyond this were still on the floor. We moved them over to cover the bedstead we'd just moved.

I suddenly noticed that it was getting light gradually. Objects which had only been implied shapes earlier suddenly became identifiable in the first light of early dawn. I looked out of our observation hole and saw that, although the sky was beginning to lighten over the tops of the mountains, the area at their base was shrouded in almost complete darkness and early morning, pre-sunlit mists.

"We have time for a smoke before we go down, don't we?" Judge asked, pulling out his package of Luckies.

We sat in the corner, our backs against the front wall. Judge handed me the pack. Crouching over and covering my head with the blanket hanging from the side of the bed, I lit my cigarette and immediately doused the light. Then, uncovering myself, I sat back up and handed Judge my already lighted smoke. He took it and, carefully cupping it in his hands, pressed the lighted end against the dead end of his own cigarette. He puffed cautiously until his was lighted. Then he returned mine to me.

We sat in silence, enjoying a peaceful break in what promised to be a hectic tour of duty on this scheduled four-day OP.

"What time did Tick say they started zeroing in?" Judge asked, looking down into his folded legs.

"He said about dawn. That's another ten or fifteen minutes, I imagine. But he said they started on that burned-out tank down there and hit the road junction after that before they started on the house. We should have plenty of time to get down."

I arose and looked out of the shell hole again.

"It's beginning to clear. Sun should come over the mountain in a matter of minutes. Uh-oh! Here they come!"

My last remark was punctuated by the scream of the first shell. It rose to an ear-splitting whistle as it roared over the house. It felt as if it missed the roof by scant inches. It landed with a loud report, bursting into long streamers of glaring white smoke against the burned-out shell of a Sherman tank, leaning dizzily into a ditch about 100 yards behind the house. Another shell flew over, hitting the same target dead center.

"Christ, I'll say they're zeroed in. That's two for two!" I said. "There's our cue, buddy. We'd better blow."

We lost no time making for the stairs. We were halfway down the steps when another shell whistled in, smashing with frightful intensity against the slate roof of our house. We didn't pause to duck the flying tiles that showered down on us and the stairway, but continued our descent, two steps at a time. We stumbled across the living room just as another shell roared in, sounding for all the world like an express train at high speed.

Instinctively, Judge passed me going into the store room, shoving me into the relatively protective depression of the fireplace just as the second shell smashed into the building. The explosion was deafening and the room was filled with smoke and debris. Years of accumulated soot and dirt from within the chimney cascaded down on me, covering me with thick layers of dirt.

"Goddamn them!" I shouted to the whole world. "They almost put that one in my back pocket!"

I assumed they were through, having hit the building clearly with both shells. As if in direct contradiction to my last thought, another whine was heard. But this one wasn't coming right at us. Instead, it sounded as if it were going right past the house instead of over it. Through the broken rear door to the barn, I could see down the slope to the road junction in the distance. The shell exploded right in the middle of the junction, about seventy-five yards distant. The next high velocity shell was on its way to the same target as I entered the small store room.

"What the hell's wrong with you guys?" Tick screamed. He had been ducking with the rest of the fellows during the few seconds of the barrage. As soon as the shelling stopped, he stood upright and looked for us. He found Judge on the floor, and me bursting through the door of the room.

"We thought for sure you had it up there. Why in the hell didn't you come down before it started?" he shouted.

I smiled and, with an exaggerated salute that indicated more bravado than I felt, I replied, "We're here, no? So what's to holler, Sergeant Boss, sir?"

"Anyway, those finks fired out of sequence this mahnin'," Judge complained. "They were supposed to hit us after the road junction."

"Well, gentlemen, I suggest you go complain to Mr. Hitler or somebody, not to me. And if you two ain't got the sense to come in out of a barrage, fuck ya!"

He looked at the others in the small room. "And the rest o' you rummies get the hell out of there from now on if you're on when it starts to get light. We don't want to lose anybody on this trip. It'd mean double shifts for everybody else," Tickler concluded, not unkindly.

"Yeah, and who'd clean up the mess?" Fortino added his two cents' worth.

Gill couldn't resist getting into the game at this point. "With my usual run of luck, I'd probably get stuck with scraping you guys off the wall. So pay attention to the sergeant, you fatheads!"

Several of the others hooted derisively. Gill's luck had been phenomenal so far. He was especially lucky at the gaming tables. Few were the men in headquarters company whose names were not entered in his little black book of debtors. I was into him for about $57.

Judge held up two canteen cups of steaming coffee. "Heah, Hal, ah fixed yuh cawfee."

I took mine and sat on the bags of grain to drink the hot, powdered muck. "Thanks, Judge. It'll hit the spot."

"Aw right, you two!" Tickler brought us back to reality. "Who the hell do you think you are? General Truscott or somebody? This ain't no rest center, and you ain't on no damn furlough. Get your asses back upstairs to that fuckin' OP! And watch your steps!" he shouted at us with a studied gruffness. We all knew this was bluff on Tick's part. He hurt every time one of our people got a slug or shell fragment wound. He died a little each time one of his men failed to return from a patrol, particularly if it had been at his order that the group went out. "C'mon, git! What if the whole regiment of Krauts was sneakin' up on us right now, and you not there to see 'em?"

"Hey, Sarge. You been seein' too many of them war movies. Anyway, let 'em come. I want to interrogate every one of them bastards till I find out which one of the sons of bitches invented that goddamn eighty-eight!" Fortino said as he blew on his coffee trying to bring it down to drinkable temperature.

"Besides," I teased, "don't worry about a thing, Tick. If there are any nasty old Krauts out there, we'll protect you." I laughed as I put down my cup and dashed out of the door just in time to escape being hit by Tickler's heavy combat boot.

Tick had been one of the few old-timers to make it this far. He'd come up through the ranks after steady combat, and had been wounded twice so far. I figured I would be due to replace him if the old fellow ever left on his long overdue rotation to the States. I was senior corporal in the platoon and, in all likelihood, would rate the next platoon sergeancy that opened. I wasn't sure I wanted it, though. There was the added, terrible responsibility of the entire platoon rather than one small squad, which was bad enough. Furthermore, I had seen many good men go down in a platoon sergeant's role. They were expendable as hell in an outfit such as this.

Tickler had replaced Sgt. Keith Taylor when Taylor was promoted to lieutenant by field commission. Before that, Rogerson was the sergeant and he failed to return from a patrol. Rogerson was the fourth sergeant to get it in close action since the outfit arrived overseas. I didn't relish those odds.

We discovered a mess when we returned to the upstairs bedroom. Pieces of the well-ventilated roof now were all over the room. The red tiles were brittle as hell and cracked into tiny pieces when they fell to the hard floor. Fortunately, the radio and scope were safe beneath the bed where we'd hidden them. Judge dragged out the scope and handed it to me. I set it up while he was getting the radio operative on the bed.

Meanwhile, I was adjusting the telescope on its bipod. Everything seemed to be in order as far as the equipment was concerned. I withdrew the scope lens cover and dusted the lens carefully. We were ready for our tour on OP duty.

"Hey, Hal, what are we hooked up to?" Judge asked.

"Regiment," I answered, without looking at him.

"The Long Toms? No kiddin'. I love those big babies. The only thing is, I gotta talk to that damn Feldstein. I cain't make head nor tail outta what he says half the time."

The Long Toms were the big 155-millimeter rifles which the Germans called "whispering death." Their whistle wasn't as loud as the howitzers, nor as raucous as and only a little louder than the chemical mortars. But their psychological impact and high explosive potency was famous throughout the theater.

Normally, Long Tom fire was directed principally by observers in tiny Piper Cub airplanes. These would hover gracefully and stubbornly over the enemy rear areas. This was because the big guns had much longer range than the howitzers. The Cubs could get much farther back than a foot soldier could. It also could get an overview that was more important than a simple ground view. The circumstances on the beachhead at this point, however, made any available type of fire direction practical for any of the weapons.

The rest of our shift passed quickly with nothing to report except an occasional Kraut soldier washing his socks in a water-filled shell hole. Nothing worth calling in artillery for, we figured.

The same was true for the rest of the day as each succeeding shift stood its three-hour tour. As dusk settled over the beachhead, Tickler announced, "OK, let's wrap 'er up for today. No point in anybody else goin' up. Can't see anything anyway. It's gettin' too dark now. Besides, the rifle company outposts are on duty."

McCullough, as a member of the last crew to stand OP, came down last. He had carefully packed the radio and scope back under the bed before leaving his post.

As soon as the six of us were reassembled in the small store room, Gill took his customary advantage. He reached into the left breast pocket of his combat jacket and removed a handful of its contents. Sorting out his rosary and a pack of cigarettes, he put these objects back into the pocket. He kept out only the blue-backed deck of Bicycle playing cards, well-worn, which had been so good to him.

"All rightee, gentlemen. Anyone for a little poker, hearts, gin, whist, or what have you? I'll play blackjack, if you like. Table stakes if you please. Remember, if you don't play, you can't win."

"Up your giggy, Josie, boy," Fortino answered. "You're into me now for three months back pay."

"OK, Frankie, m'lad. Here's your chance to get it back. What do you say, little paisan buddy?"

Fortino looked around. "Anybody else gonna play with this robber?"

Tickler and McCullough agreed to play. I offered to join the game for a short while. There was nothing else to do. The game got under way and proceeded on a fairly even basis until just after midnight.

"That does it for me," Tick finally said, stretching and yawning. "I gotta go to work in the morning." He picked up the score pad he had been using. "Come on, Judge, you and me first in the mornin'."

"No suh. You and Gill go first, remembah?"

"Oh yeah, that's right. Come on, Lucky. Wrap it up," he said, directing his attention to Gill. "You took us all for enough for one night . . . again."

Gill folded his cards and put them back in their box. Then, dropping the box in his already crowded pocket, he looked at me. "What say, buddy, a little high card out of the deck, double or nothin'?"

"Shit no," I told him. "Not me. I dropped another eight bucks tonight. That makes a total of $65 I owe you now."

"I guess you got the luck of the Irish all right," Gill teased. "And here I thought you Jews had all the money."

"Yeah, that's what I heard," I responded. "But, as the fellow said, 'We been the chosen people for long enough. Let 'em choose somebody else for a while.' "

The group chuckled as they made preparations for sleep.

Streaks of winning or losing luck weren't unusual. During the Sicilian campaign, Gill ran up a debt of more than $2,000 to one of the other men in the company. This debt was wiped out, however, by a single cut of the cards. We often would do the same thing after a particularly lopsided game. We would do it tonight, in all likelihood, before we were through, until my debt was wiped out.

Money meant nothing to us up here. The relaxation and relief from monotony, the deadly boredom of infantry service, did mean something. Even reasonable debts which could be handled out of monthly pay checks — when they were issued — often were nullified by deaths, capture, or hospitalization of either the debtor or the creditor.

The following day proved equally uneventful except for a two-truck convoy Tickler caught trying to leave Cisterna de Littoria, the village to our right and in front about a half mile away. The big guns had done their usual efficient job, coupled with Tick's dependable map coordinates. They left both trucks smashed and funeral pyres of smoke in the middle of the road.

On the morning of February 9, Judge and I drew the second watch. At precisely 11:15 A.M., Judge excitedly called me to the hole in the wall.

"Oh, man, lookee heah. Will you look at that? Ain't that a beautiful sight?"

He was pointing to the sky on our left. I followed the course of his finger and saw, in perfect formation of threes, twelve B-25 Mitchell bombers cutting across the entire front from north to south. Either they were headed for Cassino, still holding up the Allied advance, or they were headed inland to cover British activities.

I watched them with my naked eye, not wishing to take any time to adjust the scope to the high position. The planes were beautiful as they seemed to soar soundlessly across our line of vision.

Suddenly, I started, reached for the scope, and began to scan the ground directly in front of us at the base of the mountain.

"Holy shit! Ack ack!" I called to Judge, who immediately sat down at the radio and turned it on. "It's close too," I added.

I had seen several puffs of black smoke bursting among the planes. I oriented my scope on something on the ground almost directly beneath the flight until I found what I was looking for. I managed to get on target with my second sweep of the glass, just in time to see muzzle flashes from at least three guns, well covered with brush so as to resemble a stand of trees.

"I'll bet those bastards have been there all the time, camouflaged like that," I said aloud. We hadn't seen any signs of those guns in that area before. This probably was due to a lack of adequate targets for that battery so far, at least, during daylight hours. If they fired at night, they'd be harder to locate, even if our OP had been manned at night.

"Judge, get on the horn, quick. Christ! Do I have a target! And good coordinates too!" I shouted in great excitement.

Judge busied himself with the switches and dials necessary to set the radio into operation. He called in the disguised call letters to the artillery base.

"Jig, Ahtem, Thah. This is Able, Dawg, Nayan, Ovuh."

One call was enough. The boys back at regiment were anxious for targets, particularly from the area of the front in which we were operating. It had been a relatively quiet sector the past few days. The receiver crackled with Danny Barber's brittle, lower-east-side New Yorkese.

"OK, Able, Dog, Nan, this is Jig, Item, Tare. It's about time. Come on in. Whatcha got for me?"

I rechecked my coordinates on the map. Then, with my eye back on the scope, I called to Judge.

"Judge, give him the bridge at 70:45 by 31:217. Right 50! Smoke shell, quick!"

Judge relayed the message verbatim and Barber rogered it on his end of the line, telling Judge to stick around.

We heard the soft "puck" of the single gun firing over ten miles to the rear. The sound would have escaped the notice of anyone but a trained artillery observer who was waiting for it. In a fraction of a second, the huge shell whooshed overhead on its way to my coordinates. I held onto the glass excitedly, steadily, waiting for the welcome sight of smoke near the target.

"Holy God! Dead on them! Fire for effect, fire for effect!" I was shouting now. "Give us the whole goddamn battalion! Judge, give 'em the word! Tell 'em!"

Judge quickly repeated the message which, somehow, translated into Lynchburgian as "Fah foe effect, man, fah big, big, big. Yoah raht on tahget!" He returned to me as I dug my nails excitedly into the stone ledge. "What's goin' on out theah, Hal?"

"Jesus, Judge, you won't believe it! That damn smoke shell landed right smack in the middle of that battery, right on it! It blew away all the camouflage, and there they are, sittin' there like four stiff fingers, stickin' right up in the air, pointing at the sky! Four damn naked fingers! God, the Krauts are running around over there like ants on a sugar pile. Here, take a look!"

Judge leaned over to view the scene of our prospective victory, breathless. He didn't touch the scope, knowing I had it zeroed in exactly. Meanwhile, I ran to the head of the stairs.

"Hey, you guys, get the hell up here on the double. Christ Almighty, wait'll you see what we got!"

As I turned to run back to Judge, I could hear the quartets of battery guns firing. The distant foursomes cracked out their beautiful "puck, puck, puck, puck" almost simultaneously. In fact, the fourth crack had hardly sounded when another quartet of the sounds began. Just then the first of the shells whizzed over. It sounded as if each gun in the battalion had put three shells in the air before the first one landed.

I rushed to the scope and nudged Judge aside just in time to catch the entire area of the German guns disappearing into black smoke and flashes of flame. The first four explosions extended into four more until there was no conceivable way of separating the explosions. The entire valley was filled with smoke and flame now. By the time the barrage lifted, I was surrounded by the rest of the crew.

"Whatcha got, buddy?" Tick was at my side.

"Tick, I just got me a whole goddamn battery of eighty-eights! How about that?"

Tickler adjusted the scope to his eye. "How about that, indeed," he murmured.

"Here, lemme see," Gill was shouting excitedly.

"Nothin' to see for a while, Joe," Tick said slowly. "The whole damn thing just blew up over there. Smoke hasn't settled yet."

"God*damn*" Fortino said, admiration in his voice, as it came his turn to look through the scope.

Tick looked through the scope again, anxiously trying to make out the damage. I knew he still wouldn't be able to make out anything in that heavy pall of smoke. But for the experienced old hand at OP operation, the sight of the smoke was enough for vicarious excitement. No trained observer ever wasted battalion fire — especially Long Tom fire — without having an A-1 priority target zeroed in. Tick knew that.

"Now, do me again, slow-like," he said, turning to me with a big grin lighting his face. The others were crowded around the scope.

"This flight of B-25s went over, see. I was watching them. Then, all of a sudden, I see flak puffs up there, right among the planes. I traced the lines to the ground and came on those muzzle blasts flashing over there. Damned if old Barber didn't go and drop his first shell, the smoke shell, right in their lap. He blew away all the camouflage with that one shell! There they were, stickin' straight up in the air like, like . . ."

"Like peckers?" Tick said, smiling.

"Yeah, just like that!" I said, unable to calm down.

The smoke shell, normally used to give the observer an approximate idea of his coordinates' accuracy, gives him the opportunity to direct artillery adjustments, such as "fifty over," meaning, shorten the range fifty yards, or "fifty left," meaning adjust the traverse of the gun to allow for fifty yards to the right.

"Nice coordinatin', buddy boy," Tick said proudly. "Jeez, with the smoke shell, huh?"

His admiration was genuine. The thrill of a direct hit with the first exploratory shell was one which came all too seldom. It had happened to Tick a couple of times, so he understood my enthusiasm. This sort of good fortune depended on proper application of lessons learned in long and tedious practice sessions, a certain basic skill, a good deal of luck and, of course, somebody back at the artillery station who knew his ass from first base.

The excitement of my having sent a single direction to the battery and of reaching the target without having to send a single adjustment in elevation or traverse was becoming contagious.

The radio crackled. Barber's voice crackled through the frantic hubbub.

"All right, youse clowns. Do we get a cigar or what?" Of course, he knew they had hit the target. Otherwise we'd have long since been on the air with readjustments.

Judge picked up the microphone. "Man, if you was heah, ah'd kiss you, no foolin'. That wuz the most beautiful battalion fah ah evah did see."

"You'd kiss me? Big deal. Who needs it? Come on, willya? Give a little. The boys is waitin'."

"Ah sweah to you, pal, y'all just knocked out a whole battery of eighty-eights with those gohjuss Long Toms of yoahs. That's all y'all did!"

There was a slight delay as Barber relayed the message to the gunners and the rest of his crew. Then he was back on the air.

"Say, Judge. I been meanin' to ask you before, but there was so much noise here I near forgot."

"What's that buddy?"

"How do you spell 'far'?"

"Whah, ef-ay-ah."

"Then, how do you spell 'fire'?"

"Whah, ef-ah-ah-ee."

"Why don't you clunks learn to talk English?" Barber taunted. "They both sound the same to me. Fah one! Fer Christ's sake!" He imitated Judge's accent to perfection.

Judge looked genuinely hurt and angry. He retorted, "Why, you damn fool, cain't you tell the diffunce 'tween 'fah' and 'fah'?"

The resulting laughter and general elated confusion in the room cut short the conversation. Fortino excitedly handed me his binoculars which he had unsheathed for the occasion.

"Here you go, you goddamn genius you. The smoke's startin' to clear. Just look at what you done!"

I grabbed the glasses and, bolstering my elbows against the wall, looked searchingly into the thinning smoke. Most of it had either settled or blown away by now. There, in plain view, was what was left of the German death battery which every GI in Europe had come to respect and dread.

The three guns that still pointed skyward were peeled and torn, the other one pointed in a crazy, broken angle off somewhere to the east. There was nobody to fire them even if they hadn't been destroyed. I could see several vehicles, most of them large trucks, probably ammo carriers, burning in the area about the guns.

"Hey, Tick. How many men on the crews of those things?"

"They vary. Usually three, but sometimes, with ammo carriers and attached troops, I've known of as many as eight or ten. And with a battery packed as tight as that one was, buddy, I'll bet you just got yourself about thirty Heinies with that mission. Christ, from the mess over there, it looks like we got their ammo stack too."

The excitement lasted for fully an hour after the dust settled. Meanwhile, the enthusiasm generated by the successful firing mission was transmitted to the nearest foxhole outside of the house. The air was electric with the thrill of success.

The remainder of the day was anticlimactic. Occasional single or double rounds were called for when more than one German soldier appeared at one time in the same place over there. We were just wrapping the blanket which had served as our evening card table when we heard the sound of big engines. They seemed to be behind the house somewhere, toward our rear. All of us stopped breathing momentarily. We were motivated simultaneously by the same paralyzing thought — "Tanks!"

Tick was the first to speak in frightened, whispered tones. "Where the hell is that?"

"Sounds like it's out back someplace," Gill said, his head cocked toward the door of the room.

"Douse that candle," Tick ordered. It was done, and he burst through the door and through the living room toward the barn door. I was at his heels, followed by Fortino.

We crept silently to the door which hung drunkenly from one hinge. Looking through it into the barn, we were horrified by what we saw.

Two huge, two-and-one-half-ton German trucks were just pulling away from the house in the direction of the road to our rear. Three soldiers sat huddled against the closed tailgate of one of them.

In their wake stood a high pile of mortar shells measuring at least six feet in height and at least three layers deep.

"Come back here, you bastards," Tick screamed at them. "Come back here and get this crap out of here!"

Fortino and I stood horrified. The stack stood behind the house, but would be in full view of any Kraut observers on the right flank of the American sector when daylight broke within three or four hours.

"Holy Mother of God," Fortino gasped.

"Those dirty bastards! Those no-good mother-fuckers! Those good-for-shit quartermaster cocksuckers!" Tick was livid. He stamped around trying to come up with an idea, but was too furious to be lucid.

"Christ, Tick, there must be more than 500 rounds in that stack! What the hell are we going to do with them?" I asked.

"We can't cover that stack, that's for damned sure!" Tick said. "It's too damned big!"

"I wonder if we have time to move it," I thought aloud.

Tickler and I immediately looked at our watches simultaneously. Tick groaned.

"Shit," he said, "It's 4:55 A.M. That means less time than it would take to move a third of that stack before it gets light. It must have taken that crew on that truck nearly three hours to unload the goddamn load!" he said.

The truck must have backed in fairly quietly. Either that or the noise of our poker game drowned out the sound of it.

"What do we do, clear out?" Fortino asked.

"No, we can't do that. Not without checkin' with the old man."

"Well, goddamn it, let's do it!" Fortino continued.

"Nope, we're under radio silence except in an emergency."

"For Chrissakes! Don't you consider this an emergency?" Fortino's eyes were bulging at the terrifying thought of the possible consequences of that entire stack blowing at once.

The noise of our shouts and conversation apparently convinced the Germans that a patrol was in progress. The sudden explosion, followed by the whine of the swift shell coming in — the mark of the ultra-high velocity 88 — threw us to the ground defensively. The shell probably came from a tank somewhere within a few hundred yards to our front right. It barely missed the house, exploding in the field behind us.

"Tank," Tick cried from the ground. The three of us rolled rapidly into the barn. "Where'd it hit?"

"There, in the field over there," Fortino whispered, pointing to the burning bush that marked the spot.

The shell obviously had gone past the hosue near the ground. Suddenly another explosion heralded the arrival of another shell. It smashed through the wall on the far side of the house and sounded as if it had exploded just over our heads.

"Holy balls! They're shooting armor piercing!" Tick said.

These were shells that didn't explode on contact. They were of sufficient velocity, and were sufficiently hard-nosed, that they could pierce the armor of another tank before exploding. The three of us dashed into the house where the remainder of the group waited anxiously.

"Damn it, he's gonna hit somethin' if he keeps that up," Tick spat.

Two more shells ripped into the far side of the house, one exploding just above where we huddled together. Our small room was filled with flying dust particles. Then the firing stopped. We felt our way into the living room, finding the dust and smoke stifling. It was hard to breathe, and each of us could taste the acrid fumes burning our nostrils and throats.

"Let's get upstairs. The radio!" Phillips shouted. "Maybe we can catch the captain and get ordered out of here before daylight."

He and I dashed for the stairs and stumbled up them, feeling our way through the mass of broken furniture and chunks of stucco and roof tiles. We had difficulty getting to the second floor because of the new piles of debris on the steps. One of the shells had pierced the wall at the top of the stairs, showering more stone and mortar on the steps below. The second floor was even worse. It had taken three direct hits. Now there were four holes we could use for observation where before there had only been one.

The furniture in the room was smashed by large beams which had crashed down when the supporting wall was knocked out. Somewhere under all this debris was our valuable equipment. We dug furiously trying to find the radio in the dark. It was our only link with the rear and the CP. Our only hope was to retrieve it before the dreaded dawn barrage began. We searched for endless minutes. Suddenly, I found what was left of the rectangular green box.

"Here's the radio, Tick."

"Is it OK?"

"It's smashed to hell." I sat back, utterly dejected.

"Well, that's that. We're shit out of luck. Come on, let's get back down. We might be able to make it back before daylight."

Tick stopped talking suddenly as we both realized with horror that, in the frenzy of our searching, we hadn't noticed the gradually brightening sky. It was becoming daylight, right now! The barrage would be on its way momentarily. However, this morning's barrage sure as hell wouldn't be just the usual feeler operation. They would go for broke this morning with that stack of mortar ammo piled in the back yard, lying in plain view of any observer to our side.

"Get down there. Let's get those people into foxholes outside." Tick shouted, galvanizing himself into the decisive action. He had made his decision. I hoped it was in time. I took the last four steps at a single leap.

"Outside, everybody!" Tick was shouting. "Get into a hole with the riflemen outside. Get away from the building!" He was trying to herd them out of the room.

The entire group, almost as one man, was nearly at the door of the house when the first few shells roared in simultaneously. They churned up the ground and the edges of the building, turning the entire yard into an inferno of razor-sharp, white hot pieces of spinning steel. Other shells could be heard coming in, many of them from other directions. We'd had it. There was no way we were going to make it to the foxholes. The entire yard was erupting into a mass of furiously exploding metal.

We dashed back into the supply room and positioned ourselves hurriedly around its thick walls, first bracing them with the remaining bags of grain.

The shelling grew in intensity. Explosions now came so close together that it was impossible to count them. The six of us sat and stood helplessly looking at each other, undisguised fear on every face. We could do nothing but pray. There was no way we could help ourselves. Nothing could live through that barrage out there, and that cut off our only chance to leave the building. It was sure death to leave the house, almost certainly equally sure death to stay.

Fortino and Judge sat side by side against one wall of the room. I sat beneath the window with Gill lying beside me, his head resting almost on my lap. McCullough sat alone against the far wall. Tick stood in the far corner.

Tickler reached almost subconsciously into his right shirt pocket and extracted a pack of matches and a single cigarette. He applied the flame to the cigarette and dragged deeply. Then, as if a second thought occurred to him, he reached into his pocket again, withdrawing the entire pack. He tossed it to McCullough, who caught it with one hand, then took one cigarette and lit it, exhaling the smoke through his nose. He tossed the pack across the room to Fortino, who took one cigarette, and held out the pack to Judge. Fortino tossed the pack to me. I took two cigarettes, holding them side by side in my mouth. I had seen Paul Henreid do that for himself and Bette Davis in *Now Voyager* while I was at a camp in Africa.

I lighted both smokes, withdrew one and handed it to Gill, who put it in his mouth absently.

The intensity of the shelling continued undiminished.

"How long, Sarge?" asked McCullough, as if hoping Tick could call off the shelling with an order.

"Can't tell, Mac. Can't tell. Better pray they hit the stack and spread the shells all over hell and gone, rather than setting fire to it where it stands."

The silence suddenly was overwhelming. Each of us knew what was likely to be coming. None could prevent it. We waited. The shelling stopped suddenly, even though there was no major explosion. Finally, even echoes disappeared. The silence was absolutely deafening.

"What's that?" Fortino asked. He had realized the arrival of the sudden stillness.

"Now, why would they stop right in the middle . . .?" I paused to listen.

Fortino looked at me, his eyes bulging again. "Hey, do you suppose . . ."

The experience seemed soundless. The roof simply fell in, literally. There was no noise other than a hissing sound. Then there was a sudden and frightful pressure on my neck. My entire upper trunk was forced forward as if someone were behind me as I sat there, pushing with considerable force. I couldn't move.

It took forever, it seemed, for me to realize that I was buried, helpless. My helmet had been forced forward on my head so that it came down over my eyes. All I could see below the rim of it were small stones and pieces of plaster.

I felt a burning sensation in my right foot, but decided that just feeling it was a good sign. I tried to wiggle my toes. They moved within my combat boot. My leg wasn't broken, at least. My left leg was drawn up and a wiggle of those toes convinced me that it was whole too. My right arm was pinned against my side and my left was pinned in a doubled-up position in front of me. My wrist was just beneath the helmet's edge. I couldn't recall how I had been sitting those centuries ago when the event happened.

I could hear distant shouting. I couldn't make out the words. I heard groans, but couldn't tell where or whose they were. I tried to shout, but the words stuck in my throat, thanks to the queer angle at which my head had been forced forward.

I couldn't move my head up, down or to either side. There was a severe pain in my lower right back. I thought it must be from the pressure of that bag of grain that had been on the window sill. I believed at first that a shell probably had exploded in the window, throwing pieces of stone and the grain bag down on me.

"Tick," I called as loudly as I could. It came out little more than a croak. "Tick, what happened? Where are you?"

I listened, desperate. Nothing. Absolutely no sound except somebody's distant moaning. Then I heard something, nearer, more distinct. Listening carefully, I recognized Joe Gill's voice. It was muffled. Just below me and to the left slightly, his head leaned against my hip, Joe was saying something. He was alive! I couldn't decipher his words, but called out to him.

"Joe, Joe, are you all right?"

"Hail Mary, full of grace . . ."

I couldn't see anything. But I could move the fingers on my left hand a little. I moved them as far as possible, which was about to the second joint. Reaching ahead an inch and a half, I pulled a small piece of mortar out of place. Two pieces slid down to replace it. Suddenly, I was aware of a tiny, thin ray of light hanging right in front of me, filled with dust particles. Where there was light there had to be air.

"Hang on, Joe. We've got air. Can you hear me, Joe?"

". . . Hallowed be Thy name . . ."

"Hang on, Joe. Don't give up. Don't panic, Joe!"

"This is the end. Oh, Jesus, forgive me my sins. Our father . . ."

I listened in sheer desperation. Somebody had to come. Somewhere out there men were shouting. They had to come. And then, it suddenly dawned on me. There was no need to panic. Joe had air, obviously. His interminable prayers continued apace. All I had to do was live with the prayers until we were dug out.

"Hey, you guys over there. Hey, you guys. Over here. We're over here. There are men buried under here. They're alive. Hey, you . . . No, no! Over here. They're alive under here. Quickly!"

It was Tick's voice. I couldn't imagine how he managed to be able to see the people he was talking to, but it was obvious he could. I couldn't imagine, even now, how this situation looked from outside the house. But I was sure there was more than just that bag of grain pressing down on me.

I heard other voices filtering through the debris now. I could feel movement above me and occasional added weight to the burden on my back. Debris shifted about me. Tick's voice came through again, closer this time.

"Hey, take it easy. There are two guys trapped right under where you guys are standing!"

I felt rather than saw the light beam broaden. Then, suddenly, the world exploded into brightness all about my head as a large piece of masonry, then the grain bag were pulled off. I still couldn't see anything clearly, but knew that many anxious hands were working furiously to get us out.

"Donny, grab that end of the bag there," I heard a man say.

Someone lifted the helmet off my head. My head was free. I gulped huge mouthfuls of relatively clean air, seemingly unable to get enough.

"Hey, down below me to my left." I nodded my head in that direction. "There's a guy who can't breathe. Hang on, Joe, they're coming. It won't be long now!"

The men dug furiously beside me.

"Glory be to the Father . . ."

Ending the long story I had been telling Ernie and Bill, I shuddered involuntarily as I recalled the two and a half hours it took to be rescued from my living tomb.

"Did you all get out?" Ernie was asking. Both he and Bill had been sitting entranced by the narrative.

"Five of our fellows made it. McCullough's skull was crushed by part of the chimney. The roof simply opened; most of the house went about 100 feet into the air and then crashed back down. The doggies in the front lines there couldn't believe anybody lived through when those shells exploded . . . or imploded, I guess you'd have to say. Anyway, the house sort of blew in rather than out. Then we heard that there had been sixteen guys from the 1st Batallion billeted on the other side of the house. None of them were killed in that explosion. And, just think, if Tickler hadn't been standing when it happened, his head and shoulders wouldn't have been showing for him to direct the rescue and operations. You see, the entire two-story house was leveled to about four feet from the ground!" I told them.

"Jeez! And while you were being rescued, right out in the open and all like that, didn't the Krauts see the activity?" Bill persisted.

"That was the funny part of it," I said. "They couldn't have helped seeing it. The rifle company boys told us later there were about thirty GIs scurrying around, digging like mad in broad daylight and in plain sight of the Kraut lines. The whole time, though, during that entire two and one-half hours, not a single bullet or shell was fired at

226

the house from the other side. Finally, when all survivors were out, we helped each other limp back to the rear. Only then did they lay in a barrage at the next farmhouse a couple of hundred yards away. There were two tank destroyers in the yard over there."

"Christ!" Ernie said.

"You said it," I replied thoughtfully.

16. A Little Trouble Last Night

In the late news broadcast the night before, I was delighted to hear that Stuttgart had fallen to the 3rd Division. That would simplify our reentry to our own lines.

I was in a hurry to get to the hotel. It was imperative that I get Ernie and Bill briefed on the news as soon as possible.

Bruckmann was the only occupant of the dining room as I entered. The big man looked very preoccupied this morning. He sat staring into his coffee cup, oblivious to my entrance.

"Good morning," I said.

"Ah, how are you, my boy? I've been waiting for you. There is something we must discuss immediately."

"What's up?" I asked, afraid that our rumored escape might have reached his ears.

"There was a little trouble last night," he explained. "Oh, nothing serious, of course," he added hastily. A little too hastily, I thought.

"What sort of trouble?"

"*Ach,* it's that fool, Best. You know how emotionally unstable he often is. Well, last night, late, he went completely out of his head. We had a bit of an argument. It was nothing too serious, but that fool had the audacity to threaten me. Me! Can you imagine?"

"What was it all about?" I asked, trying not to appear too anxious.

"Oh, it was nothing important even. But I would be careful if I were you. You came into the discussion and I thought you ought to know that he plans to send you and your comrades back to the prison camp, or worse. And he plans to send Christianne away right away."

"Christianne? But why?"

"Well, I don't know if you noticed, but he has had his eye on her for some time. But she paid no attention to him. Then, he saw you walking with her on two, three occasions. His reason was that it isn't proper to give a prisoner of war such freedom as the three of you have."

"Well, what of it? Christianne isn't German."

"Nevertheless, you were enjoying yourself when he saw you and that is unforgivable in his eyes. Even more unpardonable is the fact that she seemed to be enjoying your company too. He puts up with you, he claims, only because I insist. My 'verdamte Amerikaner,' he calls you. He was absolutely livid. His face got all red. He simply lost his head, as you say. He must have awakened everyone in the building with his damned insane screaming. Oh, the man absolutely infuriates me!"

I had a frightening premonition. "Where is he now?" I asked.

"I don't really know. I left the hotel early this morning to avoid seeing him. He was gone when I returned a few moments ago."

"Will you tell me something, Helmut?" I asked.

It was the first time lately I had used his first name. He received it with no apparent notice. Instead, the big man simply stared dreamily into his cup.

"What is it?" he quietly asked, finally.

"Who is actually in charge here? You or Best?"

Bruckmann was silent for a moment, in studied reflection. He looked out of the window at the water rushing madly downhill beneath the bridge. The melting snow on the banks was sliding into the growing rapids. Spring was well along.

"I suppose you might as well know now," he began, wearily. "It would have to come out sooner or later. Obviously, this ridiculous uniform is merely a disguise, a subterfuge, you might say. But it was enough to make our dear *hauptstormfuhrer* forget his place for a few moments. He couldn't stand the thought that I was intelligent enough to stay out of those silly shooting companies. Instead, my brain and my experience in the diplomatic corps were utilized.

"I was transferred into the foreign ministry, the propaganda office. I have been there now four years. They sent me around Germany to organize radio stations. I was to go to Köln, er Cologne, you say, from here. At each station we organized, we used our SS engineer units to do the physical work. Those fellows know their duty. They understand their place — most of them, that is. Then, we were to move on to a new location, always just a little ahead of your troops and those of the other Allied powers. But this is the first time we have had American prisoners working for us. It was my idea because of the information about American soldiers' dissatisfaction with Sally's programs in Italy. I thought an American soldier would sound more realistic to his comrades than someone like that fool, George, in Italy.

"Well, anyhow, Best is the first combat-experienced commandant so far I've had under me. His job was to coordinate the efforts of the engineering troops here. Possibly it is because he is basically an infantry officer, not an engineer, which caused him to be the first commandant to give me any trouble. When he was so badly wounded at Ostfront, er, in Russia, they couldn't send him back into battle. So they gave him this cushy administrative post here. He hates it. His entire family was militaristic, the Prussian idiots. It goes back to his great-grandfather or somebody like that who was a general on Franz Josef's staff, or some such silly matter.

"At any rate, now that the American and French armies are so close, he is getting panicky, I think. After all, he is SS, you know, and with his recent promotion, is already a captain. And I am only a lowly Luftwaffe private when I am captured finally, eh?" He winked.

The missing pieces of the puzzle were falling rapidly into place. I was having some of my unasked questions answered well and voluntarily by the principal subject of them. Best stood a good chance of getting a fatal summary court-martial if the French got to him before the Americans, simply because of his black, lightning-bolt uniform. The Americans would probably be much more lenient, but he'd still have considerable music to face, being an officer in the elite guard.

Bruckmann, on the other hand, appeared to have the world by the tail. In his uniform, nobody would suspect he was anything but a displaced enlisted man.

"Are you going to stay here until the Allies come through?" I asked with more casualness than I felt.

"I don't know, really," he replied. "I may requisition a Volkswagen just before it becomes imminent, particularly if it is the French who occupy this area. That looks extremely likely right now, with them operating just across the Rhine from here. Well, let us not worry about that until it becomes more pressing. I'm glad we had this opportunity to talk. You are a capital young fellow and I've grown very fond of you. I wouldn't like to see you come into trouble, you understand? *Ach*, that crazy man!"

"I appreciate it, believe me. I'd better brief the boys. Now, what about Christianne?"

"I again cannot say. That may have been an idle threat on his part, or it may have been serious. In any case, I wouldn't spend too much time alone with her, particularly where you can be seen together."

Bruckmann excused himself and left the dining room. I sat alone for a few moments until von Nordenflycht entered. Inga came in shortly afterward and sat with the baron. A few minutes later, Ernie and Bill wandered in together and headed right for my table.

"Here Hal," Ernie said, handing me a piece of dried pastry he pulled from beneath his combat jacket. "I liberated this *kuchen* (he pronounced it 'kooken') last night over at the Schwann and saved this piece for you."

I accepted the unaccustomed treat gratefully. It made a worthy addition to the coffee I was drinking.

"Listen, guys. We'd better start making some serious plans and damn soon. Things are starting to blow up around here."

"Whaddya mean? What's wrong?"

"Not now. We'll talk about it later." I stopped talking suddenly as I saw Best enter the room and stand in the doorway. He surveyed the entire room and its occupants. He nodded to Inga and von Nordenflycht, who were seated together. Then, he walked toward our table, smiling cheerfully.

"Good morning, gentlemen. Did I tell you how much I enjoyed your music on the radio last night? It was excellent."

"Thank you, sir," I replied, still sitting. I couldn't be sure which of them I could trust now, Bruckmann or Best. In fact, I was sure, once the chips were down, I couldn't trust either of them.

"Now, I tell you something. Today is what, Thursday, the twenty-ninth, eh? Well, do you know what Sunday is?" Best asked coyly, apparently playing a guessing game.

I calculated rapidly in my head. "The first of April?" I replied tentatively.

"And that is the beginning of the month in which my birthday falls. Did you know that?"

"No, sir."

"Yes, indeed. On the eleventh of April, I will reach the venerable age of thirty-one. What do you fellows think of that, now?"

"Well, let me be the first, Herr Oberstormfuhrer."

"*Bitte?*" He looked puzzled.

"To wish you *fröliche Geburtstag.*"

"Ah, so, yes. Thank you so very much. But now then, the business at hand, eh? I am having a little party on the night of my birthday — for my staff here and the other guests, you know. I wish to invite everyone. It is my first birthday in recent years that I haven't spent in battle. You too, and your men, of course," he concluded without taking his eyes off mine. Then he looked at the other two. They both nodded agreement.

"Oh, and one more thing, gentlemen. I wonder if you would be so kind as to play some dance music for that night. It would be a more festive affair with some dancing, *nicht wahr?*"

"We'd be happy to," I assured him.

"Well then, it is settled. Now I must see Frau Greiner about ordering the wine. Good morning, my friends."

"I'll be damned," Ernie said. "What do you suppose got into him?"

"Probably forgot his nasty pills this morning," I replied. "But I wouldn't trust that son of a bitch as far as I could throw Frau Greiner."

Best came out of the kitchen almost immediately. He returned to our table.

"Frau Greiner is not in the kitchen now. I'll have to see her another time. By the way, have you seen Herr Bruckmann this morning?"

"No, sir," I lied. "He might be in his room, I imagine."

"Ah, so. Very well, the mountain will go to the Arab, eh? Have a good day, gentlemen. *Auf Wiedersehen.*"

Once again, he sauntered purposefully from our presence.

"I just can't figure that guy," Ernie said, puzzled.

"I'm beginning to be unable to understand any of 'em," I told him.

By now, others were coming in to breakfast. Arentz entered alone and waved to us cheerfully. He entered the office door, closing it behind him. Küttner and Trautmann entered together, doing a comic and awkward side-stepping routine of courtesy to each other.

"Here come Gallagher and Sheen," I observed.

"Who?" Ernie asked.

"The Gold Dust twins."

The pair of new arrivals were continuing their ridiculous, affected routine as they moved across the room. It started at the door as Küttner began to enter, then turned to allow Trautmann to come in first. The latter shuffled his way awkwardly past his compatriot. Then, crossing to their table, Trautmann bowed, seriously, and extended his arm as if to say, "After you, my dear Alphonse."

Küttner's reaction was completely predictable, as he bowed in turn and offered the equivalent of the complementary reaction — "No, after you, Gaston."

I nearly laughed aloud at the ludicrous picture the two oddly shaped, minimum-sized SS officers made. They were anything but the picture of the pure Nordic, Aryan stock of which their Fuhrer had boasted for so long. Neither, I recalled with amusement, were Hitler himself, or his sidekicks, Goering, that bucket of lard, or dark-haired, ferret-faced, club-footed Goebbels.

"Isn't that ridiculous?" Ernie said.

"Best probably read the military riot act to them. If he's on a discipline kick with us, as Bruckmann told me, he's probably got the same bug about his own people. Those two are officering and gentlemaning all over the place this morning."

"Do you suppose they're serious, or is that a comedy routine for the benefit of everybody in here?" Bill asked.

"Naw, those are hardly good time boys. I don't think either of them has any sense of humor, at least, no more than you'd get from a dose of clap. They're serious all right."

"Let's go get some fresh air, whaddya say?" Ernie suggested.

"Right," I agreed. "It's a nice morning. A change of pace will be welcome after the bullshit around here."

We gulped our remaining coffee, arose, and left by the rear door of the hotel. As we walked down the stairs to the outside door, I hung back, anxious to see if Christianne might be coming down the stairs from her second-floor room. There was no sign of her. Could there have been any truth in Bruckmann's story? Would Best actually send her away? Could he have done so already, before I had a chance to say goodbye?

Just as we reached the outside door, I heard footsteps descending the stairs. They were light steps.

"You guys go ahead. I'll be right with you," I said, going back up the four steps toward the bathroom on the landing. The others went outside.

Christianne reached the bottom of the stairway and looked casually around as she was about to open the door to the dining room. She saw me and smiled lovingly in surprise. I crossed the landing in one bound.

"Good morning, fair lady."

"Good morning, my cavalier."

She lifted her lips for my kiss. It was a short kiss. I didn't feel comfortable out here in the hall. There were three places from which anyone might approach — from upstairs, through the rear door, or from the dining room.

"I'd like to see you alone as soon as possible," I said softly.

"I'll be in my room just before lunch," she replied. "I have some letters to write, and this is a good morning for me to do it."

"OK if I stop by?"

"OK." She smiled.

I held the door for her as she entered the dining room. Then, closing it behind her, I turned and descended the steps to the rear of the building, opened it, and walked outside. Bill and Ernie were sitting on the back steps smoking.

The warm sun poured down, giving all of us a comfortable feeling. It would be another cloudless day. Already, much of the snow in the circle road had disappeared and grass could be seen climbing through its cover around the millpond.

"Hey, Hal, I never ast you. You married?" Ernie said.

"Naw, are you?" I responded automatically. I was a bit surprised by his reply, possibly because of his very young appearance.

"Nope. But I'm engaged to a little doll in Chicago. Shirley's her name. She's a little bitty thing, long black hair. Boy, what I wouldn't do to be with her right now. We're gonna get married right after I get home."

"How about you, Bill?"

"Nothin'. I'm gonna get me a little farm first. You cain't afford a farm and a wife both, at least not for a while, until you're settled.

Least, that's the way I figure it. Or else, I might go into the family feed business."

"Now, there's an ambitious philosophy," I observed. "What do you think about that, Ernie?"

"Hell, that's crap. I got too hot pants not to get married. You gimme my little Shirley, boy. Here, you wanna see her picture?" He pulled out his wallet and fumbled through it, flashing a celluloid-covered picture insert.

I studied the badly focused photo of a little, thin girl with a very pretty face. She was wearing a white blouse and dark, very short shorts. She had lovely legs, and the tightness of her blouse showed that she made up in pulchritude what she lacked in height.

"Whaddya think about my little Miss Zielinski?" Ernie asked, anxiously.

"Zielinski? That's not too common a name, is it? I had a buddy named Zielinski once. He was from Cleveland."

It had seemed an eternity ago that I'd last seen Joe Zielinski. A very, very long time ago.

"I don't know about that. She's German. Lots of Germans in Chicago, although she lived in a Polish neighborhood. Well, it's not really Chicago. It's kind of a suburb. A place called Hegwich. Her old man owns a lumber yard. I started workin' for him summers while I was in high school. Shirley went to a Catholic high school so I didn't meet her in school. Anyway, once I had to deliver somethin' to his house for the boss. Shirley answered the door. Boy, I tell you. She's a real doll. Jeez! What a doll. Anyway, Zielinski is just another name where she lives."

Just another name. I felt a pain in my chest as I thought about the fellow I knew with just that name. Joe and I had become very close, spending every spare moment together when we first met at the King's race track in Naples last summer. I had been sent there after my escape from German imprisonment in the north of Italy. Joe was there, having been released from the general hospital in Naples. He'd been sent there after being wounded at Cisterna on Anzio. He had a couple of weeks left before he had to report to his tank destroyer battalion. He was in the 761st, attached to my 30th Infantry Regiment.

We spent two idyllic weeks together, visiting places with ancient, exotic names — places such as Sorrento and Capri, both popularized in ballads of the day. Then there were Pompeii, Vesuvius . . .

The Neapolitan volcano had put on a spectacular show for us one night as it erupted for the first time in a generation. It showed its teeth as rivers of bright, glowing, yellow lava poured down its sides. No harm had come to the countryside around it, though, as the slithering eruption eventually stopped before touching human habitation.

I had met Joe first in the chow line at the replacement depot.

"Jeez, I wish I had guts enough to do that," I said in a friendly teasing way.

"Do what?" the good-looking, well-built fellow ahead of me replied.

"Raise one of those dusters under my nose."

Joe had smiled in mild embarrassment. "My wife likes it." As he spoke, he rubbed the pencil-thin mustache with his fingertips, very gently.

"Well, hell," I said quickly. "What better reason in the world? I tried to raise one once, but after about three weeks, I looked as if my nose was running. The damn thing never developed into much."

"Well, my wife tells me I have a weak upper lip, and Jeannie's a pretty good judge of stuff like that."

We started our friendship with as simple a conversation as that. It developed fast, and Joe and I became virtually inseparable. We toured the sightseeing routes and places together, drank wine in back street shops, saw eye to eye on the hazards of playing with Neapolitan chippies, and had an entirely sexless good time in a strange land.

Our mutual attitude on the reputedly fair sex of Naples developed one day when both of us were on pass and had tried every facility of the Red Cross service club. We were trudging side by side down one of the countless, filthy back streets of Naples, followed by several members of the legions of the Italy of the day — the kids who were bumming, begging, and stealing their way through a war that had always surrounded them. They were hustling for cigarettes, *chocolada,* or pimping for any willing female, usually the inevitable sister.

"Hey, Joe, come on. Wanna *señorina*? Hey, Joe, I gotta *sorella,* a seester. Come on, Joe. I gotta seester. First time, Joe. Come on, first time." He was directing most of his remarks to my buddy.

"Yeah, first time for me, right?" Joe laughed. Then, to me, he said, "How do you suppose he knew my name?"

"Come on," I chided. "They call every dogface 'Joe.' "

The lad, looking like a fugitive from Fagin's legion, couldn't have been over seven. But already, he was a veteran of the campaign.

He had discovered early that a ten-lire shoeshine was worth fifty to the *Americanos,* every one of whom was at least a millionaire. So thereafter he learned to charge fifty cents, hoping for more. But he also discovered that *Americanos* could be generous, dependably so, with other things than money. They had *chocolada* and cigarettes. Money obviously meant nothing to them. They preferred dirty women to clean shoes. That much this aged seven-year-old had learned. Thus, he became a purveyor of the most popular product Italy had to offer in those days. He was a top businessman who undoubtedly would die of tuberculosis before reaching the venerable age of ten.

"*Via! Via!*" I shouted at the kid, waving him away. The youngster stood for a moment, looking after us. He was a pitifully thin little guy. His buddies had left him, seeking greener pastures. This kid seemed to have as much weight hanging on him in street dirt as he appeared to carry in flesh and bone. He decided to give it one more try.

"Come on, Joe. Come with Alfredo." This time, he directed his remarks to me since I seemed to be the boss of my two-man group. At least, I was the one who had told him to beat it, and in his own language. "Hey, Joe. I gotta seester. She pretty. One real beaut, boy. Come on, Joe, first time. I promise, Joe."

"Here, kid," I tossed him a chocolate bar. "Now *prenda la strada!*" Again I waved him away.

The boy caught the candy expertly in midair. He smiled through decayed teeth and ran up the alley shouting, "*Prago,* Joe. *Molto prago.*"

"What was that you said?" Joe asked.

"What? Oh, '*prenda la strada*'? It literally means 'hit the road.' One of the cleaning women at the hospital told me that. I don't think they use it in direct translation, though. It's kind of an American idiom, you know? It looked as if the chocolate bar was what got him."

We laughed and continued past the decaying buildings of Naples which had stood for centuries, having the same type of slop dumped unceremoniously out of the open windows into the street below as was now being tossed from several ahead of us.

Ancestors of the same billions of persistent flies undoubtedly had plagued furloughing legionnaires of Caesar's day on these same roughly cobbled alleys.

We passed a large sign printed in English at the end of the alley. It was mounted on the side of the last building we passed. It said, "In 1600, the Spaniards called syphilis the disease of Naples. Let's leave it where it belongs." The sign credited the warning to the Army Quartermaster Corps.

"Does it bother you, Hal?" Joe asked.

"What's that?"

"Nookie rationing."

"Hell, it isn't rationed. Not around here, I understand."

"It is if you ration yourself."

"Well, I'll tell you, Joe, old buddy. I'm probably the world's biggest natural-born coward. When I see and hear the kind of stuff I've seen and heard around here and in North Africa, I guess I can wait a little longer."

"Oh, it's not that I'm afraid. It's just that I know Jeannie is waiting for me. She's not horsing around. I don't see where I got the right to. Know what I mean?"

"Sure," I quickly replied. "With me, it's not morals or scruples or any of those things. Hell, I love to get laid like any of those GIs. Only thing is, I've only had one girl in my life, and she's the one I'll probably end up marrying. I just don't think it's worth it to catch a dose just for a chance to shoot my wad after a couple of minutes with some poxy broad. Besides, I haven't seen any really worth takin' the chance for."

"Amen, brother. Amen to that," Joe said.

We busied ourselves for the next few days getting dreadfully drunk on frightful, overpriced, underdeveloped Italian *vino*. It took us a couple of additional days thereafter just to get over it. That included recovery time for diarrhea or dysentery, or whatever the medics had called it. We both agreed we could live happily forever without ever seeing or smelling or hearing of peanut butter again in our lifetimes. But it did the job.

In a very short time, we were back to the realities of war.

We had been patrolling in southern France for three days. This was the fourth such two-day outing we had taken since the landing at Cape Cavalier on the southern Riviera coast, three weeks earlier. Everywhere we had driven, we ran into nothing but overwhelmingly friendly French people.

When we invaded southern France, we found little active resistance on or near the beaches, and that deteriorated into a rout almost at once. We suddenly found ourselves enjoying vacation tours of some of the world's most beautiful country under near-peacetime conditions.

In our outward-bound excursions through the late summer countryside, our reconnaissance group, now working with the TD boys, visited the fabled medieval walled city of Carcassone, the lower Rhone Valley, the outskirts of Toulon and Marseilles. We saw lovely hills laced with lush vineyards and attractive, picturesque little villages, filled with pleasant, sincere, long-suffering people. The weather, too, was ideal.

This particular patrol had resulted from an intelligence report that a given village "somewhere ahead" was peopled with German military personnel. Because of the distances involved in this unique campaign so far, and the speed of the advance, we were motorized exclusively. In North Africa, Sicily, or Italy, it had been sheer insanity to venture more than a mile or two ahead of an advancing army. Here, for the first time, the enemy was outdistancing our advance in his retreat. It was not at all unusual to find an enemy patrol as far as thirty to fifty miles ahead of what would be described charitably as the "front lines."

Such patrols usually lasted three days to a week and the information found had degenerated to the routine patrol report, "No contact with enemy."

This was the tenor of the war in southern France in late summer, 1944. The American flag stitched to the right shoulder of each GI's combat jacket was enough to establish a local public holiday whenever our patrolling vehicles entered a new town. Crowds would gather on the main street, slowing our advance by the sheer force of their numbers.

Delirious civilians of all ages and both sexes, laughing and cheering, would present gifts to us of wines, fruits, bread. The old and young, male and female, exercised their historic prerogative of freely kissing whomever they chose whenever the mood struck them. And the mood struck them often and regularly these days as *les Liberateurs Americain* arrived in their towns.

Ecstatic *mademoiselles* would make sure that no liberating doggie went unbussed. It was time for pleasure, for unbridled joy, a time for relief from hostilities for all principals involved.

The Vosges Mountains loomed ominously ahead. The war was about to start again, although our patrol that day was oblivious to that fact. The impenetrable blockade of nature had prevented many advancing hostile forces throughout history from crossing it when it was being defended.

The mountains in themselves presented an adequate obstacle. But coupled with this was the presence throughout their vast, wooded hill-sides of thousands of vigorous, trained, dedicated, desperate German soldiers who knew that, if the Vosges fell, they would be backed up against and defending their homeland directly. Such men fought furiously.

Our patrol this time consisted of two jeeps, each with a mounted .50-caliber machine gun, and Joe Zielinski's lumbering tank destroyer. The huge tracked vehicle dwarfed its flanking jeeps.

In the lead jeep, I had put Fortino on the machine gun with Jeffers driving and Mahoney as observer. In my own following jeep, I manned the .50 with Ludwig driving and Sullivan observing from the front seat. Between us, Joe stood, exposed from the waist up, in his unbuttoned turret hatch, idly searching the horizon for the elusive Kraut.

We had billeted in the tiny hamlet of Le Maiz the night before and had been feted royally after ascertaining that no Boche had been in the vicinity for nearly two weeks. We were wined and dined as regal ambassadors, which, in fact, we were, I suppose.

The inn at which we had stayed was operated by an elderly Frenchman who longed to recount his recollections, now magnified with time, of turning back Le Boche at the Marne in 1918. Unfortunately, most of his French was too fast and his memory too faulty. But to compensate for the rapid-fire, unintelligible fantasies of the old man, was the presence of his granddaughter, a damsel not yet twenty. She served us our hot soup and French bread, interspersed liberally with Vin Rouge. She was a delight to the eye, even in this country so liberally sprinkled with charm and beauty.

"Man alive," Mahoney had gasped when she first entered the room. "Get a load of that, will you? Boy, I'd do her for nothin', bad as I need the money!"

Joe, the ranking non-com on the patrol as a technical sergeant, advised quietly, "Don't horse around, Mahoney. We can't afford to antagonize anybody now."

"Whaddya mean, antagonize?" Mahoney demanded in mock anger. "Why, I'll have you know that, back in Buffalo, I was considered quite a cocksman. Antagonize. Christ!"

We all laughed then as our self-admitted Lothario found that Joe's admonition was unnecessary. The young lady was willing enough to show grateful affection to her liberators, but drew the line at kissing anyone a second time. And she drew it effectively, Mahoney discovered, as he drew back a badly needle-stabbed hand with a loud yelp.

"Goddamnit! All I tried to do was pat her a little. For Christ's sake, they love it." The young lady, who obviously didn't love it, flounced out of the room toward the kitchen. She apparently carried the needle in her apron shoulder strap for such eventualities.

"Yeah, but under her skirt, Mickey?" one of the others teased.

It was a delightful evening, but it had to end because of the early start Joe wanted to make the next day. Shortly after dawn broke, we mounted our guards of two men each in two-hour shifts and roared away from the inn's courtyard.

Now we were nearly thirty miles beyond the inn and had passed through three other small villages, the first Americans to be seen in two of them for a generation.

Ahead, the road stretched straight and true and the valley began to narrow. At one point, it had been more than thirty miles wide. Now, the bordering hills were less than a mile away on either side of the road. The river that had eroded this valley over millions of years undulated gracefully about 200 yards to our right. Its banks were lined with statuesque poplar trees of varying heights and ages.

In the distance, we saw the picture-storybook layout of the next village, about two miles ahead. We were greeted first by the distinctive church spire looming upward from an accumulation of small stone houses.

For some reason, I felt a foreboding this morning. I didn't know why, but uncomfortably recalled feeling this way often before and, to date, I'd never been misguided by it. I wished to God I had been wrong on several of those occasions. Many close friends were lost on days when this unhappy sensation struck me. It wasn't peculiar to me, though. Most combat-seasoned GIs talked of their gut feelings just before an ambush, an attack call, or an enemy counterattack.

I was a sergeant now. I had been promoted shortly after our southern France invasion, at Aix en Provence, when we stopped for a few days to regroup. Fortino had moved up as corporal and second in command behind me. For purposes of this patrol, though, Joe's extra rockers gave him top billing.

Joe was riding high in the dubious vantage point, well above road level, within the steel confines of his moving fortress. The small convoy was proceeding northward in an orderly fashion at about fifteen miles an hour.

"Hey, Sarge," Sullivan called over his shoulder. "Do you suppose we can take time to stop in this town for a while? I'd like to get me a little of that French stuff before I dry up. I'm already gettin' backaches somethin' fierce."

"Simmer down, Buster," I replied, keeping my eyes on the trees that lined the stream. "You're likely to have plenty of other stuff to worry about before long. The Krauts aren't gonna run forever, you know."

Suddenly, I stiffened at my gun. I grasped the trigger handles tightly and released the safety catch. I looked again at the spot to my right front. There, where I suspected I had seen movement, I saw it again. I couldn't make a positive identification. It might be a wandering cow in the trees, or some kids playing along the bank. But something had moved in the shrubbery.

"Sully, take a look over there toward those three high poplars. No, don't look fast. Take a gradual scan to your right front. Be casual about it. Now, see the three trees sticking way up above the others?"

"Yeah."

"All right. Check the base of them. What do you see?"

"Nothin' but bushes, Sarge."

"Well, look at the bushes carefully. Better call Frank on it. I'm sure there's something in those bushes."

Sullivan picked the walkie-talkie from between his feet and clicked the switch.

"Enterprise 1, this is Enterprise 3, over."

After a momentary delay, the response came from the lead jeep. "Come in, Enterprise 3. This is Enterprise Top." It was Joe's voice in the TD just ahead of us. I couldn't imagine how he heard the radio call with all the noise his vehicle was making.

"Give it here," I told Sully, reaching for the radio. "Joe, listen carefully. Don't move fast, but take a gradual look to your right front. The three tallest poplars there along the river. See 'em?"

"Yeah, Hal. But that's all I see."

"Frankie, you on?"

The set crackled again and Fortino's voice came through. "Yeah, I'm here. Hey, I think I saw somethin' move where you said!"

I had seen movement again too.

Then I saw what I had been afraid it might be. The ugly, perforated flash hider on the snout of a small anti-tank cannon as it thrust itself out of the shrubbery.

"Joe, anti-tank gun to the right! Frank, swing around to the spot over there, quick. Under the three . . ."

The puff of smoke was seen before the muzzle blast was heard. Almost simultaneously, the explosion at the top of the TD turret obliterated Joe Zielinski. Frankie began firing his .50 at the same instant I began firing mine. Our lines of fire gradually converged on the spot where we had seen the muzzle blast. Both jeeps were now empty, the other guys wisely hitting the ditch as soon as they heard the shell whistle in. The two drivers and their observers, as soon as we began firing, crawled out of the ditch and began crawling across the grain stubble of the field toward the gun position, the live machine gun fire just over their heads.

The tracers from the two heavy machine guns laid a field of fire directly into the position of the anti-tank gun, catching the entire shrubbed area in its path. Another flash from the gun was followed by a screaming whistle as the shell zipped past my jeep, exploding a few yards beyond the road behind me.

The machine gun slugs ripped away the protective camouflage around the cannon, and I could see the three men spin as they fell away from the little 37-millimeter weapon. A fourth member of the gun crew, attempting to run from the position, was caught in the line of Frankie's fire and was flung violently forward on his face, his arms outstretched.

The rest of our crew charged across the remaining few yards of open field toward the gun position, their Tommy guns spraying the entire area. Frankie and I left our jeeps and converged on the TD. I reached the side of it first, just as the other three TD crewmen began climbing out of the rear and front hatches, dazedly looking about them. The concussion of the shell must have reverberated around the metal cage ferociously.

I climbed up on the vehicle's right track. Joe was lying over the edge of the turret, his arms dangling limply below him, swaying gently from side to side. Fortino joined me and together, we began lifting Joe out of the turret. We saw the wide red path flowing down the side of the turret, splashing into a tiny, growing pool beside the track. I saw where the bulk of the shell's explosive charge had caught Joe at the edge of the turret, in his side, just above the right hip, ripping an immense hole. I had a sudden urge to push the escaping entrails back into position as if this might prevent some of Joe's suffering. Then, realizing that Joe wasn't suffering any longer, we gently lowered his body over the side to the arms of his waiting crewmen.

We jumped to the road just as the other fellows returned. I leaned over the ditch and threw up, endlessly it seemed. I felt absolutely husked.

Jeannie Zielinski of Cleveland had just become a very young widow.

17.   No Live Music Tonight

WITH NO LIVE music scheduled for tonight's show, neither Ernie nor Bill would be needed. They decided to stay in their quarters and make plans for what supplies they might need at the last minute before our escape.

Because of the uncertainty of the specific time, I had minimized everything but prisoner messages on my last few shows. Bruckmann had presented me with a book from which I was expected to pick some light dialogue for the program. It was *Eddie Cantor's 1,000 Best Jokes*. This amused me greatly because Cantor, of course, was a Jewish American comic. I had fallen into the habit of interspersing the records and messages with occasional appropriate, topical jokes from the book. The difficulty of literally translating many of the idiomatic humorous bits and pieces, written in various examples of American vernacular, made it a wasted effort for all of the Germans who listened to the jokes, puzzled expressions on their faces. Inga was the only one who occasionally caught a punch line of a localized American story.

Tonight's show, however, was heavy on messages. There were no jokes and only three records besides the theme song. They were Gene Krupa's "Perfidia," with Howard Dulaney; "My Reverie," sung by

Bea Wayne with Larry Clinton's orchestra; and Harry James' "One O'-Clock Jump."

Other than that, I had managed to get nine messages into the limited time available by editing some of them slightly, eliminating only redundancies.

Following the completion of my portion of the show, I left the studio. The rest of the group was still on hand with about forty minutes of programming remaining until their portion of the evening's show ended.

I had a great deal to ponder. Here it was, the eve of Best's birthday party, and we were still here. April 11. I had hoped we might have left at least a week or more before this. Several conditions had arisen, however, to frustrate my efforts.

First of all, there had been a sudden unexpected snow storm which, while it wasn't long in overall time, dumped an immense amount of snow back onto the mountain which had lost nearly all of the season's fall. I wasn't sure what effect this blizzard had had on our valley to the north.

Later, as the snow was melting again, our food cache was washed away by unexpected high water running under the bridge where it was hidden. We were close to tears when we discovered our loss the next day.

Finally, the situation with Christianne had become more tense as Best made repeated attempts to be alone with her. She had managed to avoid him diplomatically so far, but I knew that nothing but trouble would come from this situation eventually.

As I approached the hotel, I noticed that the dining room was practically in total darkness. I didn't want to go to the Schilli house just yet.

I noticed with some surprise that the light was on in the dining room level room that served as the SS company office. It was a room in the rear corner of the building. My heart beat faster as I thought of the possibility of finding Christianne there alone. I walked past the hotel entrance to the street below. Best's room overlooked this street. I followed the line of windows on the second floor with my eyes until I counted to the third one from the rear of the hotel. This was Best's room. It was dark.

I returned to the front door of the building, climbed the stairs to the glassed-in porch, and looked through the dining room window nearest the door. The only light in the room was a small table lamp on the sideboard.

Opening the door quietly, I held it as I closed it, to prevent any sound. Mounting the front stairway silently, I reached the dining room floor and cautiously approached the door of the office. I knocked quietly, twice.

"Come in," Christianne's voice was soft, but I heard it because I wanted to so badly. She had responded in German.

I opened the door and quietly closed it behind me. I stood staring at her as her eyes held mine.

"Oh, Hal, he's sending me back to Munich," she said, her eyes brimming.

"I know. Bruckmann warned me. When do you leave?"

"I don't know. He invited me to his birthday party tomorrow night, so it won't be tomorrow anyway. Probably the day after."

She rushed into my arms, tears now cascading down her cheeks. I held her tightly a few moments, then tenderly kissed her upturned lips.

"What were you doing here?" I asked.

"Waiting. I hoped you would come tonight. Oh, Hal, I need you so much."

I kissed her again. Then, reaching up, I pulled the chain controlling the single, shaded light hanging from the chandelier at the center of the ceiling. The room plunged into immediate darkness. We stood together, holding each other tightly, gradually becoming accustomed to the darkness. The reflection of the moonlight through the window panes formed small squares of light on the now black floor.

I began moving my hands across her back, her shoulders, down her sides. I rested them momentarily on her hips, hungrily kissing her lips all the while. I felt the button on the left side of her skirt and began pushing it through its buttonhole.

"Not here," she said in a gentle whisper, guiding my hand away from its objective.

She gently took my hand and turned me around to face the door. She stepped in front of me and opened the door slightly, listening, into the hall. Hearing nothing, she turned back to me and, throwing her arms around my neck, placed her lips against my cheek.

"Remember, my room is directly across the hall from this one, one floor above. Give me five minutes. I will wait for you." She slid out of my close embrace and through the partially opened door, closing it quietly behind her.

I stood waiting nervously, then paced to the front window of the dining room. I looked up the hill toward the school. Some of the others were leaving that building.

Damn, I thought. *I'd better get out of here before some of them come up looking for something.*

I estimated that Christianne had been gone for about three minutes. I watched the group from the school approaching the hotel, unaware of my presence at the window. Then, as they began mounting the stairs, deeply engrossed in conversation, I walked quickly to the back door of the dining room and let myself into the hallway. The corridor was silent as a tomb. I waited until I heard voices as the others entered the hotel foyer. With the dining room closed, they had no reason to stay downstairs. They would be going up to the second and third floors immediately.

I quickly climbed the stairs as quietly as possible, unable, however, to avoid an occasional creek of tired, old boards. I knew that the others could reach the top of the front stairs within seconds of my reaching the top of the rear steps. I had to move quickly.

I went to the first door, which should be Christianne's, and listened at the door, hearing nothing. I rapped quietly and the door opened, allowing me to enter the darkness beyond. The door was pushed shut behind me.

Christianne threw herself into my arms with a sob. I held her without speaking, kissing the top of her head, her forehead, her eyes. I moved my lips tenderly across her cheek as I raised her face with my forefinger under her chin.

"Chris. Oh, Chris, I want you."

By way of answer, she inserted her tongue into my mouth and pressed more tightly against me.

She pulled her head away slightly. "Oh, Hal, love me. Love me!"

I gently pushed her backward against the side of the bed. I sat beside her, holding her in my arms. She clutched my shoulders tightly as she gave me her lips. Slowly and carefully, we fell back together on the bed. She took my hand and placed it on her breast. I caressed her tenderly, wordlessly. We weren't aware of how long we'd been lying there, but we obviously were aware of the buildup of emotions.

The hotel was quiet. The only sound was the wind blowing outside of the room's lone, small window and the panting of two young lovers.

I turned above the girl, half leaning on her. My hand moved down the side of her leg until it reached the hem of her skirt. Exploring with a featherlike touch, my hand moved up the length of her leg which she had drawn up, knee bent. I found the button on the side of her cotton underpants and undid it. Then, shifting my position without breaking the bond of our lips, I placed both hands under her skirt at her waist and began gradually removing her panties. She arched her back to help me. Then, lifting one leg at a time, she encouraged the last few inches of the downward rout.

I stood and pulled her gently to her feet. Slowly, methodically, I removed one piece of her clothing at a time, punctuating each with a long, deep kiss. Her sweater and skirt joined the underpants on the floor. A single snap was all that held her brassiere in place. I unlatched it with the thumb and forefinger of my left hand, letting it, too, fall to the floor. She was completely nude now, shivering slightly. She unbuttoned my shirt and slid it over my shoulders.

She crawled into bed, the covers of which already had been turned down. I finished undressing as she lay watching me intently in the reflection of the moonlight that filtered into the small room. She made no move to cover her slim, lithe body which lay stretched on the bed, only her feet and ankles hidden beneath the eiderdown.

I stood before her a moment, drinking in her incredible beauty in the dim light. She held out her arms for me, and I went to her. We held each other tightly for several moments before all the pent-up frustration and ferocity of our short-lived, young love burst forth. We were to be separated. We both knew she was leaving. She didn't know that my escape was imminent. Together we lay immersed in our last desperate hours, sharing a frantic, exhausting embrace.

Much later, she fell asleep, her head nestled on my arm, her long, dark hair tangled over my shoulder. Christianne looked very young and beautiful in the half light. I leaned over and kissed her softly so as not to wake her. Suddenly, she turned her body to face mine, pressing the length of herself against me, her arms around my neck. She invited me again with a long, drawn-out kiss.

Finally, completely sated physically, we lay back and touched each other softly, intimately. She arose and walked slowly across the room, straight and lean. I admired the perfection of her body as I watched her step before the mirror over her dresser. She turned on the small lamp and picked up the comb lying on the dresser top. Turning partially toward me, she began combing her auburn hair, holding her arm deliberately high, it seemed, so as to accentuate the upward swell of her full, firm breasts. She stood upright, open, unashamed, welcoming my devoted gaze.

I had seen many of the peculiar kidney-shaped porcelain bowls in other buildings in France, but never fully understood the intimacy of their use on the low, three-legged stools which held them. I had heard them called *"bidets."*

With typical, unembarrassed aplomb, fastidiousness, and thorough objectivity, Christianne demonstrated its use, almost as if she were unaware of my presence. It seemed a perfectly natural thing to do at the time.

It was becoming light as the first full rays of dawn began breaking over the forests and valley. I managed to descend the front stairs of the hotel quietly, find an unlocked window to the porch, open it and crawl through it, closing it silently behind me. I made my way back to the Schilli house, physically exhausted, but exalted in the knowledge that we had said the happiest of farewells.

18.   Lot of Weird Guck

BBC HAD ANNOUNCED the fall of Stuttgart. The way was clear now. In all likelihood, the advancing Allied armies would move southeasterly. There was nothing of particular military significance directly south toward Schonach, Triberg, or Villingen. In fact, the maps showed nothing but flyspeck villages throughout this area.

Our chances of leaving after the party tonight probably were the best we would find in the near future, I was sure. There was certain to be a great deal of heavy drinking, perhaps enough to incapacitate all or most of the guests. I glanced at the clock on the wall of the living room. It said 5:30. In another hour, Herr Schilli would be arising to leave for work. I didn't want to talk to either of my kind hosts this morning. I felt that the fewer people who had a clue about the escape plans, the better. And Frau Schilli had proved herself amazingly perceptive in interpreting my moods of late. She knew full well when I was feeling homesick, when I was worried about the war, when I was mooning in lovesick silence over Christianne. She didn't know who the girl was, but Frau Schilli knew there was a girl.

I held the earphones to my ear again. The BBC announcer was continuing his analysis.

"Prime Minister Churchill explained earlier this week that several independent attempts have been made to lay the groundwork for separate peace with the Western Allies. None of these has had the blessing of Soviet Russia, however. The government of Prime Minister Stalin has been most insistent on total surrender or no terms. This, Mr. Churchill has called a difficult decision, but one in which he must concur with the Soviets inasmuch as the enemy must fall completely and utterly rather than piecemeal. Only then, the prime minister has said, can there be total peace . . ."

I never failed to thrill at the mention of the little, heavy-set, bald, bulldog of a man at 10 Downing Street. My earliest recollection of Mr. Churchill had been created during an assignment in my current events Civics class in high school several years before, when the British hero had distinguished himself in other fields than wartime leadership.

The BBC newsman's voice droned on as I recalled the one occasion on which I had seen the little British leader close enough to shout a greeting.

The sleek landing craft pulled away from the Pozzuoli harbor, stern first, in order to clear the prow of the next ship, tightly jammed in behind her. I had observed many combat vessels in my numerous amphibious landings, and never failed to admire the distinct similarity in silhouette between the svelte LCI on which I stood and the submarines I had seen surface in other harbors.

My squad and I had arranged to claim squatter's rights on the fantail afterdeck of the ship. From here, we could observe the entire dramatic panorama, the thousands of war vessels of every shape and size, which filled this corner of the Tyrrhenian Sea. There were battleships, carriers, cruisers, and submarines, and a profusion of landing craft of all shapes and sizes — LICs, LSTs, LCTs, and Higgins Boats. Little efficient-looking destroyers darted about among their bigger sisters.

We pulled into a corner of the harbor to await our rendezvous with the remainder of the huge convoy. With plans for an overall rendezvous farther out at sea already established, the ships cruised their leisurely, zig-zag course into the deeper water.

I stood on the afterdeck among several men from my platoon. In the distance, a small speck, barely visible, and hardly distinguishable as some sort of craft, was approaching rapidly. We could tell it moved at high speed by the feathers and wake it spewed about it. It drew closer and we could make it out to be a sleek, speedy patrol craft. One figure was prominent in its foresection. He stood erect, disdaining to maintain his balance by a handhold.

As the boat approached to within a few hundred yards of our LCI, a few soldiers stared unbelievingly. Then the cry went up.

"It's Churchill!"

The cry was taken up and echoed throughout the ship. Soldiers and sailors crowded to the port side of the vessel.

The short, stubby figure stood straight. His thinning, white hair blew awry. As the little launch drew nearly abreast, he waved. Then the doughty little warrior raised his right hand to form, with two fingers, the V-for-victory sign — the symbol of hope and determination which, two years and more before, he had raised and flaunted at the power of the then mighty German war machine. The United States troops cheered and waved back.

Prime Minister Winston Churchill, in Italy to confer with Italian Minister Bonomi, had been unable to resist seeing off the invasion convoy, now starting with his blessings and with some of his direction. He came to wish God-speed and a quick, successful victory to the U.S. troops. There seemed to be a feeling of relief among the admiring troops. It was a favorable omen, we seemed to feel.

The little launch finally made its rounds among the many vessels in the armada, came about, and sailed back to its favorable harbor. My ship continued on her wavering course until, by sunset, it was a part of the massive formation which was to become the largest military convoy of World War II, we had been told.

The entire night was spent in port and starboard deviations with scarcely an hour devoted to a straight course. My entire section was delighted at the caution being shown by the skipper. It meant that U-boats would have a tough time targeting us.

The fumes of the rear-mounted diesel engines swept over the afterdeck occasionally, adding to the already potent combination of fright and mild seasickness which infected every man aboard.

Even the luxury of a card game was denied us. From our relatively plush quarters on the open fantail, we enjoyed the unusually airy freedom denied those cramped in confined quarters below decks. Any light could be seen for many miles at sea and could illuminate a ship adequately to make an ideal torpedo target.

As a result, we of the I&R platoon reveled in our good fortune without the bonus of man-made diversions. We settled ourselves for an open-air sleep in our sleeping bags on the hard, cold, metal deck.

Unable to sleep, I spent most of the night looking out into the moonlight-silver wake, remembering horrendous adventures of the past.

As dawn broke, I shook myself awake. I had dozed off beside the 40-millimeter anti-aircraft gun mounted on the rear deck. As I looked around, I discovered that most of the section apparently had gone down to breakfast which, this morning, was slated to be S.O.S. — Shit on a Shingle, Same Old Shit, or any other combination of socially unacceptable words to describe chipped beef on toast. I never talked about S.O.S. I liked it!

I couldn't stand anything this morning, though. Instead, I settled for a couple of slices of white bread and two cups of coffee, even though I had to fight my way through the line twice for the privilege.

The sea was glassy calm in every direction. In the distance, to the right front, land loomed on the horizon. It was Corsica. We spent a considerable portion of the morning approaching the coast of the little island close enough for the inexperienced sailors in olive drab costumes to recognize its features and landscape. The hillsides were, or appeared to be, devoid of vegetation and frightfully steep. Nevertheless, they were heavily dotted by thousands of sheep. Corsica's grass apparently wasn't green, but a sickly tan shade.

The few villages visible to us were congregations of little stone buildings literally flung against the mountainsides. One small village in particular stood out, probably because of its precarious perch at the water's edge. It seemed to be ready to slide into the well-designed, natural scimitar-shaped bay. The natural harbor protected calm, smooth, deep blue water.

At approximately 11:00 A.M., the convoy drew to a halt, covering hundreds of square miles of the Mediterranean's surface. The ships weren't bobbing or riding swells. There were no swells — only smooth, glassy, incredibly blue water.

The order passed down the ship: "Swimming time will be allowed here in the harbor of Bonifacio. We will be anchored here for the rest of the day."

At once, the landing ramps, bracketing the bow of the ship, slid forward, coming to rest less than a foot out of the water on either side of the ship's nose. They extended nearly thirty feet beyond the foremost part of the ship's bow.

Virtually immediately after the word had come over the amplifying horns of the public address system, hardly a man was wearing a shred of clothing. The naked bodies were being flung off the side of the ship, fifteen feet through the air and into deep, clear, thoroughly refreshing water.

We spent the rest of the day diving from the ship's side, surfacing and swimming to the ramps up front. We'd climb aboard the nearest ramp and walk uphill to the deck to begin the process all over again. So the endless cycle continued.

In this way, much of the psychological pressure and emotional strain of combat-bound men, especially experienced ones, who were headed for a known hostile shore to perform the most hazardous of military maneuvers — the amphibious frontal assault against a strongly held beach — were alleviated, at least for part of a single day.

Toward the time that the sun disappeared over the smooth horizon, over there where France was, we were recalled to our deck positions to prepare for an anxious evening and night; anxious because of the lights-out regulations; anxious because of the fear of the known and unknown but suspected fate that dawn had in store for us.

I resumed my post against the heavy coil of steel wire lying on the fantail. Fortino and I sat alone. The others were scattered about the deck, smoking, talking or simply staring into the peaceful beauty of the sea and surrounding panorama.

"Frankie," I said absently, an implied question in my voice.

"Yeah?"

"Have you ever thought you wouldn't come out of this, or that you might not?"

"I don't know. I suppose. Like everybody else, I guess I don't like to think about them things. I guess I wanted to ignore it and hope it would go away."

"You know, Frank, that's a funny thing. Not once since I joined the army, not once in all the months of combat, or in the dozens of times we've been close enough to death to taste it . . . all those times when guys died all around us. Not once in all that, did I actually think I was going to die over here," I said. I really meant it. I never thought, throughout the entire war, that it would kill me.

"Yeah? Well, that's you, buddy. Me, I thought about it plenty."

"Oh, I've thought about it too. But what I mean is that I never thought I'd actually be killed. I've been afraid of being maimed, severely wounded, you know, in the gonads or having your spine split, or that kind of stuff. Something that would make a lifetime cripple out of a guy. But actually being killed . . . it never bothered me. It won't happen, I'm convinced."

"I'll think of that tonight when I say my rosary, pal."

"Yeah? Say a couple of go-rounds for me, will you? You know what? Here, look."

I opened my shirt front and pulled out my dog-tag chain. In addition to the two metal tags attached to it, there were two other items — a mezuzah and a round disk. I held out the St. Christopher medal for Fortino to see.

"This was given to me by my girl's best girlfriend. She's Catholic."

"Yeah, I imagine," Frank said with a grin.

"Well, anyway, this gal said to me before I left home, 'Hal,' she said, 'Take care of yourself. Here's something that is blessed. Wear it and come home safely to Nana.' Wasn't that great? That Alice is some kind of doll."

"Lotsa people wear lotsa weird guck at times like this. You know, rabbit's foot and like that."

"Well, this is no rabbit's foot. Is that all you Catholics think about it?"

"Oh, shit, no. That ain't what I meant. But you know, there are those guys that are . . . whaddyacallit . . . fatalists. They figger if you're gonna get it, you're gonna get it and nothin' you do about it will change nothin'."

"I don't know, Frank, I still think my number isn't coming up in this round!"

"Well, you know what else they say. That you never hear the one with your number on it. Maybe that's for the best too. I could stand some of heaven, I tell you, after the lousy way I was brought up back home."

"You mean actual heaven? Like heaven and hell and purgatory?"

"Look, buddy," Frank said, almost defensively. "Right now, I don't know what in hell I mean. I mean, it's been a rough war. Christ, you know that as good as anybody."

"I know. The only thing is, what does a guy do when he doesn't believe in all that? You know, like heaven and hell." I thought for a few seconds. "Or God, maybe?"

"What do you mean, you don't believe?"

"Well, you know, every time one of our guys got it, we always felt kind of sorry he was gone, but at the same time, we thanked God it wasn't us, right?"

"Sure."

"Then I started thinkin'. If there was a God, would he let this kind of thing happen? Would he let so many guys get killed and mutilated so horribly? And what about the Krauts? Their goddamn belt buckles even say *'Gott mit Uns'*!"

"That's right. I never thought of that."

"Anyway, I was brought up to believe that Jews don't believe in an afterlife."

"You're kidding."

"No, really. No heaven or hell."

"Then what happens when you die?"

"Who knows," I replied. "It's kind of like going to sleep, I suppose, only you don't wake up. Just kind of nothingness after that."

"Oh, shit. No way, man. Not for me. I gotta believe there's somethin' better out there. I really do, hey."

Frank shook his head as he looked down at the deck between his folded knees. Then, without another word, he simply dropped to the deck, stretched out, and wrapped his blanket about him. He was asleep almost immediately.

He was rudely awakened by a sudden burst of blue-black exhaust fumes spewing out of the side of the ship just below where we sat. The engines roared to life as the Navy crew secured the steel lines that guided the ramps. Other ships in the convoy were beginning to be set into motion. They began cruising as we did, in erratic patterns again, making no specific immediate sense, but moving inevitably toward that horizon over there, where France waited.

The sun now had disappeared entirely. Dusk was settling rapidly over the sea. Frank and I stretched out on the unyielding metal deck and tried to rest.

We slept fitfully, tossing, turning, and moaning, both of us. The only reason we didn't awaken the other men in the platoon was that this proved to be a universal condition on this, the eve of another amphibious assault against an enemy-held shoreline. A challenge of the unknown again, plaguing our subconscious.

The first flush of rockets zooming high and noisily into the sky and their clear arc of flight awoke us with a start. We gained consciousness quickly, in time to see the flashes in the sky. The tails of the rockets poured out flames and sparks, making them look like meteors descending into the distance.

I was amazed by the number of ships which had been equipped to fire multiple rockets for this invasion. A few hundred yards to our right was an LST with heavy rocket installations mounted on its upper forward deck. From all sides, hundreds of powerful weapons were firing explosive charges high into the air to curve into the enemy-held beaches. The view of flashing white contacts was followed in seconds by distant explosions.

Then the Navy's big guns opened up. Two or three large naval vessels were well out in the sea, beyond our LCI. The heavy roar of their twelve- and sixteen-inchers rolled across the water as the scream of those immense shells flew overhead.

The knowledge of such activity, intended to soften up whatever was in front of us, always buoyed the morale of the infantrymen assigned to the early waves in an invasion. Invariably, such heavy concentrations of fire promised to wipe out everything in its path, opening the way for a safe, effective, amphibious landing.

Due to the volume of fire laid down for this, our fifth division-wide landing and the seventh for many of the men in my regiment, there would appear to be no enemy left alive in our direct path anywhere near the beach itself.

Yet, within two hours after the first Higgins Boat tore out its bottom trying to get the doggies ashore with dry feet, I knew of twenty-seven men in my regiment who were dead. Of them, eighteen had been the victims of German machine guns. The rest fell to Kraut artillery and mines.

Another "routine," safe landing had been effected.

19. "Cover me and fall back"

I BEGAN UNDRESSING slowly. Stuttgart had fallen. What possibilities that opened for our escape! This would make any approach to Allied rear lines much simpler than having to make a move through two sets of combat positions — theirs and ours.

I hung my shirt over the corner bedpost, my trousers from the top drawer in the small chest of drawers, their cuffs held tightly inside the closed sliding panel. Clad only in my underwear, I sat on the side of the bed.

The heavy, steady snoring of Herr Schilli lulled me into another daydream. Such dreams had been recurrent lately. I wondered how long after the war, after I returned home, such thoughts would stay with me. Normally, they weren't particularly morbid thoughts, despite the fact that I had lost a great number of buddies, some of them quite close. Instead, they were nothing but recollections of exciting adventures relived, all the more thrilling because I escaped serious injury or worse.

Some of them were humorous, too, I recalled. In fact, one such crossed my mind momentarily, causing me to chuckle aloud. I listened carefully then, but heard no evidence of having disturbed the Schillis.

Then, I thought of other times, other places. I thought of Christianne and her warm, young, complete love. I thought of the idyllic setting of Schonach and my desire to return here in another day, with no thought of war or wartime situations. It wouldn't be the same, though. This I knew.

Then a nagging thought crept into the background. Was all this romantic fantasy? That is, was Christianne's love really any more than normal sensuality, loneliness, positive chemistry between her and an appealing contemporary? Was Schonach really all that beautiful, or was it that it was so much more attractive than the place from which I had come? And might it not have been that the treatment here, so unique in itself, was so vastly different from that in Waldkirch and other prison compounds in which I had found myself?

I believe I was more disturbed at thinking such thoughts than I was at the possibility of what their answers might be. But, I had to admit after careful reflection, Schonach was, indeed, a most beautiful setting. And Chris . . . certainly we had needed each other during this short adventure. We had fulfilled each other's needs. Was that so bad?

I placed my underwear beneath my pillow so it would be warm in the morning. Lying back, I pulled the eiderdown close about me. Before I dropped off to sleep, my thoughts reeled with faces.

The dissatisfaction of returning to Schonach in some distant postwar era, looking for the familiar faces, would be a nostalgic experience. I vowed I would return, knowing full well I never would. The beauty of the place would pale without some trace of the familiar staying with me. Besides Christianne, Inga would be gone. So would von Nordenflycht, Trautmann, Best, Bruckmann, Arentz, Küttner — all of them gone. Even Frau Greiner probably would be only a memory, as would the Schillis.

I would return to find an empty shell of a distant experience, if a long lost memory. The meat would have been removed and I would stand, hungry in my sadness, looking at the bare bones of the never changing millpond.

These were sad thoughts for me, on what had to be the eve of my last day in this place.

Then, as I pictured an imaginary path through the forest, I could see myself looking up at the towering evergreens. This faded into the fleeting, amusing recollection I had just finished, the one that had caused the chuckle. It was one of the few experiences of a terrifying war which had an element of true humor in it, an element of justification

260

for some of the irresponsible acts that occurred under the pressure of combat.

2nd Lt. Roger M. Ellis, 4th Infantry Division, had won the Distinguished Service Cross at Mouglinay, France, on October 21, 1918, after charging single-handedly into an enemy machine gun emplacement and, despite several serious and painful wounds, shooting it out in face-to-face violent combat with the crew. Then, charging up the same heavily wooded hill still further, he wiped out a German mortar position and two more enemy machine gun emplacements before his weakened, bloody body collapsed, and he was evacuated to an American field hospital in the rear.

His heroism and intrepidity at the extreme risk to his own life had saved his entire battalion, which had been pinned down all morning.

His son, 2nd Lt. Donald L. Ellis, 3rd Infantry Division, dearly sought to emulate his late father somewhere in France on October 21, 1944, exactly twenty-six years after the original act of heroism. He had been overseas for nearly a month and came to the 3rd as a replacement officer. He replaced Lt. Terry Harris, who had been sent home with a million-dollar wound — one that got him out of combat. Harris' left leg, below the knee, was considered a small enough price to pay for such a privilege. That is, it was considered such by everyone except Lieutenant Harris.

The young officer had been the victim of a German artillery shell which was completely irreverent, entirely without prejudice of rank, and which had torn flesh and bone away indiscriminately in its furious bursting. In addition to frightfully wounding Harris, it had taken the lives of the four other men with him in his bunker, all members of our I&R unit.

Lieutenant Ellis was a likeable enough young fellow. His manner was jovial in the few rear areas we were privileged to see occasionally when on reserve duty, although such occurrences were few and far between and their duration pitifully short.

Every man in the platoon sincerely hoped Lieutenant Ellis would win his coveted DSC, and soon. The only trouble was that the dangerous patrol duty which was likely to do it for him, and for which he continually volunteered so cavalierly, proved to be more than one-man affairs. This meant that the well-intentioned men of the platoon would have to accompany the officer on his heroism-bound assignments.

Such was the case on the morning in question. The forward elements of the regiment on our right flank had sighted an enemy roadblock about a mile ahead of our advancing columns. The message, relayed to our CC by radio, advised him that the roadblock consisted of a single small tank and several troops, probably with a machine gun. The regimental commander relayed the message to our battalion commander, who got it to our company commander. He, in turn, passed it along to our section.

Lieutenant Ellis' immediate response was, "Yes sir. We'd be delighted to check it out." Jesus! Shades of the football hero with the "Put me in, Coach" complex. Except, this Ellis asshole didn't seem to realize there was lots of war still ahead and he'd have ample opportunity in the normal course of events to earn his goddamn medal!

But there it was. He'd gone and done it again. He'd volunteered us. Or some of us.

The lieutenant, flushed with victory at the thought of having beaten out other junior officers at getting the mission, returned to the platoon positively aglow. Everyone groaned silently at the sight of his advancing, jauntily striding form. Ellis smiled victoriously, showing his straight, even, white teeth.

"Sergeant, alert your section."

"Yes, sir," I said wearily. The lieutenant was right, of course, chronologically. The other section had pulled the last patrol into the wooded area immediately above St. Die. The fact that the last three patrols pulled by the second section had been milk runs with no enemy sighted failed to budge the lieutenant in his desire for equity. "We take our fair turns, men," he had advised during his introductory policy speech. I had just finished complaining to him that the guys in my section were worn out and deserved a little relief. We had run into fire fights on every single patrol we pulled in the past month. The last two, in fact, had been veritable hornets' nests which had cost us three men wounded.

The road along which we proceeded now ran in a straight line for about a quarter of a mile, very gently sloping downhill. We obviously had crossed the ridge of this hill and were on the far slope approaches. It was hard to tell exactly where we were because of the intensely heavy forest on both sides of this Vosges Mountain roadway. The trees reached sixty feet and higher into the sky.

Then the road disappeared around a curve to the right among some heavy evergreen concentrations. Nothing could be seen among the thickly wooded areas ahead of us, and the map had proved exceedingly sketchy as far as short sections of road were concerned. This proved intensely burdensome to those of us who had to explore such stretches which, while appearing as an eighth of an inch on a piece of colored paper, proved, more often than not, to be several hours worth of hellish activity, often resulting in serious injury and death to too many of the men involved.

We came upon a road sign nearly hidden by overhanging branches of heavy shrubbery. The lieutenant pulled aside the branches to reveal a sign proclaiming "Remiremont 14 Km." and an arrow pointing in the direction we were going.

I sent Simmons ahead as lead scout. I took second scout position myself. Simmons crawled down the ditch until he could see around the bend in the road. Then, rising to his feet, he waved the rest of us on. This indicated that all was well, I assumed. As I came up to him, about fifty feet ahead of the lieutenant and the rest of the men, Simmons said, "Hey, Sarge, I can't see nothin'. The road is pretty level for about a hundred yards then seems to dip downhill. I can't see what's over the hill there."

I immediately signaled caution to the others. What we really didn't need here was laughter and loud talk from men who thought a signal meant all was well.

I moved to the spot just vacated by Simmons and looked for myself. The next stretch of visible road was, as he had said, relatively level, then seemed to drop over the edge on its downhill path. It lay under a heavy green umbrella of overhanging branches from the huge trees.

While the lieutenant was consulting his map board, I signaled Simmons, and he led out with the rest of us following at about ten-yard intervals. The lieutenant now was third in line, followed by seven rifle company men who had been attached.

Simmons dropped into the ditch before reaching the end of the level stretch of road. He gingerly checked the five-foot embankment on his left. Rising, he walked back to me as the lieutenant came forward to us.

"I can't rightly see, Sarge. There's a rise in the road just over the edge there, before it drops off again down into the valley. I can't see nothin' over that rise. I didn't hear nothin' either."

Lieutenant Ellis dashed anxiously up to our conference.

"What is it, Sergeant?"

I apprised him of the facts as relayed by Simmons. The lieutenant pondered but a split second. Then, charging out into the middle of the road, he strode boldly over the hump and directly down the highway in full view of anybody who might be down there.

"All right," he said firmly. "We can't tell until we look, can we?"

I signaled the riflemen back around the bend in the road and began looking for a sheltered space over the embankment.

Ellis walked down the new stretch of road until he stood in the middle of it, looking ahead and down the hill. With no sign of fear whatever, he calmly proceeded to assume the prone position and, unsheathing his binoculars, raised them to his eyes very deliberately.

"Sergeant, there's a light tank down there and a log barricade. I can see at least thirty or forty German soldiers wandering around the position. We had better move closer if we are to dispose of the roadblock."

"We were only supposed to reconnoiter, sir," I called to him, trying desperately not to shout.

"That crazy son of a bitch is gonna get us all killed!" Simmons croaked. He was now a battle-hardened veteran of a campaign and a half in a war which required less than a day in action to create veterans.

"Simmons, take three men and make your way through the trees on the other side of the road until you're as far down there as the lieutenant is. Don't show yourselves, though. I'll take the rest of 'em down this side in the trees. You should be able to cross over back there at the bend without being seen. That dropoff is more than fifty yards away."

Simmons nodded. "Right." Then, grumbling under his breath, he headed back to where I had sent the riflemen. He led his three across the road into the thick forest on the other side. Almost immediately, they disappeared, although I could hear them picking their way through the undergrowth.

The other riflemen were walking tentatively toward me along the edge of the road on my side. I signaled them up over the bank into the trees. The lieutenant, ignoring my admonition, still was lying full length in mid-road, watching the enemy through the glasses.

As I moved my people through the trees, I stayed as close to the road as I could without being seen, just so I could keep tabs on the situation. I took another look out at the lieutenant. We were practically abreast of him now. There he was, lying there as if he were watching some sailing regatta on an inland lake.

I hand signaled my men behind trees. There really was nothing to be seen because of the vastness of the forest's thick growth. We couldn't see more than ten feet ahead of us.

Suddenly, the lieutenant moved on hands and knees to the ditch on the far side of the road and stood up in the heavy growth just beyond it. I squinted through the overhanging trees and saw the lieutenant reach out and take a rifle from someone. I couldn't see the other person, but it must have been one of Simmons' riflemen. The weapon was an M1 and we carried Tommy guns.

Then Ellis stepped bravely down into the ditch again, went down on one knee, and called across the road to me.

"Sergeant Lister."

"Yes, sir," I acknowledged his call, sotto voice. At this point, he and I were directly opposite each other, some forty feet apart.

"There seems to be a foot patrol of Germans headed up this way in the ditch on your side of the road. They are carrying axes and other equipment besides their weapons. They're probably going to chop down some trees to delay us until they can get away."

"How many of them are there, sir?"

"I would judge about twenty."

"How far away are they?" I asked with increasing nervousness.

"Not far now," Ellis replied, raising his rifle. He sighted deliberately from his exposed position and began firing single rounds at the approaching enemy which still was invisible to me.

All at once, immediately ahead of me and not more than ten to fifteen yards away, a large party of surprised German soldiers burst into the underbrush.

"Jesus Christ! That goddamn fool!" I muttered in amazement.

"Cover me and fall back," Ellis yelled. I could hear the four men over there charging through the trees.

"Oh, that crazy bastard!" I fired one short burst in the general direction of the sounds of confusion just ahead of me. My men opened up.

Groans could be heard, and shouting, just beyond the trees in front of us. I waved my Tommy gun from side to side, just spraying in the general direction of the sounds.

The firing began again from across the road, this time about thirty feet behind us. It was Ellis, I guessed. I waved my men back. They broke and ran in a crouch position as the ripping of machine pistols sounded from the Germans. The Krauts couldn't see any better than we could, but they had much greater firepower in their 1,100-rounds-per-minute burp guns than we did in our 400-rounds-per-minute Thompson submachine guns. With that kind of firepower they really didn't need accuracy. One of their slugs could kill any of the men with me, or me, I thought bitterly.

We stopped and took cover behind trees again as we heard the group across the road stop firing. Then they could be heard crashing through the brush. This leap-frog procedure continued for two more short laps which brought the entire group together on the road behind the bend from which we had started. Several German bursts had split bark from the trees behind which I had taken cover.

The actual firing time for the entire episode was just over eight minutes. The volume of enemy fire, now more than sixty yards distant, had slowed considerably. I had emptied four clips of thirty rounds each and, like a fool, hadn't taken the time to recover them. As one emptied, I simply dropped it and grabbed another off my belt.

Ellis bounced jauntily toward me from the roadway where he and the men with him had crossed.

"Well, we have our information," he beamed. "They have a log barricade down there about half a mile away. That patrol should be starting back with its casualties soon."

"Begging the lieutenant's pardon," I said aloud in full hearing of all the men. I really should have moved in close enough so that only Ellis heard it. "That was the biggest horse's ass trick I've ever seen pulled in combat!"

"Sergeant?" Ellis said, his forehead pulled into a frown of confusion.

"I mean, exposing yourself like that in the first place. Then firing alone at an armed group that size without laying a plan of attack. We didn't know what in hell was going on! We couldn't see a thing and you were talking out loud with them that close! What if your rifle had jammed over there? You'd have given away your own position and those of those men."

"What's the matter, Sergeant? Chicken? I thought you'd been through a lot of combat." His smile was one of extreme insolence.

"Yes, sir, and what brought me through it was not pulling bonehead stunts like yours back there."

"Careful there, Lister," Ellis snarled. "I could have . . ."

He was interrupted by the whiz of a high-velocity tank shell. All the enlisted men dropped into the ditch beside the road. Ellis and I stood our ground. However, as the second and third shells roared in, I decided discretion was in order. I, too, dropped into the ditch.

Actually, we were in no position to be hit directly. We were around a bend. The tank was down at the bottom of the long, straight road, firing up that alley. His shells would have to be able to swing around corners to hit us directly. But the trees they were hitting down there at the place where the road turned were being scarred badly, branches were being broken off, and shell fragments were flying everywhere.

The lieutenant stood boldly, defiantly, leering at the enlisted men, contempt written all over his face. Apparently the fact that the tank was in no position to score a direct hit gave him a sense of false security.

Razor-sharp pieces of spinning, white-hot metal flew through the air, striking indiscriminately at trees, bushes, rocks.

Suddenly, Ellis grunted in surprise. He dropped to the road, lying on his side. "I'm hit! I'm hit!"

"Simmons. Give me a hand, quick! The rest of you stay down. Oh, you, soldier." I pointed to the one farthest from me. "Get back to regiment as fast as possible. Tell 'em to bring a jeep up here. On the double!" The man was on his feet and away.

The firing stopped. I nodded to the others. "You might as well go back too."

The men all stood up and began moving quickly toward the rear.

Lieutenant Ellis lay where he had fallen, his head cushioned in his folded arms, an expression of pain and mute amazement on his face. He was in agony.

Simmons and I checked him for blood stains. We found them. We removed our cartridge belts and began taking off our first aid packs. As we did, we looked at each other and smiled slightly.

Lieutenant Ellis wouldn't be winning his DSC, not for a while, at least. He would receive a medal, though — the Purple Heart. He had sustained a long, fairly deep, very painful, badly bleeding, but not eternally significant cut across the entire width of his rather adequate buttocks.

20. Ninety Rounds Per Man

ERNIE AND BILL had left me alone in the dining room earlier. Ernie had heard of an opportunity to trade a concentrated chocolate bar for a half bushel of apples. His appetite being insatiable, he reasoned that this would be a logical move. His slender frame continually amazed me in the face of his constant hunger, to say nothing of the volume of food he put away at a sitting.

"Hello, my friend. Have you finished or will you have another cup of coffee with me?" Arentz said as he entered the dining room to find me seated by myself.

"Sit down, Emil. Glad to see you. Are you coming to the party tonight?"

"*Jah. Der Oberstormfuhrer* and Lieutenant Küttner have ordered me to put chairs in the room. When that is done, they said they will allow me to have some wine with the other guests."

"Well, it should be fun."

"*Ach,* I don't know. I don't like so much this army life, I tell you this. Not like some of those others. Heller has been in a uniform since he is a boy. Now he gets old. Und der Spiess . . . *ach,* that one. He is already eighteen years a soldier. That's too much for me. I want to go back to the farm."

"Maybe it won't be too much longer," I tried to encourage him. This attitude was most unusual for Arentz. He usually effervesced constantly, no matter what shitty duty he was assigned. As he cleaned out and polished garbage cans, he could be seen smiling broadly and singing to himself. So today's doldrums seemed most unlikely to me.

"The war, you mean?" he asked.

"Yeah. It should be over pretty soon."

"Who do you think will be victorious?" Arentz asked in a flat, quiet, confidential tone.

I was surprised at the question. With the recent news of the Allied advances on all sides, bracketing Germany; American and British troops already well across the Rhine; the Russians deeply into the eastern portion of the Reich, I hadn't thought that anyone, even an SS storm trooper, could have any honest doubts.

"Are you serious?" I asked.

"Of course, serious. We are told our armies are repulsing the enemies everywhere they attack us. Soon we shall be fully victorious, *nicht wahr*? We don't hear the radio, of course, and they don't let us see anything from outside in our letters from home."

"You mean they censor your incoming mail?"

"Of course," he said, matter-of-factly.

"Then you ought to listen to Allied radio, my friend. I'll tell you the truth. There's where you'll get the true picture."

"*Um Gottes willen!* That is *verboten!* You know this already," he said, shocked.

"Now look, Emil. In almost no time, all the rules will be changed, mark my words." I leaned forward and confided quietly, "You remember what I say. The Greater Third Reich will throw in the towel within a month or so, or I miss my guess."

"Towel?"

"Give up. Surrender."

"Deutschland defeated? Never. No, Hal, you shouldn't say such things." He looked around nervously over his shoulder toward the office. "If the wrong person hears you talking so . . . you are in *schrechlich* . . . frightful danger."

You are in frightful danger. How familiar that sounded suddenly, especially with the thick accent Arentz effected. I thought back to the last time I had heard an identical phrase muttered anxiously.

"You are in frightful danger, Signor Lister," Giovanni had said, worry lines deepening on his face. "Your back is still not strong enough. I should take your place. You should not go. I know the terrain better anyway. And the *tenente* told you you didn't have to go on this patrol."

Giovanni Scalzi had been a volunteer guide for the division ever since Marshall Bodoglio's capitulation of the Italian army. He had been invaluable as a guide throughout the campaign up the costly ankle of the Italian boot. He spoke the dialects of the southern provinces and was personable in his approach to the suspicious natives.

During the Anzio campaign so far, his services had been much more valuable to the division in regimental headquarters where he had proven extremely adept at reading and interpreting enemy maps and documents we had captured.

He had become a highly capable cartographer and entered into the intelligence work with vigor and fervent interest. He hated the Nazis with a venomous fury, showing intense impatience whenever one of our patrols would pass toward the rear any group of captured Germans, sending them to the evacuation area instead of shooting them once they had answered our questions.

"Prisoners make no sense," he would say. "They are Nazis. They should be dead! That's for all the *Tedeschi!*" He would touch the old-fashioned trench knife whose handle was a set of brass knuckles. He kept the knife in the top of his combat boot which, we all felt sure, must have been uncomfortable with the knife's four-inch blade rubbing his ankle. Still, it had a certain psychological value on occasion during an interrogation of prisoners. I didn't know where Scalzi got his trench knife, but I knew of nobody in the area who used this weapon as regulation equipment. It was World War I vintage. I had found one months ago, but got rid of it because it was just too heavy to carry.

With the fall of Cisterna de Littoria to the division's right front, the way had been cleared for breaching the mountains which had held us all stalemated captives for the past four bloody months.

Giovanni was becoming nervous being out of action for so long. He had been a good soldier in combat, I was sure, although what I had seen of the Italian army in action hardly justified such an opinion. The man, however, had shown indomitable courage on the few patrols we had pulled together, always willing to give just a little more than the Americans who weren't fighting to liberate their own homelands. He never took prisoners, preferring to stand in virtual face-to-face confrontation with a Kraut machine gunner against his own tiny carbine, rather than take cover and pick off the German gunners. He was a furious opponent of *Tedeschi.*

Under either artillery or small-arms fire, Giovanni had exhibited apparently limitless endurance, fired by his intense hatred of the enemy and what they had done to Italy. He had taken to me as his favorite and clucked about me as a mother hen would about one of her chicks.

Scalzi's constant worry since I had returned from the hospital was the weakening of the incompletely healed back wound I suffered in that house explosion in February. I had returned to the beachhead from the mountaintop convalescence hospital at Venafro, my upper trunk still encased in a partial plaster cast from just below my breast to my hips. The manpower situation being as desperate as it was, I felt I was needed, despite my dread of returning to the hell of combat on Anzio. A feeling of utter loyalty to my outfit, possibly a stronger emotion than I ever felt in my life, forced me to sell the doctors on the lie that I felt much improved.

Scalzi had hovered about me ever since I returned a month and a half earlier. He performed menial tasks to prevent aggravation of my injury. I really was grateful for the relief from many of my heavier physical burdens that Giovanni provided.

Weber had observed wryly at one point, "Hell, you're as important as the colonel, by God. You got your own personal dog-robber. Hey, Sarge, does he warm your shit paper for you on these cold mornings like the colonel's number-one boy does for him?"

But the chiding was good-natured. Every man in the squad knew of my affliction and my reason for prematurely returning to the outfit. Tickler had been evacuated to the States. The rest of the crew from the explosion were still in the hospital in Naples. Mixed emotions greeted my return. The men and I knew that my value to the platoon could be nullified if I allowed my nerves to act up during a vital patrol action. Still, the men seemed to respect my effort to continue doing what I could to lighten their load.

Velletri lay in the saddle between two massive mountains directly ahead of us. Velletri itself was a little to our left front. To the right of the gap between the two hills was Cori, well up on the mountainside. In fact, it was from Cori that Bill Mauldin later drew his famous cartoon showing his heroes, Willie and Joe, looking back toward the sea from up on the mountain.

"Geez," Willie's captioned observation went, "They wuz here

and we wuz there." This just about summed up the feelings of every Anzio Beachhead veteran who made it up the mountain that far. The unbelievable advantage the Krauts had had in observation, firepower, defensive position . . .

Cori had been abandoned, we were advised by returning recon patrols from the 7th Infantry, our sister regiment, although, with the extremely static nature of the "front" and the constant encroachment and infiltration by German units, nobody could be completely certain.

Only Giulianello left any doubt as to its status as abandoned or occupied by the Krauts. It was a tiny village beyond the pass, on the far side of the hill mass which faced us immediately to our front. Giulianello had to be checked out and its condition affirmed before the regiment was ready for an overall advance through the gap.

The village was an unknown factor with strong defensive possibilities. It could be the site of heavy concentrations of enemy armor or a perfect, zeroed-in artillery target, or it might be ringed by machine gun nests and enemy infantry. On the other hand, it might be entirely free of any German troops, providing us with an enjoyable and rare respite from the shooting war for the hour or two it would take to go to and through it and up into the hills beyond. Nothing could be seen with any clarity by aerial reconnaissance due to extremely heavily forested areas surrounding the village itself.

Now that the combined firepower of every unit on the beachhead had been lined up virtually hub-to-hub in an all-out breakout attempt — the longest continuous firing since the British turned Rommel's forces and began the route at El Alemein in Libya a year before — the Anzio Beachhead had threatened to explode in two directions, the east and the north.

American infantry units were making contact with beachhead forces already along the coastal highway from the south where, after months of stalemate, they finally bypassed Cassino and came up the shortest, fastest route. Now it was a truly allied force which threatened to burst through former enemy positions, punching its way off the tabletop flatlands and pushing on to Rome, some thirty-five miles to the north.

My platoon had drawn the assignment of leading reconnaissance activity into Giulianello. Since Tickler left, I had been hospitalized for over a month. Upon my return, I was given my third stripe. I still felt terribly anxious whenever a stray shell flew over, and the sound of a plane flying above sent me into internal paroxysms of fright. I didn't know if the others noticed it. I'm sure I would in anyone else. Still, they stuck with me. The thrill of finally breaking out of the hell of Anzio Beachhead outweighed everyone's fears now.

Lieutenant Borden had ordered me to pick my ten men for the patrol. Cpl. Frankie Fortino would be next in command behind me. Scalzi was begging for a chance to go, either as a patrol member or in my place, even if it meant taking the point position throughout the entire area to be covered.

"Look, Giovanni, I have to go. The lieutenant said so. But let me see what I can do. I'm supposed to pick the patrol. Why don't I just include you in it?"

"*Grazi, grazi, il Sergenti mio!*" the little Italian shouted, jubilant at the thought of facing more *Tedeschi*. He pounded my shoulders in his pleasure.

"Hey, take it easy!" I winced.

"Oh, *Sergenti* . . . I forgot your back. Forgive me, please. Forgive me." He was desolate in his apology.

"Lister, got your patrol?"

"Yes, sir. I've included Scalzi if that's all right. He's going wacky from rear echelonitis. Besides, he knows part of the territory."

"Fine. That's fine. He's a good guide and he does know the country. Here, now. Here's the final on the map," the lieutenant continued.

Major Colby stepped up to our small group. "How's the back, Sergeant?"

"It'll be OK, sir. I'm fine."

"Good. Now look here, men . . ." He pointed over Borden's shoulder to a spot on the map. "Here's Cori. We expect it to be cleared. Your mission is to make sure one way or the other. Keep in constant radio contact, Lieutenant. You'll approach on the main highway here. Over here is Velletri. You'll be making your way around this point behind the city, back toward that road junction just below Giulianello. Velletri is enemy-occupied. We know that. We're still taking some artillery fire directed from there. They have at least two guns on the top of that mountain above the city. If everything goes well, you should get your information and be back by late tomorrow. Be careful."

The major saluted in response to the lieutenant's salute. The major obviously was through with his contribution to our patrol and had stepped back upon completion of his last admonition. He turned and left us.

"You know, Lister, this may not be as smooth as he thinks," Lieutenant Borden said. "We have definite information that the Hermann Goering Division or elements of it are still somewhere in this area. At least, they were two days ago, according to prisoners we've been taking throughout this entire sector. They've moved out of the spot in the gap here, according to aerial photographs. We know that much. We'll have to find out where they are or where they've gone."

I nodded. "Yes, sir. As I understand our mission, we are to climb to Cori, circle back behind it, behind Roca Massina, then through this wooded area to Giulianello, and return through the same saddle."

"Right. But you're forgetting the guns."

"Guns, sir?"

"Those two or more guns above Velletri that still are firing on us. We also have to find them."

"Christ, sir. That's meat for a whole other patrol. It'll take us a full day just for that part of it."

"Then we'll just take the extra day, Sergeant. Now check out rations for three days, just in case. And advise your men of the mission, Lister."

"Yes, sir."

I gathered my people and explained as quickly and clearly as I could where we were going. "You'll each take rations for five or six meals at the most. Travel as light as possible."

"Oh, and Sergeant." The major had turned back. He stopped and faced me without returning to us. "Remember, depending on what you run into, you might be out of radio contact for a period of time. That's especially likely in that heavily wooded section shown just to the east of Giulianello. Take plenty of ammo, though, just in case you run into anything. Try to have your top radio man on at all times. We'll try to stay on you around the clock, but it's imperative that we know as much as possible about what's in there before the regiment takes off. And try to pick up a prisoner or two. We don't know where in hell these Heinies have spread themselves during the last few days. They're all over hell and gone."

"What about that prisoner B Company took yesterday, sir? He said something about a paratroop outfit, didn't he?"

"Naw. Well, yes, he did, but I don't believe him. In fact, the 15th Infantry had a patrol partway up that hill last night. If there were any Krauts there then, they seem to have taken off like big-assed birds since. The area seems to be clean as a whistle now. We're just trying to be extra cautious."

The interview was ended. Everything that had to be said was said. The major stood erect, immense at his full six and one-half feet and 240 pounds. He extended his hand, first to Lieutenant Borden, then to me. "Good luck. See you in a few days."

We all exchanged salutes and separated.

"Lieutenant?" I asked, once we were out of earshot of the major.

"Um?" the lieutenant asked, absently. He appeared to be lost in thought.

"I'm worried about that mountaintop gun position thing, sir."

"Me too, Lister. Me too."

"Well, we'd better hop to it if we're gonna cover all that territory in three days."

"Right, Sergeant. Better saddle 'em up now. We'll move out as soon as everyone is equipped."

"Yes, sir." I moved over to the waiting men. "OK, you guys. Fall in. Everybody checked out on canteens and ammo, Frank?"

"Right," called Fortino. He was at the rear of the group handing out the last three extra, loaded Tommy gun clips. "That's ninety rounds per man plus the thirty they're carrying in their pieces, Hal."

"Jesus. They'll be all pooped before they've gone a mile, Frank. Those damn clips get heavy as hell, you know."

"Not as heavy as a body once it runs out of ammo," Fortino reminded me.

"I suppose you're right, but it's still gonna be a hell of a load. Anyway, I hope they'll be just as heavy on the way back. What about chow?"

"Everybody's eaten just now. They all have three chocolate bars — the concentrated stuff. And a can of cheese with two packs of crackers. That'll have to last 'em, I figure. Myself, I'd rather have the extra ammo."

The lieutenant was approaching, his carbine hanging limply from his left hand at the balance.

"All set, Lieutenant."

"All right. Move 'em out, Sergeant." The lieutenant took the lead, his long legs biting gigantic, spirited strides with each swing of his hips.

"All right, men. Movin' out. Five-yard interval as soon as we get to the railroad tracks."

The men spread themselves into their prearranged order. I ran the few yards that brought me close to the lieutenant. Fortino was right behind me, struggling along on his short, stubby legs. He was swearing under his breath at the extra weight he had selected to carry in the form of the Browning automatic rifle. In a separate bag slung over his shoulder, he carried six clips of ammo.

For the first quarter hour, we enjoyed a hitherto unknown luxury on the Anzio Beachhead — the opportunity to walk openly along a road with no enemy shells falling about us, no German machine guns ripping trails through the air in search of us. Each of us was too in-grained with the habits of violent combat we had known, though, to take full advantage of the current lax situation.

This thing was far from over, and death might lurk as close as the high railroad embankment we were approaching. Each man in the patrol was tensed for a quick, automatic dive into a ditch at the first hostile sign.

We reached the embankment on which lay the badly chewed tracks across which we would go for our first real worrisome test on this mission. We had crossed it often in the past few months, but always in the dark. Now, for the first time, we were able to see a great distance on all sides as we topped it. But we didn't stay to enjoy the view, silhouetted as we were atop the bank. Entire sections of the rail had been torn askew by repeated artillery hits and bombs over the past five months, artillery from both sides. Just before the lieutenant reached the top of the bank and ventured over it, he looked back over the strung-out patrol.

"Close 'em up a little more, Lister," he called back to me as he jumped down the far side.

"Keep it five yards, not twenty!" I yelled back to the men who shoved forward to try and close the gap between them. Then I, too, vaulted the tracks, followed by each man singly until the entire dozen were over. This could present a perfect target, making it vital for no two men to rise at one time.

Burke, right behind Fortino, had the radio strapped to his back. The column worked its way down the ditch on the far side of the tracks, up the far embankment and across Highway 6. Another fifty yards and we reached the steep road leading a serpentine trail up the mountain to Cori.

"Hey, Hal, lookee theah," shouted Judge Nottingham, who was in sixth position.

I looked back and then in the direction he was pointing. There, less than 100 yards from us, at the edge of a wooded area, were the remains of the battery of 88s we had knocked out more than a month ago. We could see the three still pointing upward, looking very much like partially peeled bananas. They were shattered, as was the area around them.

The climb took an exhausting forty minutes. The sun was out in full now, the temperature hovering in the eighties. Each man's shirt showed dark wet wherever it touched his body tightly. Perspiration ran down our backs, our sides, our legs, into our combat boots. And from under our helmets, a literal torrent poured over our brows, noses, and cheeks.

The lieutenant stopped us, and we sent Fortino and Judge out to reconnoiter the outskirts of a tiny village of ancient stone buildings cramped together in typical Italian fashion, and dropped against the dull, unproductive stone of the cliffside.

Lieutenant Borden gave the rest of the patrol a welcomed break in the shade of the trees until the two returned. He and I checked map coordinates with them against the panorama before us. The two men reported that Cori did, in fact, appear to be completely deserted.

Of course, that was no true assurance. Back in February, during the counterattack that had nearly done us in, the Rangers on our right had tried to enter Cisterna de Littoria after being informed that it was cleared. The outfit was destroyed when the entrenched Krauts killed, wounded, or captured most of them.

The lieutenant sent Keller and Freeman above the road on the high side as outposts. Then he rejoined the rest of the patrol to permit the men to finish their nervous smoke. It was too quiet so far, uncomfortably peaceful compared to what we all knew had to be in these mountains somewhere nearby. At least, every one of us was sure. We had learned to develop these gut feelings in numerous campaigns.

"OK, let's move 'em out, Sergeant." The lieutenant stood and immediately continued the climb up the road. He was a tireless campaigner, a tough old soldier for his rank. He had more than twenty years of service behind him.

In fact, the romantic story about the lieutenant, which had made its way via latrine-o-grams from regimental headquarters, was that Lieutenant Borden, now a first lieutenant, had been a major in the

45th Division during the Sicilian campaign. The story went that he had lost the better part of a battalion in a single, ill-advised, frontal attack against overwhelming odds in an impossible position. The attack had been at the direct order of his regimental commander. Major Borden had ordered his men out against his better judgment, but a score of years in OD had taught him to behave like an automaton in such circumstances.

Covering for the colonel's poor judgment, however, the major had been broken to his permanent rank of first lieutenant and promptly cashiered from his division. He had been reassigned to the 3rd Division as an Intelligence and Reconnaissance platoon leader as an alternative to a court-martial. We didn't know how much truth was in that story. However, there wasn't a man among us who considered it completely apocryphal.

The lieutenant was a sad-eyed, soft-spoken, stern-visaged Oklahoman whose quiet, undemonstrative humor had endeared him to us. I always thought of him somehow as "The Major."

The remainder of the morning was occupied with the climb up and around the mountain, often on the narrow road, much of which had been bombed or shelled away into the abyss that yawned beside and beneath them. In places, the remnants of the road clung tenaciously to the mountainside by roots of roadside trees, with no other visible support.

At one spot, we passed a line of burned-out German tanks . . . big ones. They apparently had been strafed from their vulnerable rear, the hot slugs entering the thinner rear deck metal surrounding the motor and fuel area. I had seen many tanks explode internally when the fuel — gasoline in American tanks; diesel fuel in the German vehicles — ignited. They became sealed cremation chambers for their crews in such cases.

Shortly before noon, we paused for a break beside a wooded hill below and behind Velletri. Defensively, the men moved nervously and automatically backward, edging into the shade of the forest.

"Lister," Lieutenant Borden called. "This looks like the place where we're supposed to go in." He pointed to a horseshoe-shaped clearing at the edge of which we were sitting. In the center of the approximately acre-sized clearing was a field of grain, yellow and leaning away from a soft, warm breeze. It resembled wheat and stood about three feet high. Trees ringed the wheat field on three sides. We were to enter the clearing from the open end of the horseshoe, as determined by our map. Then, we were to follow a very wide pathway into the forest.

"We'll have to be doubly alert from here on," Borden reminded me, unnecessarily. "No tellin' what kind of troop movement they've got going on in this area. We'd best stay in the woods as deep as possible, understand, Sergeant?"

It was a rhetorical question.

"I'll get them moving, sir." I arose and turned to the patrol. "OK, off your dead and on your dying. Keep your eyes open from here on. Watch both sides of the path and unsling your pieces."

The group slowly stood, and Tommy guns and BARs were brought off shoulders and into anxious hands, action-ready. Thumbs moved anxiously toward safety catches as the nerve-tingling sensation of entering the absolutely unknown again assailed each of the combat-hardened men in the group.

The twelve of us skirted the grain field rapidly, eager to get under the protective cover implied by the high, heavy trees. We watched the undergrowth on both sides of the wide path. We were in an intensely vulnerable position with no appreciable cover for the few moments it took us to cross the clearing.

We entered the forest at the position indicated earlier by Lieutenant Borden and found ourselves in a densely covered glade with a few narrow, dust-filtered beams of sunlight reaching the soft, leaf-covered forest floor. The huge trees on both sides of the twenty-foot-wide path formed a vast, thick umbrella over us.

The depth, natural beauty, and peaceful serenity of the place infected each of us. We stood for a moment, gazing high into the branches, astounded to hear the carefree sound of birds again after so long. It was strange, I realized, that we hadn't noticed the lack of bird sounds all these months.

Except for the birds and the occasional rustling of the leaves, kissed by the gentle, soft, treetop breezes, no sound could be heard. It was as if the war had completely ignored this little corner of a tortured country. An occasional tiny forest creature scurried frantically across the path ahead of us as our heavy feet announced our approach.

Violent deaths had occurred within a few hundred yards of this quiet setting in recent months, but no sign of that could be seen here. It was truly the forest primeval. Lieutenant Borden immediately sensed the false security that such a location could engender in his men. He called the patrol close about him, signaling the two outpost men to stay where they were.

"Keep your eyes open more than ever now," he said in a loud whisper. Every man tensed upon hearing the tone of the officer's words. It implied a knowledge of imminent danger. "This is an ideal situation for an ambush," Borden reminded us quietly.

As if awakening from a daydream to the frightful reality of our vulnerability, each man stumbled to alertness and into position, automatically taking the recommended and traditional five-yard interval between him and the next man. Everyone now was completely alert to the danger implicit in this idyllic setting.

"Keep it quiet now," Borden ordered. "No speaking aloud, no smoking, no laughing — nothing that could give away our presence. Got it?"

We all nodded assent. Borden moved out, his long legs swinging well ahead. We moved through the dark wood for another hour and a half. Again, the tension of too much silence began to pall on the men. The only slight solace we received was the sound of the birds, now louder and more numerous than ever.

Suddenly, Lieutenant Borden stopped his own forward progress and deterred the men behind him with a hastily upraised hand. Instinctively, every man in the patrol moved off the path to alternating sides, their eyes on the officer. Frankie and I moved forward, quickly and quietly until we were beside Borden. He pointed well up the left wall of the deep "V" through which we were walking. He had seen movement up there somewhere.

Then Fortino and I saw it too. It was too far away for us to make out clearly through the trees, but there definitely was movement in the brush about 350 feet above us on the steep slope.

Silent hand signals immediately were sent down the column, indicating the course each man was to follow as the lieutenant wordlessly showed Frank and me where he wanted the men positioned. They were distributed strategically throughout the area, each man well camouflaged.

I waved to Keller and Freeman to accompany me as I advanced up the slope. We headed gradually across the front of the hill toward the upper right, a path intended to bring us up and around that side of whatever we were stalking. Our eyes riveted on the now nearby spot where we had sighted the movement. We began our steady climb, pausing every few yards behind thick tree trunks.

Simultaneously, Fortino started up toward the left, followed closely by Scalzi and Judge. The lieutenant squatted behind a twin-trunked berth with Burke and the radio just behind him. Steve Bogacz, Mooney, Johns, and Mitkiewicz were scattered along the bottom of the pathway, their eyes trying to focus on the nebulous target.

Carefully picking my way up the steep slope, taking precautions not to step on dried twigs, I continued my ascent. Far to my left, I could see Fortino and his two men circling in the opposite direction, their weapons alertly at port.

For a panicky moment, I lost sight of the spot we were seeking, then recognized the naked rock formation that jutted out just below it. Our goal seemed to be some sort of promontory or ledge, covered with mossy grass. Heavy shrubbery protected its forward edge. I could make out nothing more from my present position, almost on a level with the spot. No movement was visible there at the moment.

Keller and Freeman, both about ten yards below me, watched me intently.

We had completely lost sight of the other three now because of the thickness of the trees through this elevation. We were sure, however, that they had reached a point almost as high if not higher. I tried to stop to get my bearings, looking up and down the hill in both directions. Nothing was moving anywhere. The path far below seemed totally deserted.

Suddenly, I heard Fortino's voice, quiet, but with an excited laugh. Presently, the little Italian corporal approached the edge of the ledge, carrying a tiny, black-haired girl in his arms. She couldn't have been more than two years old. She was wearing a tattered blue dress and was covered with dirt.

The two men with me and I dashed across the intervening space to reach the ledge in time to find an amazing sight. A cave extended deep into the hillside and this ledge served as both front porch and entryway for a settlement of terrified Italian civilians, threadbare and frightened as they sat huddled within the cave's opening. They appeared to be evacuees from one of the beachhead towns, judging by the pitifully meager bundles of personal effects they had with them.

I moved to the front of the ledge, signaling those waiting far below that all was well. Lieutenant Borden and the others immediately began climbing toward us at full speed. Finally, the entire patrol was grunting its breathless way up the last few feet of the steep slope.

We spent as long with the now delighted and relieved civilians as was needed to interrogate them. The people, four old men and eight women of varied ages, with five little children, had run away from Velletri three weeks earlier. They had been living on the small store of staples they had been able to bring with them, supplementing their diet with roots, herbs, and berries. They were all related to each other in some way. Their young men had been drafted into the Machi, they told Scalzi.

"What's that?" Borden asked.

"Machi. That's the resistance movement, sir," Scalzi said. "You know, *partigianos.*"

"Ah, partisans." The lieutenant nodded understanding.

Scalzi immediately turned back to the children with whom he was playing delightedly, and started distributing his meager supply of rare and invaluable concentrated chocolate bars. He was among his own again and reveled in the opportunity to play with the children and shake the welcoming hands of the older men and women. They conversed animatedly with much hand-waving.

"OK, here's the story, Lieutenant," Fortino said as he pieced together what he had been able to obtain of military significance from the refugees.

He squatted with the lieutenant and me at the edge of the stone outcropping. Frankie diagrammed the situation, as he understood it, in the dirt with a stick.

"There's some sort of clearing up topside of this hill. According to the old man back there, there's at least one artillery piece up there. He doesn't know the size. He says every time one of them ever gets close to it, you know, when looking for berries and like that . . . the Krauts would fire a machine gun over their heads. The last time they heard the gun fire was last night, just after dark."

"From what direction did these people approach it?" Borden asked. Fortino returned to the oldest of the women who had just come out of the cave. She animatedly pointed around the hilltop to the far side, on our right.

"She says the hill straight above here is much too steep with mostly rock outcroppings, sir," Fortino advised us. "So they found a narrow path about forty feet up there and followed it around to the first vertical path . . . really two wagon ruts. I think that must be the way the Krauts got the gun up and supplied the position, don't you, sir?"

"Very likely," said the lieutenant, "particularly if that's the direction in which their defensive field of fire has been set up. They aren't likely to be defending these steep cliffs that way, not expecting anybody to come up this way."

"Er, Lieutenant," I faltered. "Now that we know where the position is, why would you be picturing a way of getting up there?"

Of course, before I asked, I knew . . . and, by the look on his face, so did Frankie. The lieutenant had decided on another goddamn suicide mission. Not satisfied with learning the enemy's artillery emplacement whereabouts, he was going to go after it! I couldn't help wondering how many of these deals we were going to come across before we got out of the war alive . . . if we did.

"Oh yeah, another thing, sir. The old lady there said something else too. Every so often a Kraut patrol has been comin' down that path we came in on, in the direction we came from."

"You mean going in the opposite direction to ours?"

"Yes, sir."

"How often?" the lieutenant asked.

"Well, according to these people, they don't do it very regular. One day it's in the morning, another time, in the afternoon."

"How about vehicles?"

"Only once, sir. They saw a guy on a motorcycle with a sidecar going back into the woods along the path."

"How big has the patrol been that came through here?" the lieutenant continued.

Fortino again asked his informant. A hurried, whispered exchange occurred during which Fortino repeated twice, *"Quando Tedeschi?"* The reply brought forth a shoulder-shrugged reply, *"Otto."*

"Eight, Lieutenant," Frankie called, holding up all five digits on his right hand, the thumb, forefinger and middle finger on his left, in typical European style of finger counting.

"Hell, I wish I knew what was going on up there," Borden said. He was staring up the hill. "They might have anything from a single gun to a battery. See if you can find out any more about this situation, Fortino. I'd hate like hell to have a large Kraut concentration move in between us and home."

Frank talked to the old woman and her husband, who had joined us on the ledge. They knew no more than they had told him before, it seemed, except that there was another narrow path that bisected the one just above us. It cut down the hill on a gradual decline. It was pretty overgrown, the old man said, which probably was why the Germans didn't use it as a supply route.

The lieutenant and I snapped our heads around the second this information came out. "You mean the Krauts don't know about it?" he asked.

This seemed to be the case. It was relatively unused, the old man said. The children had found it one day while out playing along the horizontal path. The road was about fifty yards back in the direction from which we had come, he added.

"Well, we have to check the damn thing out," Borden announced decisively. "That sounds like a logical way up. Lister, you take three men and get down there to check out that path. Be careful, and try to work your way up to the top. We'll start up along here slowly. I don't want to alert them by running into a machine gun outpost."

I picked Keller, Bogacz, and Freeman. We moved up the steep hill to the horizontal path. Then, able to stand upright on it, we turned left and headed in the direction indicated. This was a pretty well-established path, much of which actually had been cut into the mountainside. As we reached a bend in the path, about sixty yards from the cave, we looked back. The lieutenant and the others, in two groups, had begun to climb diagonally through the trees above the cave. The two groups, in a sort of skirmish line, formed a shallow "V" as they climbed, taking occasional cover behind trees.

My group turned and continued along the path until we came to the vertical path running diagonally down the hill. The upward part of it was harder to see, it was so overgrown.

It took about fifteen minutes of steady climbing before the ground leveled off slightly. Shortly after reaching what seemed to be the level hilltop, we crossed another path which ran along the ridge line of the mountaintop. Far to our right, we saw movement through the trees which we quickly identified as some of our other patrol members. We waited until the lieutenant had assembled them and moved them toward us, keeping within the tree line.

"Did you see anything on the way up, Lister?"

"No, sir. Only that this path goes all the way to the wide roadway at the bottom."

We were whispering. The rest of the men, fully aware of the precariousness of our position, didn't have to be told to keep absolutely silent. The safety on every weapon had been switched off.

"Apparently, whatever's up here is dead ahead of us on this level. But, as I see it, we're to its side rather than its rear," Borden said. "Sergeant, you and Fortino get us some information."

I nodded, and Frankie and I moved out cautiously, keeping as low as possible. We carefully avoided loose limbs or twigs on the ground, or any hanging branches. The foliage was so thick just ahead of us that our vision was limited to roughly twenty feet or less. The rough path we were following curved several times before we reached what resembled a widening of the path. This might be an approach to a clearing. I put my hand on Frankie's arm and nodded to the left. We made our way silently in that direction to the edge of the trees.

"Holy Christ," Frankie whispered excitedly. "Will you look at that?"

Ahead of us stretched a clearing easily two acres in size. Beyond the far edge of it, a man-made swath had been cut into the trees, giving the gunners a direct sighting view down into the beachhead. From as far back as we were, Frankie and I could see much of the beachhead area below the clearing, including the harbor and the road junctions we had crossed so often.

"Jeez, no wonder they could drop them fuckin' things right in our pockets!" Frankie hissed. "Them sons a' bitches!"

What interested me right now was the gun emplacement itself. It stood just about in the center of the clearing, dug into a pit which appeared to be about two feet deep. The cannon was an ancient 75-millimeter piece with large wooden-spoked, iron-rimmed wheels. The crew was busily engaged in moving a stack of ammunition from a former emplacement, now empty, to a spot beside the present hole.

One German soldier was in the pit. I could see five more moving between the holes, moving the ammo. I assumed there might be one or two more on some sort of outpost. I saw no sign of a machine gun emplacement.

"Frank, get back to the lieutenant, quick. Tell 'em to be quiet coming up here!"

Fortino crawled away and disappeared from view. In a few moments, he was back with the lieutenant in tow. The other men in the patrol hovered back in the trees. Together, the three of us surveyed the situation.

After his initial survey, during which I briefed him of the personnel I had seen, the lieutenant asked quietly, "What about that machine gun emplacement the old lady told us about? There must be at least two more Germans with it, maybe further down the hill over there. Tell you what, let's get three groups out. Lister, take two men around to that far side of the clearing in the trees so you can hit 'em from over there. Fortino, you take three men and go back along that path. Try to find the machine gun nest. You'll probably come in on it from behind. Keep the element of surprise in your favor. I'll take the rest of the men along this side of the clearing until we're abreast of the gun. I'll start firing up there. Check your positions before firing so you aren't shooting into us. Fortino, better give Judge your BAR and take his Tommy gun. It's just as efficient at close range and a lot easier to transport. Besides, I want the heavier firepower up here. And remember, we need a prisoner or two. Now move!"

The curt, whispered instructions stopped as the lieutenant waved us back to the others.

Frankie picked Scalzi, Freeman, and Keller. They started tiptoeing along the path, moving into the heavier trees. Mooney and Johns answered my finger instructions and followed me. The others gathered around Borden.

We made our way silently through the trees to approximately the place suggested by the lieutenant. I looked through the leaves into the clearing. The Krauts apparently were still unaware of our presence.

We could see the gun clearly now. We were approximately thirty feet from the muzzle and about forty feet from the nearest German soldier, the man in the gun pit. They certainly had picked an admirable spot for a gun emplacement. And I wondered if, with the extreme height, it wasn't virtually untouchable by American artillery even if we'd known it was here. The camouflage netting also managed to keep the site hidden from prying Piper Cubs.

I couldn't see any of the others across the clearing, but, as I was scanning the far side through eyes squinted against the bright sun, BAR fire burst out of the woods way over there. The first long burst caught the Krauts flat-footed. Two of them fell immediately over the boxes they had been carrying. Others began running toward the gun pit. One of them was caught and fell just as he reached the edge of it. Tommy gun fire now could be heard farther back. That would be Frankie's group attacking the machine gun nest. Other guns now joined in the one-sided battle as my group began firing at the survivors.

One of the Germans turned and aimed his burp gun in our direction but, before he could fire, Johns pinned him against the gun carriage with a single shot from his Tommy. The two surviving Krauts threw down their weapons and held their hands high in the air.

One of Frankie's men, I couldn't make out who it was at this distance and in the bright sunlight, ran out and herded the pair toward the far side of the clearing. I scanned the entire field of the short battle and cautiously began edging out of the trees.

At the same time, Judge left the lieutenant's group and carefully entered the clearing, too, his BAR in firing position, resting on his right hip. Keller also entered the open area, just five yards behind Fortino, who was standing about ten yards into the opening.

We cleared the trees and, satisfied there were no more Krauts in the surrounding underbrush, began our dash across the clearing to the point from which we'd started. Suddenly, midway across, we encountered the oilcloth-ripping sound of the German burp gun from the left somewhere.

Judge and I were closest to it and we turned simultaneously as two Krauts entered the clearing from the forward slope of the hill. In the brief but furious exchange of fire, both of them went down. Judge sustained a minor flesh wound to his left shoulder, but it wasn't bleeding badly and required just minimal first aid.

The entire patrol gathered about the lieutenant, Scalzi, and Freeman standing guard over the two kneeling prisoners.

"Where in hell did they come from?" the lieutenant asked, indicating the two latecomers.

"Out of the trees down there. They might have been an OP for a forward gun position, sir," I said.

"Yeah, or they might have been the forward element of some relief unit. Let's clear the hell out of here," Borden urged.

I thought his reaction a bit unlike the lieutenant. He wasn't one to panic, and those last two could hardly have been leading a relief column coming from the direction they did. I wasn't sure what was going through Lieutenant Borden's mind.

"Want us to spike the gun, Lieutenant?" Fortino asked.

"No, we don't have time. I don't imagine they'll be using it again anyway. Come on, let's make tracks."

Going back down the steep path was a lot easier than the uphill climb had been. Furthermore, the possibility of large enemy forces circulating throughout this general area spurred our steps. We reached the wide path at the bottom of the hill, and the lieutenant turned sharply to the right, back toward the American lines.

"We have all we need with these guys," he said. "We'll stop down the road a way to interrogate them briefly."

I nodded my understanding. The patrol moved about half a mile along the path when Lieutenant Borden called a halt. The men broke to the side of the path, sitting against trees in the soft grass.

"Giovanni, bring the prisoners up here," Borden called in a loud whisper.

Scalzi, looking after his charges with rare enthusiasm, pushed them ahead of him until they stood before the officer, their hands clasped behind their necks. Giovanni actually looked disappointed. I assumed it was because he hadn't been authorized to end their lives with his trench knife. But he followed orders despite his frustration. Perhaps, after Signor Tenente finished with the questions . . .

I signaled Keller, who rushed forward. He did most of our field interrogating of Germans because of his three years of the language in high school. I had picked up considerable German myself, but still lacked enough grammatical knowhow to converse easily.

"Keller, find out their outfit," Borden ordered.

"*Du. Wie heisst deine Regiment?*" he asked.

The first prisoner, a hard-looking man in his early forties, stared at us stonily. The ribbons and medal decorations placed about his uniform jacket with no apparent plan indicated that he had seen considerable service. He wore the oval laurel wreath which corresponded to our Purple Heart, for wounds received in action against the enemy. This was worn on the left side of his uniform jacket, midway between waist and shoulder. He also wore a small ribbon across the buttons of his jacket, high on his chest. It was tan and red, identifying him as a member of the Afrika Korps. Just below it was another small piece of ribbon folded between two buttons, one I had seen often among prisoners. The Iron Cross first class for heroism. He looked back at Keller, his face expressionless.

"*Heinrich Gerber, Unteroffizier, Nummer drei, sieben, vier, acht, acht, swei,*" he muttered.

"What was all that?" Borden asked.

"That, sir, was name, rank and serial number."

"Try the other one."

"*Du. Deine Regiment, bitte? Los! Los! Antworten, bitte!*"

"*Ein und Zwanzigste Hermann Goering Fallschirmjaeger,*" the younger man answered, nervously.

"Goering?" the lieutenant asked, suddenly more interested.

"Paratroopers," Keller explained. "21st Hermann Goering Paratroop Regiment."

"Jesus, they aren't supposed to be here," I interjected. "Last I heard, they were in Yugoslavia. Find out where their CP is, Keller."

"*Du, wo den ist dein Kommandaturie?*"

"*Hinten, vieleicht dreizehn Kilometre,*" stammered the man. His companion sat staring sullenly at the ground now.

"*Sind sie auch ein Fallschirmjaeger?*" Keller asked the first, older man. The prisoner nodded affirmation without looking up.

"They're both paratroops, sir. Their CP is about thirteen miles back that way." He nodded in the direction of the German rear area, the opposite of our present route.

"All right, see if their entire outfit is there, or if they are from a separate detached unit."

"*Du,*" Keller turned his attention again to the younger, more talkative prisoner. "*Ist deine ganze Regiment hier?*"

"*Weis nicht,*" the young man replied.

"He says he doesn't know, Lieutenant."

"Probably doesn't, not the way he's been willing to talk up till now. And he still looks kind of scared. Well, that's about all we could have found out anyway just now," Borden said, looking around. "Let's get these people back to division. They'll get more out of 'em. Boy, they'll be happy we brought these birds back with us." Then, more to himself than to us, the lieutenant said aloud, "Hermann Goering, huh? My God, we wiped them out in Sicily and again at Valmontone. I had no idea they had regrouped this soon."

I remembered the 21st Paratroops too. We also had faced them in North Africa. While the 3rd Division had defeated them soundly both times, it was at awesome cost. The lieutenant wouldn't have been aware of the African confrontation, having been with the 45th then. They hadn't come into the war until Sicily.

"Sergeant, space your men so these two are in the middle with one of ours between them. I don't want them feeling comfortable enough to exchange information. Keep 'em nervous."

I arranged the column so that I followed the lieutenant and Burke followed me with the radio. Then came, in order, Fortino, Scalzi, Judge, Bogacz, Keller, the older German prisoner, Johns, the younger prisoner, Mitkiewicz, Freeman, and Mooney.

"Let's go," the lieutenant whispered. "And watch your interval."

The silent trek began. We had about five miles to go before reaching the clearing from which we had entered the path. Our mission accomplished, we would cut over half a day off our patrol time. We walked rapidly toward home.

21. "Johnny, can you hear me?"

W E WERE APPROACHING the clearing from which we had entered the forest. We could see the waving yellow wheat in the midst of the cleared spot. The return journey had taken about an hour and a half so far, including two short map-checking breaks. The lieutenant had sent Freeman ahead to check the condition of the clearing and the level ground beyond. Lieutenant Borden was absolutely paranoid on the subject of the movement of enemy troops. He saw Krauts behind every tree, we all felt sure. Freeman returned to report seeing nothing suspicious.

"OK, same order of march, except, Lister, I want you to bring up the rear," the lieutenant said. "At this rate, we'll be home before sundown. That's fine with me. I don't relish coming up on our lines in the dark, not with the situation as it is right now."

"Yes, sir," I said, waiting until the others had passed me. Then I fell in line and followed them around the grain field.

As the fellows in the line went by me, I noted Johns shoving the nose of his Tommy gun into the older prisoner's back a little too enthusiastically. "Lay off, Johns," I said quietly. Both German prisoners were looking around nervously. Probably afraid of going out into the open without tree cover. They had been so badly shelled whenever they had done that lately, this was understandable, I thought.

Our group filed around the grain field, close to the outer fringes. The lead element turned the far corner and was headed toward the trees on the far side when all hell broke loose.

It was impossible to tell immediately where they were. In fact, they seemed to be everywhere! Several German machine guns had opened up on us. I heard a grunt and saw the lieutenant spin around and sit down. He didn't lie down. He simply sat there, his head on his chest. I instinctively fell and rolled into the grain. I could hear others bustling into the field too. It wasn't cover, but it might shield me from gunners' eyes at least until I could get my bearings.

The firing was coming from several directions. Individual rifle fire was going on too. The automatic rapid fire of heavier weapons echoed back and forth across the small grain field. Bits of wheat clipped by bullets were falling all around my head. I felt a tug at my right heel and dug deeper into the ground with my face, trying all the while not to make any bodily motion that would divulge my location.

My Tommy gun was held crosswise, across the front of my head, to help ward off any bullets coming from that direction.

Occasional groans filled the air. The seemingly endless fusilade of bullets ripped through the field from side to side and end to end. Thousands of slugs tore across the cramped little area for what seemed like hours. Actually, the entire episode took roughly three minutes.

The ambush had been eminently successful. Apparently, the Germans had moved into position surrounding the field while we were in the forest. Neither they nor we knew the other was there until we had exposed ourselves in the open. They made no move until our entire patrol was exposed, then opened up on us with machine gun fire from three sides. The riflemen also had had a field day.

The firing stopped. Suddenly, I realized that my heart was pounding fit to escape through my mouth. My throat was unbelievably parched and dry. My hands were shaking. It had been an eternity.

I turned my head cautiously and became aware of his presence. Our older prisoner of a few moments ago was standing over me, pointing his burp gun at my back, a smile on his face. He waved me to my feet with the weapon.

I struggled up and placed my clasped hands behind my neck. This was the position automatically demanded of our prisoners, so I assumed it was what they would want of me.

Looking around the field as I was being conducted out of it, I saw more Germans rounding up a few other members of my patrol.

Keller and Mooney were standing together on the far side of the clearing, guarded by two Krauts. Freeman and Fortino were being marched out of the grain field toward them. All had their hands clasped as I had mine.

Judge sat beside Keller, holding his left knee in both hands. His hands were bloody. I started to walk, but felt a sharp, stabbing pain in my heel. I limped toward the others, my guard directly behind me.

As I left the grain field, I saw Lieutenant Borden sitting where he had fallen. It was eerie. He simply looked as if he were resting, except for the two neat little holes through the right temple of his helmet and the pool of blood forming beside his right knee.

Then I passed Bogacz' body. It apparently had been hit by the first burst, and he lay spreadeagled on his back. Several successive machine gun bursts had run lines up and down and across his liberally perforated corpse. Nearby, Burke, his radio smashed to bits, lay, also on his back, staring at the clear, bright sky with sightless eyes, mouth agape. Three running red spots showed clearly on his throat. Already the busy black flies had begun congregating. They were thick about the bleeding wounds. I wanted to wave them away but realized the futility of such an act.

As I approached the others, still limping, I passed the still, stiff bodies of Mitkiewicz and Johns, both lying face down, several holes clearly visible in their shirt backs. They, too, obviously were caught in the crossfire.

Two Germans called to the ambulatory Americans, waving them back into the field. Keller, Fortino, and I were closest. We found Giovanni Scalzi lying on his back in the grain, bloody spots showing where his shirt met his belt buckle. He was clasping his midsection with bloody hands, his face contorted in agony. We carried him to a protected area back on the path from which we'd just emerged only moments before. We laid him down at the side of the path where our guard indicated.

I knelt beside Giovanni, trying to comfort him. His babbling was incoherent, and he was somewhere besides with us at that moment.

"Johnny," I called softly to him, holding the little Italian's shoulder tenderly. "Johnny, can you hear me?"

Scalzi frantically whipped his head from side to side, groaning. He was unaware of my presence. I stood and looked about, trying to survey the casualties. Of the twelve men who had emerged from the forest, only Fortino, Keller, Freeman, Mooney, Judge, and I remained alive or likely to survive, and Judge and I were wounded. Scalzi was sure to be dead in a matter of hours, if he lasted that long. So, that meant six killed, six captured, two of them wounded. Judge's bad knee was being tended to by Fortino and Keller.

Only then did I remember my own heel which still stabbed painfully. I sat on the ground and unbuckled my combat boot. The laces were ripped open, and I pulled the heavy shoe off. My heel was bleeding, the entire end of my sock soaked in blood. The bullet had penetrated the entire rubber heel. Had the shoe heel not slowed its progress, the bullet could have ripped all the way through my foot, shattering several bones.

I forced the slug out of my heel. Most of the bullet had cut into my foot, but its base still held in the rubber of the heel. I put the boot back on and laced and buckled it. The Germans, meanwhile, were organizing burial details. They apparently planned to stay here for a while. Each prisoner was given an assignment and all were busy for the next two hours. We used donated German trenching shovels which were smaller and clumsier to use than ours.

Fortino and I were assigned the lieutenant and Bogacz. We began digging shallow excavations in a neat line. Keller and Mooney were digging two other holes beside ours. Freeman and one of the German soldiers were busy carrying bodies to the burial place. The limited facilities and precarious position in which we found ourselves necessitated hasty burials with complete lack of any ceremony. Just as I completed patting the pile of dirt on Bogacz' grave and laying his helmet on the mound, one of our captors called from the far side of the field, excitedly pointing into the sky. Every man on the field looked up. Flying slowly in a small circle was a Piper Cub. He was at about 1,000 feet, but the circle of observation almost was certain to indicate that he had spotted this activity in the open field.

We barely had time to place helmets on each grave with the appropriate dog tags tied inside the liners. We finished our macabre obligations and dashed back onto the path under the cover of the high, arched tree limbs. We had just enough time to crawl under the hollow overhanging bank beside the path.

Scalzi had been placed further down the path under a slightly deeper overhang. No attempt was made to comfort him now. He was barely conscious. He was crying and calling softly, *"Mama mia . . . Mama mia . . ."*

"Fantazieren," observed one of the German soldiers, clinging to the bank on the other side of the path. He pointed to Scalzi with a nod of his head, indicating that it was the dying man to whom he had referred, not unkindly.

Scalzi's cries had become more quiet in the past few moments, then they stopped as a gurgle of blood bubbled over his lips and down his cheek onto the rough pallet, then to a growing little pool in the mud beside the path. He lay stiffly on his back, his eyes staring into the green, leafy umbrella overhead. He didn't see it. His left arm was paralyzed in a doubled-up position in the last second of his life.

Suddenly, the fear we all felt was justified as the Cub's message apparently reached a distant artillery position and was relayed to anxious gunners, lanyards in hand.

The shells literally cascaded down on the forest glen, many of them bursting in the treetops, spraying their deadly pieces in all directions. The screams of the shells were joined by the cries of the wounded Germans further up the path where most of the damage was being done. The barrage ripped huge pieces of bark from immense, multi-centuried denizens of the forest. Whole branches crumbled or were torn off under the fury of the attack. Then, as suddenly as it had begun, the barrage ended. The combined troops there in that heavily wooded glade still clung to their protective, slightly roofed walls for several minutes until it was obvious that no more shells would be coming in, at least for a while.

An officer stamped down the path, followed by a retinue of variously ranked enlisted men. He busied himself ordering the still cringing troops into activity. His screamed commands caused every German soldier to jump toward the rear area along the path. The lieutenant then looked over the American survivors. Turning to one of his sergeants, the officer ordered Scalzi's body buried among the trees just off the path. Then he bent down and gently examined the area of Judge's injured knee.

"Are you able to walk?" he asked.

"Ah don't think so, suh," Judge replied, wincing. He tried to rise.

"Stay," the lieutenant said. Then he turned to me. "Sergeant, you and your men will take him back on a litter. Are your other men all right?"

"Yes sir, I believe so."

"Good. Then you will go to the rear with some of my men as soon as the burial squad completes its work. Several of my men were killed just now by your artillery." He turned to acknowledge one of his enlisted men who approached him from the rear. *"Bist du fertig?"*

"Jah wohl, Herr Leutnant," the man answered, saluting.

"Wie viel Hatben wir vorloren?" the officer asked.

"Neun tot, vier verwundet."

The lieutenant frowned at the thought of his nine dead, four wounded.

I couldn't help but feel somewhat pleased at the retribution just visited on these people. It hadn't been a very good trade, of course. It never was. But at least the enemy also knew what I felt when I realized I had lost six men and had another wounded. The Germans' thirteen casualties compensated somewhat.

"Come now, you will go to the rear. For you the war is over, eh?" The lieutenant had a trace of a smile at one corner of his mouth. One of his men ran up with a folded canvas litter with wooden poles as side handles.

Keller and Fortino carefully placed Judge on the stretcher and the sad procession started toward the rear. We were sandwiched between the German litter bearers and two guards who brought up the rear of the parade. Two more Krauts walked ahead of us, one turning back periodically to check on us.

Occasionally, as we passed over a particularly uneven stretch of the path, we jostled the stretcher unavoidably, causing Judge to grimace or grunt in pain. But immediately, he would smile up at his buddies to let them know there were no hard feelings.

We walked for nearly three hours, pausing only five times to permit a few moments of rest and the exchange of litter bearers. Finally, we came upon a very large clearing. The entire area was covered with a roof of tree limbs more than forty feet in the air. Several eight-man pyramidal tents were spaced about the area and behind some of them were vehicles of various descriptions, each covered with camouflage netting. This obviously was the command post about which we had heard, but it was only about five miles from our earlier position, rather than thirteen, as our prisoner had told us.

The German litter men disappeared behind a group of tents with large red crosses on their roofs. The other Germans in the clearing all were busily engaged in packing and loading vehicles. It was apparent that the CP was in the progress of bugging out. One of our guards had gone into a nearby tent, probably the orderly room. He emerged a moment later and conferred with the other guard.

"Now listen carefully," I whispered to the five men gathered about me and on the stretcher. "They look like they're pulling out. That means we won't be likely to take a lot of interrogating. They probably won't have time. Now remember, we don't know a thing. Play it dumb all the way. Tell 'em about the Kraut tanks we saw above Cori if you want, but nothing about the breakout."

"Hell, ah cain't tell 'em nothin' when I don't know nothin', kin I?" Judge asked, smiling.

The men all nodded understanding. I felt relief when I realized suddenly that all the survivors of my patrol were old-timers who knew their way around. All of them had been in the outfit in combat through at least two campaigns. Freeman was the most recent to join and he came in before Cassino. We had gone through enough prisoner preparation for interrogation to know generally the type of questions likely to be asked, and had been given enough time together since our capture, with no talking restrictions, to formulate answers which wouldn't help the enemy.

The tent flap was pulled aside and a heavy-set, short man came out. He looked about fifty, I thought, and wore the epaulets of a full colonel.

"Oh Christ, the top honcho himself," Fortino whispered over my shoulder. We all, except Judge, stood at attention as the officer approached us, two guards flanking him.

The little man withdrew a pack of German cigarettes from his tunic pocket and passed it around, giving each of us one. He was deliberate in his stalling, and I felt more comfortable suddenly, realizing that we were going to be given the sugar treatment rather than being intimidated with threats.

"How iss your friend, Sergeant?" the colonel asked finally.

"He's been hit in the knee, sir," I replied.

"We will have our medical officer look at him, *nicht*? Meanwhile, I want you to come with me, Sergeant." He turned and walked back toward the tent.

Upon entering the structure, I noted that the field office was comfortably appointed despite the packing which had disrupted part of it. The interior was much more spartan than similar frontline quarters for an American colonel would be, I observed with mixed emotions. The colonel indicated a wicker rocking chair in front of his desk as he walked around to his own chair.

"Please be seated, Sergeant. Now, then, suppose you tell me your name, rank, and number." He seemed to enjoy my recitation. "And now," he continued, "let us discuss the purpose of your patrol."

"To find you, sir."

"To . . ." The officer stared at me for a moment. Then he stood and walked around to my left side, staring at my blue-and-white-diagonally striped shoulder patch. "Ah, I thought I recognized your unit. Sird Infantry Division, *nicht wahr?*"

I said nothing. I didn't have to.

"Ah yes," the colonel continued. "Almost old friends we are by now, eh? Twice we have met before."

"Three times, Herr Oberst," I corrected him, suddenly realizing as I said it that it probably was a mistake to do so.

"When was that?"

"In North Africa, sir."

"Oh, but I was not with the division in those days. But you knew, did you, that we were here."

"Yes, sir."

"But tell me, Sergeant, how did you know we were here?"

"I don't know, sir. Possibly from a prisoner. I only followed orders," I lied.

"Oh, come now, Sergeant. Do you expect me to believe this? We are old friends, after all. Surely a man of your rank would be more conversant with such matters."

"I don't know, sir."

"Let us not pursue the matter. Now, tell me about armor."

"Armor, sir?"

"*Jah,* armor. Panzers, er, tanks. Are they moving from the Nettuno front with the infantry and, if so, which way do they plan to go through the mountains?"

"I really don't know, sir. I'm in the infantry."

"You mean to say you have seen no tanks since your large attack the other day? After all, the Nettuno front provided the first major opportunity for your armor to operate in Italy. Surely you have seen many tanks!"

"Oh, yes, sir. I saw six of them yesterday morning."

The colonel smiled at the expected victory. He was mentally wringing his hands; I could feel it. "Ah, that is more like it. And where were they?"

"On the road behind Cori, sir."

"Behind Cori? In the mountains?" The colonel turned and consulted the map behind his desk, mounted on a tripod. He turned his head to me, keeping his right forefinger on a spot he found on the chart. "Behind Cori? What were they doing there?"

"Nothing, sir. They were all burned out."

"Burned out already? But I've heard of no tank battle up there. What kind of tanks were these?"

"I think Mark IVs, sir."

"Mark IVs?" he asked, seeming increasingly surprised.

"Yes, sir. They were German tanks."

He sputtered briefly and, in his fury at the unexpected reply, knocked his heavily braided, stiff-visored field cap to the floor. Gasping for breath, he laboriously bent over and retrieved it, giving himself a chance to regain composure somewhat by this maneuver.

"Now then," he continued with strained patience, "we wish to know about the Japanese. Word has come that they have joined your division in this attack."

"Japanese, sir? Oh no, we're fighting the Japanese, too, in the Pacific."

"*Ach,* this I know, you fool. I am talking of the Japanese fighting with you here in Italy!"

Of course, he referred to the intrepid little band — the Nisei combat team — the 100th Infantry battalion, attached to the 34th Division. Most of the boys of Japanese extraction from Hawaii, and some from the West Coast, were outstanding infantry troops. They had sustained frightful casualties in marking up one of the truly memorable records of the European war. Later, they were combined with other recently transported Nisei in France, to become the 442nd Regimental Combat Team.

"No, sir," I said, shaking my head in apparent confusion. "I never heard of any Japanese on our side. We have an Indian chief in our regiment, but no Japanese."

"*Ach,* you are a fool. A fool, do you hear me? How did you ever get to be a sergeant?" The colonel was red-faced by now. "Send in your next in command," he ordered.

I stood, saluted, and retired. I was warmed by the knowledge of the German officer's frustration. I approached the group and nodded toward the colonel's tent.

"You're up next, Frankie. Play up the Kraut tanks we saw. Oh, and he's interested in the 100th Infantry. You know, the ones we don't know about?"

"Check. I'm one ignorant son of a bitch," Fortino grinned as he headed for the colonel's tent with the guard who had accompanied me back from there.

I squatted among the others and, trying to appear as nonchalant as possible, briefed them on the questions I had been asked. I told them my answers. The remainder of the interrogations took about a half hour. Apparently, the officer hadn't varied his questions and, as he stormed out of his tent at the end of the session, it was obvious that his disposition wasn't improved by the replies.

He climbed into a command car and, as several enlisted men lifted the long poles which held up the camouflage netting, his driver slowly edged the awkward vehicle out of its parking place and down the rutted road beyond, disappearing into the trees.

We often analyzed what happened to us that day and agreed on one point — it had been extremely foolish of us to take such liberties with the high-ranking German officer. After all, he was not in his position because he was a fool. It was just that we had been given ill-advised freedom to discuss matters among ourselves when we were captured and no effort had been made to intimidate us. We simply had become overconfident. Fortunately for us, the colonel hadn't had time to deal with us as he might have.

It was nearly completely dark now, and my companions and I were wondering where we would be bedded down for the night. Just then, a non-commissioned officer approached us and ordered us into a truck that was being readied to pull out. The camouflage net already was up and we were being herded aboard. We slid Judge's stretcher to the front of the truck deck and placed ourselves around it. One of the two guards posted at the rear of the vehicle edged forward to look at my arm. He was an older man, obviously uncomfortable in his ill-fitting uniform.

"*Sie sind ein Feldwebel, nicht wahr?*" the man asked in a friendly tone.

"*Jah,* I'm a goddamn *Feldwebel,*" I shot back at him.

"*Sind sie verwundet?*" the man persisted.

I shook my head negatively.

"*Wie lang sind sie in Armee?*"

"*Drei Jahre,*" I replied.

"*Was ist dein Civilist Beruft?*"

I began to warm to this harmless-appearing old fellow. I was about to go through an elaborate description of my civilian salesman's job when the man interrupted me with a misinterpretation of a remark and, realizing how unimportant my answer really was in this conversation, I admitted to being a radio announcer.

"Hey, Sarge," Keller spoke up as the guard returned to the rear of the truck bed. "You should have seen that colonel's face when I gave him that shit about us fightin' the Japs. I thought he'd blow a gasket." Keller was choking with laughter.

"Same with me," I said. "And I kind of played out that story about those burned-out tanks behind Cori too."

We enjoyed a good laugh for the first time in days.

"Where do you suppose they're takin' us?" Frankie asked me.

"Can't say, Frankie. Probably some prison camp somewhere ahead, although I doubt it's anywhere we'll be very long. It looks like our people are movin' for keeps now. They'll probably take Rome in the next week or so."

The truck lumbered slowly along the highway, now in almost total blackness. Behind us, the sky was lighted with reflections of occasional muzzle blasts during artillery duels. The dull booming rolled across the mountains seconds later, resembling distant thunder.

A battle was on somewhere to the south, that much was obvious, and it proved a comforting thought somehow to the weary group of prisoners.

After about an hour's drive, the truck turned into a gravel driveway leading back into a huge staging area. Barbed wire fences surrounded the yard, in the center of which stood an imposing, shadowy structure resembling an immense airplane hangar. The guard at the gate approached the truck as it squealed to a halt, checked the driver's credentials, and signaled to another guard to open the gate.

Once inside, the truck stopped again, and the two guards dismounted. They called us to the ground. Other German guards came out of the sentry building at the gate and relieved the two soldiers who had accompanied us. That pair now climbed back onto the truck which made a U-turn and drove off into the night.

We were marched across the open areaway to a large sliding door at the front of the vast building. We waited while two Germans slid the door open enough to permit us to enter. Once inside, we found the door sliding shut behind us.

Straw-filled burlap bags were lying everywhere. The only light in the vastness before us came from a few widely scattered candles burning every thirty feet or so. A pile of blankets beside the door beckoned appealingly to us and we each got one. Then, out of a habit built during long periods in combat, we stood holding the edges of the blankets behind us in our extended hands, and brought our arms together across our chests, encircling ourselves with the blankets. Then we just lay down to get as much rest as the balance of the dark hours would afford.

22. A Circle of
Corporate Stockholders

"*APPEL! APPEL!*" THE call came, awakening me from the soundest sleep I'd had in months. At first, it seemed to come from a great distance. Then, as the haze of sleep wore away, we awoke to find ourselves among hundreds, perhaps thousands of stirring men. Daylight seeped in through high windows on the side of the building just below the roof line, perhaps thirty feet from the floor.

The building measured at least 200 feet in length and nearly 100 feet across. The high, arched ceiling, at its peak, looked all of sixty feet from the floor.

I observed men in many Allied uniforms, including Americans, British troops dressed in tan desert uniforms, other Britons attired in the heavier wool uniforms, Indian Gurkhas, their beards trim and neat despite their present circumstances, and several Anzacs — Aussies and Kiwis from down under, identifiable by their informal and distinctive wide-brimmed campaign hats, the brim on the left side folded up and held in place by regimental cap badges.

The call came again and the sliding door was pushed open from outside. The man who entered was extremely heavy-set, his jowls wobbling as he looked down at the clipboard nestled in the crook of his arm.

"Appel!" he shouted. *"Appel! Jeman aufstehen! Los! Los!!"*

The prisoners began edging slowly out the door. Columns of four were established as if by long custom. We made our way into the line of American prisoners.

Three fully armed and manned machine gun towers covered the area in which, I estimated in daylight, fully 500 prisoners of several nationalities were milling in a loosely knit formation. A German officer marched up and down before the line while two non-coms stopped before each file of four men deep, counting in fours in a half-aloud murmur to themselves. I smiled at the unusual sound of rapidly running numbers in German.

"Acht und zwanzig, zwei und zwanzig, drei und zwanzig . . ."

The count by the first man and subsequent recheck by his companion took nearly an hour. Finally, satisfied that all were present or accounted for, at least in number, the lieutenant ungraciously accepted the salute of his two men, turned, and left the area. The non-coms faced the prisoners and screamed German commands at the lines of bedraggled Allied troops.

"Also, fertig, fertig. Appel ist fertig. Freizeit jetzt. Freizeit!"

With that, the ranks broke and began mingling in informal conversation. Several American and British soldiers congregated about us, anxious to hear about the progress of the war which many of them had left long ago.

" 'Ey, Yank. What's 'appenin' with the war?" asked a short, chubby Englishman wearing the cap badge of the Northumberland Fusiliers.

"Starting when?" I asked.

"Bloody 'ell, I 'eard nowt since we got the rumor a few months ago that there was an invasion somewheres near 'ere. I reckon it was about thirty miles away, accordin' to the stories I've 'eard. We've 'ad no new ones in 'ere, though, for over four months, and they come up from Cassino."

"Four months? How long have you been here?" I asked the Tommy.

"Me and me mates was took at Tobruk in '42. But these Yanks over 'ere, they been 'ere only about six months, eh, lads?"

The small group of GIs, most of them wearing patches of the 36th and 45th Divisions, nodded almost in unison. I looked over the group before me. Further away from our immediate group, I saw patches from other familiar American outfits — my own, the 34th, the

1st Armored, the 82nd Airborne. The group, it turned out, had been taken piecemeal in North Africa, Sicily, and Italy. For some reason I couldn't figure, no Anzio Beachhead prisoners had been brought to this particular compound, or so it seemed. The place, I was told, had been an abandoned movie studio. This came from the little Britisher who, with nineteen months behind barbed wire, had become nearly permanent cadre.

More questions and answers were exchanged. Prisoners of long standing exercised their seniority by providing expert advice to the newcomers. Such information as the advisability of " 'opping it when Jerry gives an order," and "Don't trust nobody where your food is concerned," was rampant. The suggestion was to wolf one's food either before Jerry could change his mind and take it back, or before one of your starving buddies "nicked" it.

" 'Ey, mate. Got a fag on yer?"

Keller reached into his left shirt pocket. He began extracting a package of Luckies. At once, the entire crowd immediately surrounded us and began pressing in.

"Watch yourself, buddy," yelled a corporal wearing the gray-blue arrowhead of the 36th Texas Division. "Hang onto your butts. They're the most valuable things you got. And for Christ's sake, make 'em last."

We understood what he meant within a few days. We learned various survival techniques quickly. For example, we learned that only one man in a group would light a cigarette that had been carefully hoarded. He'd take two drags, then pass it around in a closely confined circle of corporate stockholders. Each of them would, quite honorably, pass it on after taking only two drags of his own. Following this solemn ritual, the butt was carefully snuffed out and returned to the original soldier's pack to become part of future makings.

Following the *Appel* about five days after our arrival, the assembly was not dismissed as usual. Instead, we were held in formation while a guard conference went on among the officers and staff of the Kraut cadre.

Finally, one of the non-coms, apparently elected because of his obviously self-admitted command of English, stepped out of the cluster of his colleagues and stood before the prisoners. We all stood in expectant silence. The air was electrically charged with anticipation, or foreboding. This was the first break I had seen in the dull, deadly, daily routine and obviously deserved our full attention.

"You men," began the Kraut corporal. Then, smiling at the stillness his opener had caused to hang over the assemblage, and proud of his center stage position, he began his halting announcement. "You men. All of you will leave here this morning. You are being taken north to Chermany. We have no transport for you so you will walk with the convoy. Keep in lines of six across. You will start with the Englanders first. You have ten minutes to gather your personal belongings."

He returned to his compatriots, satisfied that, with true Teutonic thoroughness, he had said what had to be said. There should and could be no questions.

Many of the prisoners, having no possessions except what they wore, stood about expectantly while the old-timers among them, especially the British, dashed inside the studio building to retrieve precious blankets, tin cans, and other trinkets which might spell the difference between survival and death.

Three truckloads of German troops pulled up outside the gate. There were about ninety of them in all who disembarked and formed two long lines bordering the driveway down to the road. All carried burp guns. I had no idea of what was coming, but was sure it would be no picnic.

The march began shortly before noon. The entire group headed northward toward the Eternal City. Although latrine-o-grams had persisted since the Allies hit Italy, it was amazing to our ragged group that Rome hadn't been bombed. As we entered the southern suburbs, we saw no buildings pockmarked with bullets or shell holes or craters. This was almost unheard of in Italy, which the Germans called the "*Meterkampf*" — the yard-by-yard war in which virtually every square inch of ground, every building was fought over and bitterly contested.

Our route through Rome took us around some of the most famous tourist attractions in the pre-war world. We passed the immense Tomb of the Unknown Soldier, covering a full city block and every bit as high, I estimated, as a six-story building. The tremendous life-sized statuary, spread all over the huge monument, was breathtaking, even from the distance at which we viewed it.

As we were being marched around another street corner nearby, we came in full view of the outer wall of the historic Coliseum. The structure, several stories high, consisted of row upon row of large arches through which could be seen the sky over the arena itself.

I recalled pictures and diagrams I had seen of the huge, oblong arena within the edifice. The overwhelming size of the stadium building from outside the walls seemed unbelievable to me. The path of our march took us around the base of the outside walls for about two blocks, then turned us in a northerly direction.

Throughout the days and nights that followed, I had several occasions to witness brutality at its worst as the Germans, in their frenzied rush to escape the oncoming Allied armies, stood for no malingering, either real or implied.

Many of the prisoners, weakened by sustained hunger, were held up and supported on the brutal march by comrades on either side of them. Otherwise, they might collapse and suffer the fate of soldiers who had fallen so far. At least six such unfortunates had died at the hands of their guards, following vicious beatings from the short-tempered, frantic Krauts. Several other prisoners were shot where they fell rather than cause the procession to slow.

The final blow came early the next morning when we passed a horse watering trough. Several of the British soldiers up ahead of us broke ranks to dash for the trough and grab a fast drink. They were shot where they stood, about eight of them. No effort was made to see if the wounds were fatal. They simply lay where they fell while the rest of the column was shunted quickly past the watering trough.

Time was becoming all-important to the escaping Germans. Food was scarce and the occasional break we were given was hardly enough to rest us for the ensuing two- or three-hour stint among the German military vehicles in the convoy that packed the road from side to side.

No rail traffic remained in central Italy, at least, none of any consequence which could suffice for the mass exodus of German troops and equipment. The crowded highway was jammed with every conceivable type of moving object.

Besides the straggling German troops who had given up the attempt to retain a semblance of military structure, hundreds of horse-drawn wagons loaded with indiscriminate supplies and military equipment were interspersed among wood-burning trucks, man-drawn carts, bicyclists, and tanks. Amid this conglomeration there staggered our ragged army of Allied war prisoners.

Throughout the daylight hours now, British Spitfires circled and occasionally buzzed us. Fortunately, the pilots appeared to have recognized this enormous, indefinable group as Allied prisoners. The message apparently had been relayed to their air bases because, as long as we were on the road, no attack was made on the crowded highway.

The first indication we had of the RAF plan was early one morning when the German guards appeared to tire of carrying their weapons and equipment and called for a short break. They herded us all off the highway and into an adjoining field. The welcome rest period came at the end of an all-night march in which several more men had been left to die beside the road. The break permitted the rest of us to climb off the road and collapse, footsore and bone-weary, on the bare field beside it.

Keller, Fortino, and our British friend who seemed to have attached himself to our little contingent, moved as far off the road as our suspicious guards would permit. I led the way and stopped the group when the nearest guard unshouldered his burp gun.

"Hey, Hal, does it look like we'll make it all the way?" Frankie asked.

"I wouldn't worry about it too much right now. We're in pretty good shape for a march like this compared to some of those other poor bastards," I replied.

"That's the truth, me lad," our English colleague said. "Some of the lads I started with 'ave bloody well 'ad it, I tell you. That mob of Wogs will be droppin' out next, mark my words."

"Wogs? Who the hell are they?" Keller asked as he followed with his eyes the direction indicated by the Briton's nod.

The group referred to were eight Arab soldiers from North Africa. Wearing American uniforms, these men had served as part of an advanced unit from the French army in the last stages of the African campaign.

Normally disinclined to obesity anyway, these men had become emaciated during their sixteen months of short rations under German imprisonment. The fact that they represented an "inferior race" to the Aryan "supermen" caused them to suffer even more than did the Caucasians, either British or American.

"Wogs. 'Aven't you 'eard that before? You know, 'Worthless Oriental Gentlemen,' " the Tommy continued.

"They still look pretty tough to me," Keller observed.

"Yeah, but how much more of this crap can they take?" Frankie countered. "They only get half rations now."

The four of us stared across the field at the Arab contingent. The North Africans kept exclusively to themselves, never conversing with any of the other prisoners. They stoically accepted whatever privation the Germans devised for them.

Our observations and conversation were terminated by a sudden roar from the rear of the column. We turned our heads quickly, just in time to catch the glint of the early morning sunlight on metallic wing-tips as the first Spitfire zoomed by just above treetop height. I looked quickly into the sky and discovered that the planes that had been circling above our parade now had roared down to the attack.

The speed of the first plane took it well past us before we could identify the source of the roaring motor. Scant seconds later, the second, third, and fourth planes whipped by, their machine guns spurting in long, concentrated bursts.

Immediately opposite my position, on the road where our prisoner assemblage had been standing only moments before, was a heavily laden old wooden wagon, its wooden-spoked, iron-rimmed wheels creaking slowly as its elderly, uniformed driver patiently waited for the two antique horses to move at a better pace.

Seemingly oblivious to the race against time which was in progress all about him, the driver sat hunched forward on the seat, his tunic collar up around his neck, despite the high temperature of early June. It was almost as if he considered the high collar protection against the bullets converging behind him.

The roaring of the first plane as it passed over him seemed for a frightening split second near enough to touch. It momentarily jerked him out of his lethargy. He looked up and ahead at the disappearing fighter, then back over his shoulder.

For the first time in the few moments I had been observing him, his weather-beaten, leathery face showed marked emotion. It twisted in understandable abject terror . . . fear of violent, painful death and fear of his own physical inablility to move out of the way in time.

The man's frightened amazement turned to a paralyzed horror as he saw the second plane approaching. The Spitfire kept steadily on course, the fire from its six .50-caliber machine guns converging at a spot some 300 feet ahead of it in a single, frightful blast that ripped down the center of the road, destroying everything in its path.

My fellow prisoners and I watched in horrified fascination as the line torn along the road by the heavy machine gun slugs ripped through a truck, cut a path along the middle of the road approaching the old man's wagon, smashed through the center of the wagon and beyond, then caught a heavy tank in its vulnerable rear, causing an immense explosion that incinerated the crew.

In the wake of the strafing attack lay the two horses that had been pulling the old man's wagon — mortally wounded. Both had been torn into a mass of quivering flesh. One of them kicked spasmodically in its death throes. The old man himself had literally disintegrated before our eyes under the furious onslaught of hundreds of pieces of high-velocity, hot metal. All that remained of him on the driver's seat was a gory pile of bloody meat, mingled with pieces of burning cloth. The man was completely unrecognizable as a human being who, less than ten seconds earlier, had sat with his hands ineffectually raised before him to ward off the anticipated blow.

"Bloody 'ell!" gasped the British soldier.

"Jesus Christ!" murmured an American GI standing near him.

Another GI, a few feet away, began crying. He stopped only long enough to retch. His dry heaves caused me to feel sick. The guards, their faces ashen, ran frantically among the prisoners, pounding us back onto the highway amid the carnage. Other planes could be seen farther down the line to the rear, but they were pulling out of their runs several hundred yards behind us.

As long as we were on the road, it was assured that no such attack would be repeated. The combination of malnutrition, fright, and the singular smell of death caused several of the prisoners to vomit. We picked our way around the burning equipment and among the bodies of dead Germans lying everywhere. Many of the dead had lost their faces, others were badly mauled by the large bullets that had ripped through them. Parts of bodies could be seen lying on the roadway and I nearly stepped on what remained of a leather jackbooted leg, the owner of which must have been one of several dead Germans lying nearby. It was impossible to make out where one corpse began and another ended, so completely torn were the cadavers whose blood ran freely and mingled abundantly in depressions in the road where bullets had dug out the macadam.

For several miles, we grew increasingly sickened at the enormity of the destruction and the procession itself. Those vehicles that hadn't been hit were moving at all possible speed as if to get out of range of future attacks. Unscathed foot soldiers left their comrades where they had fallen. Whenever possible, German officers with drawn pistols forced unwilling enlisted men to heave together to pull bloody carcasses of horses off the road, or to shove wagons and carts aside in their frenzied desire to expedite their escape.

Hours later, we still walked amid destruction. The hot sun now bore down mercilessly on the slaughter scene. The putrifying stench filled the air, announcing that many more dead lay ahead.

By this time, many of the horses and men who had been destroyed began to bloat. Most of them lay on their backs, a fact that puzzled me as I looked back on it later. The horrible, blackened corpses were bloating almost to the point of explosion, filling with gases which caused even those inured to violent death to turn their faces away. The stench, unbearable in its volume, became increasingly nauseating.

It took nearly six hours of steady marching, of breathing in short gasps into dirty handkerchiefs or the cloth of our sleeves, to leave the area of maximum destruction. Much of what we saw apparently was the residue of strafing attacks from earlier days. The writhing, crawling forces of nature already had performed their congenitally assigned duties, leaving behind little of the carrion but bones and pieces of uniform, some with bits of valourously earned medals and colored ribbon attached.

Darkness was approaching and this augured well for us. Darkness permitted longer breaks for us and for our guards, improving dispositions and gaining all a much needed rest.

Meanwhile, the survivors of the air strikes took advantage of the cover of night to gain as many miles as possible. Their efforts usually proved futile, but they tried, spurred on by the dreadful scenes they were leaving.

With each passing hour, the Allied troops wheeled north to close the gap forever. Artillery and tank fire could be heard in the rear now, several miles away. Counterfire lighted the night skies to the near south of the procession.

Despite the decimation of the enemy equipment during the air blows, the column continued to grow as each road junction we passed brought its share of new arrivals, escapees disgorging into the main line of traffic. The Allied air umbrella had become a routine occurrence during the preceding six days of the march. Breaks became more infrequent since the strafing strikes began because they invited attack.

We all longed for breaks for two reasons. We badly needed rest after tiresome hours of incessant marching along the Appian Way. But more important was the knowledge that, in some way, our taking advantage of these rest periods was contributing to the shortening of the war. Only when we were resting beside the road would the planes do their deadly work on the remaining military strength of the German forces in this part of Italy.

Recently the Spitfires had been joined in their attacks and surveillance of the column by American P-47s and the beautiful P-38s, their split tails identifying them long before their sting was felt.

Late on the evening of the sixth day, during a much-needed rest period, my companions and I lay about fifty yards off the road in a field of unmown hay. We relished the unaccustomed luxury of lying openly, flat on our backs, the fresh smell of the fields permeating the air around us. I stared at the clear, black sky dotted with myriad twinkling lights.

"Hal," whispered Fortino.

"Yeah, Frankie?" I whispered in reply, my eyes still pointed heavenward.

"What do you suppose they'll do with us? They sure as hell won't ever get us into Germany at this rate."

"I imagine they'll try," I said, suddenly feeling very sleepy.

"Like 'ell they will," interjected the little Tommy. His name, we had discovered, was, of all things, Bill Lister. He was from Bradford, Yorkshire. When he introduced himself, I said to him, "Bill Lister? That was my father's name." He had replied, "I'm not your bloody father!" We became fast friends after that.

"They'll bloody well do us all in, you mark my words. They'll never get us to that bloody Brenner Pass. Why, the British and the Yanks are on their bleedin' tails right now, you know. They'll 'ave to shoot us to get out of it themselves."

I had been pondering just this situation myself and had come to much the same inescapable conclusion two days earlier. The only rail system which could possibly accommodate a crowd this size was well to the north, much too far to walk in the time which remained before the narrowing gap between the Allies' forward elements and the Germans' rear guard disappeared entirely.

Little Bill might not have been the greatest sage in the world, but I believed he was voicing the fears of every prisoner who had given the matter any thought. We debated several possibilities of escape. The only difficulty heretofore had been the width of the valley through which we were walking. Lately, however, the mountains on either side of us had been drawing closer as the valley narrowed noticeably. We were approaching northern mountain passes.

Two nights earlier, a few men, including two Gurkhas, who were excellent night fighters, had tried to sneak away in the dark from the rest of the prisoners. They were intent on running once they reached a point far enough removed from their guards to prevent easy recapture. They were seen before they cleared the immediate area. Automatic rifle fire from a dozen outpost guards cut them down. They were left where they had fallen.

"We'll just have to watch for our chance," I said finally. "I think the most logical time would be during a strafing run."

"Yeah, that's right!" Frankie said. "They'll be too busy duckin' to worry about us."

The immediate group surrounding me consisted of my own men, Fortino, Keller, Freeman, and Mooney. Judge had been taken away by ambulance a few days earlier. Little Bill Lister also was with us. The plan we devised, roughly, was to put our group as far from the road as possible during the next break. This would give us a head start when the confusion of the air strike began. We took advantage of the remaining fifteen minutes of our break to indulge in fitful sleep. There would be little enough opportunity to store up rest for some time, I feared.

Early the following morning, before the intense heat of the midsummer Italian sun reached us, we were off again, northwest bound. The hills to our right were less than a quarter mile away now. A roadside sign announced an upcoming village as "Vignanello." It had the sleepy, crowded look of all the other Italian villages we had seen. The nearest stone buildings were less than half a mile away when the guards called us off the road for a rest break.

My group of would-be escapees made sure we were first off the road in our sector, and walked far away from the road itself so that the rest of the prisoners would fill in the distance between us and the road. We were more than seventy-five yards from the road when the planes swooped down. The nearest German vehicle was a lumbering old truck about 150 yards behind where we had left the road. Behind the truck, a unit of straggling foot soldiers was leading a procession of horse-drawn vehicles. All were more than 300 yards from us.

This time, the pilots reversed the usual procedure and swept in from the front of the column, the sun at their backs. They began their fire just about the time they were passing us. The chatter of the guns and roar of the engines were deafening. Four P-38s swooped in, tearing parts of the convoy to shreds.

While our guards and the rest of the prisoners dug themselves as close to the earth as possible, attention was diverted from us by the furious action along the road.

"Now!" I called, loud enough for those around me to hear. As a man, we arose and began the mad dash to the nearby wooded area at the foot of the hills.

I still favored my injured heel a bit and was hobbling along, threatening to slow the entire group. Fortino and Keller each grabbed one of my arms about their shoulders, serving as crutches, dragging me along with them. Finally, I was able to step out and land on my toes. This facilitated my progress considerably.

We were nearly 200 yards from the nearest German when the guard noticed us. He opened up with his machine pistol, soon to be joined by others. Fortunately, we were well out of range of this weapon for any practical purposes.

Certain that the Krauts' flight northward precluded the possibility of pursuit of our small group, I led the group to the trees. Once in the shade of the forest, we luxuriated in a rest, each of us leaning against a tree trunk.

Fortino was lying beside me while Mooney and Keller moved to the edge of the trees to keep watch on the column over at the road. The other prisoners had been hurried back into the column and everyone was moving off again.

"Christ, that group looks small, doesn't it?" Frankie said. "How many you figure are left out there, Hal?"

"Oh, I would guess no more than 350 by now," I said, thinking of all the good men who had been gunned down along this line of march.

We had left the movie studio in Rome with a roll call count of *Fümf hundert acht und dreizig* — 538 prisoners. Nearly a third of them had died so far. To the best of my knowledge, ours was the first successful escape from the column.

23. Fire From the Valley Floor

Fortino HAD GONE out on point to lead our patrol back to the base of the mountains so we could find some sort of escape route to the rear. He came out of the shrubbery and waved us on.

We moved into the small clearing in which Frankie stood. We reached him and all sat down in the shade to rest. Turning to look back toward the highway, I could see the road clearly and the long line of German traffic which clogged it. The column of prisoners had disappeared from sight, having rounded a bend into Vignanello.

"Hal, don't move," Frankie suddenly whispered.

"Huh?" I turned my head to look at my friend. He was staring at the brush to the side of the clearing. Following his gaze, I saw two men in civilian clothing standing just inside the line of trees. Each held a German machine pistol pointed directly at us.

"Oh shit!" I moaned quietly. "Do you suppose they're fascists?"

As if in reply, three more armed civilians came out of the trees. Fortino stood silently, being exceedingly careful not to move too quickly. He stared at the man standing in the center of the newest group of arrivals.

"*Tedeschi?*" the man asked, sneering. He seemed to be the leader of the group. His frown was frightening to behold, it was so intense.

He had on his face an expression that advertised the delight he would feel in cutting us down where we stood.

"No, no, *Americano*," Frankie replied quickly. "*Americano soldati, ay uno Inglese soldat*," he pointed to Bill Lister. "*Priggionari de Guerra!*"

The faces of the five Italians suddenly broke into wide smiles. They rushed in on Frank, embracing him. They pounded his back, showering him with rapid-fire questions in a dialect not entirely familiar to his Sicilian tongue. He valiantly struggled with the language in order to explain the Americans' situation clearly.

"*Ashpet, ashpet, uno momento*," he pleaded. Then, as they quieted down, he slowly and methodically described our capture, brief imprisonment, and subsequent death march. Then he told of the strafing missions that led up to our escape. The story was delivered in the tongue of his parents — Sicilian, a language not to be spoken slowly.

This incongruity, plus the fact that the accent was new to these Florentine-area natives, caused considerable amusement among the five Italians. However, the details of the story and the sudden discovery that I had a slight wound yet, prompted agonized sighs from them. Handing their weapons to Frankie, two of them lifted me gently, one holding me under the knees, the other under my armpits. They carried me into the forest as their leader directed the rest of our group to follow.

Fortino was busily engaged in describing in Italian his many adventures to a rapt audience as we walked. He turned to me after one particular exchange.

"They're Machi," he said. "That's partisans. They've been fightin' the Krauts while living in the hills for a couple of years. They use captured Kraut weapons mostly. These guys have been fighting a hell of a war, using whatever they can get their hands on. They've been disrupting German communications and supply routes pretty badly."

I viewed these brave people with new admiration. Reprisals against them had been many and severe. But they doggedly continued their guerrilla fighting, patiently waiting for their day of liberation. There were men cast in the mold of Giovanni Scalzi, I knew.

We followed a path up the mountainside, reaching the crest of the hill, and then descended the other side along a cleverly concealed network of footpaths until we reached an encampment at the base of the reverse side of the hill.

There, with tender care, they laid me down in the entrance to a cave. Several more caves had been enlarged by tedious hand digging, and others had been started from scratch by such primitive measures. Many other civilians were circulating busily about the camp. It appeared to be a well-organized military installation except for the lack of uniforms. Other men rushed up to us to discover our identity. All were well-armed with German materiel.

I went to the others as soon as my carriers left me. I stood next to Frankie, now deeply engrossed in animated conversation. Finally, we were shown to the cave we first entered and handed bowls of a heavy, thick stew. The entire group ate heartily of the first solid food we had tasted in nearly a week. We wanted to savor every bite, but recent training caused several of us to wolf it down. We washed the delicious meaty meal down with red vino, of which there seemed to be plenty. The potent wine was sour and its tartness was a shock upon first taste.

"Wow, this is the life, eh?" Frankie said, speaking around a gigantic piece of meat which he had stored in his right cheek, giving him the appearance of a nest-bound squirrel about to cache a large nut.

We were bedded down for the night in a large cave, over the door of which hung a large tarpaulin. I recognized it as a German truck cargo cover. This permitted us the luxury of a light and the chance to sit in conversation, free from fear. It was a unique experience for us after so much time over the past few months, during which we were surrounded by active danger and immense fear.

We enjoyed the position of relaxed, valued guests for three more days. The food was plentiful, the wine freely given, equipment in apparently good and plentiful supply. Our hosts proved extremely amiable, and grateful for the news that their liberators were fast approaching from the south.

On the morning of our fourth day in the partisan camp, Bill Lister came running up the hill from the river where he had been washing parts of his uniform. He burst excitedly into the cave.

" 'Ey, you blokes. It sounds like there's a bleedin' battle goin' on up there." He pointed up the hill from the river . . . up above where our cave was located. We all dashed out to join the Italians who had emerged from their caves and stopped their activities to listen to the exchange of heavy gunfire just above our location. It sounded very close. Two partisans charged down the forest path and engaged in excited conversation with their anxiously waiting comrades.

"What's goin' on, Frankie?" I asked Fortino.

"Hold it," Frankie said. He listened carefully, and then turned back to us. "They say there's a tank battle going on up at some bridge up there. Apparently it's the bridge that crosses this valley just beyond that bend. The British tanks caught the Kraut panzers just as they were about to cross the bridge."

The furious battle raged above us and beyond the bend in the valley, each exploding shell reverberating the length of the valley which served to magnify the sounds. Machine gun fire exchanges now joined the fight. Then a new sound entered the picture. It was much closer than the other noises. It was the muffled *pock, pock, pock* of mortars being fired.

The attitude of the entire gathering changed instantly when the mortar fire was heard. This was a new threat that hadn't been expected. These had to be German mortars and they sounded as if they were just around the bend on the valley floor. Obviously, they were firing over the hilltop into the approaching Allied armored column. If they were that close, they also presented a distinct threat to the partisan position.

The camp became the scene of feverish activity as the Italians pulled open the entrance to the largest of the caves. This was their munitions storehouse. Two men rushed inside and began handing weapons and ammunition out to their waiting companions. Frank and I exchanged glances.

"How about it?" I asked him.

"Fuckin' A," Frankie replied. We rushed to the cave entrance, where Frankie engaged in a short verbal exchange with one of the partisans, a man we had decided was a leader. Happy nods greeted his requests, and a shouted command brought out two more rifles and bandoliers of ammunition which were handed to us.

"OK, you slobs, what about us?" Keller and Mooney had been watching the exchange. Frank and the partisan leader looked at each other. The guerrilla chief grinned and shrugged his shoulders.

He ordered ammo and rifles for the two new recruits too. Bill Lister preferred to stay behind. He blushingly admitted to having been a company cook in the desert before being captured.

Our group was ready now for its attack and in well-coordinated movements, divided into three units as if it had been working together for years. The chief indicated that Frankie, Keller, Mooney, and I were to accompany him and three of his men. Freeman was asked to stay behind and help organize the stockpile of weapons and ammunition in order to expedite replacement as the fighters returned to replenish their stock.

The leader started out closely following the wall of the valley on which the caves were established. The bend of the river valley was a little over 150 yards away. We reached it shortly, unobserved. We cautiously made our way along the tree-sheltered path. Continuing to follow the path in the direction of the now heavy mortar fire, we arrived in sight of the high bridge spanning the valley. The leader stopped us and pointed to the base of the bridge. There, less than fifty yards from us, were the three tubes.

We counted sixteen German soldiers hovering about the three weapons, carrying ammunition, dropping shells into the tubes, completely oblivious to anything but their current assignment. They obviously were members of the well-trained, experienced mortar crew. Their operation was smooth and efficient. The last thing in the world they expected was an attack from the bottom of this valley which, technically, was behind German lines.

The rifle fire began from across the valley floor as another partisan patrol got into position. The first volley dropped two of the Germans in their tracks. The others immediately turned and dashed for their stacked rifles.

The leader of our group aimed carefully and fired at the first Kraut to reach the weapons. The man stopped still and spun forward onto his face, knocking over the stacked rifles. His companions pushed him aside and grabbed their weapons, opening fire immediately.

We were all firing now. Our fire was joined by a third partisan group farther up the hill. By now, there were nine German soldiers lying on the ground, either dead or badly wounded. They still couldn't see any of us. Two more fell, and another ran toward the woods on the far side of the valley. His hands were extended over his head as he screamed, *"Kamrad, Kamrad!"* The leader shot him right through the back of his head.

The remaining four Germans began running toward the shelter of the huge, concrete bridge supports. They still were too far from this cover, however, to escape the withering fire of the vengeful, long-suffering Italians. All four were dispatched in a furious fusillade of fire from both sides of the stream.

The fire above was slackening. Only one German tank was still visible from the valley floor. It was at the far side of the bridge, burning furiously. A heavy, black cloud of smoke hung over the end of the bridge, indicating that another tank was burning there. Occasional bursts of machine gun fire and individual rifle fire could be heard in the distance, indicating that the Allied troops were engaged in mop-up operations. The partisan leader, whose name we had learned was Maurizio Laurenti, motioned to Fortino, and the two held a hurried conference.

Frank turned to me and said, "He wants to know if we would like to stay with them for a while, or if we are anxious to return to our own people."

I pondered the question. I had no intense desire to return to combat, but these past three weeks had been a long time. I was anxious to get back to the outfit. I looked at Keller and Mooney. Both shrugged as if to put the responsibility for the decision squarely and exclusively on my shoulders.

"Thank him for us, Frankie, but we have to go back right away. Tell him we appreciate everything they've done for us."

Frank relayed the message and, in return, received and transmitted a message of thanks from the Italian leader for the gallantry of the *Americanos* who had lent him their services in the matter of the mortar crew. I smiled as I wondered what gallantry was involved. It had been a turkey shoot.

The partisans showed us the easiest way to reach the top of the cliff. Two of them went with us. We reached the top in time to witness the roundup of the last few German prisoners who had been captured in the short but furious battle. At first glance, I saw six British Sherman tanks lined up on the street, a column of heavy trucks lined up behind them. Tommies were moving through the village, systematically flushing out remaining small pockets of resistance and snipers.

Welcomes and greetings were exchanged by the Britishers and our group of returning prisoners. We were loaded aboard a truck for the high-speed ride southward. The travail of the bitter period had ended. We were free to return to our own people.

24. The Heart Has Its Reasons

"JAH, HAL, DREADFUL danger. I fear for you. You must be more careful," Arentz was saying. He shook his head soberly.

I realized that I had been getting a lecture on political morality, German style, from this young fellow. Then I remembered what day this was — I was on the verge of another escape, also intended to return me to my own people. This time, however, the war was approaching an indisputable conclusion.

Bruckmann entered the dining room silently and crossed to the sideboard, helping himself to coffee. He looked worried. I arose and crossed to sit beside him at his table.

"What's the matter, Herr Bruckmann?"

"Oh, it's that fool, Best. He has threatened me again this morning. He insists that I attend the stupid birthday tonight, and I simply do not feel like that."

"Why not? After all, it's his birthday, and the price of the booze is right. You probably would have a good time."

"After the past few days, I simply don't feel comfortable in the same room with the man," Bruckmann said petulantly.

I nodded in understanding and looked away just in time to see Best entering the dining room. "Watch it, here he comes."

Bruckmann and I stood as the *oberstormfuhrer* approached us. He smiled broadly.

"Well, well, and are you getting ready for my party?" he asked ecstatically. "I am anxious for it all to go well." He seemed like a child on Christmas Eve.

"I'm sure it will, sir," I said.

"And Helmut, my dear friend," Best turned to Bruckmann directly. The big man stood by awkwardly, uncertain as to the other's next move. It was the first time since meeting him that I had seen Bruckmann in anything but complete command of the situation. Now he was speechless.

"Sit down, Helmut. Sit, sit, my friend," Best said, sitting.

Bruckmann realized suddenly that he was still standing while Best and I had taken seats. He cleared his throat nervously and ran his left forefinger around his collar. He sat nervously opposite the captain.

"Mr. Lister, have you spoken to your men about playing tonight?" Best asked me, peering intently into my face.

"Yes, sir. We're going to play mostly slow dance music."

"And waltzes?"

"Right. Waltzes too."

"Ah, excellent, excellent. I enjoy waltzing." The *oberstormfuhrer's* face clouded suddenly. It was as if the recollection of the days when he loved to waltz proved painful to him. Then, with a shake of his head as if to dispel unpleasant memories, he returned to the present and the joviality he had expressed earlier. "I mean," he said, "I used to love to waltz. That was before . . ." He indicated his legs with a wave of his hand. Then he stood and turned to leave. "Don't forget now, eight o'-clock sharp." He turned and left the dining room.

Bruckmann stared at the tablecloth on which he was drawing pointless concentric designs with his spoon. He was in another world. I felt useless and uncomfortable in Bruckmann's presence this morning. Without being noticed, I stood and looked down on the now stoop-shouldered Bruckmann. It was almost as if the once-proud high executive had tasted his first real defeat. I smiled to myself. Even the mighty must fall, I mused. Still, I felt sorry for the man, in a way. He just wasn't accustomed to such staggering setbacks.

Trautmann entered the room as I was preparing to leave. He reminded me that I still had his book. I had brought it to the hotel this morning in the large side pocket of my combat jacket. I pulled it out and handed it to the lieutenant.

"Thank you, Herr Lieutenant. I enjoyed reading it immensely."

Trautmann looked up, his kindly eyes smiling before his lips did. Still, there was a sadness about the smile. He picked up the thin little volume on the cover of which, in large, Spencerian script appeared the title: "Unhappy Far-off Things," by Lord Dunsany.

"And what did you learn from it, Mr. Lister?" he asked, a slight crack noticeable in his voice. "One should never engage in any activity, you know, without having learned something in the process of the experience, even if it teaches him only that he shouldn't have indulged in this particular activity."

"What did I learn? Nothing new, really. Oh, I learned that the author felt about war as I do. I learned that he says things much better than I could say them. Oh, and I learned that it made me curious as to why you'd have such a book in your library."

The lieutenant picked up the book and turned it over thoughtfully. He looked up at me with an unhappy expression I had only inferred earlier.

"Lord Dunsany felt for a wounded nation. He felt for France, and he hated war," the lieutenant explained. "I suppose if we are honest, we'd all have to admit we hate war."

I had the unpleasant feeling that I had been excluded from participation in the discussion, not rudely, but simply because the lieutenant suddenly seemed to be completely alone.

"Is something wrong, Lieutenant?" I asked, uncertainly.

"Wrong? What is wrong, my boy? I spent sixteen years trying to get young men to realize that each definition is different in light of the circumstances in which it is applied. Wrong?"

"I mean you seem to be worried about something this morning."

"Yes, isn't it true?" Trautmann turned away from me. "You will excuse me." He left the room, looking at the Dunsany book, his head bowed, shoulders hunched forward. He had the look of a man completely and suddenly defeated. Something very definitely was amiss at the Hotel Lamm this morning. Both Helmut Bruckmann and the lieutenant had acted as if they held the weight of the world on their shoulders.

I didn't know how long Inga had been standing in the doorway or how much of my conversation with Trautmann she had heard. Apparently, she had entered when he left the door open during his exit. She, too, shared the unhappiness of this hour, according to her facial expression.

What a hell of a party this is going to be tonight, I thought. *We'll be lucky to get it off the ground at all.*

I crossed to Inga, intending to greet her cordially in an effort to brighten her morning. She turned from me and walked to the coffee urn, pouring herself a cup thoughtfully. Then she turned and passed me again with her full cup in a trembling hand. She sat at a corner table. I followed and sat opposite her.

"Hey, what's with everyone this morning? You'd never guess there was a party scheduled for this evening."

Inga looked up from her coffee cup, her eyes brimming with tears. "Haven't you heard?" she asked. A single tear escaped her left eye and rolled, undisturbed, down the roundness of her cheek.

"Heard what?"

"Lieutenant Trautmann's family. He received word this morning. His wife and two children were killed in a bombing raid on Berlin last week."

A pall hung over the group. Trautmann's tragedy meant, of course, he was absent. Everyone was aware of it. Nobody seemed in any mood for a party. Best's festive evening promised to die aborning. Even the *oberstormfuhrer* himself, circulating among the tables, failed to raise many spirits. He crossed the room toward the three of us.

"Mr. Lister, could you have your men play something cheerful? We can't help poor Trautmann, but we can enjoy the evening anyhow. Do you think you could do that?"

I looked at Bill and Ernie. Bill checked the piece of paper on which he and Ernie had listed their repertoire. He studied the list for a moment.

"How about 'Sunny Side of the Street'?" he asked finally.

"Yeah, that should do it. Let's give it this beat, though."

I started the rhythm at an excessively fast pace, even faster than the customary rapid pace of the song.

Ernie kept more than adequate pace at the piano, and Bill was in rare good form. He played melody throughout the first chorus, throwing in several riffs. Ernie took the proferred solo as the second chorus began, and Bill interjected several harmonic rides. They gave me an eight-bar break which I filled in loudly, using my brushes and highboy exclusively. I reintroduced Bill's horn with a heavy brush roll on the snare, using the rubber-tipped reverse ends of the brush handles. We wrapped up the number with a raucous flair. It was truly the best effort we had made and the best single result achieved since we started playing together.

Scattered applause greeted our effort and the general tenor in the room seemed to be brightening gradually. Best led the applause, enthusiastically slamming his palms together in an awkward, effeminate way. Before it died down, Best signaled Frau Greiner to bring on the wine. She was standing in the kitchen doorway waiting for his signal. When she received it, she immediately pushed the wheeled tea cart into the dining room. On it were seven large buckets, each holding two bottles of iced wine. The beverages were accepted, and drinks were poured all around. Best crossed to me with a full bottle.

"Here you are, gentlemen, for a job well done. I think perhaps you have improved morale around here already." He handed me the bottle and reached to a nearby table for three glasses. As he saluted us we raised our glasses in a toast.

"Happy birthday, Herr Hauptstormfuhrer," I said simply.

Best acknowledged the greeting, sipped from his glass, then left us to return to the other guests.

"What was that?" Bill asked.

"Just a birthday smile," I said. "He's happy tonight."

In the far corner of the room, Charlie Schwedler, apparently with a good head start on the party, sat alone, his head rolling in a pendulum motion. A drop of spittle slid out of the corner of his mouth and rolled down his chin, reflecting the light of the candle on his table. He wanted to look around the room, it seemed, but he couldn't lift his head enough to do so. He finally gave up and fell forward, his head falling on his folded arms on the table.

Christianne had been seated with Arentz and von Nordenflycht during the early part of the evening. Inga sat with them much of the time. Chris had danced with Arentz twice, which seemed to please Best. It appeared that he might feel more confident competing with one of his lowest subordinates than with an independently-minded prisoner of war, especially one who was needed by these *verfluchte* propaganda people.

Christianne hadn't paid any attention to me throughout the early hours. She had matched Best and Arentz drink for drink, and her voice grew louder as she laughed at some secret joke Emil whispered intimately in her ear.

Suddenly, she stood beside her table and, while Arentz and von Nordenflycht exchanged another confidence, moved away from them. She seemed a bit wobbly on her feet, apparently feeling the effect of the young Rhine wine. She walked uncertainly toward the improvised bandstand as I watched. She swayed slightly. She was smiling enticingly as she stopped directly in front of the bass drum, staring at me.

"*Bon soir, mon Sergeant, ce va? Bien?*" Her words were slurred. I stood and walked around the set of traps, standing beside her. Taking her arm, I guided her gently to a nearby table.

"Take ten, guys," I called to Ernie and Bill.

A casual glance across the dance floor told me that nobody seemed to have noticed me with Christianne. Everyone was too busy setting new drinking records. They appeared to be trying to overwhelm the gloom of the evening all at once.

"What is it, Chris? You don't seem yourself tonight."

She grinned at me drunkenly. Then, leaning against my shoulder and laughing softly, she said, "I am having fun on my last night, *mon* Sergeant. Is that wrong?"

"No, I suppose not. I'm glad we had a chance to be together last night, though. I'll miss you, Chris."

"Will you, *mon* Sergeant?"

"Chrissy, what's gotten into you?"

She suddenly seemed bitter. It was apparent that her resentment over having to leave here, of being frustrated in what had developed into a wonderful love affair, of several other disillusionments, had become too strong for her to handle alone. And, within a matter of hours, I wouldn't be here to help even if she were to stay.

"Chris, what did I do? Did I do something wrong?"

She leaned across the table to me, wagging her forefinger slowly before my eyes.

"No, *mon* Sergeant. You did nothing wrong. But do you realize that tomorrow I shall leave here? Not once have you told me you love me!" Her tongue was thick now, her conversation becoming more slurred with each phrase.

"Do you really need to be told in words? Haven't I showed you?"

"A woman must be told," she said, her head inadvertently rolling forward, her long hair falling about her beautiful face, cameolike in the dim candlelight.

"Chris . . ." I whispered softly.

She made the effort and raised her head. Brushing her hair out of her eyes, she stared at me seriously. No trace of a smile remained about her mouth now.

"Yes, *cheri* . . ."

"We both knew when it began that it couldn't last, didn't we?"

"Yes, darling, we both knew that."

"And we took our happiness when and where we could, didn't we?"

She was thoughtful. Then, after what seemed like an interminable delay, she breathed a deep sigh. *"Oui,"* she said softly.

"Didn't we?" I persisted.

"Hal, when you return to your home and marry, you will think back of Christianne in Schonach, won't you? Sometimes. Tell me you will, please."

"Of course I will."

She smiled softly to herself. Then, barely loud enough to be heard, table, touching her hand gently.

She smiled softly to herself. The, barely loud enough to be heard, she murmured, *"La Coer a ses raison, que le raison ne connait pas."*

"What was that?" I asked.

"It means, 'The heart has its reasons which reason knows nothing of.' " Smiling warmly again, she stood up and, brushing my cheek with her soft palm, left me and staggered back to her table.

Arentz was engaged in animated conversation with Best, who was sitting drunkenly in Christianne's former chair. Both men looked up, pleased at her return. She placed her hands on Arentz' shoulders and rubbed the top of his head with her cheek.

He pulled his head around so his mouth was beside her ear and whispered something to her. She nodded, smiling sadly. He stood up and, arm in arm, they crossed to the door. Arentz opened it for her and, just as she was about to go through it, she turned and looked at me. Our eyes met, and I saw tears sparkle in the corner of hers. Leaving the door open behind them, they weaved drunkenly up the stairs.

Best had become quite loud and, in a drunken attempt to make a speech, stumbled over a chair. He fell to the floor with a crash. The others rushed to his rescue. He was all right and he indignantly told them to back off. He stood erect among his retinue, brushing himself clean of dust. The clandestine conversations returned to normal.

Frau Greiner had turned off the overhead lights earlier in the evening and now the only illumination in the large dining room came from four candles on occupied tables.

Best lurched to his feet and staggered out the door. He fell twice as he mounted the stairs, but finally reached the landing in front of his room.

Bruckmann sat moodily by himself, drowning his sorrows in wine. He, too, would feel physically unhappy in the morning. In fact, I decided, practically everyone in the hotel would vie for the grand-daddy of all hangovers the following morning. I had taken only a little sip of the Rhine wine and found it terribly sour. It had been bottled much too early, I assumed.

One by one, the guests either passed out or made their way to the stairs in order to get to their rooms as soon as possible. Finally, Ernie and Bill remained alone with me. We shared the room with four others, all of whom were fast asleep at their tables. The party had lasted for nearly five hours. The clock over the kitchen door was just about to strike one o'clock.

"Well, gents. That does it. Our good captain has hit happy thirty-one. What say we toast him?" I suggested.

I poured wine in three glasses and handed one to each of the others. "Here's to our very own *oberstormfuhrer*," I said, holding my glass high.

"And may all his troubles be beauts," Ernie added.

"Here, here," Bill contributed with a smile. We downed our drinks in a single gulp each. Then, with a smirk, Ernie teased Bill by saying, "Hey, buddy, don't you hate to leave your boyfriend?"

I suddenly looked around. We hadn't seen Humphreys throughout the entire party. I began to wonder how safe our escape plans might be under the circumstances. Perhaps Best wasn't as boiled as his actions indicated. Maybe he was out with the Englishman right now, setting a trap for us. Humphreys had suspected us of planning to leave for some time. Still, I thought, despite the series of disappointments, the loss of our food cache, the possibility of another ambush, perhaps we could still get away with it.

"Ernie," I suggested. "Better load up with rations from the kitchen. I'll take a look around. Bill, you help Ernie gather some chow."

The two men headed for the kitchen as I walked across the dining room, first to the rear door where I listened carefully for any sounds from above. Hearing none, I turned and walked out to the porch. The same boxes of ammunition and revolvers which I had seen several days earlier were piled beside the door. I broke open the top carton of each pile and withdrew a P38, the long-barreled Luger, for each of us, and two clips of ammunition for each.

Returning to the dining room, I handed Ernie and Bill their weapons.

"Keep these stashed in your belts and cover them with your jackets. We'll use them only in case of trouble."

The two men took their pistols hesitantly, stuck them in their waistbands, and buttoned their jackets over them. Only minor bulges indicated the presence of the automatics.

"Well, what do you say, shall we?" I asked, looking around the room.

Bill picked up the musette bag he'd found in the kitchen.

"I got two loaves of black bread and six potatoes," he said.

"And I found two bottles of that rotgut sour wine," Ernie added.

"Well, if we're careful, we can stretch it for four or five days. God knows we've had worse rations than that in their lousy prison camps," I suggested.

"Hey, Hal," Bill interrupted. "Have you seen the Limey tonight?"

"Humphreys?"

"Yeah. I didn't see him at all."

"Now that you mention it, neither did I," Ernie said.

"Well, I'm still sweatin' out that son of a bitch," Bill said. "He tried it again two days ago."

"He made a pass?"

"Yeah. He invited me up to his room for some cognac."

Ernie snorted. "Did you go, chubby?"

Bill glared at him. "Now you just listen here . . ."

"OK, now, simmer down. He's just riding you. Lay off, Ernie. Let's get one thing straight. If this thing is gonna work, we have to get away clean. So knock off this bullshit squabbling. We sure as hell won't help ourselves if you two keep fighting."

"No offense, Bill," Ernie said.

"OK, let's blow," I urged. We looked around the room once again. Then, turning toward the door, we walked out into the rear hallway of the hotel, out of the door at the bottom of the stairs, and down the street toward the bridge.

When we reached the bridge, I looked down into the swirling black water reflected in the pale moonlight. I thought about the weeks of preparation and the storing of supplies, all wasted by a single heavy waterflow down the steep hill. Then, resigning myself to the shorter rations we had with us, I smiled at my two companions. They smiled back, confident of the success of our mission.

"Well, gentlemen, we seem to be on our way."

"Don't we just?" Ernie said, laughing.

We started off, jauntily stretching our legs along the smooth, paved raod. We approached the footpath up which we planned to go over the mountain.

Suddenly, a shadowy figure stepped out of the shadows. My heart began to pound. I was sure that Best had posted a guard along the most obvious escape route, although rational recollection would have reminded me that there was nothing to tip our hand for tonight, specifically.

Closer examination of our silent adversary proved it to be Humphreys. The little Englishman apparently was more perceptive and considerably more sober than were any of the others at the station. He stood straight and firm before us, almost demanding in demeanor. He ignored Ernie and me entirely and concentrated his stare on Bill.

"I'd like a few words with you, my friend."

Bill looked at me, desperately. I stepped forward, my hand on the grip of the automatic pistol in my belt.

"Maybe Bill doesn't want to talk to you."

"You know, of course, that I could present a danger to you," Humphreys sneered. "If the *oberstormfuhrer* were to hear about your escape plans . . ."

"If you had the opportunity to tell him, that is," I said.

"What do you mean?" Humphreys' voice took on a strained tone.

"Look, little friend. You came out for a walk tonight. Now you can enjoy your walk. Only now you'll have company. You might as well come along with us, at least for a while."

"I have no intention of walking anywhere except back to the hotel!" Humphreys insisted, suddenly seeming to acquire confidence.

"Well, start intending, little friend. Ernie will be right behind you. If you behave yourself, we'll let you come back here about dawn. And, by the time you get back here, we'll be away."

With a show of defiance, Humphreys turned as if to return to the hotel — only he found Ernie blocking his path, his pistol drawn. Ernie had edged around to Humphreys' rear while we were talking. Ernie said nothing, simply waved the weapon.

With almost servile capitulation, Humphreys turned around and began walking up the hill into the woods behind Bill, followed by Ernie.

I brought up the rear, keeping a steady lookout over my shoulder for any signs of pursuit. There were none. The village slept quietly.

We climbed the hill toward the spot where the road branched off to the east. Leaving the roadway at the spot where I noticed, with a slight pang, the three-sided shelter stood, we lost all trace of moonlight. Humphreys, Ernie, and Bill plowed ahead on the path into the woods. They could follow it at this point because it was marked clearly by a wide lane through the trees.

I turned and looked back at Schonach from the edge of the clearing. The small, white houses, distributed neatly about the circular main road, in the center of which reposed the beautiful calm millpond, looked almost ghostly in the eerie light of the full moon. The spire of the Catholic church stood firm and erect against the night sky. I saw the square block of the school silhouetted, then forced my glance down to the Hotel Lamm. I stared at the building, large, white, imposing in the moonlight.

No lights showed in any of the windows except the dining room, where dim candlelight was visible. I wondered what each of the occupants of the hotel was doing at this moment. I wondered if any of them had the slightest inclination of the escape. What, I wondered, would be the reactions tomorrow morning when our absence was discovered?

"Chris. Oh, Chris," I murmured, looking at the darkened window of her room.

I turned and followed the others into the forest.